Network Processor Design
Issues and Practices
Volume 2

D1475435

Network Processor Design

Issues and Practices

Volume 2

Edited by

Patrick Crowley

Mark A. Franklin

Haldun Hadimioglu

Peter Z. Onufryk

AMSTERDAM • BOSTON • HEIDELBERG • LONDON
NEW YORK • OXFORD • PARIS • SAN DIEGO
SAN FRANCISCO • SINGAPORE • SYDNEY • TOKYO

Morgan Kaufmann is an imprint of Elsevier

MORGAN KAUFMANN PUBLISHERS

Senior Editor   Denise E. M. Penrose
Publishing Services Manager   Simon Crump
Senior Developmental Editor   Marilyn Uffner Alan
Editorial Coordinator   Alyson Day
Editorial Assistant   Summer Block
Project Editor   Sarah Manchester
Project Management   Elisabeth Beller
Cover Design   Ross Carron Design
Cover Image   Getty Images
Text Design   Windfall Software
Composition   Newgen Imaging
Technical Illustration   Newgen Imaging
Copyeditor   Daril Bentley
Proofreader   Jennifer McClain
Indexer   Steve Rath
Printer   The Maple-Vail Book Manufacturing Group

Chapter 18, "Implementing Voice over AAL2 on a Network Processor," by Jaroslaw Sydir, Prashant Chandra, Alok Kumar, Sridhar Lakshmanamurthy, Longsong Lin, and Muthaiah Venkatachalam, copyright © 2002 *Intel Technical Journal*, Vol. 06, Issue 03 (August 2002). All rights reserved.

The programs, procedures, and applications presented in this book have been included for their instructional value. The publisher and authors offer NO WARRANTY OF FITNESS OR MERCHANTABILITY FOR ANY PARTICULAR PURPOSE and do not accept any liability with respect to these programs, procedures, and applications.

Designations used by companies to distinguish their products are often claimed as trademarks or registered trademarks. In all instances in which Morgan Kaufmann Publishers is aware of a claim, the product names appear in initial capital or all capital letters, or in a specific combination of upper- and lowercase letters. Readers, however, should contact the appropriate companies for more complete information regarding trademarks and registration.

Morgan Kaufmann Publishers
An imprint of Elsevier
500 Sansome Street, Suite 400
San Francisco, CA 94111
www.mkp.com

Library of Congress Control Number: 2003213186
ISSN: 1545-9888
ISBN: 0-12-198157-6

This book is printed on acid-free paper.

About the Editors

Patrick Crowley received his B.A. from Illinois Wesleyan University, where he studied mathematics, physics, and computer science, and his M.S. and Ph.D. degrees, both in computer science and engineering, from the University of Washington. Crowley's research interests are at the intersection of computer systems architecture and networking, with a present focus on the design and analysis of programmable packet-processing systems. He is an active participant in the architecture research community and a reviewer for several conferences (ASPLOS, ISCA, INFOCOM) and journals (*IEEE TOCS, IEEE Network*). He was an organizer and member of the program committee of the HPCA Workshop on Network Processors in 2002 and 2003. In Autumn 2003, Dr. Crowley joined the faculty of the Department of Computer Science and Engineering at Washington University in St. Louis.

Mark A. Franklin received his B.A., B.S.E.E., and M.S.E.E. from Columbia University and his Ph.D. in electrical engineering from Carnegie Mellon University. He is currently at Washington University in St. Louis where he is in the Department of Computer Science and Engineering. Dr. Franklin holds the Hugo F. and Ina Champ Urbauer Chair in Engineering. He founded the Computer and Communications Research Center and, until recently, was the director of the Undergraduate Program in Computer Engineering.

Dr. Franklin is engaged in research, teaching, and consulting in the areas of computer and communications architectures, ASIC and embedded processor design, parallel and distributed systems, and systems performance evaluation.

He is a fellow of the IEEE, a member of the ACM, and has been an organizer and reviewer for numerous professional conferences, including the Workshops on Network Processors 2002 and 2003. He has been chair of the IEEE TCCA (Technical Committee on Computer Architecture), and vice-chairman of the ACM SIGARCH (Special Interest Group on Computer Architecture).

Haldun Hadimioglu received his B.S. and M.S. degrees in electrical engineering at Middle East Technical University, Ankara, Turkey and his Ph.D. in computer science from Polytechnic University in New York. He is currently an industry associate professor in the Computer and Information Science Department and a member of the computer engineering faculty at the Polytechnic University. From 1980 to 1982, he worked as a research engineer at PETAS, Ankara, Turkey. Dr. Hadimioglu's research and teaching interests include computer architecture, parallel and distributed systems, networking, and ASIC Design. He was a guest editor of the special issue on "Advances in High Performance Memory Systems," *IEEE Transactions on Computers (Nov. 2001)*. Dr. Hadimioglu is a member of the IEEE, the ACM, and Sigma Xi. He has been an organizer of conferences, workshops, and special sessions, including MICRO-35 (2002), ISCIS-17 Special Session on Advanced Networking Hardware (2002), the ISCA Memory Wall (2000), ISCA Memory Performance Issues (2002, 2001), and HPCA Workshop on Network Processors (2002, 2003).

Peter Z. Onufryk received his B.S.E.E. from Rutgers University, M.S.E.E. from Purdue University, and Ph.D. in electrical and computer engineering from Rutgers University. He is currently director of the New Jersey design center at Integrated Device Technology, Inc., where he is responsible for system architecture and validation of processor-based communications products. Before joining IDT, Dr. Onufryk was a researcher for 13 years at AT&T Labs-Research (formerly AT&T Bell Laboratories), where he worked on communications systems and parallel computer architectures. These included a number of parallel, cache-coherent multiprocessor and dataflow-based machines. Other work there focused on packet telephony and early network/communications processors. Dr. Onufryk is a member of the IEEE and has been a reviewer for numerous professional conferences and an organizer of special sessions and workshops, including the HPCA Workshops on Network Processors (2002, 2003). He was the architect of several communications processors as well as the architect and designer of numerous ASICs, boards, and systems.

Contents

Preface

This is the second book in a series of texts on network processors. These volumes are an outgrowth of the annual Workshop on Network Processors, the second of which (NP-2) was held in conjunction with the Ninth International Symposium on High-Performance Computer Architecture (HPCA-9), in Anaheim, California, on February 8 and 9, 2003. This volume carries forward the structure of Volume 1: Part I presents research results introduced at the workshop, while Part II describes current industrial products and techniques. Interest in network processor-related research is growing, a fact illustrated by the strong growth in both workshop attendance and the number and quality of NP-2 submissions. Accordingly, our goal was to provide a useful text that balances current research and industry practices.

This book owes a great debt to the people who made NP-2 possible, beginning with the workshop's program committee. The committee consisted of the four editors of this book and 11 additional distinguished researchers and practitioners in the fields of networking and computer architecture: Anant Agarwal (MIT), Andrew Campbell (Columbia University), Kenneth Mackenzie (Georgia Tech), Bill Mangione-Smith (UCLA), John Marshall (Cisco Systems), Daniel Mlynek (EPFL, Switzerland), Mohammad Peyravian (IBM Corporation), Dimitrios Stiliadis (Bell Labs), Mateo Valero (UPC, Spain), Tilman Wolf (University of Massachusetts), and Raj Yavatkar (Intel Corporation).

The workshop program also included a keynote address by Jonathan Turner, of Washington University in St. Louis, an invited talk by Ravinder Sabhikhi, of the IBM Corporation, and an industry panel session moderated by one of the editors, Mark Franklin. The panel consisted of Prashant Chandra (Intel), Marco Heddes (Transwitch), Gary Lidington (Xcelerated Packet Devices), Michael Miller (IDT), and Keith Morris (AMCC). The panel, whose title was *Network Processors— Challenges and Implications*, focused on a range of network processor topics from an industry perspective. These included programming and applications of NP-based systems, as well as the impact of current economic conditions on industry.

We would like to extend our thanks to the workshop program committee members, the keynote speaker, the invited talk speaker, the authors who presented papers at the workshop, the industry panelists, and the HPCA-9 organizers. We would also like to offer particular thanks to those authors from industry and academia whose contributions appear in this book; indeed, this edited volume would not exist without them.

Our special thanks go to those at Morgan Kaufmann Publishers who diligently walked us through the process of producing this book. These include Denise E. M. Penrose, senior editor; Marilyn Uffner Alan, senior developmental editor; Alyson Day, editorial coordinator; Summer Block, editorial assistant; and Elisabeth Beller, production editor.

Patrick Crowley[1]
Mark A. Franklin[2]
Haldun Hadimioglu
Peter Z. Onufryk

1. Patrick Crowley's work was supported by NSF grant CCR-0072948.
2. Mark Franklin's work was supported in part by NSF grant CCR-0217334.

1 Network Processors: Themes and Challenges

Patrick Crowley
University of Washington

Mark A. Franklin
Washington University in St. Louis

Haldun Hadimioglu
Polytechnic University

Peter Z. Onufryk
Integrated Device Technology, Inc.

The objective of this second volume on network processor (NP) design is the same as that of the first [1]: to survey the latest research and practices in the design, programming, and application of network processors. The term *network processor* is used here in the most generic sense and is meant to encompass everything from task-specific processors—such as classification, encryption, and traffic management engines—to more general-purpose and programmable packet or communications processors. In all of these, the objective is programmable packet processing whether this be on a high-speed core router line card or on a comparably low-speed device such as consumer cable or DSL gateway.

The main theme of Volume 1 was on meeting the real-time processing performance required for high-speed networking. While technology advances continue to enable increasingly faster networks, the telecommunications downturn has slowed the rate of deployment of these new technologies as the oversupply of network capacity built during the boom years is brought in line with demand [2, 3]. This, in turn, is changing the focus of network processor design. Equipment vendors no longer view performance as the sole differentiator among network processors, but consider other factors—such as ease of programming and application development—as, if not more, important.

Network processors are increasingly finding their way into higher-layer protocol-processing applications and services. This expansion in the application space beyond traditional router line card forwarding may be signaling the general acceptance of NPs. As programmability is gradually introduced into the network through the deployment of systems containing these devices, the view of network processors simply as replacements for fixed-function application-specific integrated circuits (ASICs) is slowly shifting to one in which these devices are viewed as enabling new networking protocols, applications, and services. This expansion is challenging the designers of network processors. While packet-forwarding applications are relatively straightforward and often require relatively few lines of code, these new higher-layer applications and services require larger amounts of instruction memory, stateful packet processing (i.e., processing during which state information must be maintained and passed between packets of a given flow, or across flows), and deeper and more complex packet inspection. Thus, the work of network researchers, protocol designers, software developers, and network processor architects is becoming increasingly interwoven.

As with Volume 1, this book is organized into two parts. The first part presents research in the design, programming, and use of network processors. The second part details state-of-the-art products and techniques from industry. Our goal has been to balance the forward-looking and sometimes theoretical view of leading-edge research with the challenges faced by practitioners in the field and current solutions. Conceptually, the contributions of this book fall roughly into three domains: technology, software, and applications reflecting the shift in emphasis from raw performance toward ease of use and new applications. The remainder of this introduction reviews this book's contributions in these areas.

1.1   TECHNOLOGY

While astounding network growth claims—such as the doubling of Internet traffic every 90 days, made by former Federal Communications Commission Chairman Reed Hundt—may have contributed to the dot com and telecommunications bubbles, the fact remains that (when viewed over a decade) traffic doubled yearly [4]. Recent economic conditions may have virtually halted the deployment of high-speed networking technologies; however, there is reason to believe that this condition is temporary. Thus, while performance may no longer be the single driving focus of network processor design, it remains nonetheless extremely important.

Memory latency has always been a challenge in the design of network processors, but as network processors move to higher-layer processing applications that are typically *stateful*, the effects of memory latency become even more significant. Chapter 6 presents an architecture for stateful networking applications that uses massive multithreading to tolerate memory latency rather than to try to reduce it.

As with general-purpose processors, the architecture of network processors is likely to evolve into a very few dominant approaches surrounded by many variations and diverse designs suited to the multiplicity of niche applications. We may be seeing the first signs of the evolution of such a dominant approach. Many of today's network processors contain multiple internal execution "cores." These cores may be organized as a pool of processors, as a pipeline of processors, or as some combination of the two. While no definitive conclusions can yet be reached, the authors of Chapter 7 suggest that a pool of processors is the preferred organization. This organization is used in a processor, described in Chapter 2, designed for storage area networks. It is also used in the network processor described in Chapter 15, where the network processor consists of three execution cores organized as a pool of processors, with each processor core capable of executing 24 threads. The programmer's task is simplified on this network processor by a programming model in which a single program is run to completion on each packet. In Chapter 3, the authors describe analytical performance and power models for network processors built using multiple pools of processors. These models may aid in the design space exploration of future network processors.

As line rates increase, so does the challenge of packet classification. Packet classification, determining the flow or class associated with an arriving packet, is typically the first task performed by a network processor and determines the subsequent operation(s) to be performed on the arriving packet. In Chapter 13, the authors argue that future classification algorithms will need to exploit the structure and characteristics of packet classification rules. Chapter 17 presents the architecture of a specialized commercial search engine for packet classification that addresses this challenge today.

1.2 PROGRAMMING

The performance requirements of high-speed packet processing have been addressed in most network processor architectures through the use of multiple internal execution cores and specialized hardware accelerators. The challenge of programming parallel processors with hardware accelerators is in itself daunting, but when coupled with the added requirement of meeting real-time constraints the task can become overwhelming. The task of programming a network processor falls into two related areas. The first is developing a functionally correct program. Since network processors typically contain multiple execution units, powerful software development tools are needed to ensure correctness. Once functional correctness is achieved, the next challenge is to meet the real-time constraints imposed by the packet-processing application. Highly accurate performance prediction techniques are needed to deal with these constraints.

One NP programming model and associated tool that has been developed and has become popular for handling both of these issues is the Click [5] tool set. Chapter 9 examines the challenge of developing applications for network processors from a research perspective. It explores use of the Click programming model in a commercial processor environment. The emphasis in this work is on software productivity. In Chapter 10, which tackles the same application development challenge, a different sort of model is developed, with an emphasis on performance (see Figure 1.1). Chapter 20 examines the programming challenge from an industry perspective and describes a product that aids in this challenge.

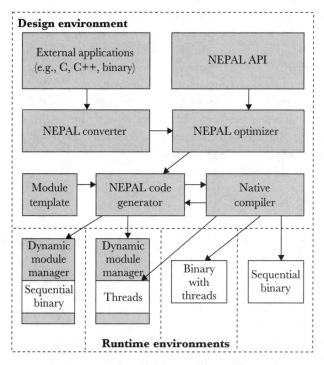

1.1   The NEPAL environment (from Chapter 10).

FIGURE

Network-processing applications have inherent time constraints, and thus when one develops a network-processing application it is important to be able to predict its real-time performance. Chapter 4 presents a technique for determining the worst-case execution time of a program on a network processor by transforming the problem into an integer linear programming problem. The solution yields worst-case performance and provides a guide to where the application program may be modified. Chapter 7 uses real-time calculus to model the performance of complex configurations of network processor cores. Chapter 11 presents a system performance-modeling scheme that captures the integrated behavior of applications and the workload. Finally, Chapter 5 shows how ideas originally developed for multiprocessor scheduling can be used with network processors for service guarantees.

1.3   APPLICATIONS

As discussed earlier, there is a growing awareness that merely transferring bits among network nodes at line rates is no longer the principal challenge in network processor design. While it is difficult to predict what impact, if any, higher-layer protocol-processing and service applications will have on the architecture and design of future network processors, the potential exists for it to be significant.

An emerging trend is to view networks from an application-centric perspective where distributed applications and new network services can be deployed. Jonathan Turner, in his keynote address at the recent Workshop on Network Processors [6], presented one view of how network programmability, as enabled by NPs, relates to the deployment of network services and, more generally, networking research. Turner argued that technology research in the nineties closed the gap between networking performance and existing application needs, but that large challenges remain in providing quality of service, stimulating the development of new services, and deploying those services. To meet these challenges, Turner suggested a shift toward application-centric networks, in which network elements—in addition to end hosts—participate in application-level protocols.

While quality of service (QoS) is required to build such an application-centric network, it is also an important application in today's networks. A single unified network for voice, video, and data can not only reduce carrier network operating costs but also offer the potential for the creation of new applications and services. Chapters 16 and 19 describe approaches for implementing QoS mechanisms on commercial network processors, while Chapter 14 describes the architecture and algorithms for traffic management on a 10-Gb/s commercial network processor. Chapter 16 presents a new queue management algorithm that is implemented on a commercial network processor. Finally, in Chapter 18, the authors describe the implementation of Voice over AAL2 on a commercial network processor.

Network security is becoming an ever more important application as reliance on the Internet for critical applications continues to grow. In Chapter 12, the authors describe the use of a network processor in the design and implementation of a system that mitigates distributed denial of service (DDoS) attacks.

As local area network (LAN) data rates continue to increase, the processing of network protocols on the main CPU (central processing unit) is becoming a bottleneck. Even when the main CPU is able to process protocols at the required rate, the overhead of this processing takes away from system and application processing. As a result, new processors, commonly referred to as TCP offload engines (TOE), are being introduced. Chapter 8 explores the architecture of such a TOE. Whether used to accelerate end systems or within a network for advanced services, such as those requiring TCP reassembly, there exists a growing need for network processors to efficiently process higher-layer protocols. Ravinder Sabhikhi described network processor requirements for processing such protocols in his invited talk at the Workshop on Network Processors [7].

1.4   CHALLENGES AND CONCLUSIONS

The performance aspects of network processor design continue to be challenging. Additionally, there are now other concerns of growing importance that focus on software and new applications for network processors. In this introduction, we have touched upon these themes. The design and application spaces are very large. Programmability remains a substantial challenge due to the different types of NP architectures, the evolution of networking standards and applications, and the unavailability of a unified and widely accepted set of software development and performance prediction tools.

As you read Part I of this book, you will find papers addressing research issues on processor design, modeling, scheduling, programmability, security, and classification. Part II contains industry papers that describe commercial products and applications. Taken as a whole, this book conveys the vibrancy of network processor-related research and development, within both academia and industry.

REFERENCES

[1]   P. Crowley, M. Franklin, H. Hadimioglu, and P. Onufryk, *Network Processor Design: Issues and Practices, Volume I*, Morgan Kaufmann, San Francisco, CA, 2003.

[2]   S. Romero, "Once-Bright Future of Optical Fiber Dims," *New York Times*, June 18, 2001.

[3]   "The Great Telecoms Crash," *The Economist*, July 18, 2002.

[4]   A. M. Odlyzko, "Internet Growth: Myth and Reality, Use and Abuse," *iMP: Information Impacts Magazine*, Nov. 2000.

[5]   E. Kohler et al., "The Click Modular Router," *ACM Transactions on Computer Systems (18)3*, Aug. 2000, pp. 263–297.

[6]   Jonathan Turner, keynote address: "Extensible Networking—Transforming the Internet," Workshop on Network Processors, 2003, *www.cs.washington.edu/ NP2/jon.t.keynote.pdf*.

[7]   Ravinder Sabhikhi, invited talk: "Network Processor Requirements for Processing Higher-layer Protocols," Workshop on Network Processors, 2003, *www.cs .washington.edu/NP2/ravi.s.invited.talk.pdf*.

PART I

DESIGN PRINCIPLES

A Programmable, Scalable Platform for Next-Generation Networking

Christos J. Georgiou, Valentina Salapura, Monty Denneau
IBM T. J. Watson Research Center

In recent years, configuring computer systems with shared storage accessed via a network has become increasingly popular because of performance, cost, and availability advantages over the traditional way of directly attached dedicated storage. Storage attached via parallel SCSI (small computer systems interface) connections is being replaced by Fibre Channel storage area networks (SANs) operating at bandwidths of up to 2 Gb/s. In the next few years, the migration to networked storage is going to continue at an accelerated pace, embodied both in Fibre Channel SANs and in other emerging networking architectures, such as iSCSI and Infiniband [1, 2, 3]. iSCSI involves transfers of block data over TCP/IP networks, typically built around Gigabit Ethernet, while Infiniband is a new server interconnection architecture, designed to replace the PCI (peripheral component interconnect) bus. Transmission bandwidths of 10 Gb/s will be used, providing significantly better performance.

The proliferation of multiple networking architectures suggests that at network interface points protocol conversions may need to take place. For example, a server system interconnected via Infiniband, PCI-X, or some other host attachment scheme may use storage that is part of a Fibre Channel SAN (see Figure 2.1). The controller at the interface between the two networks must not only handle the endpoint functionality required by Fibre Channel and Infiniband (or whatever the host connection may be) but also perform packet resizing and reformatting. As a result, significant processing power is required, especially when considering that protocol handling must take place in full-duplex mode at 10 Gb/s.

Another example may involve iSCSI transfers to an Infiniband interconnected server via a Gigabit Ethernet LAN. Implementing iSCSI/Infiniband

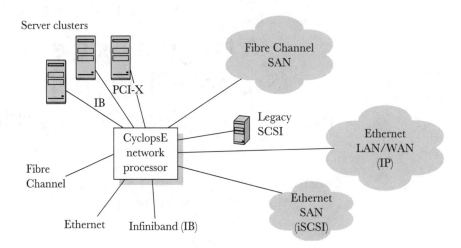

2.1   Multiprotocol network adapter.

FIGURE

protocol conversion may require implementation of TCP/IP termination. This requires the implementation of several layered protocols (i.e., the TCP/IP protocol stack, as well as the iSCSI functionality on top of it), which results in a more complex solution than having the Fibre Channel/Infiniband conversion alone.

The complexity of multiprotocol processing suggests that a programmable solution would be more suitable than a hardwired one. Programmability ensures ease of implementation of the various protocol functions, resulting in faster time-to-market [4]. It also provides great flexibility in accommodating changes to the networking architecture (common in evolving and emerging standards), without having to redesign ASICs, a costly and time-consuming process. An additional advantage in using a programmable solution is that product differentiation is enabled through software customization. In this way, the same hardware platform can be deployed for the implementation of the various networking architectures, thus reducing development, production, and maintenance costs. A second point that must be considered is the performance requirements imposed by the 10-Gb/s line speed, as the time budget available for processing each packet is limited. For example, in a 10-Gb/s Fibre Channel network, the time available for processing a minimal-size packet (36 bytes) is only about 50 ns (this includes the minimum required interpacket gap). This means that in the worst case of a stream of minimal-length packets a Fibre Channel protocol handler must process about 20 million packets per second. On the other hand, if a stream of maximal-length packets (2112 bytes) is to be received, the protocol handler must ensure memory bandwidth of 4 Gbyte/s for delivery to a host in full-duplex operation [5].

These processing and memory bandwidth requirements make the use of off-the-shelf general-purpose processors impractical because of limited performance. For example, recently available top-of-the-line general-purpose uniprocessors are still too slow for processing packets at 10-Gb/s link speed. Even assuming a superscalar 3-GHz processor with a sustained CPI of 0.5 (which is unrealistic given the memory latencies involved), this would allow only 75 instructions per package received at the peak packet rate. From our experience, it takes at least 500 instructions to process a single packet. Besides, the cost, power consumption, and packaging form-factor of high-end microprocessors prevent them from being an attractive alternative, even if they were to have the right performance characteristics.

Current versions of network processors may not offer sufficient levels of performance for protocol termination and conversion at the endpoints of the network at 10-Gb/s speeds, as they have been typically optimized to handle packet-forwarding functions in the middle of the network [6, 7, 8, 9]. IBM's network processor [6], which integrates an embedded PowerPC core and 16 protocol engines, can handle up to 4-Gb/s line bandwidth. The C-5 NPU from Motorola [7] contains 16 channel processors and 5 coprocessors to accommodate 2.5-Gb/s line bandwidth. Vitesse Prism IQ2000 has four processing units and can handle line rates of up to 2 Gb/s [9]. All of these NPUs combine processors, memory, and I/O on a single chip. Their on-chip memory is in the range of 100 to 500 KB, the processors are RISC cores augmented by specialized instructions, and operating frequency is up to 200 MHz. Note that simply increasing the frequency of these processors to a frequency comparable to our design does not provide the processing power required by the aggregate line bandwidth of 20 Gb/s for full-duplex operation, as our architecture does.

The next generation of Intel network processors (e.g., IXP 2800 [10])—although having some similarities with our design philosophy (as we discuss in material to follow) and claiming capability at handling 10-Gb/s line speeds—does not exhibit a level of scalability that would easily enable it to handle higher line bandwidths or very complex protocol processing tasks. Similarly, Cisco's Toaster3 network processor [11] combines four serially connected chips to achieve the processing power required to handle 10-Gb/s line speeds, something we achieve with only one, much smaller, chip. In addition, the use of assembly language makes very difficult the development and maintenance of applications in the ever evolving world of network protocols.

The previously cited limitations of current architectures led us to the development of a programmable, scalable platform that is easily reconfigurable in terms of processing power and memory capacity. The approach is based on the BlueGene/Cyclops cellular architecture [12] and involves the system-on-a-chip integration of many simple general-purpose processors, multiple banks of embedded memory (SRAM or DRAM), and network interfaces interconnected via a crossbar switch. The combination of high aggregate processing power and massive bandwidth to embedded memory, coupled with the scalability offered by the crossbar switch, allows the realization of very high-performance network processors.

This chapter is organized as follows. Section 2.1 presents an overview of the network processor architecture. Section 2.2 describes the application pipelining approach used to efficiently exploit the architecture's multithreading capabilities. Section 2.3 presents a sample application of protocol conversion; that is, Fibre Channel to Infiniband. Simulation and performance analysis for the sample application are discussed in Section 2.4, followed by Section 2.5, Conclusions.

2.1   THE NETWORK PROCESSOR ARCHITECTURE

As previously pointed out, the required network processor computing power at 10 Gb/s can be very high (up to 20 GIPS [giga instructions per second] for full-duplex operation), a level of performance by far exceeding the capabilities of any general-purpose processor currently available. This performance gap could have rendered programmable solutions impractical, if it were not for two key characteristics of networking processing:

+ Network processing is a matter of throughput capacity rather than latency; that is, the time it takes to process each packet is not as important as having the capability to process all incoming packets at line speed without interruptions. For example, it does not matter if it takes 500 ns to process a 50-ns packet, as long as all incoming packets can be processed within a reasonable time window with no packet overruns. This suggests that aggregate processing power is more important than unit processing power.

+ The locality of data references (a key consideration in designing cache hierarchies in general-purpose processors) is not found in network processing, as networking data typically show low temporal and spatial locality. This means that while large data caches improve general-purpose processing significantly, this is not the case for data-streaming processing. Streaming data typically are not used repeatedly, resulting in low cache hit rates. This suggests that data caches can be avoided, thus reducing complexity by not having to implement directories and cache coherency protocols.

The previous observations motivated us to follow, in designing the network processor architecture, the multiprocessing approach adopted by the BlueGene/Cyclops architecture [12]: many simple cores with a reduced, but general-purpose, instruction set of about 40 instructions derived from the PowerPC architecture. Each processor core has its own register file, ALU, and instruction sequencer. The processor cores have a single-issue architecture with a simple, four-stage pipeline. Four cores share a local SRAM, for storing their stack and local variables, and parts of packets that need to be processed, such as header fields. Although this SRAM effectively "caches" information, it does not require any of the usual attributes of a processor data cache, with its inherent design and validation complexity and area overhead (typically, a cache requires 2x area compared to a same-size SRAM). Two four-processor clusters share an instruction cache. The i-cache bandwidth to the processors is sufficient to prevent instruction starvation. As most working sets of the processor fit in the i-cache, sharing of the i-cache does not cause cache trashing and increased instruction miss rate. Our implementation of Fibre Channel protocol shows that less than 4 KB of i-cache were sufficient per processor to get instruction hit rates of more than 98%, because of the small footprint of the code.

The small instruction set and simplicity of features allow the processor cores to be of minimal size while delivering a high ratio of MIPS/mm^2 of silicon area (of the order of 250 MIPS/mm^2, including i-cache and local SRAM, for 0.13 process technology). This makes possible the placement of many cores on a chip of a rather small footprint, to exploit thread-level parallelism.

Another feature of our network processor is the use of embedded memory for storing data packets, connection information, and programs. Usage of embedded memory (SRAM or DRAM) is advantageous, as significant amounts of memory can be placed on a chip without excessively increasing its size. In addition, embedded memory has short and predictable access times, which can be accounted for in the time budget for the processing of a single packet. Compared to conventional off-chip memory, embedded memory offers significant performance advantages. Moreover, storing data packets on the chip, as opposed to buffering them in the off-chip memory, reduces the overall traffic on the internal interconnect, resulting in fewer resource collisions and less performance degradation and power consumption.

The on-chip memory has to be carefully sized to ensure normal operation of the controller and to provide overflow protection in case of temporary speed mismatch between input and output paths. In addition to storing data, we maintain current control, status, and routing information in the embedded memory. Since in some applications memory requirements may be of the order of tens or hundreds of Mbytes, thus exceeding the available on-chip memory, we employ off-chip DRAM connected via a high-bandwidth DDR memory interface. The external DRAM may store statistics and archival information, as well as provide congestion buffering.

In our network processor, the intent is to implement most protocol functions in software. However, some highly time-critical functions at the lower level of the network protocol are implemented via hardware accelerators. Hardware accelerators handle low-level protocol tasks, such as data encoding/decoding, serialization/deserialization, link management, and CRC and checksum calculation. These tasks are performed on every byte of the transferred packets and would be very computationally intensive if implemented in software. The hardware implementation of these functions requires a small silicon area, typically under 50,000 gates. In our design, we have included hardware accelerators and network interfaces for Fibre Channel, Gigabit Ethernet, and Infiniband.

The network processor internal interconnect is a crossbar switch that interconnects processors, memory blocks, and I/O interfaces, as shown in Figure 2.2. The crossbar switch has 64-bit data paths and provides several words worth of pipelining and token signaling to avoid data overflows. The four processors in a cluster share a port to the crossbar, and thus a crossbar with 16 ports is sufficient to interconnect up to a 32-processor system.

The architecture is cellular, meaning that it allows the design to be custom scaled, depending on the application requirements. For example, endpoint functionality of Fibre Channel requires less computational power than the more complex TCP/IP termination with iSCSI protocol conversion to Infiniband. In our design, the number of processor cores and embedded memory blocks can be easily adapted to the application requirements without making significant design changes.

Because of the simplicity of the processor cores, an eight-processor cluster with its associated 32 KB of SRAM and 32 KB of i-cache occupies about 8 mm^2 in 0.13-μm process technology, as shown in Figure 2.3. Thus, a design integrating 16 processor cores, 500 KB of global embedded SRAM, and network interfaces and hardware assists for Fibre Channel, Gigabit Ethernet, and Infiniband would result in a chip size of only about 40 mm^2. Chips of that size have excellent yields, resulting in a low-priced solution for network interface controllers.

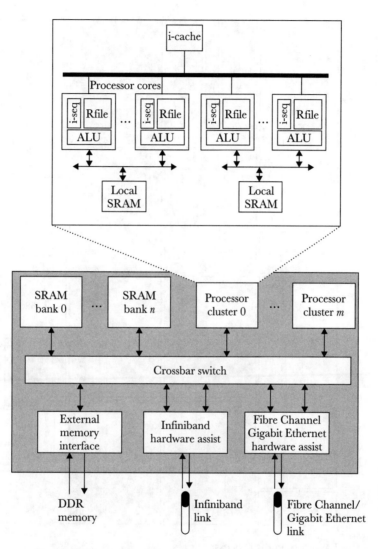

2.2   Network processor architecture.

FIGURE

2.2   PROCESSOR SCHEDULING

Packet processing on multiple processor cores could be done either by following a run-to-completion approach, in which a packet is assigned to a single
processor that carries out all processing operations, or via pipelining, whereby

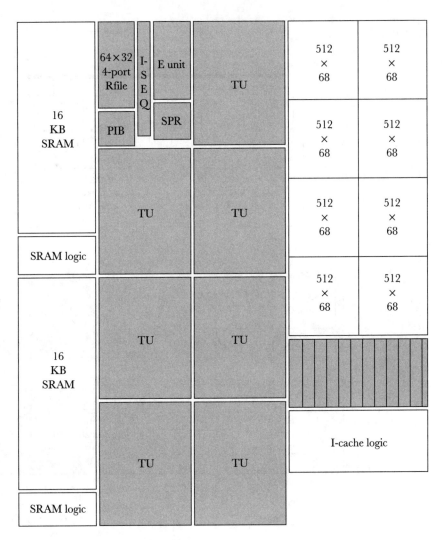

2.3   Layout of eight processor cores.

FIGURE

the packet-processing operations are partitioned into multiple pipeline stages assigned to separate processors. In our implementation, we chose the pipelined approach because of better utilization of hardware resources, such as i-caches. Examples of network operations that can be assigned to separate pipeline stages are header handling, packet validation, generation of an acknowledgment response, packet reordering and message assembly, and end-to-end control.

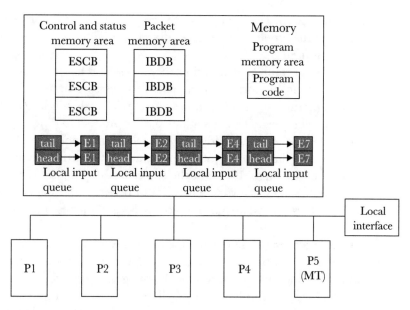

2.4   Memory structures in network processor.

FIGURE

The scheduling of protocol tasks to processors is done statically during initialization; that is, each processor executes the same set of operations on various packets. Likewise, to avoid overhead associated with dynamic memory management, such as garbage collection, static memory management is used. All memory structures used are initialized during system bring-up. These include memory areas for storing data packets, control and status information of existing network connections, program code, and work queues. The various memory structures used in the architecture are illustrated in Figure 2.4.

The memory area that stores data packets is organized as a linked list. An incoming packet is stored in the next free buffer obtained from the linked list. During packet processing, only the pointer to the memory area where a packet is stored is passed between processors. When packet processing is completed, the packet is transferred to the outbound network interface, and the buffer is returned to the list of free buffers.

Processor synchronization is done in the form of message passing via work queues (see Figure 2.4). In this approach, each processor is associated with a work queue that stores the pointers to the packets waiting to be processed by that thread. When the processor is ready to work on the next packet, it gets the pointer of the next pending packet from its work queue. When it finishes processing, it places the pointer to the packet into the work queue of the next thread in the pipeline. To ensure correct operation in memory access collisions, locking is used.

An important consideration in processor scheduling is that all pipeline stages may not require the same packet-processing time and, furthermore, the processing time at each pipeline stage may vary, depending on the packet context. For example, in Fibre Channel, packet-processing time depends on whether the packet is the first, middle, or last packet in a sequence of packets, whether it carries the link control information, and whether it belongs to a solicited or unsolicited message. If one of the stages of the pipeline is significantly slower than other stages, its work queue could become overloaded, becoming a bottleneck. This is remedied by employing several processors to work on the same pipeline stage in parallel.

As processing time in the pipeline stages may vary among packets, all processors may not be fully utilized. However, this is not a concern, as processor utilization was not our primary design goal. Instead, we tried to achieve a matched throughput between pipeline stages by providing sufficient buffering and decoupling logic. Historically, computer architects and logic designers have assumed that computation is expensive and communication is cheap. But this is no longer valid when the figure of merit is performance in terms of MIPS per mm^2 and processor design is limited by wire and not logic delay.

The assignment of multiple processors to work on the same task requires the introduction of a task-dispatching processor (designated "MT" in Figure 2.4). The packet assignment method must be simple, so that it executes in a short processing time, and must not lead to performance degradation through resource contention and locking. For the latter reason, we have discarded round-robin and first-come, first-serve sorting methods. These approaches may assign packets from the same flow to separate processors, resulting in performance degradation, as the processors would be competing to access the flow status information from the same memory locations.

Instead, for the Fibre Channel implementation, a bin-sorting algorithm is used that results in the processing of all packets belonging to the same context group by a single processor. Information about the current context is cached in the register file of the processor, reducing resource contention and average access time for fetching this information. The sorting overhead is kept low by using a simple hash function. In our implementation, packet sorting and processor assignment tasks introduce about 50 instructions. As there may be more active context groups than processors in typical network traffic at any given time, several different contexts can be assigned to a single processor at the same time. It is possible in the worst case that all packets could be assigned to only one processor, causing it to overload. However, our analysis of network traffic running real applications shows that this is not a problem, as the context groups are distributed evenly among the processors operating in parallel.

2.3   FIBRE CHANNEL/INFINIBAND IMPLEMENTATION

Two networking architectures we intend to support are Fibre Channel and Infiniband. In our prototype system we have implemented the required endpoint functionality, as well as the packet resizing and reformatting needed for conversion between these two protocols. The basis for our implementation is the partitioning of the protocol operations so that they can be handled by different resources on the chip. We assign each protocol operation to a processor (or a group of processors), except for some time-critical functions close to the network physical interfaces that are implemented, as previously pointed out, by means of hardware accelerators.

The packet and processing flow can be described as follows. The received packet and some status information are transferred from the inbound FIFO buffer to embedded memory by DMA (direct memory access) logic that has already received a pointer to an empty memory area from a list of free buffers. The packet header is examined to determine the packet context and to switch current context, if necessary, by obtaining control information from memory or by generating new control information in case the packet is the first one of a new exchange. In addition, the received packet is validated to ensure that it complies with the class of service of the exchange it belongs to. If an acknowledgment for the received packet is required to be sent back to the source (e.g., class 2 service in Fibre Channel), an acknowledgment packet is generated. The corresponding header information for the acknowledgment packet is assembled, and the packet is sent to the outbound Fibre Channel network interface.

In the meantime, an Infiniband packet header is generated for the received packet, and the packet is resized according to the Infiniband network protocol. The newly formed packet (or packets) is transferred to the outbound FIFO buffer in the Infiniband network interface hardware module. Similar tasks take place for performing the opposite protocol conversion; that is, transferring packets from the Infiniband to the Fibre Channel network.

The logical representation of our prototype Fibre Channel/Infiniband implementation is illustrated in Figure 2.5. This implementation uses 14 processors, with those operating on the Fibre Channel–to–Infiniband conversion being on

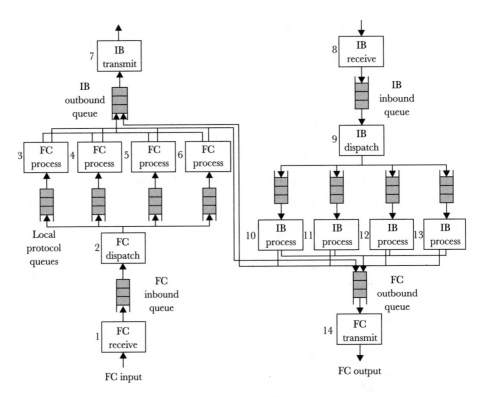

Implementation of the Fibre Channel/Infiniband protocol converter.

the left, while the reverse conversion takes place on the right. The assignment of protocol tasks to hardware resources is done as follows: processor 1 takes care of the Fibre Channel inbound DMA setup and target memory area assignment; processor 2 dispatches packets to one of the four processors 3 to 6, based on the packet header information, which perform context switching, packet valida- tion, and acknowledgment packet generation (if required); processor 7 performs Infiniband header generation, sets up data transfer to the Infiniband outbound network interface, and returns memory area blocks no longer needed to the linked list of free buffers. Similarly, the packet flow from the Infiniband network to the Fibre Channel network is handled by processors 8 to 14. Pointers to the packets to be transmitted to the Infiniband network are placed in the work queue located at the upper left side, and pointers to packets to be sent on Fibre Channel are placed in the Fibre Channel outbound work queue, located on the bottom right side.

Other network protocols, or protocol conversions, can be easily implemented in a similar fashion. For example, in implementing the TCP/IP protocol stack, the existing code for uniprocessor implementations can be reused, requiring only a modest programming effort to adapt it to the architecture. More specifically, the tasks of packet dispatching and collecting (processors labeled 2 and 7 for the receiving path shown in Figure 2.5, and 9 and 14 for the transmitting path, respectively) have to be implemented, but the network protocol could be run almost unchanged in parallel, on processors labeled 3 to 6 and 10 to 13. The number of processors running protocol tasks in parallel has to be scaled according to task complexity to meet the timing requirements.

2.4 PERFORMANCE SIMULATION AND ANALYSIS

The performance simulation and analysis were done concurrently at the application and hardware architecture levels. Using extensive testing with typical and worst-case network traffic samples, which we describe in this section in detail, we were able to develop a functionally correct application independently of and in parallel with the hardware architecture design effort.

The implementation of the Fibre Channel protocol functions was done in C language. The code is highly modular, allowing the reuse of common functions among various processors. An added advantage of this modularity is the localization of the particular implementation of functions that are subject to change in evolving network protocols, such as next-generation 10-Gb/s networks.

The available time for processing a single packet is a function of the Fibre Channel packet length, and varies from as little as 50 ns for minimum-size packets to $1.8\,\mu s$ for packets of maximum size. Since in our implementation an average of 500 instructions is needed to process a packet, a single processor configuration would be capable of handling packets of 1000 bytes or larger only. But by employing multiple processors working in parallel, the overall performance increases almost linearly, despite the overhead introduced by the packet sorting and processor assignment based on the packet context. For example, by using four processors in the packet-processing stage, as previously described, it is possible to handle a sustained stream of packets as small as 256 bytes, as shown in Figure 2.6. In the figure, the curve showing available time indicates the time bound of processing a packet of a given size at 10 Gb/s, while the horizontal lines indicate how long a uniprocessor or a four-processor system takes to execute 500 instructions at the given clock rate of 500 MHz.

To verify the functional correctness and processor synchronization of the implementation, we simulated a storage subsystem configuration consisting of

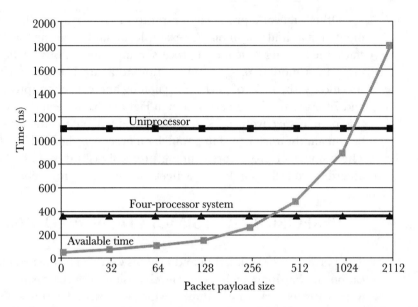

2.6

FIGURE

Performance of multiprocessor network architecture versus a uniprocessor implementation for various packet sizes.

a host connected to a disk, both using our network processor. A multithreaded simulation environment using POSIX pthreads was used. The simulation vectors were traces from real Fibre Channel network traffic captured between a host and an IBM Shark storage system exchanging SCSI commands and data, as well as from Microsoft's Windows 2000 disk stress test, both scaled to 10 Gb/s (by adjusting the time scale of the 1-Gb/s traces by a factor of 10).

An analysis of the workload characteristics of the collected traces from the Shark test system is shown in Figure 2.7. About half of all packets exchanged are 68 bytes long or smaller, carrying commands and acknowledgments, while the other half are large packets (40% of all packets are of maximum size) carrying data. This means that on average the available time budget for packet processing is more relaxed than for the worst case of a sustained series of minimal-size packets. As a result, the number of processors implemented was sufficient to handle the workload. Similarly, the Windows 2000 disk stress test was easily passed, even though it consisted exclusively of small packets, as the interframe gaps provided additional time for packet processing.

For applications requiring more processing power or having more demanding packet traffic characteristics, configurations with more processors can be

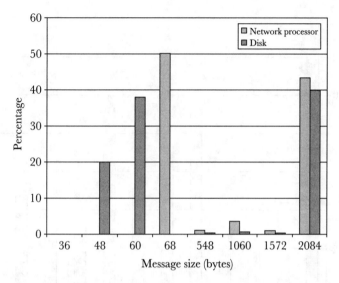

Sample of SCSI commands over Fibre Channel traffic characteristics.

used. For example, 24- or 32-processor chips can be built that would still fall within the sweet spot of the yield and cost curves of the silicon technology.

Additional studies were performed using a cycle-level simulator in order to obtain more detailed information on the instruction mix, register usage, and overall processor performance. The C compiler we have used throughout the design is based on the *gcc* compiler from the GNU tool family, and implements all of its optimizations. Compiled code is very compact and well optimized, but for time-critical parts it is possible to use hand-optimized assembler code instead. However, we prefer to improve and optimize the application at the high level instead of making changes at the assembler level. This ensures that the application is portable and well documented, easing further code development, adaptation, reuse, and maintenance.

The analysis of the dynamic instruction mix for the processing of a series of packets shows that only about 30 instructions were used during program run-time. Of those, only 14 instructions contributed 84% of all instructions executed (see Figure 2.8). The most frequent instructions used are integer arithmetic and logic operations, compare operations, load stores, and control flow operations. In addition, instructions for memory locking were used. For example, the load and then set true to memory (i.e., $L = SETT\ RT, RA$) first loads a word from memory addressed by the contents of register RA into register RT, and then sets

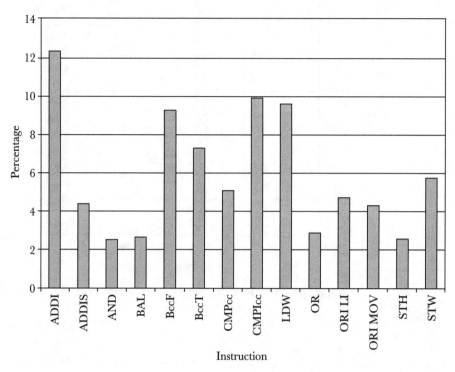

Instruction histogram.

the memory location to all ones as an atomic operation. The small number of instructions used proves the validity of our original assumption that in networking applications it is advantageous to use many simple processing cores with minimal instruction sets, each occupying a small silicon area, instead of more complex uniprocessors.

2.5 CONCLUSIONS

This chapter described a scalable parallel network processor architecture for handling next-generation storage networking at line speeds of 10 Gb/s or higher. By using many simple but general-purpose processors and embedded memory, high levels of processing power per mm^2 of silicon area can be achieved, making this architecture ideally suited to the computationally intensive conversion of protocols required by current and emerging storage networks. The coarse-grain parallelization of protocol tasks and synchronization via queues and message passing are a good match for the parallel processor core environment. Our simulations have shown that a chip with fewer than 16 processor cores can easily handle the protocol conversion between 10 Gb/s Fibre Channel and Infiniband networks. Larger configurations may be used for the implementation of iSCSI protocols.

ACKNOWLEDGMENTS

We would like to acknowledge the contributions of Henry S. Warren, Jr., toward the development of the compiler, linker, assembler, and other software tools for the network processor architecture.

REFERENCES

[1]   T11 Technical Committee, "10 Gb Fibre Channel Standard," Draft v1.91, Oct. 2001.

[2]   Infiniband Trade Association, *Infiniband Specifications*, vols. 1 and 2, Release 1.0.a, June 2001.

[3]   IEEE 802.3ae Task Force, "10 Gigabit Ethernet," IEEE Draft P802.3ae/D3.3, Oct. 2001.

[4]   P. G. Paulin, F. Karim, and P. Bromley, "Network Processors: A Perspective on Market Requirements, Processor Architectures and Embedded S/W Tools," *Proceedings of Design Automation and Test in Europe, Conference and Exhibition 2001*, Munich, Germany, Mar. 2001, IEEE Computer Society, pp. 420–427.

[5]   C. J. Georgiou and C. J. Li, "Scalable Protocol Engine for High-Bandwidth Communications," *Proceedings of International Communications Conference, ICC'97*, Montreal, Canada, June 8–12, 1997.

[6]   M. Heddes, "IBM Power Network Processor Architecture," *Proceedings of Hot Chips 12*, Palo Alto, CA, Aug. 2000, IEEE Computer Society.

[7]   D. Husak, "The C-5 Digital Communications Processor," *Proceedings of Hot Chips 12*, Palo Alto, CA, Aug. 2000, IEEE Computer Society.

[8]   H. Shimonishi and T. Murase, "A Network Processor Architecture for Flexible QoS Control in Very High Speed Line Interfaces," *Proceedings 2001 IEEE Workshop on High Performance Switching and Routing*, Dallas, TX, May 2001, IEEE Computer Society, pp. 402–406.

[9]   S. Sheafor and C. Lindsay, "Vitesse Network Processors: Optimizing Architecture for Bandwidth and Flexibility," *Proceedings of Hot Chips 12*, Palo Alto, CA, Aug. 2000, IEEE Computer Society.

[10]   M. Adiletta et al., "The Next Generation of Intel IXP Network Processors," *Intel Technology Journal*, vol. 06, issue 03, Aug. 2002.

[11]   P. Glaskowsky, "Toaster3 Pops Up at MPF," *Microprocessor Report*, Oct. 2002.

[12]   F. Allen et al., "Blue Gene: A Vision for Protein Science Using a Petaflop Supercomputer," *IBM Systems Journal*, vol. 40, no. 2, 2001.

3 Power Considerations in Network Processor Design

Mark A. Franklin
Department of Computer Science and Engineering,
Washington University in St. Louis

Tilman Wolf
Department of Electrical and Computer Engineering,
University of Massachusetts at Amherst

Over the last several years, network processors (NPs) have become important components in router designs. By providing for programmability, they permit adaptation to new functional requirements and standards. Additionally, NPs provide a powerful single (or a few) chip multiprocessor architecture, typically containing logic components and instructions specialized to the networking environment, to satisfy a range of performance requirements. At this point, there are over two dozen companies producing a variety of network processors [5, 9, 10, 13].

At the hardware level, there are four key concerns in the design of NPs.

+ *Computational power*. The NP must be able to perform the required computational tasks fast enough to keep up with input line speeds.

+ *Functional power*. The NP must be able to perform the required functional tasks associated with its targeted environment (e.g., packets, cells, IPv4, IPv6, and MPLS).

+ *Cost*. The cost of the chip should be reasonable. In this chapter we deal with manufacturing costs only, and consider chip area to be a proxy for these costs.

+ *Electrical power dissipation*. The NP must not consume an excessive amount of power.

In this chapter we consider the prototypical NP architecture shown in Figure 3.1. It contains a number of identical multithreaded general-purpose

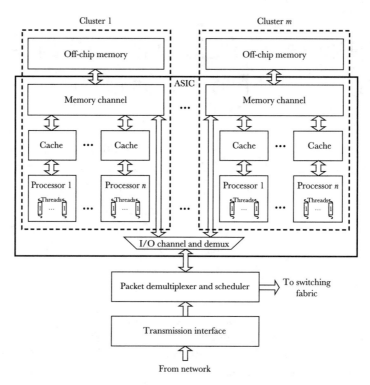

3.1
Overall network processor architecture.

FIGURE

processors, each having its own instruction and data caches. To satisfy off-chip memory bandwidth requirements, groups of processors are clustered and share a memory interface. A scheduler assigns packets from independent flows to the different processors. Thus, after assignment of a flow to a processor, all packets of the same flow are routed to the same processor. Speedup and computational power are achieved by exploiting parallelism at the flow level. Note that additional speedup can be obtained by also exploiting packet-level parallelism; however, this is not considered here. All of the processors are assumed to be identical and capable of executing the necessary NP functions.

In our previous work [6, 14, 16] we have developed performance models in order to find the optimal configuration of components associated with this architecture. The performance metric utilized in this prior work involved both computational power and chip area. Computational power is measured by the total IPS (instructions per second) available from the NP, and area is measured by the number of square centimeters required for a given chip configuration.

A configuration consists of a selection of the instruction and data cache sizes, the number of processors, the number of clusters, and the multithreading level associated with each processor.[1] Other design options, such as channel bandwidth and use of on-chip DRAM, were also considered.

In this chapter we extend the model presented earlier to include the important component of power dissipation. As line rates and clock frequencies have increased, power dissipation considerations often affect design decisions. In a router environment, there may be one or two NPs per line card, with the card holding various other components (e.g., optical-electrical converters, line drivers, memories, CAMs, and various interfacing chips). A group of line cards (e.g., 16, 32) is generally placed within a single rack or cabinet, and in such an arrangement aggregate heat dissipation issues become important. Thus, although many current commercial NPs consume 10 or more watts, designing for increased performance while restraining power dissipation is a constant concern.

This chapter presents the development of optimal designs that provide for the maximum IPS while at the same time minimizing metrics involving power consumption, chip area, or a combination of the two. The components involved in the process are shown in Figure 3.2. Using a benchmark of networking-oriented programs, called CommBench [15], we obtain an application workload that is representative of the network processor environment. This workload is simulated with the SimpleScalar [2], Wattch [1], and Cacti [12] tool sets to derive workload and power parameters, which are necessary for the analytic models. Analytic models consist of a model for processing power and chip area and a model for power consumption. Individual analytic power dissipation models for the main architecture components (e.g., ALUs, clocks, and caches) are developed in this work. The results of various performance metrics from the models are used to find the optimal configurations for the system of Figure 3.1 by iterating over the design space. The simulation environment is also used to verify the accuracy of the analytic models derived in our work.

Section 3.1 presents the model used in determining the processing power for the NP. The workload for our analysis is based on the CommBench benchmark, briefly discussed in Section 3.1.1. Section 3.2 develops the power model and explains the usage of various simulation tools to obtain model parameters. Section 3.3 describes the area model utilized and the set of performance metrics to be considered. Section 3.4 presents the results of overall model optimization and examines how performance changes as selected parameters are varied.

---

1. While most commercial NPs employ multithreading, for simplicity we consider single-threaded processors in this chapter. The processor model can be readily extended to the multithreaded case [6].

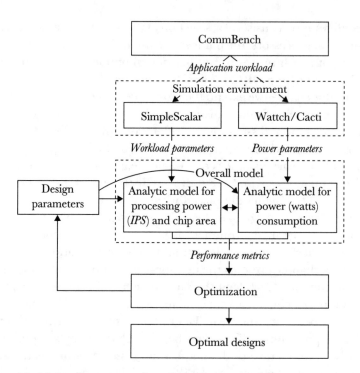

3.2

FIGURE

Model development and optimization process.

The final section contains a summary of the results and a number of design conclusions that follow from the analysis.

3.1   COMPUTATIONAL PERFORMANCE MODEL

For a single processor, processing power can be expressed as the product of the processor's utilization, ρ_p, and its clock rate, clk_p. The processing power of the entire NP can be expressed as the sum of processing power of all processors on the chip. If all processors are identical and run the same workload, then in an NP with m clusters and n processors per cluster, on average the processing power is:

$$IPS = m \cdot n \cdot \rho_p \cdot clk_p. \tag{3.1}$$

A key question is how to determine the utilization of the processors. For ideal RISC processors where significant hazards result principally from cache misses, processor utilization can be expressed as:

$$\rho_p = \frac{1}{1 + \tau_{mem} \cdot p_{miss}}, \tag{3.2}$$

where τ_{mem} is the memory access time and p_{miss} is the cache miss rate.

We assume the memory channel implements a FIFO service order on the memory requests in such a way that they can be interleaved in a split-transaction fashion. The total off-chip memory request time, τ_{mem}, thus has three components: the bus access time, τ_Q; the physical memory access time, τ_{DRAM}; and the cache line transmission time, $\tau_{transmit}$ (all represented in terms of numbers of processor clock cycles):

$$\tau_{mem} = \tau_Q + \tau_{DRAM} + \tau_{transmit}. \tag{3.3}$$

The DRAM access time, τ_{DRAM}, is determined by the external DRAM specifications. The cache line transmission time, $\tau_{transmit}$, depends on the cache line size, $linesize$; the memory channel width, $width_{mchl}$; the processor clock frequency, clk_p; and the memory channel clock frequency, clk_{mchl}. The queuing time, however, depends on the load on the memory channel. We have shown earlier [6] that the M/D/1 queuing model is a reasonable approximation of the memory channel queuing time τ_Q. Thus, for a channel utilization of ρ_{mchl} and an average service time of $E(s)$, the bus access time, τ_Q, is given by:

$$\tau_Q = \frac{\rho_{mchl}^2 \cdot E(s)}{2(1 - \rho_{mchl})} = \frac{\rho_{mchl}^2}{2(1 - \rho_{mchl})} \cdot \frac{linesize}{width_{mchl}} \cdot \frac{clk_p}{clk_{mchl}}. \tag{3.4}$$

With a fixed DRAM access time, τ_{DRAM}, and a transmission time of

$$\tau_{transmit} = \frac{linesize}{width_{mchl}} \cdot \frac{clk_p}{clk_{mchl}}, \tag{3.5}$$

we can substitute in Equation 3.3 to obtain the memory access time:

$$\tau_{mem} = \tau_{DRAM} + \left(1 + \frac{\rho_{mchl}^2}{2(1 - \rho_{mchl})}\right) \cdot \frac{linesize}{width_{mchl}} \cdot \frac{clk_p}{clk_{mchl}}. \tag{3.6}$$

The remaining component needed to evaluate the utilization expression (Equation 3.2) is the cache miss rate, p_{miss}. For a simple RISC-style load-store processor running application a, the miss probability is given as [8]:

$$p_{miss,a} = mi_{ci,a} + (f_{load_a} + f_{store_a}) \cdot md_{cd,a} \cdot (1 + dirty_{cd,a}), \tag{3.7}$$

where $mi_{ci,a}$ and $md_{cd,a}$ are the instruction and data cache miss rates for application a with respective cache sizes ci and cd. The parameters f_{load_a} and f_{store_a} are the frequency of occurrence of load and store instructions also for application a. The parameter $dirty_{cd,a}$ is the probability of the dirty bit being set on a cache line requiring that the cache line be written back to memory. Section 3.1.1 discusses the applications from which these parameter values are derived.

The expression for miss rate, p_{miss} (Equation 3.7), and for total memory access time, τ_{mem} (Equation 3.6), can now be substituted into Equation 3.2 to obtain processor utilization. To do this, the memory channel load, ρ_{mchl}, needs to be fixed because τ_Q depends on ρ_{mchl}. Thus, with the memory channel load given, we can determine the utilization of a single processor. This gives us the memory bandwidth, $bw_{mchl,1}$, required by a single processor:

$$bw_{mchl,1} = \rho_p \cdot clk_p \cdot linesize \cdot p_{miss}. \tag{3.8}$$

With $width_{mchl} \cdot clk_{mchl} \cdot \rho_{mchl}$ being the bandwidth associated with the selected memory channel utilization, the number of processors, n, in a cluster corresponds to the number of processors that can share the memory channel without exceeding the specified load. Thus, n is given by:

$$n = \left\lfloor \frac{width_{mchl} \cdot clk_{mchl} \cdot \rho_{mchl}}{bw_{mchl,1}} \right\rfloor. \tag{3.9}$$

Having considered the memory channel, we now turn our attention to the I/O channel used to input and output packets from the network. From monitoring execution of an application a (or a benchmark of applications), one can obtain a parameter, $compl_a$, referred to as "complexity." The application complexity corresponds to the number of instructions required to process a packet of a certain length. That is:

$$compl_a = \frac{instructions\ executed\ in\ the\ application}{packet\ size}. \tag{3.10}$$

For an I/O channel operating at a load of ρ_{IO}, the I/O channel bandwidth, bw_{IO}, for the entire NP is:

$$bw_{IO} = 2 \cdot \frac{IPS}{compl_a \cdot \rho_{IO}}. \tag{3.11}$$

The number of pins on the NP package can also be determined by summing the pins required for I/O and memory channels with the pins required for control and power. The number of memory channel pins is obtained directly from $width_{mchl}$, while the number of I/O memory pins can be obtained from a knowledge of bw_{IO} and the I/O channel clock frequency.

3.1.1   The Benchmark

To properly evaluate and design NPs it is necessary to specify a workload typical of the environment. This has been done in the development of the benchmark CommBench [15].

Benchmark Applications

CommBench applications represent typical workloads for both traditional routers (focus on header processing) and programmable routers (perform both header and stream processing). Thus, the applications can be divided into two groups: header-processing applications (HPA) and payload-processing applications (PPA).

A desirable property of any application in a benchmark is its representativeness of a wider class of applications in the domain of interest. Therefore, a key focus is on the "kernels" of the applications, which are the program fragments containing the set of most frequently used instructions. The application kernels associated with W1 and W2 applications are shown in Table 3.1.

Workload	Name	Type	Application	Kernel
W1	RTR	HPA	Radix tree routing	Lookup on tree data structure
	FRAG	HPA	IP header fragmentation	Packet header checksum computation
	DRR	HPA	Deficit round-robin	Queue maintenance
	TCP	HPA	TCP filtering	Pattern matching on header fields
W2	CAST	PPA	Encryption	Encryption arithmetic
	ZIP	PPA	Data compression	Compression arithmetic
	REED	PPA	Reed-Solomon FEC	Redundancy coding
	JPEG	PPA	JPEG compression	DCT and Huffman coding

3.1   Benchmark applications.

TABLE

For each application, the properties required for the performance model have been measured experimentally: computational complexity ($compl_a$), load and store instruction frequencies (f_{load_a}, f_{store_a}), instruction cache and data cache miss rate ($mi_{ci,a}, md_{cd,a}$), and dirty bit probability ($dirty_{cd,a}$). These parameter values were obtained with a processor and cache simulator (Shade [3] and Dinero [4], and verified with SimpleScalar [2]) for cache sizes ranging from 1 KB to 64 KB. A 2-way associative write-back cache with a line size of 32 bytes was simulated. The cache miss rates were measured such that cold cache misses were amortized over a long program run. Thus, they can be assumed to represent the steady-state miss rates of these applications.

Workload

For our model, we use two workloads, W1 and W2, which are aggregates of the applications in CommBench. A list of the applications is given in Table 3.1. Workload W1 is a combination of the four header-processing applications. Workload W2 consists of the four payload-processing applications. The applications within the workloads are weighted such that each application processes the same number of instructions over time. W1 applications process packet headers only and are generally less computationally demanding than W2 applications that process all data in a packet.

The average values for the model parameters were obtained for each of the benchmarks (W1 and W2) by averaging over the benchmark application values assuming equal probabilities for each application. Table 3.2 shows the aggregate complexity and load and store frequencies of the workloads. Note that the complexity of payload processing is significantly higher than for header processing. This is due to the fact that payload processing actually touches every byte of the packet payload (e.g., transcoding, encryption). Header processing typically reads a few header fields only and does simple lookup and comparison operations. The other benchmark parameter values can be found in [15].

The aggregate cache miss rates for instruction and data cache are shown in Figure 3.3. Both workloads achieve instruction miss rates below 1% for cache

Workload	$compl$	f_{load}	f_{store}
W1 (HPA)	3.77	0.2118	0.0838
W2 (PPA)	203	0.1822	0.0569

3.2

TABLE

Computational complexity and load and store frequencies of workloads.

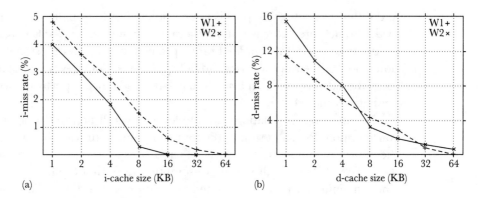

Aggregate cache performance of workloads: (a) instruction cache; (b) data cache.

sizes of above 8 KB. The data cache miss rates for the workloads drop below 2% for 32 KB.

With all workload parameters defined, the processing performance of the network processor system can be determined. Section 3.2 explores how to derive other system metrics.

3.2   POWER MODEL

The IPS metric is one of three that must be obtained in determining the "best" NP architecture configuration. The second critical metric relates to the power consumption (watts) associated with the design. The third is the NP chip area, considered in the next section.

3.2.1   Overall Power Model

The principal components considered in the power calculations are:

+ Processor ALUs
+ Processor clock
+ Processor instruction and data caches (level 1, on-chip)
+ Off-chip memory and I/O bus

Since we are interested in relative performance of alternative configurations for the architecture of Figure 3.1, power associated with off-chip components and with driving the chip pins is not considered. Additionally, the contribution of the branch predictor is ignored because for simple NP RISC cores it is not necessary to perform complex branch prediction and, overall, system power is dominated by memory accesses and I/O operations. Complex superscalar processors, where a mispredicted branch may have a significant performance impact, are not considered.

For all of our simulations, we model the overall network processor power consumption, P_{NP}, as a sum of the four components previously listed (scaled to the appropriate number of processors and sizes of caches). This makes up for 94 to 97% of the overall power consumption (ignoring the branch predictor). The remaining 3 to 7% is consumed by register files and miscellaneous control components.

For CMOS technology, dynamic power consumption P_d is defined as:

$$P_d = C \cdot V_{dd}^2 \cdot a \cdot f, \tag{3.12}$$

where C is the aggregate load capacitance associated with each component, V_{dd} is the supply voltage, a is the switching activity for each clock tick ($0 \leq a \leq 1$ and can be considered to be the utilization of the component), and f is the clock frequency. The energy expended per cycle is:[2]

$$E_d = C \cdot V_{dd}^2 \cdot a. \tag{3.13}$$

By obtaining parameter values for Equations 3.12 and 3.13, the power consumption models for each of the components is determined. The sum of these models yields an overall power consumption model for the NP. Most of the parameters are based on usage of the Wattch toolkit [1] and Cacti [11, 12]. These values correspond to the use of an Alpha 21264 processor [7] and a .35-μm technology. Since we are primarily interested in comparative NP configurations and what they illustrate about NP design, smaller-feature-size technologies are not initially considered. However, the analytic models presented apply with adjustments of the parameter values for other technologies (e.g., .18-μm and $V_{dd} = 2.0$ volts).

To verify the analytic power model, power results are compared to the power results obtained from executing Wattch over the benchmark discussed. This is considered in Section 3.2.6. Once the model has been verified, optimal NP configurations are then obtained analytically without resorting to the use of Wattch simulations.

---

2. The power modeling does not account for leakage currents and associated power, which become more important as feature sizes shrink below .15 μm.

3.2.2   ALU Power Model

ALU power depends on the voltage, V_{dd}; processor clock frequency, f; the ALU utilization, a_{ALU}; and capacitance:

$$P_{ALU} = C_{ALU} \cdot V_{dd}^2 \cdot a_{ALU} \cdot f. \tag{3.14}$$

Using Wattch, the capacitance for .35-μm technology (the process specification of an Alpha 21264 [7] simulated by Wattch) can be obtained as 310 pF. V_{dd} for this case is 2.5 volts.

The value for a_{ALU} (that corresponds to the ALU utilization, ρ_{ALU}) used by Wattch is 1. As discussed later, this value is used to verify the analytic power model by comparing model results with the results obtained from Wattch. However, by using a value of 1, the Wattch simulator assumes that the ALU is busy on every cycle. This is not true during stalls due to cache misses. Thus, the value used in our optimization studies (as contrasted with the power model verification work) is obtained from Equation 3.2 ($a_{ALU} = \rho_p$) and reflects the effects of cache misses on component utilization.

3.2.3   Clock

In a similar fashion, clock power consumption can be obtained:

$$P_{clk} = C_{clk} \cdot V_{dd}^2 \cdot a_{clk} \cdot f. \tag{3.15}$$

Since the clock is changing state in every cycle, $a_{clk} = 1$. From Wattch, we obtain $C_{clk} = 3.33\,n$F. With differing cache configurations, the clock power consumption can vary by up to $\pm 8\%$; however, the model does not consider this effect. As will be shown in Section 3.2.6, overall power consumption that is predicted corresponds well to that obtained with Wattch.

3.2.4   Caches

The expression for cache power consumption is:

$$P_{c_i} = C_{c_i} \cdot V_{dd}^2 \cdot a_{c_i} \cdot f. \tag{3.16}$$

The dynamic power consumption of caches is due to memory accesses. For the instruction cache, the i-cache is accessed for each instruction. Additionally, the

Cache size (KB)	i-cache capacitance (nF)	d-cache capacitance (nF)
1	0.369	0.378
2	0.397	0.406
4	0.440	0.450
8	0.541	0.570
16	0.708	0.739
32	0.957	1.030
64	1.368	1.412

3.3

TABLE

Cache capacitance for .35-μm technology. The cache line size is 32 bytes and associativity level is 2. For instruction caches, one read/write port and one read port are assumed. For data caches, two read/write ports are assumed.

i-cache is accessed after each pipeline stall due to i-cache misses or branch misprediction (we do not consider misprediction effects on cache power in this analysis). Adding in the effects of cache usage occurring after a miss, one obtains:

$$a_{c_i} = \rho_p \cdot (1 + mi_{ci,a}), \tag{3.17}$$

where $mi_{ci,a}$ is the instruction cache miss probability associated with application a and instruction cache size ci.

The data cache is accessed for each read/write (load-store) instruction and for each d-cache miss, thus:

$$a_{c_d} = \rho_p \cdot ((f_{load_a} + f_{store_a}) \cdot (1 + md_{cd,a})). \tag{3.18}$$

The cache capacitance, C_{c_i} and C_{c_d}, is shown in Table 3.3. These numbers are given by the Cacti tool [12] for .35-μm technology.

3.2.5   Memory and I/O Bus

The same approach taken in Wattch is used to calculate the power consumption of the memory and I/O busses. The memory channel is characterized by its width, $width_{mchl}$; physical length on the chip, $length_{mchl}$; clock frequency, f_{mchl}; and utilization, $a_{mchl} = \rho_{mchl}$. As part of the optimization procedure, the channel utilization, as used in performance model Equations 3.4 to 3.9, is varied to find its value associated with the optimal configuration.

The capacitance, C_{mchl}, is based on the width and length parameters and is given by:

$$C_{mchl} = 2 \cdot C_{.35\,\mu m} \cdot width_{mchl} \cdot length_{mchl}. \tag{3.19}$$

The factor of 2 is due to the coupling capacitance between wires. The length of the memory channel is taken to be $length_{mchl} = 5\,mm$, which is the expected distance to a processor from the edge of a chip. We also explored a larger channel length, of 20 mm. This, however, only affects the overall results by about 1%. The width is set to 32 bits. The capacitance parameter associated with using .35-μm technology is obtained from scaling the capacitance associated with Wattch's "result bus," yielding $C_{.35\,\mu m} = 0.275\,fF/\mu m$.

3.2.6 Validation

To compare the validity of the previously cited power model, the energy results obtained with Wattch are compared with the model results. In the validation experiment, all applications in the benchmark were executed for cache configurations ranging from 1 KB to 64 KB. Figure 3.4 shows the Wattch results versus the model results. Ideally, each cross point would lie on the dashed line, which corresponds to the model and Wattch having the same results. It should be noted that Wattch simulates a complex superscalar processor. To make a reasonable

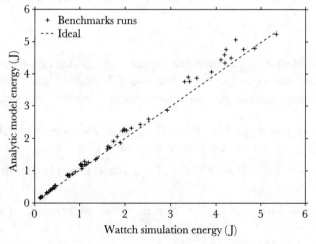

3.4

FIGURE

Comparison of benchmark application execution energy for Wattch toolkit and analytic model.

comparison to the RISC core we are modeling, only the ALU, clock, and cache access power from Wattch were considered. Since there is no shared memory bus modeled in Wattch, we cannot compare the results for this component.

The maximum error is 15.8% for the smallest cache size. This is due to differences in the results from the Cacti toolkit versus the Wattch results. For larger caches, the differences are much smaller. With an average error of only 8%, the analytic approximation of power consumption is a useful tool for NP design space exploration.

3.3 PERFORMANCE METRICS

We use several performance metrics to evaluate design choices. Processing performance comes at the cost of power consumption and chip area. To be able to capture the chip area cost, A, we use the following expression (see [6]):

$$A = s(io) + m \cdot (s(mchl) + n \cdot (s(p) + s(ci) + s(cd))), \tag{3.20}$$

where s is the area of a processor ($s(p)$), the caches ($s(ci)$ and $s(cd)$), the memory channel ($s(mchl)$), and the I/O channel ($s(io)$). For .35-μm CMOS technology, we assume $s(p) = 4\,\text{mm}^2$, $s(c) = 0.5\,\text{mm}^2/\text{KB}$, and $s(mchl) = 28\,\text{mm}^2$ (20 mm^2 for the channel and 8 mm^2 for memory channel logic).

With an expression for processing performance (IPS), power consumption (P), and chip area (A), performance metrics of the following form can be derived:

$$Performance = IPS^{\alpha} \cdot A^{\beta} \cdot P^{\gamma}. \tag{3.21}$$

In particular, we are interested in the metrics that consider area and power consumption as a cost ($\beta, \gamma \leq 0$) and $\alpha < 0$. For the design results in Section 3.4, the following common processor performance metrics are used:

+ *Processing/power or IPS $\cdot P^{-1}$*. This metric assumes an equal weight to processing performance and power consumption.

+ *Processing/(power)^2 or IPS $\cdot P^{-2}$*. In this case, power consumption is weighted higher.

+ *Processing/area or IPS $\cdot A^{-1}$*. This metric considers only area, and no power consumption (as used in [6]).

+ *Processing/area/power or IPS $\cdot A^{-1} \cdot P^{-1}$*. This combines both area and power costs.

3.4 DESIGN RESULTS

In this section, design results based on the "optimal" design for a given metric are considered. To obtain this "optimal" design, the entire design space is examined and the best configuration of cache sizes ($ci, cd = 1$ KB ... 64 KB), number of processors ($n \geq 1$, limited by maximum memory channel load), and memory channel utilization ($\rho_{mchl} = 0 \ldots 0.999$) is obtained. The processor clock frequency is 600 MHz, and the memory channel clock frequency is 240 MHz.

3.4.1 Performance Trends

Figure 3.5 illustrates the basic trends for the components of the performance metrics from Equation 3.21. To illustrate basic trends, the cache sizes in this figure are set to 8 KB for both the instruction and data caches. The number of processors, n, that share a memory channel (i.e., processors in a cluster) is shown on the x axis. The y axis shows the increase in processing performance, power consumption, and area relative to a configuration with a single processor ($n = 1$).

As expected, the area curve, A, increases linearly with the number of processors (the slope depends on the proportion of processor and cache sizes to

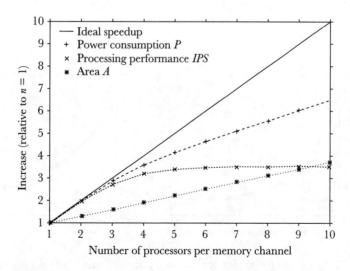

Number of processors per memory channel

3.5

FIGURE

Trends of processing performance, area, and power. The workload is W1 and cache sizes are $c_i = 8$ KB and $c_d = 8$ KB.

the memory channel). The instructions-per-second curve, *IPS*, initially increases more rapidly than A, but then at about six processor levels out. This is due to the fact that with increasing numbers of processors the shared memory channel load, ρ_{mchl}, increases due to processor contention for use of the channel. However, at saturation, the memory responds to requests at its maximum rate and hence the *IPS* remains steady.

The trends depicted in Figure 3.5 show that power consumption grows fastest. The faster growth of power is due to memory channel contention. If more processors share a memory channel, the processor stall time on a cache miss increases. During a stall, the processor does no useful computation, but still consumes energy. As a result, the total processing performance does not increase very much, but power consumption does. These trends are very similar for all cache configurations. The plateaus for processing performance are higher for larger caches since miss rates are lower and thereby contention on the memory channel is less. In all cases, however, power consumption grows faster than processing performance.

The effect on the performance metrics is shown in Figure 3.6, where each metric is shown versus a range of processors for both workloads. Figure 3.6a shows the trends for both power-related metrics (*IPS/P* and *IPS/P²*). Because power increases faster than processing performance, the performance drops with an increasing number of processors. This means that from the point of view of power consumption fewer processors per memory channel are preferable. Looking at the impact of area in Figure 3.6b, however, fewer processors are

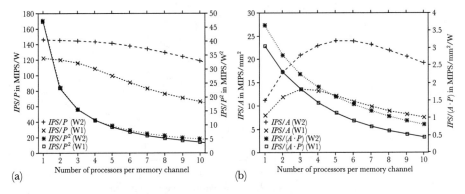

Performance trends for various performance metrics and workloads: (a) power-related (*IPS/P* and *IPS/P²* and (b) area related (*IPS/A* and *IPS/(A · P)*). The cache sizes are set to $c_i = 8$ KB and $c_d = 8$ KB.

not necessarily best. There is a clear optimum for three (workload W1) or six (workload W2) processors. The differences between the workloads are due to different cache miss rates. When combining both area and power, again, power consumption dominates the cost and causes a clear drop in performance for more processors.

The implications for network processor design are the following:

+ An increasing number of processors per memory interface increases the relative power consumption for the network processors. This comes from power dissipation of the clock during stall cycles while waiting for memory access and suggests that fewer processors (ideally one) per memory interface is best in terms of power consumption. However, that is not realistic from the point of view of the number of external memory chips that would be required. Thus, there is the trade-off between power dissipation, which requires few processors with high utilizations and many interfaces, and the costs and engineering constraints (e.g., pin limitations) associated with having many memory interfaces.

+ When considering area constraints in the design, having only one processor per interface is not optimal. Instead, the optimum is reached when a few processors are clustered to share a memory interface. The optimal configuration depends on the workload and technology parameters.

+ Other measures can be taken to avoid energy consumption during memory stalls. Multithreading allows a processor to switch to a different task when encountering stalls. Clock gating can be used to reduce the power consumption of components that are not in use.

One main observation from our design results is that a significant amount of power is lost through processor stalls. For the optimal configurations, shown in Table 3.4, the processor utilization, ρ_p, ranges from 30% to 50%. This emphasizes the importance of multithreading support in network processors. With additional hardware threads and zero-overhead context switching, the processing power can be increased significantly. In our previous work [6], we have shown that the processing power improvement for two threads easily makes up for the additional area cost associated with multithread register files.

3.4.2 Optimal Cache Configuration

One key question for system-on-a-chip design is how to find a good balance between processing logic and on-chip memory. Network processor designs are constrained by the maximum chip size. More processing engines mean more

Metric	Workload	Chip configuration					Total IPS (MIPS)	Total P (W)	Throughput (Gb/s)
		m	n	$m \cdot n$	ci	cd			
IPS/P	W1	10	1	10	8	8	3181	26.0	6.75
	W2	10	1	10	8	8	4499	30.8	0.18
IPS/P^2	W1	10	1	10	1	4	2095	19.7	4.45
	W2	11	1	11	1	4	2293	19.9	0.09
IPS/A	W1	4	4	16	16	8	5360	48.7	11.37
	W2	4	6	24	8	8	9603	69.2	0.38
$IPS/(A \cdot P)$	W1	11	1	11	4	4	2652	22.6	5.63
	W2	10	1	10	8	8	4499	30.8	0.18
$IPS/\sqrt{A \cdot P}$	W1	5	3	15	16	8	5406	47.7	11.47
	W2	4	5	20	8	8	8448	59.6	0.33

3.4

TABLE

Chip configurations and throughput results. This table shows the optimal configurations for various optimization metrics for a 400-mm^2 chip.

processing cycles, but also smaller caches, higher cache miss rates, more memory contention, and higher energy consumption. Using our model, we can find the optimal cache configuration for a given metric. The design space is relatively small, and an exhaustive enumeration of the design options can be used to obtain the optimum design. Figures 3.7a through 3.7d show the performance of various cache configurations for the various performance metrics.

The following observations can be made regarding the optimal cache size:

+ For IPS/P (Figure 3.7a), the optimum lies at $ci = 8$ KB and $cd = 32$ KB. Since processing power increases with larger caches (due to fewer memory stalls), the optimum configuration uses a large data cache.

+ For IPS/P^2 (Figure 3.7b), the optimum lies at $ci = 4$ KB and $cd = 4$ KB. Even though the optimization metric is based on power (as is IPS/P), the optimum configuration yields small caches, which is quite different from the optimum for IPS/P. Because of the quadratic cost for power consumption, larger caches cost more than they can contribute in terms of processing power.

+ For IPS/A (Figure 3.7c), the optimum lies at $ci = 16$ KB and $cd = 8$ KB. For this metric, small caches cause inefficient processing and large caches cost

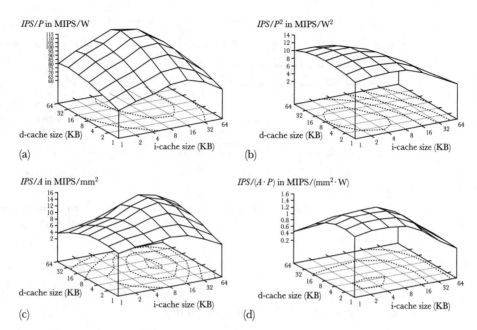

IPS/P in MIPS/W

IPS/P² in MIPS/W²

d-cache size (KB)

i-cache size (KB)

(a)

(b)

IPS/A in MIPS/mm²

IPS/(A · P) in MIPS/(mm² · W)

d-cache size (KB)

i-cache size (KB)

(c)

(d)

3.7

FIGURE

Performance of cache configurations for various performance metrics. The work-load is W1 and the number of processors per memory channel is set to four: (a) IPS/P; (b) IPS/P^2; (c) IPS/A; (d) $IPS/(A \cdot P)$.

too much in terms of area. Thus, there is a clear optimum for a medium configuration.

✦ For $IPS/(A \cdot P)$ (Figure 3.7d), the optimum lies at $ci = 4\,\text{KB}$ and $cd = 4\,\text{KB}$. Here, the optimum configuration again uses small caches, because both area and power contribute to the cost. The larger caches contribute to a better IPS performance but at the same time cost in terms of area and power.

From these observations, we can conclude that for both IPS/P and IPS/A there are clear optima for which the network processor can be configured. Using any combination metric involving power as a cost function (e.g., P^2 or $A \cdot P$) yields very small cache configurations, since the IPS improvements cannot keep up with the cost for larger caches. If a metric for both area and power is desired, it might be more suitable to use $IPS/\sqrt{A \cdot P}$, as it keeps a balance between performance and total cost.

The values for the optimal instruction and data cache sizes as a function of the number of processors per cluster are shown in Figures 3.8a and 3.8b. There is

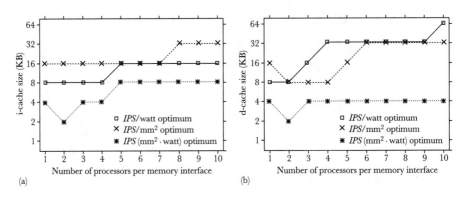

3.8

FIGURE

Optimal cache configuration for various numbers of processors per memory channel: (a) optimal instruction cache size; (b) optimal data cache size. The workload is W1.

a slight trend toward larger caches for more processors, as again more processors cause more load on the memory channel.

3.4.3   Chip Configurations

Table 3.4 shows overall chip configurations for a 400-mm^2 chip. The table shows the optimal configurations in terms of number of memory interfaces, m, and processors per memory channel, n. For all metrics and workloads, the overall throughput of such a system is also shown, which is determined by the complexity of the workload and the overall processing power (*IPS/compl*). Note that the complexity for workload W2 is about 50 times higher than that of W1, which results in the large differences in throughput. Thus, while header-processing applications can achieve throughput rates in the gigabit range, payload-processing applications have rates well under a gigabit for all performance metrics. This is consistent with the notion that these types of applications (e.g., encryption) often require special-purpose processors and logic to achieve high throughput rates.

For power-related metrics, the trends shown in Figure 3.6 result in optimal configurations with only one processor per interface. This, however, yields a lower throughput than when optimizing for area only. On the other hand, power consumption for the area-optimized configuration is about twice as high as that for power-optimized configurations. The $IPS/\sqrt{A \cdot P}$ metric is a good combination of area and power. It yields configurations with four to five memory interfaces and good throughput (e.g., for workload W1, $IPS/\sqrt{A \cdot P}$ yields higher throughput with less power consumption than IPS/A).

The overall power consumption of the optimal configurations with 20 W to 70 W is higher than current commercial systems, which consume on the order of 10 W. This is due to commercial NPs using more advanced CMOS technologies with smaller feature sizes and overall chip sizes (e.g., Intel IXP2400: .18 μm versus .35 μm and 1.3 V versus 2.5 V [10]).

3.5   SUMMARY AND CONCLUSIONS

This work develops an analytic model for power consumption of network processor systems-on-a-chip. Combining this with the performance model we have developed in previous work, we show how both models can be used to yield an understanding of power issues for these systems. Our power model was verified through comparison with the Wattch toolkit, with an average error of only 8%. Using a workload derived from our CommBench benchmark for model parametrization, we obtain quantitative results for various performance metrics. This enabled the determination of optimal network processor configurations in terms of cache configurations and number of processors per memory interface. We believe this is an important step toward developing network processor architectures that yield high processing power, but are also within the power constraints of realistic systems.

Currently, we are refining the models and methodology presented. In particular, we are expanding the analysis to reflect multithreading. Additionally, we are investigating the use of more accurate power, associated capacitance models, and incorporation of limitations on the number of external memory chips that can be used.

ACKNOWLEDGMENTS

The research has been supported in part by National Science Foundation grant CCR-0217334.

REFERENCES

[1]   D. Brooks, V. Tiwari, and M. Martonosi, "Wattch: A Framework for Architectural-Level Power Analysis and Optimizations," *Proc. of ACM ISCA-27*, Vancouver, BC, June 2000, pp. 83–94.

[2]   D. Burger and T. M. Austin, "The SimpleScalar Tool Set, Version 2.0," Technical Report 1342, Department of Computer Science, University of Wisconsin in Madison, June 1997.

[3]   R. F. Cmelik and D. Keppel, "Shade: A Fast Instruction-Set Simulator for Execution Profiling," *Proc. of ACM SIGMETRICS*, Nashville, TN, May 1994, pp. 128–137.

[4]   J. Edler and M. D. Hill, *Dinero IV Trace-Driven Uniprocessor Cache Simulator*, 1998, *www.cs.wisc.edu/~markhill/DineroIV/*.

[5]   EZchip Technologies Ltd., Yokneam, Israel. *NP-1 10-Gigabit 7-Layer Network Processor*, 2002, *www.ezchip.com/html/pr_np-1.html*.

[6]   M. A. Franklin and T. Wolf, "A Network Processor Performance and Design Model with Benchmark Parameterization," *Network Processor Workshop in Conjunction with Eighth International Symposium on High Performance Computer Architecture (HPCA-8)*, Cambridge, MA, Feb. 2002, pp. 63–74.

[7]   M. K. Gowan, L. L. Biro, and D. B. Jackson, "Power Considerations in the Design of the Alpha 21264 Microprocessor," *Proc. of 35th Design Automation Conference*, San Francisco, CA, June 1998, pp. 726–731.

[8]   J. L. Hennessy and D. A. Patterson, *Computer Architecture—A Quantitative Approach* (2nd ed.), San Francisco, CA: Morgan Kaufmann, 1995.

[9]   IBM Corp., *IBM Power Network Processors*, 2000, *www.chips.ibm.com/products/wired/ communications/network_processors.html*.

[10]   Intel Corp., *Intel IXP2800 Network Processor*, 2002, *http://developer.intel.com/design/ network/products/npfamily/ixp2800.htm*.

[11]   G. Reinman and N. P. Jouppi, "CACTI 2.0: An Integrated Cache Timing and Power Model," Technical Report WRL, Research Report 2000/7, Western Research Laboratory, Palo Alto, CA, Feb. 2000.

[12]   P. Shivakumar and N. P. Jouppi, CACTI 3.0: An integrated cache timing, power and area model. Technical Report WRL Research Report 2001/2, Western Research Laboratory, Palo Alto, CA, Aug. 2001.

[13]   Silicon Access Networks, San Jose, CA, *iFlow Family Overview*, 2002, *www.siliconaccess .com/products/iFlow_DP3_PB_2.6.pdf*.

[14]   T. Wolf, "Design and Performance of a Scalable High-Performance Programmable Router," Ph.D. thesis, Department of Computer Science, Washington University, St. Louis, MO, May 2002.

[15]   T. Wolf and M. A. Franklin, "CommBench: A Telecommunications Benchmark for Network Processors," *Proc. of IEEE International Symposium on Performance Analysis of Systems and Software (ISPASS)*, Austin, TX, Apr. 2000, pp. 154–162.

[16]   T. Wolf and M. A. Franklin, "Design Trade-Offs for Embedded Network Processors," *Proc. of International Conference on Architecture of Computing Systems (ARCS) (Lecture Notes in Computer Science)*, vol. 2299, Karlsruhe, Germany, Apr. 2002, Springer-Verlag, pp. 149–164.

4

Worst-Case Execution Time Estimation for Hardware-Assisted Multithreaded Processors

Patrick Crowley, Jean-Loup Baer
Department of Computer Science and Engineering,
University of Washington

Network-processing systems are real-time systems: if packet-processing times exceed inter-arrival times, system instability will result (e.g., due to input buffer overflows). Consequently, network-processing systems must process packets at network line rates. When a packet-processing function is implemented in hardware, the packet-processing rate, or throughput, is typically fixed and evident in the circuit timings. However, when such a function is implemented in software on a programmable processor, such as a network processor, the packet-processing rate becomes variable (e.g., because of differing packet lengths).

To provide some estimate of throughput in the presence of this variability, some model, or trace, of expected traffic is used to measure packet-processing rates. Examples of such traffic include minimum-size packets or traces gathered in networks where deployment of the system is anticipated. This provides the designer with an expected level of performance, referred to here as an expected packet-processing rate.

In this chapter, we propose a complementary approach that bounds packet-processing rates in a traffic-independent fashion. Our approach determines the peak performance attainable under worst-case circumstances, thus setting a bound on the processing rates for which we can ensure that the system will deliver packets at the advertised rate. There are two additional reasons to follow such an approach: (1) traffic can vary widely and expected performance might not be characteristic, and (2) the relationship between program performance and traffic characteristics is poorly understood and it is thus, in general, difficult to know how changes in traffic will affect performance. We see great value in being able to accurately describe both the expected and worst-case performance of software-based network-processing systems.

Our interest is in determining the worst-case packet-processing rate for a network-processing system built around a programmable network processor (NP). This goal involves certain challenges: (1) programs can have complex control flow, (2) the packet-handling process is generally structured as a software pipeline, and (3) NPs typically employ multiple multithreaded processors to implement functionality. The method described in this chapter deals with these challenges as follows.

The basic method used here to deal with the complexity of programs employs an implicit path-enumeration technique (IPET) [7] to find a bound on the worst-case execution time (WCET) of a program. IPET reduces the problem of finding the WCET to that of finding the most expensive path through a network flow graph, a problem readily solved with integer linear programming methods.

If the packet-handling process is structured as a pipeline of programs, and if parallel resources (such as multiple processors) can be used to exploit pipeline parallelism between packets, then we can determine the worst-case throughput of the pipeline (e.g., the worst-case packet-processing rate) by finding the pipeline stage with the greatest WCET. This slowest pipe stage determines how quickly packets may safely enter the pipeline; the inverse of this WCET is the worst-case packet-processing rate.

Modern NPs feature multiple embedded processors and thus facilitate this parallelization of pipeline stages. Furthermore, many NPs—notably Intel's IXP and IBM's PowerNP—include hardware-assisted multithreading in each embedded processor. This multithreading provides low- or zero-cost context switches, so that as one thread begins to stall (waiting on some long latency operation, such as a DRAM read) another thread can be swapped in to use the otherwise idle processor resources. Multithreading increases resource utilization and can therefore increase system throughput, with the potential danger of increasing the latency (i.e., worst-case processing time) of an instance of a packet-processing function. The method proposed in this chapter takes this flavor of multithreading into account when determining the worst-case packet-processing rate.

The general theme of this chapter stems from the realization that it is important to describe the worst-case performance for software-based implementations of network-processing systems. To this effect, we introduce and evaluate a method for bounding worst-case performance on a programmable, multithreaded network processor. The evaluation in this chapter targets the Intel IXP1200 NP; worst-case processing rates for a number of programs are compared to some corresponding simulated processing rates.

The remainder of the paper is structured as follows. Section 4.1 first provides greater background on the structure and implementation of functionality on multithreaded NPs, and then sketches the method used to bound system performance in such systems. Section 4.2 introduces the base method of determining a program's worst-case throughput by finding its WCET. Section 4.3 introduces the multithreading extension to the base method by considering the case of two threads; Section 4.4 discusses the case of four threads. Limitations and future work are discussed in Section 4.5. The chapter concludes with a summary and discussion of contributions in Section 4.6.

4.1   BACKGROUND AND MOTIVATION

Both the sequential (e.g., pipelined) nature of packet handling and the parallel, multithreaded organization of modern NPs are dominant factors in determining a system's worst-case packet-processing rate. In this section, we explore both factors and then discuss the flavor of multithreading considered in this chapter.

4.1.1   Handling Packets with Software Pipelines on Multithreaded Chip Multiprocessors

The steps involved in handling a packet are inherently sequential. When a packet arrives, it must first be moved from the external transmission medium into memory. Once in memory, packet processing begins and typically proceeds according to the layers in a protocol stack. When a TCP/IP packet is received over Ethernet, for instance, the Ethernet headers are processed first, followed by the IP headers. Such processing can proceed up the networking stack, including application-specific processing in the data payload (e.g., such as HTTP URL parsing). Once all processing has completed—including classification, modification, next-hop lookups, and any other application-specific processing—the packet must be transmitted out of memory and onto the appropriate output link. These steps in the packet-handling process can be described as stages in a pipeline. This pipelined nature can be exploited for increased performance: if stages can execute in parallel (say, on different embedded processors) and if the amount of computation in each stage is balanced, then throughput can be increased by exploiting pipeline parallelism.

Since modern NPs feature multiple processors, pipeline parallelism can be exploited. Such an arrangement suggests that a packet will be processsed by several processors (one for each pipe stage). This is no requirement, however. Another approach would be to simply implement the full packet-handling process on each processor and let them proceed in parallel without any pipelining. This certainly has scalability benefits over the pipelining approach, since the parallelism available with a pipeline is limited to the number of pipe stages. However, it also has greater costs. One practical consideration is the increased amount of control store needed by each processor; modern NPs typically have small control stores available at each embedded processor, which cannot hold the programs necessary to handle all packet-processing functions. Thus, NPs tend to favor pipelined or pipelined/parallel hybrid implementations over fully parallel ones.

Regardless of whether a given processor implements the full pipeline or only one stage, we can view the software it executes as a program that processes packets. The rate at which this program processes packets will influence the worst-case processing rate of the entire system; either it will determine it completely if the program implements the entire packet-processing pipeline or it will contribute to it as a single stage.

Modern NPs are multithreaded to help hide the long latencies required to access memory and other external resources. Thus, throughput can be improved by running multiple copies of the packet-processing program in different threads on the same processor. Again, this applies regardless of how the pipeline is mapped onto processors.

In this chapter, we consider replication of identical threads (i.e., replication of pipeline stages), but the method is applicable to the other arrangement as well.

4.1.2   Non-Preemptive, Hardware-Assisted Multithreading

The flavor of multithreading we consider in this chapter can be described as non-preemptive and hardware-assisted. The term *non-preemptive* refers to how threads are scheduled: it is up to each thread to yield control to the scheduler. This is in contrast to a preemptive scheduler that can interrupt the execution of one thread to switch control to another. The term *hardware-assisted* refers to both the hardware scheduler and the resources provided to each thread. When multithreading is hardware-assisted, each thread is allowed to save its architectural state (control and data registers, PC, and so on) in private hardware. This is opposed to a thread having to save its state to memory prior to a context switch.

This chapter assumes a threading model identical to that found in the Intel IXP1200. Each processor has support for up to four threads of execution, and context switches require a single cycle (which can be hidden via delayed execution, as is common with branch instructions). On the IXP1200, all long latency operations, such as memory operations, accept an optional parameter requesting a context switch. Since the arbiter is non-preemptive, the programmer, or compiler, must include these optional parameters often to keep any one thread from monopolizing the processor.

4.2   PROCESSING THROUGHPUT OF A SINGLE THREAD OF EXECUTION

Our approach for determining the worst-case packet-processing rate of a program begins with determining the program's WCET. In this chapter, we use the implicit path-enumeration technique (IPET) from [5, 6, 7]; this is one, and in our view the most promising, of a number of recent results in the area of determining WCET on modern processors [2, 3, 8, 9, 10]. For a program running on a single threaded processor, the worst-case processing rate is the inverse of the program's WCET.

4.2.1   WCET Analysis via Implicit Path Enumeration

The WCET of a program depends on two factors: the path of instructions to be executed and the microarchitecture of the processor. In IPET, the possible, or feasible, execution paths through a program are described implicitly with a set of linear, network flow constraints extracted from the program's control flow graph (these constraints describe how often each basic block in the program can be executed).

To determine the execution cost, in cycles, of each basic block, the microarchitecture of the processor must be considered. The work in [7] describes how to account for pipelined execution units, as well as for instruction and data caches. Since the NPs we consider in this chapter have no caches, we do not consider cache-related effects; we return to this topic when discussing future work, in Section 4.5. When pipeline stalls might occur or when delayed branch operations (present in the NP engines that we model) are used, we assume the worst cases; these assumptions introduce some pessimism into the WCET estimate.

Once the execution costs for all basic blocks are known, they can be combined with the flow constraints to form an integer linear program. To find the WCET, the objective function, which sums the product of basic block frequencies and costs, is maximized subject to the constraints via integer linear programming.

For this optimization problem to be decidable, we must place certain restrictions on how programs are written. This set of sufficient restrictions has been described by [4, 12]. The restrictions are: (1) no recursion, (2) no dynamic data structures, and (3) no unbounded loops. These are not overly restrictive conditions, as we are concerned with applications for NPs that for precisely the same reasons do not generally have these restricted features.

We now show how to construct the linear program from a program's control flow graph. We illustrate this construction with a small program. For a more complete discussion, see [7].

4.2.2   Constructing the Linear Program

Suppose we have N basic blocks, B_i, in our control flow graph (CFG). Let the variable x_i represent the execution frequency of block B_i, and let c_i represent its execution time, or cost, in processor cycles. The program's total execution time can be expressed as:

$$\text{Total execution time} = \sum_i^N c_i x_i. \tag{4.1}$$

The purpose of the linear program is to find the set of feasible x_i values that maximizes the objective function (Equation 4.1). The x_i variables are constrained by the feasible flow in the control flow graph. Figure 4.1 depicts a program fragment and its associated CFG. This code checks an array of integers, of size *datasize*, for any negative numbers. If a negative number is found, the function immediately returns a 0; otherwise, it examines all entries and returns 1. Each basic block has an execution frequency variable as well as some number of in and out edges (denoted d_i), which describe the flow between basic blocks.

There are two types of constraints in the graph shown in Figure 4.1: structural and functional. The *structural* constraints require that the flow into a node equal the flow out. In general, we have

$$x_i = \sum d_l = \sum d_m, \tag{4.2}$$

where the d_l are the incoming edges and the d_m are the outgoing edges.

The following equations describe the structural constraints that can be automatically extracted from the CFG shown in Figure 4.1b.

$$d_1 = 1 \tag{4.3}$$
$$x_1 = d_1 + d_6 + d_8 + d_9 = d_2 + d_3 \tag{4.4}$$
$$x_2 = d_2 = d_4 + d_5 \tag{4.5}$$
$$x_3 = d_4 = d_6 \tag{4.6}$$
$$x_4 = d_5 = d_7 + d_8 \tag{4.7}$$

$$x_5 = d_7 = d_9 \tag{4.8}$$

$$x_6 = d_3 = d_{10} + d_{11} \tag{4.9}$$

$$x_7 = d_{10} = d_{12} \tag{4.10}$$

$$x_8 = d_{11} = d_{13} \tag{4.11}$$

The *functional* constraints constrain flow through the graph according to the program semantics. Loop bounds are the principal example and are indeed the only required functional constraints. In the code fragment, we see that the *while* loop will be taken between 1 and 10 times. The following equation expresses this constraint.

$$10d_1 \geq x_1 \geq 1d_1 \tag{4.12}$$

Other information may also be present in the program's semantics to obtain a tighter WCET estimate. For instance, the block B_3 can be executed at most once each time we enter the code fragment. We can add the following constraint to express this condition.

$$x_3 \leq 1d_1 \tag{4.13}$$

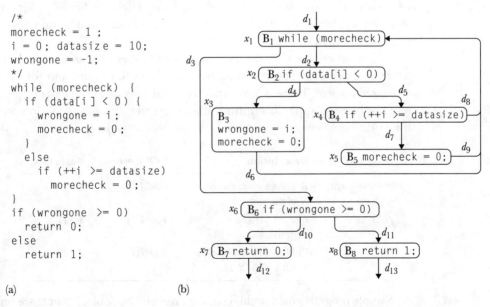

```
/*
morecheck = 1 ;
i = 0; datasize = 10;
wrongone = -1;
*/
while (morecheck) {
   if (data[i] < 0) {
      wrongone = i ;
      morecheck = 0 ;
   }
   else
      if (++i >= datasize)
         morecheck = 0 ;
}
if (wrongone >= 0)
   return 0;
else
   return 1;
```

(a)   (b)

4.1   (a) A sample code fragment and (b) corresponding CFG (control flow graph).

FIGURE

Once the objective function and structural and functional constraints have been constructed, the program may be solved with an LP solver. Many such solvers exist; in this chapter, we use the publicly available program *lp_solve* (*ftp://ftp.es.ele.tue.nl/pub/lp_solve*). As these optimization problems are network flow problems, solutions are found very quickly; problems with hundreds of basic blocks are solved in a few seconds on a modern PC.

There are other complicating factors, not described here, such as the proper handling of procedure calls. For a more complete treatment of the IPET method, see [7].

4.2.3   Benchmarks and Single-Threaded Results

In this section, we describe our simulation and analysis methodology, present WCET estimates for a selection of programs, and compare those estimates to simulated execution times gathered on the Intel IXP1200 cycle-accurate simulator. These programs, along with descriptions and code size when compiled for the IXP1200 microengines, are listed in Table 4.1.

These programs are all written in C. We use the Intel IXA microengine C compiler, version 2.01a, to generate assembly code. The same assembly code that gets assembled and executed in the simulator is used as input to our WCET estimation tool. This tool constructs the control flow graph from the assembly code, determines the cost of each basic block, formulates the linear program (user must provide loop bounds and other functional constraints), and calls *lp_solve* to find the WCET estimate.

The microengine C compiler supports a number of optimization levels. We present results for programs compiled without optimization and for programs optimized for size. There is also a speed optimization, but some of our programs were too large to apply this optimization correctly, and hence we do not report those numbers here.

Program	Description	IXP μ-words	Basic blocks
reverse_array	Reverses an array of N elements	60/54	14/13
chk_data	Checks array for negative values [11]	70/61	16/17
sort	Bubblesort of worst-case input $(-1, -2, \ldots)$	103/70	23/23

4.1

TABLE

Sample programs used in this chapter. Sizes and basic block counts are reported for unoptimized and size-optimized compilation, respectively.

Program	Unoptimized		Optimized for Size	
	Simulated WCET	Estimated WCET	Simulated WCET	Estimated WCET
reverse_array	718	733	659	699
chk_data	795	807	530	568
sort	211339	423125	134794	274002

4.2

TABLE

Simulated and estimated WCETs for unoptimized and size-optimized programs.

In the simulations, each program has been given input as close to algorithmic worst-case input whenever possible. For instance, the program *chk_data* has been given an input with no negative numbers, so the entire array gets traversed.

The results can be seen in Table 4.2. The WCET estimate is generally within a factor of 2 of the simulated execution time. Smaller programs, with fewer loop iterations, are quite close; longer running programs with more complex control flow yield more pessimistic estimates. For the case of *sort*, it is difficult to closely model the algorithmic worst case with only two nested loop bounds; thus, the sort estimate is overly pessimistic. The algorithmic worst case for an initially sorted array in reverse order has $N^2/2$ comparisons, while the two-nested-loops model results in a pessimistic n^2 comparisons, and hence the factor of 2 increase in the estimate. Note that the constraints could be tailored for a better fit. In general, greater care in the construction of functional constraints can increase the tightness of the bound.

4.3   PROCESSING THROUGHPUT OF TWO THREADS

The method described in the previous section applies to a single-threaded program. As noted previously, NPs typically provide hardware support in each embedded processor for multiple threads of execution. In this section, we introduce our method for finding the worst-case packet-processing rate of a program running two threads on a multithreaded processor.

Our method extends the IPET method for estimating WCET to accommodate multiple threads. The principal goal of our extension is to support control flow and latency hiding between threads, notions that are not present in the original IPET method. To handle inter-thread control flow, we introduce yield nodes and edges; to handle latency hiding, we keep an accounting of the portion of a thread's memory latencies that is hidden via execution in another thread.

When considering the performance of a multithreaded program, two natural metrics arise: (1) the worst-case execution time of any one thread and (2) the worst-case throughput of the system. In this section, after describing yield nodes and their construction and how concurrency is modeled, we show how the linear program may be formulated to model either of these metrics.

4.3.1 Yield Nodes and Edges

Basic blocks consist of sequences of instructions with single entry and exit points. When memory operations invoke a context switch, they in essence fragment their enclosing basic blocks (the context switch is an exit point). Figure 4.2 depicts

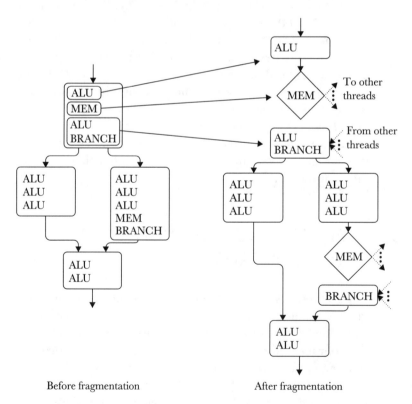

Before fragmentation   After fragmentation

4.2 CFG fragmentation due to yield operations.

FIGURE

a control flow graph before and after fragmentation. This fragmentation step introduces *yield nodes* into the CFG, which are basic blocks containing the yielding operation only. Furthermore, each yield node has some number of outgoing *yield edges*, which represent the transfer of control from this thread to another. Control returns to this thread, specifically to the yielding operation's subsequent basic block, by returning along a yield edge from another thread. In the single threaded case there was no other thread to yield to, so control proceeded directly to the subsequent node. In the multithreaded case, this flow gets routed through one or more other threads.

A yield edge begins at a yield node within one thread and, generally, ends at a basic block that follows a yield node in some other thread. A yield edge connecting two nodes within different threads has a precise meaning; namely, that once the source thread executes the yield operation it is possible that the target node will be the next basic block to execute. To construct all yield edges for a given yield node, then, we must determine which nodes might next execute. This involves two questions, which we consider in order: which threads might next be scheduled, and which nodes within those threads might next be executed.

Yield edge placement and thread scheduling policies

Yield edges are placed between threads according to the scheduling policy employed by the thread scheduler. That is, a yield edge is placed between threads *A* and *B* if and only if the thread scheduling policy would allow thread *B* to be scheduled immediately after thread *A* yields control. In this chapter, we consider a strict round-robin scheduling policy only, where strict round-robin means that the order in which threads get scheduled follows a fixed round-robin pattern. In Section 4.5, we discuss other possibilities, such as the non-strict round-robin policy of the IXP1200, in the context of future work.

Note that our assumption of strict round-robin is a good first approximation. In particular, if all threads yield only when accessing the same external resource, then the completion of those external resources will typically be serialized, and thus so will the thread scheduling order. In other words, if we restrict our benchmark programs to use only a single external resource, such as one of either DRAM or SRAM, then the microengine scheduler will produce something similar to a strict round-robin scheduling pattern. However, it will not necessarily be a precisely strict round-robin pattern. In any case, we assume that any difference due to a non-strict schedule will only improve performance. Thus, our worst-case bound will still be valid.

A strict round-robin scheduling policy means that each thread will yield to one other only. Thus, yield edges need be constructed only between each thread and the one that follows it in the strict round-robin schedule. For example, if we have N threads, and the round-robin schedule is $1, 2, \ldots, N$, yield edges must be constructed between thread i and thread $(i + 1) \bmod N$.

Yield edge placement and target nodes

Once we have established the yield edge destination thread, we must find the target nodes within that thread. As previously mentioned, yield edges begin at yield nodes and end within another thread, usually at nodes following yield nodes. Each thread's entry node also receives yield edges. This determines the major source of our target nodes: we must add a yield edge from the source yield node to each node in the target thread that follows a yield block, as well as the target thread's entry node. An example of the case of two threads is shown in Figure 4.3.

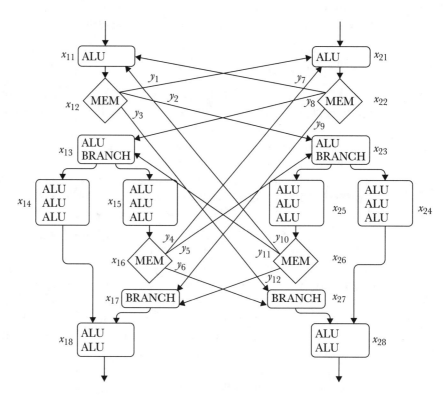

4.3

FIGURE

CFG fragmentation due to yield operations. Exit nodes and their corresponding yield edges are not pictured.

Although not pictured in Figure 4.3, a thread's exit node is also treated as a yield node. This is in order to permit threads to restart if the structural and functional constraints allow it to do so. This models the completion of the thread (and the satisfaction of its structural and functional constraints) and allows more flow to enter at the start node. We return to this subject in Section 4.3.3.

Linking yield edges to basic block frequencies

The fragmentation due to yield node edges has an important effect upon the structural constraints of the graph. Specifically, there are no d edges linking yield nodes to their subsequent basic blocks. To repair intra-thread constraints, in addition to the expected flow conservation constraints linking node execution frequency to flow on yield edges (denoted y_k) we require that the sum of yield flow out of a yield node equals the sum of yield flow into the subsequent basic block. In general, we augment the remaining structural constraints (from Equation 4.2) with

$$x_i = \sum y_k \tag{4.14}$$

$$x_j = \sum y_l, \tag{4.15}$$

where x_i is a yield node, the y_ks are outgoing yield edges from x_i, x_j is a node following a yield node, and the y_ls are incoming yield edges ending at x_j.

For the example in Figure 4.3, we have the following yield flow constraints.

$$x_{11} = y_7 + y_{10} \tag{4.16}$$

$$x_{12} = y_1 + y_2 + y_3 \tag{4.17}$$

$$x_{13} = y_8 + y_{11} \tag{4.18}$$

$$y_1 + y_2 + y_3 = y_8 + y_{11} \tag{4.19}$$

$$x_{16} = y_4 + y_5 + y_6 \tag{4.20}$$

$$x_{17} = y_9 + y_{12} \tag{4.21}$$

$$y_4 + y_5 + y_6 = y_9 + y_{12} \tag{4.22}$$

$$x_{21} = y_1 + y_7 \tag{4.23}$$

$$x_{22} = y_7 + y_8 + y_9 \tag{4.24}$$

$$x_{23} = y_2 + y_5 \tag{4.25}$$

$$y_7 + y_8 + y_9 = y_2 + y_5 \tag{4.26}$$

$$x_{26} = y_{10} + y_{11} + y_{12} \tag{4.27}$$

$$x_{27} = y_3 + y_6 \tag{4.28}$$

$$y_{10} + y_{11} + y_{12} = y_3 + y_6 \tag{4.29}$$

In the single-threaded case, we began "execution" by setting the entry node's incoming d edge to 1 in the set of structural constraints. Likewise, for multiple threads we will set the first thread's incoming d edge to 1, but we must arrange that the first node of each of the other threads be reachable via yield edges.

4.3.2   Modeling Concurrency

The purpose of fine-grained multithreading is to increase resource utilization by overlapping one thread's memory accesses, or other long latency external operations, with another thread's execution. In this method, yield edges describe the possible flow of control between threads; specifically, each yield edge connects a yield operation with basic blocks (which consist of non-yielding operations) that might execute concurrently.

To model concurrency for our target system, we begin with the observation that total runtime has two components: execution time and stall time. Since no computation occurs in parallel, execution time is simply the sum of the execution times of all computation blocks in all threads. This can be computed by totaling the effective execution time of those blocks along the worst-case path. Stall time results when a long latency yield operation cannot be completely overlapped with execution in another thread. This is our key to modeling concurrency: we will account for the portion of each yield operation that in the worst case forces a thread to stall. To this end, we will assign values to yield edges, and add those yield edges to the objective function, in order to calculate each yield operation's contribution to stall time, and hence total runtime. Only rarely will a yield operation's full latency contribute to stall time. For example, if a yield operation with a 30-cycle latency contributes only 10 cycles of stall time along a given path, then the yield edge value would be set to -20, so that when the yield latency and yield edge value are summed in the objective function the true contribution to execution time (namely, 10 stall cycles) will be represented.

To calculate the stall time contribution for a yield operation, we make the conservative assumption that the only cycles of overlap are due to the minimum number of execution cycles that can take place at the yield edge destination. The equation for determining the yield edge value is as follows. Note that the *min* function ensures that no amount greater than the source yield latency will be

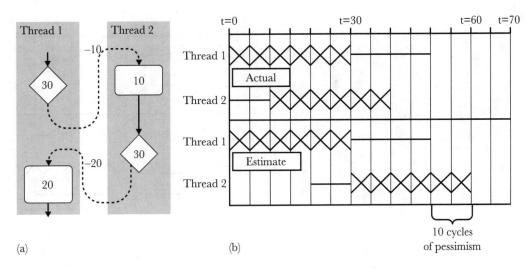

(a)   (b)   10 cycles
                                                                                      of pessimism

4.4

FIGURE

Modeling concurrency with yield edges: (a) CFG with yield edge values. In the timeline, the Xs denote memory operation and the horizontal lines denote execution: (b) execution timelines: actual versus estimate.

hidden in the case of large execution sequences (this avoids negative stall times).

$$\text{Yield edge value} = -\min (\text{minimum destination execution cycles,}$$
$$\text{source yield latency}) \qquad (4.30)$$

As we show, this approach in determining a yield node's stall time contribution is conservative in two ways. We illustrate them beginning with a simple example, shown in Figure 4.4. It depicts two threads, each with one yield operation. The first source of pessimism is present in Figure 4.4. Since we assume that only the destination execution cycles overlap with the source yield operation, we imply that no overlap occurs between yield operations. Since the IXP1200 supports pipelined SRAM requests, this is a safe but pessimistic assumption. This assumption results in 10 cycles of pessimism in this example. Furthermore, the pessimism seems unwarranted in this simple example. Indeed it is, in this particular case, as we clearly see that the first 20 cycles of thread 2's yield latency are overlapped with thread 1's yield operation. We see this example clearly because each of the two yield nodes has only one incoming edge. In general, however (as shown in Figure 4.2) each yield node will have many incoming edges, and it will not be clear how to choose a safe amount of overlap between yield operations.

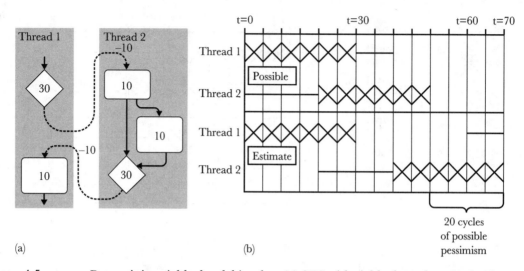

(a)   (b)

4.5

FIGURE

Determining yield edge debit value: (a) CFG with yield edge values. In the time-line, the Xs denote memory operation and the horizontal lines denote execution: (b) possible versus estimated timeline.

This approach for determining a yield node's stall time contribution is conservative in a second way, as shown in Figure 4.5. There, we see the potential pessimism due to choosing the minimum number of execution cycles in Equation 4.30. In general, we must base our stall time contribution on the minimum number of execution cycles, rather than the maximum, because we only get to choose one value for each yield edge. This value must make a conservative contribution to execution time, taking into account all possible paths. In the case of Figure 4.5, the yield edge from thread 1 to thread 2 is followed by two possible paths: one with cost 10, the other with cost 20. Since during the course of execution flow may follow either path, we base our stall time on the conservative value of 10.

One might be tempted to choose to use the value of 20, since that is the costlier exit path from thread 2; after all, our method is meant to find the worst-case path. Note, however, that the structural and functional constraints might require that the shorter path be taken (e.g., at a loop exit). In this case, a value of 20 would overestimate the amount of overlap and lead to an underestimate of execution time.

These figures have depicted simple target execution paths; that is, Figure 4.4 has only a single path, while Figure 4.5 has two. In general, however, the control flow could be arbitrarily complex, involving loops and branches. To find a safe value for each yield edge, we must first find the minimum-cost exit path for each yield edge destination node. The procedure for determining this is a simple iterative breadth-first traversal in which cumulative cost is maintained for each path. At each step, we compare the cost of the newly extended path to the minimum-cost completed path seen so far. Any paths with cost greater than the minimum are discarded; any completed path with a lesser cost becomes the new minimum. The procedure completes when no paths remain with cost less than the current minimum.

When all yield edge credit values are found, they must be added to the objective function to accurately model the cost of flow through the CFG. The updated objective function is shown in Equation 4.31.

$$\text{Total execution time} = \sum_{i}^{N} c_i x_i + \sum_{j}^{M} c_{y_j} y_j, \qquad (4.31)$$

where c_{y_j} is the yield edge value for yield edge j, and y_j is its frequency.

4.3.3   Worst-Case Latency Versus Worst-Case Throughput

When a stage of our packet-processing pipeline is implemented in software on a multithreaded processor, we will be interested in both the worst-case latency that a packet might experience and the worst-case throughput achievable by the pipeline stage. Note that these are indeed different metrics. The worst-case latency for a single packet might arise when the other threads in the system achieve very short latencies; so, despite one packet in the system experiencing worst-case latency, overall throughput might still be good. The case is the same for worst-case throughput. An individual thread might not be experiencing its worst possible latency because doing so would shift the contention for resources in such a way as to *improve* the latency of some other thread by a greater amount. Our method distinguishes these two target metrics by constraining each thread's entry and exit frequencies in different ways.

To target the worst-case latency of a single thread (e.g., packet), we constrain the entry and exit node frequencies for the first thread to be 1, as shown in Equation 4.32. Intuitively, this constraint allows the maximum possible amount of time to be spent in the second thread between the time execution enters and exits the first thread.

$$x_{\text{first thread entry}} = x_{\text{first thread exit}} = 1 \qquad (4.32)$$

To target the worst-case throughput, we constrain (1) the entry nodes for all threads to be 1 or greater and (2) the exit nodes of all threads to be 1. These constraints are shown in Equations 4.33 and 4.34. Intuitively, these constraints allow the maximum possible amount of time to be spent in all threads, provided that each thread only completes once. A thread completion corresponds to a packet completion, and thus, in the case of two threads this worst-case path through the combined CFG corresponds to the worst-case time needed to process two packets.

$$x_{\text{thread } i \text{ entry}} \geq 1 \qquad (4.33)$$
$$x_{\text{thread } i \text{ exit}} = 1 \qquad (4.34)$$

In our benchmarks, we have found no cases where targeting worst-case latency produces a significantly different result from targeting worst-case throughput. This is likely due to the memory-bound nature of our programs; that is, with two threads, the computational resources are generally idle for half the total cycles. For this reason, along with the difficulties in comparing such an estimate to a measured result, we report only worst-case throughput results in this chapter.

4.3.4 Benchmark Results with Two Threads

The worst-case execution time estimates for dual-threaded versions of each of the programs, along with their simulation times, are shown in Table 4.3. In each case, two copies of the same thread are sharing processor resources. With the exception of *sort*, all estimates are near the worst-case simulation time. The differences are, as expected, slightly larger than those seen in the single-threaded case because of the pessimistic assumptions explained previously. For *sort*, as was the case for a single thread, the estimate is greater than the simulated result by more than a factor of 2. This is again due to the pessimistic mismatch between the loop constraints and the actual worst case achievable by *bubblesort*.

It is also interesting to note that these dual-threaded programs require approximately the same amount of time as their single-threaded counterparts (in the "Simulated WCET" column). This implies that the second thread, in each case, is taking advantage of idle resources without impacting the performance of the first thread. In these cases, multithreading has doubled throughput.

Program	Unoptimized				Optimized for size			
	Simulated WCET	Estimated WCET	Basic blocks	Yield operations	Simulated WCET	Estimated WCET	Basic blocks	Yield operations
reverse_array	731	1162	23	7	675	1102	23	7
chk_data	822	1302	30	8	564	904	26	6
sort	210291	633786	33	7	133447	407700	31	6

4.3

TABLE

Simulated and estimated WCETs for dual-threaded programs. The basic block and yield operation counts indicate the number of each per thread. These times indicate the number of cycles needed for both threads to complete.

4.4 PROCESSING THROUGHPUT OF FOUR THREADS

The method for estimating the performance of dual-threaded programs described in Section 4.3 scales and applies directly to versions with four threads. The reason is that none of our assumptions change. Yield edges are drawn between neighboring threads according to the round-robin schedule (e.g., $1 \rightarrow 2 \rightarrow 3 \rightarrow 4 \rightarrow 1 \ldots$). Yield edge values, which account for the stall time contributions of their source yield nodes, are still based on estimates of the minimum number of execution cycles that will occur at the yield edge destination. None of this requires inspection of any threads but those joined via a yield edge. Had we taken a less conservative approach in Section 4.3—one that, say, tried to tighten the bound by accounting for the amount of overlap between subsequent yield operations—we would almost certainly require a change in strategy.

The simulation results and estimates for four-threaded versions of the programs are shown in Table 4.4.

The estimates are roughly within a factor of 2 of the simulation results. The program *sort* is once again the exception; its WCET estimate is approximately four times the simulated result, for reasons similar to those seen in the previous section.

4.5 LIMITATIONS AND FUTURE WORK

The objective of this line of research is to provide tight and safe bounds on the performance of multithreaded network-processing programs. The method described in this chapter represents a first attempt at bounding performance for

Program	Unoptimized				Optimized for size			
	Simulated WCET	Estimated WCET	Basic blocks	Yield operations	Simulated WCET	Estimated WCET	Basic blocks	Yield operations
reverse_array	1083	2326	23	7	896	2204	23	7
chk_data	1201	2612	30	8	985	1808	26	6
sort	282973	1267570	33	7	192789	817980	31	6

4.4

TABLE

Simulated and estimated WCETs for four-threaded versions of the unoptimized and size-optimized programs. The basic block and yield operation counts indicate the number of each per thread. These times indicate the number of cycles needed for all four threads to complete.

a limited class of such programs under restricted circumstances. Each of these limitations represents directions for future research. We now discuss these limitations and then consider additional opportunities for extending our approach.

4.5.1 Limitations

Multiple yield resources and other scheduling policies

The method presented in this chapter requires that all threads yield on the same external resource. So, for example, it is not possible for threads to yield on accesses to both SRAM and DRAM. We plan to extend the model to accommodate multiple yield resources in the near future.

Additionally, our approach pessimistically requires that threads execute according to a fixed round-robin schedule. This is a fundamental limitation to our approach, since this choice determines how yield edges are constructed between threads. In the near future, we plan to restate the problem as a generalized linear program, in which some coefficients are described with systems of equations, in the hopes of alleviating this limitation.

Asynchronous events

Certain network-processing tasks are activated by external, asynchronous events. For example, in response to a packet arrival a packet-receive routine might allocate a buffer, perform record keeping, and then move the packet into memory. The present method does not consider any events that are not synchronized with, or requested by, a thread.

Thread Interdependencies

The present method has assumed that threads have no interdependencies. This precludes, for example, implementing mutex regions within the threads to limit access to shared state. Such protections are critical for some important functions, and as such this is a high-priority area for future research.

4.5.2 Additional Future Work

Caches and other architectural features

The established method for modeling caches is one benefit of using IPET to bound worst-case performance. In future work, we plan to incorporate the caching techniques into our extension. Caches are generally lacking in the NP embedded cores for two reasons: (1) conventional wisdom holds that there is insufficient locality available, and (2) caches introduce nondeterminism and complicate worst-case analyses. Providing sufficient worst-case bounds for a system with caches would help address both of these issues.

Formal verification

We would like to establish the formal correctness and validity of our bounds. This will become more important as the method grows in complexity.

Restatement as a generalized linear program

Tighter worst-case bounds could be achieved if some flexibility could be retained in the description of cost coefficients in the objective function. Having to choose a single constant to serve as a coefficient for yield edge costs, for instance, is more restrictive than strictly necessary. We feel the problem can be recast as a generalized linear program [1] in which certain coefficients can be described with systems of equations rather than constants.

4.6 CONCLUSIONS

In this chapter, we have introduced the problem of estimating worst-case performance for network processing programs running on multithreaded processors. We have described an initial estimation method suitable for a limited class of programs executing under a restricted set of conditions. The method, which is based on the IPET approach [7] for worst-case program execution time estimation, casts the worst-case estimation problem as an integer linear program. To evaluate the method, worst-case processing rates for a number of programs running on Intel IXP1200-like microengines were compared to some corresponding simulated processing rates for that network processor. Results were presented for programs with one, two, and four threads. In the multiple thread cases, the estimates were found to be between 40% and four times greater than the results gathered via simulation. The program *sort* is an outlier due to a pessimistic bound on the number of worst-case nested loop iterations.

In future work, we plan to address the current limitations and restrictions in order to broaden the class of programs supported by the method. Additionally, we plan to explore compatible extensions to the model, some of which have been described in the literature (such as cache analysis), in order to investigate whether certain nondeterministic architectural features can be shown to provide sufficiently good worst-case performance to warrant inclusion in network processors.

ACKNOWLEDGMENTS

This work was supported by gifts from Intel Corporation and NSF grant CCR-0072948.

REFERENCES

[1]   G. B. Dantzig, *Linear Programming and Extensions*, Princeton, NJ: Princeton University Press, 1963.

[2]   J. Engblom and A. Ermedahl, "Modeling Complex Flows for Worst-Case Execution Time Analysis," *Proceedings of the 21st IEEE Real-Time Systems Symposium (RTSS'00)*, 2000.

[3]   C. Ferdinand, F. Martin, and R. Wilhelm, "Applying Compiler Techniques to Cache Behavior Prediction," *Proceedings of the ACM SIGPLAN Workshop on Language, Compiler and Tool Support for Real-Time Systems*, 1997, pp. 37–46.

[4]   E. Kligerman and A. D. Stoyenko, "Real-Time Euclid: A Language for Reliable Real-Time Systems," *IEEE Trans. on Software Eng.*, 12(9):941–949, Sept. 1986.

[5]   Y.-T. S. Li and S. Malik, "Performance Analysis of Embedded Software Using Implicit Path Enumeration," *Workshop on Languages, Compilers, and Tools for Real-Time Systems*, 1995, pp. 88–98.

[6]   Y.-T. S. Li, S. Malik, and A. Wolfe, "Efficient Microarchitecture Modeling and Path Analysis for Real-Time Software," *IEEE Real-Time Systems Symposium*, 1995, pp. 298–307.

[7]   Y-T. S. Li, S. Malik, and A. Wolfe, "Cache Modeling for Real-Time Software: Beyond Direct Mapped Instruction Caches," *Proceedings of the IEEE Real-Time Systems Symposium*, 1996.

[8]   S-S. Lim et al., "An Accurate Worst-Case Timing Analysis for RISC Processors," *Software Engineering*, 21(7):593–604, 1995.

[9]   S-S. Lim, J. H. Han, J. Kim, and S. L. Min, "A Worst-Case Timing Analysis Technique for Multiple-Issue Machines," *Proceedings of IEEE Real-Time Systems Symposium (RTSS)*, 1998, pp. 334–345.

[10]   G. Ottosson and M. Sjödin, "Worst-Case Execution Time Analysis for Modern Hardware Architectures," *ACM SIGPLAN 1997 Workshop on Languages, Compilers, and Tools for Real-Time Systems (LCT-RTS'97)*, 1997.

[11]   C. Y. Park, "Predicting Deterministic Execution Times of Real-Time Programs," Ph.D. thesis, University of Washington, August 1992.

[12]   P. Puschner and C. Koza, "Calculating the Maximum Execution Time of Real-Time Programs," *The Journal of Real-Time Systems*, 1(2):160–176, Sept. 1989.

Multiprocessor Scheduling in Processor-Based Router Platforms: Issues and Ideas

**Anand Srinivasan, Philip Holman, James Anderson,
Sanjoy Baruah, Jasleen Kaur**
Department of Computer Science,
University of North Carolina at Chapel Hill

With the commercialization of the Internet, there is a growing need for network providers to enhance their service offerings. Deployment of new services often requires making changes to switches and routers, which are the basic building blocks of wide-area networks (WANs) such as the Internet. Traditionally, routers have been built using application-specific integrated circuits (ASICs) that enable high-speed packet switching. Unfortunately, ASIC designs take months to develop, and routers built using them are costly to deploy. To enable router extensibility in a rapid and cost-effective manner, significant effort is now being invested in a different approach: implementing routers using programmable network processors (NPs) [1, 2, 3, 33].

There are three main shared resources in a software-based programmable router: *link capacity* (which is shared by traffic destined for the same outgoing link), and *memory capacity* and *packet-processing capacity*,[1] which are shared by all traffic arriving at a router. Two trends are expected to guide the manner in which these resources are managed in next-generation routers:

✦ *Growing demand for sophisticated resource-allocation mechanisms*. The current Internet mainly supports just a single service class; namely, best-effort delivery. In this model, there is no assurance of when, or even if, a packet sent by a data source will reach its destination. While this model has worked well for traditional applications, such as e-mail and web browsing, it is not

---

1. The term *packet processing* refers to functions that are performed for every incoming packet, such as computing checksums, route lookup, and packet classification.

adequate for many emerging network applications that require quality-of-service (QoS) and timeliness guarantees. Such applications require that both link and packet-processing capacities be multiplexed across different applications in a *fair* manner, even at short time scales.

✦ *Increasing disparity between link and processor speeds.* Link capacities are increasing rapidly, almost doubling every year [16]. On the other hand, processor speeds are increasing less rapidly [4]. This gap is further heightened by the fact that the processing demands of new applications, such as encryption/decryption and transcoding, are increasing. For these reasons, routers must be instantiated as *multiprocessor platforms* that process multiple packets simultaneously. Further, to keep up with large volumes of Internet traffic [16, 26] router mechanisms must incur *very low overhead*.

In the last decade, a significant amount of research has been conducted on scheduling mechanisms for fairly allocating link capacity [11, 12, 18, 19, 20]. However, considerably less work has been done on designing mechanisms for allocating packet-processing capacity. The reason for this is simple: conventional routers, built using ASICs, perform only simple packet-processing functions that are likely to execute faster than the time it takes to transmit packets between ports. As such, link capacities are assumed to be the only resources in a network for which flows must contend. However, routers built using programmable NPs are destined to implement more complex packet-processing functions in software, making packet-processing capacity a critical resource to be managed.

Unfortunately, techniques developed in prior work on link scheduling cannot be directly applied to the problem of fairly allocating packet-processing capacity in multiprocessor routers. There are two reasons for this. First, link-scheduling algorithms are typically devised to manage just a single outgoing link; that is, link scheduling is fundamentally a *single*-resource scheduling problem. Second, some assumptions usually made in work on link scheduling (e.g., unbounded buffering capacity and processing bandwidth) are unreasonable to assume on router platforms connected to high-speed links.

Given the trends previously noted, and the limitations of prior work, there is a significant need for research on the problem of fairly allocating packet-processing capacity in multiprocessor routers. Fair scheduling on multiprocessors has been a topic of recent research in work on real-time scheduling, and several fair-scheduling algorithms have been developed [6, 9, 10, 22, 36]. However, due to various assumptions made in this work, these algorithms cannot be applied directly in multiprocessor routers. In this chapter, we explore some of the issues that arise in applying these algorithms to routers, and describe some approaches to handling them.

The rest of this chapter is organized as follows. In Section 5.1, we consider the problem of scheduling packet-processing capacity in routers in more detail, and describe past work on multiprocessor scheduling in real-time systems. In Section 5.2, we consider requirements unique to router platforms and outline some of the issues in applying existing multiprocessor scheduling schemes to routers. In Section 5.3, we present some ideas for addressing these issues. In Section 5.4, we present an experimental methodology to evaluate our approach. Finally, we summarize in Section 5.5.

5.1   RELATED WORK AND CONCEPTS

In this section, we formulate the problem of multiprocessor scheduling in routers and describe prior work on multiprocessor scheduling.

5.1.1   The Problem: Limited Packet-Processing Capacity in Routers

Figure 5.1a depicts the high-level architecture of a typical wide-area packet-switched network. When a packet arrives on an input link at a router, the router determines the *next* hop on the end-to-end path of that packet, and transmits the packet on the corresponding output link.

To understand the need for scheduling mechanisms in routers, consider Figure 5.1b, which depicts the architecture of a typical router platform built using

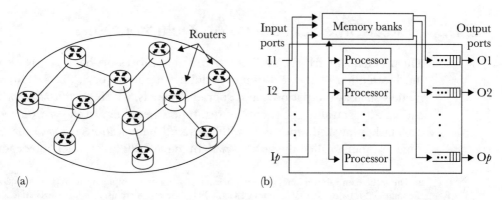

(a)   (b)

5.1   Typical architectures of (a) a network and (b) a programmable NP-based router.

FIGURE

programmable NPs.[2] Each incoming packet is stored in memory, is processed at one or more of the M processors, and is transmitted on an outgoing link. The processing required for each packet includes such functions as checksum computation, packet classification, route-table lookup, and queue maintenance.

As mentioned earlier, there are three main resources for which the packets of different flows contend: (1) processing capacity within the multiprocessor bank, (2) transmission capacity of the outgoing links, and (3) buffer space in the high-speed memory banks. To provide delay and throughput guarantees for the packets of a given flow, the router must employ sophisticated scheduling mechanisms to arbitrate access to the first two resources, and mechanisms to allocate, in a fair manner, buffer space. In this chapter, we focus only on the problem of allocating processing capacity.

Research on designing scheduling mechanisms for routers over the past decade has focused mainly on the second resource identified previously; that is, outgoing link capacity [12, 18, 19, 20, 32, 38]. Indeed, in most work on link-scheduling algorithms, buffer space and processing capacity within routers are assumed to be unlimited. These assumptions have been justified by the fact that conventional routers, built using ASICs, have very fast interconnects between input and output ports, and perform simple packet-processing functions implemented using fast hardware. Consequently, it is reasonable to assume that packets require queuing only while accessing outgoing links. However, because of the two trends mentioned previously—the growing disparity between link and processor speeds, and an increasing need for more sophisticated resource-allocation mechanisms—it is not reasonable to assume that queuing occurs only at outgoing links in software-based router platforms built using NPs. In this chapter, we focus on the problem of fairly allocating processing capacity in multiprocessor routers.

5.1.2   Real-Time Scheduling on Multiprocessors

The problem of fairly scheduling tasks on multiprocessors has recently received much attention in the real-time scheduling literature [6, 8, 22, 31, 36]. Task models such as the periodic and sporadic models, which permit *recurrent* execution, are central to the theory of real-time scheduling. In the *periodic* model, each task is invoked repeatedly, with consecutive invocations (or *jobs*) spaced by a fixed amount, called the task's *period*. In the *sporadic* task model, job deadlines

2. The architecture shown here, in which streams arriving on multiple input links are processed in the same NP, is based on that of Intel's IXP1200 [1]. Some NPs are used in line cards attached to a single link. In such architectures, the streams shown in Figure 5.1b arrive and depart on a single link.

are defined similarly, but a task's period defines a *lower bound* between successive jobs. In the variant of these models considered here, each task's *relative job deadline* is equal to its period: each job of a task must complete execution before the current period of that task has elapsed. In both models, the *weight* or *utilization* of a task T, denoted $wt(T)$, is defined as the ratio of its per-job execution requirement and its period.

Multiprocessor scheduling techniques in real-time systems fall into two general categories: *partitioning* and *global scheduling*. Under partitioning, each processor schedules tasks independently from a local ready queue. Each task is assigned to a particular processor and is only scheduled on that processor. In contrast, all ready tasks are stored in a single queue under global scheduling. A single system-wide priority space is assumed; the highest-priority task is selected to execute whenever the scheduler is invoked, regardless of which processor is being scheduled.

Partitioning has two main advantages: migration overhead is zero (since each task runs on only one processor), and simpler and widely studied uniprocessor-scheduling algorithms can be used on each processor. Unfortunately, finding an optimal assignment of tasks to processors is a bin-packing problem, which is NP-hard in the strong sense. In addition, partitioning is inherently suboptimal: task sets with utilization at most M exist that cannot be partitioned on M processors. Furthermore, partitioning is quite problematic if tasks can be created and terminated dynamically. In particular, every new task that joins can potentially cause a repartitioning of the entire system.

Because of the limitations of partitioning, there has been much recent interest in global multiprocessor-scheduling algorithms that ensure *fairness* [8, 13, 14, 22, 36]. In the following subsection, we present an overview of this work.

5.1.3   Pfair Scheduling

Fairness is defined with respect to a basic *fluid-flow model*. Given a resource that is shared among several data streams (or tasks) in specified proportions, the goal of a fair-scheduling algorithm is to allocate the resource so that each stream's allocation is always "close" to its designated proportion. Ideally, one would like to treat the data streams as fluid flows and continually assign an appropriate fraction of the available bandwidth to each stream. This idealized scheme is referred to as *generalized processor sharing* (GPS) [32]. In practice, supporting ideal fluid flows is not possible, and hence scheduling schemes that closely approximate GPS must be used. Fairness in such schemes is usually measured by determining *lag bounds* that reflect the extent to which actual behavior deviates from the idealized GPS behavior.

Proportionate fairness (Pfairness) is a fairness constraint introduced by Baruah et al. [9, 10] as a way to optimally schedule periodic tasks on multiprocessors. Some of the key concepts arising in this work are described in the following sections.

Assumptions and terminology

Most prior work on Pfairness has focused on periodic tasks with hard real-time execution requirements, where processor time is allocated in uniform time units (called *time slots* or *quanta*). Let $T.p$ denote the period of task T, and let $T.e$ denote its execution requirement within each of its periods. Then, $wt(T) = T.e/T.p$ is the processing-rate requirement of T. In satisfying this rate requirement, T may be allocated time on different processors, but not at the same time (i.e., migration is allowed but parallelism is not).

Pfairness

Pfairness is defined by focusing on the *lag* between the amount of time allocated to each task and the amount of time that would be allocated to that task in an ideal fluid system (i.e., GPS). Formally, the *lag of task T at time t*, denoted $lag(T,t)$, is defined as follows:

$$lag(T,t) = wt(T) \cdot t - allocated(T,t),$$

where $allocated(T,t)$ is the total processor time allocated to T in $[0,t)$. A schedule is *Pfair*[3] iff

$$(\forall T, t :: -1 < lag(T,t) < 1). \tag{5.1}$$

Informally, the allocation error associated with each task must always be strictly less than one quantum. It is easy to show that Equation (5.1) ensures that each job completes before the next job of the same task is released.

Baruah et al. [9] proved that a periodic task system τ has a Pfair schedule on M processors iff

$$\sum_{T \in \tau} wt(T) \leq M.$$

This expression is in fact a feasibility condition for all the task models considered in this subsection.

---

3. A lower bound of 0 for $lag(T,t)$ (as in most uniprocessor fair-scheduling schemes) is not sufficient to guarantee all deadlines on multiprocessors.

Pfair-scheduling algorithms

Baruah *et al.* presented two optimal Pfair-scheduling algorithms, called PF [9] and PD [10]. In these algorithms, a task T is divided into a sequence T_1, T_2, ... of quantum-length *subtasks* to be executed sequentially. Both algorithms schedule subtasks on an *earliest deadline first* basis, where the deadline of a subtask T_i ($i \geq 1$), denoted $d(T_i)$, is computed as follows:

$$d(T_i) = \left\lceil \frac{i}{wt(T)} \right\rceil. \tag{5.2}$$

These deadline assignments respect the lag bounds given in Equation (5.1). The lag bounds in Equation (5.1) also imply a *release* time for a subtask; that is, the earliest time at which the subtask can be scheduled. Thus, we obtain a time interval for each subtask during which that subtask must be scheduled. This interval is referred to as the subtask's *window* (see Figure 5.2a).

PF and PD differ in the way in which ties are broken when two subtasks have the same deadline. (Selecting appropriate tie-breaks turns out to be *the* most important concern in designing correct Pfair algorithms.) In PF, ties are broken by comparing a vector of future subtask deadlines, which is somewhat expensive. In PD, ties are broken in constant time by inspecting four tie-break parameters. In recent work, Anderson and Srinivasan presented an optimized variant of PD, called PD^2 [6, 8], which was obtained by eliminating two of PD's tie-breaks. PD^2 is the most efficient Pfair-scheduling algorithm currently known. We now examine the PD^2 tie-breaks in more detail.

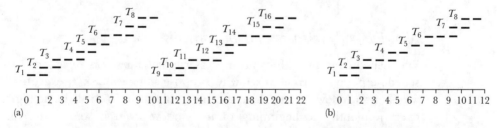

(a)

(b)

5.2 FIGURE (a) Windows of the first two jobs of a periodic task T with weight 8/11. These two jobs consist of the subtasks $T_1, \ldots, T_8$ and $T_9, \ldots, T_{16}$, respectively. Each subtask must be scheduled during its window, or a lag-bound violation will result. (b) The Pfair windows of an IS task. Subtask T_5 becomes eligible one unit late.

PD² tie-breaks

The first PD^2 tie-break is a bit, denoted $b(T_i)$. As seen in Figure 5.2a, consecutive windows of a Pfair task either are disjoint or overlap by one slot. $b(T_i)$ is defined to be 1 if T_i's window overlaps T_{i+1}'s, and 0 otherwise. For example, for task T in Figure 5.2a, $b(T_i) = 1$ for $1 \leq i \leq 7$ and $b(T_8) = 0$. PD^2 favors a subtask with a b-bit of 1 over one with a b-bit of 0. Informally, it is better to execute T_i "early" if its window overlaps that of T_{i+1}, because this potentially leaves more slots available to T_{i+1}.

The second PD^2 tie-break, the *group deadline*, is needed in systems containing tasks with windows of length two. A task T has such windows iff $1/2 \leq wt(T) < 1$. Consider a sequence $T_i,...,T_j$ of subtasks of such a task T such that $b(T_k) = 1 \wedge |w(T_{k+1})| = 2$ for all $i \leq k < j$. Scheduling T_i in its last slot forces the other subtasks in this sequence to be scheduled in their last slots. For example, in Figure 5.2a, scheduling T_3 in slot 4 forces T_4 and T_5 to be scheduled in slots 5 and 6, respectively. The group deadline of a subtask T_i is the earliest time by which such a "cascade" must end. Formally, it is the earliest time t, where $t \geq d(T_i)$, such that either $(t = d(T_k) \wedge b(T_k) = 0)$ or $(t + 1 = d(T_k) \wedge |w(T_k)| = 3)$ for some subtask T_k. For example, subtask T_3 in Figure 5.2a has a group deadline at time 8, and subtask T_7 has a group deadline at time 11. PD^2 favors subtasks with later group deadlines because *not* scheduling them can lead to longer cascades.

Anderson and Srinivasan have shown that if either PD^2 tie-break is eliminated, then tasks can miss their deadlines. To see that the b-bit is necessary, consider Figure 5.3. In this schedule, the tasks of weight 1/3 are favored over those of weight 4/9 at times 0 and 1, even though the former have a b-bit of 0. Note that $\frac{8}{3} + \frac{4}{3} = 4$. Thus, all four processors are fully utilized, which implies that no processor should ever be idle. However, in [2, 3], only three tasks can be scheduled, implying that a deadline is missed in the future.

Allowing early releases and late arrivals

Pfair-scheduling algorithms are necessarily *non-work conserving* when used to schedule periodic tasks. To see why, suppose some subtask T_i executes "early" within its window. Then T_{i+1}, the next subtask of T, will be ineligible for execution until the beginning of its window, even if some processors are idle. To enable more efficient use of processing capacity, a work-conserving variant of Pfair scheduling, called *"early-release" fair* (ERfair) scheduling, was recently proposed by Anderson and Srinivasan [6, 8]. Under ERfair scheduling, if two subtasks are part of the same job, then the second subtask becomes eligible for execution as soon as the first completes. For example, if T_3 in

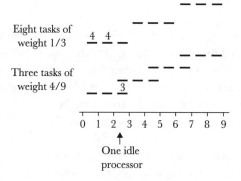

Eight tasks of
weight 1/3

Three tasks of
weight 4/9

One idle
processor

5.3

FIGURE

Eight tasks of weight 1/3 and four tasks of weight 4/9 scheduled on four processors (tasks of a given weight are shown together). The Pfair window of each subtask is shown on a separate line. An integer value n in slot t means that n of the corresponding subtasks are scheduled in slot t.

Figure 5.2a were scheduled in slot 2, then T_4 could be scheduled as early as slot 3.

In other recent work, Anderson and Srinivasan extended the early-release task model to also allow subtasks to be released "late"; that is, there may be separation between consecutive subtasks of the same task [7]. The resulting model, called the *intra-sporadic* (IS) model, generalizes the sporadic model, which allows separation between consecutive *jobs* of the same task. An example of an IS task is shown in Figure 5.2b, where T_5 is released one slot late. Note that an IS task is obtained by allowing a task's windows to be right-shifted from where they would appear if the task were periodic. Thus, we can define an IS task by associating with each subtask an *offset* that gives the amount by which its window has been right-shifted. Let $\theta(T_i)$ denote the offset of subtask T_i. Then, from Equation 5.2, we have the following:

$$d(T_i) = \theta(T_i) + \left\lceil \frac{i}{wt(T)} \right\rceil. \qquad (5.3)$$

These offsets are constrained so that the separation between any pair of subtask deadlines is no less than the separation between those deadlines if the task were periodic. Formally, the offsets satisfy the following: $k \geq i \Rightarrow \theta(T_k) \geq \theta(T_i)$. Anderson and Srinivasan have shown that IS (and hence early-release) tasks can be correctly scheduled by PD^2 on M processors if total utilization is at most M [36].

Heuristic approaches

In recent work, Chandra et al. considered fair multiprocessor scheduling algorithms that use variable-size quanta, use mechanisms that discourage task migrations, and allow tasks to join and leave dynamically [13, 14]. Their work is entirely experimental in nature. In particular, they provide no formal correctness proofs for the algorithms they consider. Nonetheless, their results demonstrate convincingly the utility of using fair-scheduling algorithms on multiprocessors.

In other recent work, Jones and Regehr proposed and evaluated a reservation-based multiprocessor scheduler implemented within a research version of Windows NT, called Rialto/NT [25]. While their results show that reservations and real-time execution can be effectively implemented on multiprocessors, Jones and Regehr, like Chandra et al., present no formal analysis of their scheduling algorithm.

5.2 ISSUES IN USING PFAIR SCHEDULERS IN ROUTERS

We now examine how real-time task scheduling concepts can be applied to the problem of packet processing on multiprocessor routers. In Pfair terms, the arrival of a packet for a given connection would cause a task (corresponding to that connection) to release one or more subtasks that encompass the packet-processing functions to be performed.

While the notion of a Pfair weight was defined previously based on the per-job execution cost and period of a task, these weights can be viewed more abstractly as denoting *maximum processor shares*. In packet scheduling, each backlogged flow must instead be guaranteed a *minimum* share. If the workload to be scheduled never changes, then the share of each flow remains fixed and there is no real distinction between the notion of a maximum and a minimum share. However, in a dynamic system—in which flows may join and leave or become inactive—it is desirable to increase a task's share if there is available spare capacity. In fact, this very issue was one of the key problems addressed in prior work on fair link scheduling.

Of the task models considered previously, the IS model is the most suitable for scheduling dynamic flows within a router. Due to network congestion and other factors, packet arrivals may not be periodic, and packets may arrive late or in bursts. The IS model treats these possibilities as first-class concepts. In particular, a late packet arrival corresponds to an IS delay. On the other hand, if a packet arrives early (as part of a bursty sequence), then eligibility times of the corresponding subtasks will be less than their Pfair release times. Note that the Pfair release time of a subtask determines its deadline. Thus, in effect, an early packet arrival is handled by postponing the deadline of the subtasks to where they would have been had the packet arrived on time. This is very similar to the approach taken in the (uniprocessor) virtual-clock-scheduling scheme [39].

The observations made previously suggest that Pfair-scheduling schemes that allow IS task execution are capable of providing provable service guarantees, while being an efficient and flexible choice for multiprocessor router platforms. We now examine this choice in greater detail. In the following section, we describe several issues that indicate that existing Pfair-scheduling algorithms need to be refined for use in multiprocessor routers.

5.2.1 Applicability Issues

Some assumptions made in Pfair-scheduling theory are not valid in the context of packet processing in routers. Specifically, in all prior work on Pfair algorithms, quanta have been assumed to be uniform, and to always align on all processors (see Figure 5.2). However, the execution costs of packet-processing functions in routers can vary significantly. In particular, packets (even from the same flow) may vary in size, and the complexity of some processing functions (e.g., validating the checksum of a packet) is a function of packet size. Furthermore, if different threads are responsible for different subsets of processing functions, the execution cost across threads may vary substantially. Hence, if a fixed-length quantum is used, then some quanta will almost surely be partially wasted. Specifically, waste will occur whenever packet-processing functions complete before the next quantum boundary.[4] In addition, with aligned quanta there may be excessive memory contention at the beginning of each quantum. Thus, to enable efficient use of resources *multiprocessor scheduling schemes used on routers should allow nonuniform and nonaligned quanta*.

A second key assumption in prior work on Pfair scheduling is that task migrations are unconstrained. However, on a router, such migrations may need to be constrained to reduce the number of (off-chip) memory references made per packet. Migrations may also be constrained by the processing architecture. For

---

4. Note that it is possible to reduce this loss by scheduling a new thread for the rest of the quantum. However, the loss that we are considering here is the loss due to inflating execution costs to a multiple of the quantum size. For instance, if $T.e = 1.5$ and $T.p = 3$, then $wt(T)$ (which determines the utilization reserved for task T) would be defined as $2/3$ instead of $1/2$. This reduces the total number of tasks that will be accepted by the scheduler, and hence reduces the utilization of the system.

instance, if different processing functions are pipelined, then the task corresponding to the processing of a particular packet may necessarily migrate in a constrained (not arbitrary) pattern. Therefore, current multiprocessor scheduling theory needs to be extended to *operate under constrained models of migration*.

5.2.2 Flexibility Issues

Unlike many real-time applications built for stand-alone embedded systems, packet arrivals for a given flow at a router are not likely to be periodic. Packets may arrive at a rate less than or greater than the rate reserved by the flow, and may end up creating or utilizing spare processing capacity.

In contrast, even in the most flexible task model used for Pfair scheduling (namely, the IS model), subtask deadlines are computed according to a strictly periodic schedule of packet arrivals. Scheduling algorithms designed specifically for periodic flows may penalize flows that use spare capacity to transmit at more than their reserved rates, by denying them allocation at their reserved rate during a subsequent time interval. To see this, consider again Figure 5.2a. Suppose that early releases are allowed, and there is spare capacity prior to time 11, but not afterward. Then, T could potentially execute in each of slots 0 through 10. These 11 subtasks "use up" the first 11 subtask deadlines of T. Thus, if T has another eligible subtask at time 11, then it uses the subtask deadline associated with T_{12}, which is at time 17. Thus, while each subtask of T *should* have a deadline two or three time units after its release, this particular subtask has a deadline six time units after its release. In general, the extent to which deadlines can be postponed in this manner is unbounded.

This property of penalizing flows for using spare capacity is undesirable in networks for two reasons. First, for many network applications that have timeliness requirements, it may not be feasible to predict accurately the exact rate to reserve. (Consider, for instance, the problem of transmitting a variable-bit-rate-encoded video stream over the network.) The performance of such an application may be significantly enhanced by allowing it to utilize spare capacity. Second, allowing applications to transmit packets in bursts enables networks to provide low average delays and to increase network utilization due to statistical multiplexing gains. Thus, it is important to *devise fair allocation schemes for multiprocessors that do not penalize flows for using spare processing capacity in the past*.

5.2.3 Performance Issues

Network link capacities are increasing at almost double the rate at which router processing speeds are increasing [4, 16]. To keep up with high link speeds, packet-processing functions must be implemented in a highly efficient manner. Deadline-based scheduling algorithms, on the other hand, impose nonnegligible computational complexity. In particular, these algorithms require routers to maintain a sorted queue of packet descriptors (sorted according to deadlines); this leads to a per-packet complexity that is a function of the number of packets (or flows). Therefore, to enable routers to operate efficiently in high-speed networks, *the complexity associated with packet sorting should be eliminated, while ensuring that meaningful deadline guarantees are still provided*.

5.2.4   Scalability Issues

To compute deadlines, routers need to maintain state [for instance, $\theta(T_i)$ in Equation 5.3] for each active flow and perform flow classification for all incoming packets. However, the complexity of these two per-flow operations limits the scalability of routers as the number of flows increases. This is especially true for routers in the core of a network, which aggregate and handle a large number of flows originating from different edges of the network, and are also required to operate on high-speed links. Thus, it is essential to *eliminate the complexity associated with these per-flow operations in the core routers of a network*.

5.3   MULTIPROCESSOR SCHEDULING IN ROUTERS: KEY IDEAS

In this section, we discuss some approaches we believe will address the issues outlined in Section 5.2. Many of the ideas presented in this section exploit a key difference between the timeliness requirements of traditional real-time applications and emerging network applications. Network applications have to be designed to tolerate the least possible network delay, which is given by the sum of link-propagation and transmission latencies on end-to-end paths. These minimum end-to-end latencies are themselves of the order of a few *milliseconds*. Unlike hard real-time applications that have no tolerance for deadline misses, these applications are capable of operating well even if deadlines are not strictly adhered to, as long as deadline misses are bounded by a quantity less than, say, a fraction of a millisecond. Hence, the use of PD^2 is not warranted and a simpler algorithm may be used.

The EPDF Pfair algorithm is similar to PD^2, but *uses no tie-breaks*. While deadline misses can occur under EPDF (refer to Figure 5.3), based upon preliminary evidence (presented in the following), we believe that the impact of such misses will be extremely limited.

5.3.1   Deadline Guarantees Under EPDF

The *tardiness* of a scheduling algorithm indicates the extent to which a deadline can be missed. To determine how frequently deadlines are missed under EPDF, and by what tardiness threshold, we recently constructed a series of EPDF schedules for randomly generated task sets [35]. Out of approximately 200,000 generated task sets, *no subtask ever missed its deadline by more than one quantum*. Moreover, single-quantum deadline misses were very rare. For example, on systems of five or more processors the miss rate was about 0.1%. This evidence indicates that EPDF (and variants considered in Section 5.3.2) may be ideal for use within multiprocessor routers.

Currently, we are trying to establish *formally* that EPDF guarantees a tardiness of one. To date, this has been proved for systems that satisfy the following constraint [35].

(M1) The sum of the weights of the $M-1$ heaviest tasks is at most $(M+1)/(2M-3)$.

Note that this restriction only applies if there are tasks with weight greater than $1/2$, and that it imposes no restrictions on systems of four or fewer processors. It may seem that eliminating such a liberal condition is not important. After all, a flow with weight exceeding $1/2$ may seem quite unlikely. However, one of the scheduling schemes considered later (in the section "Limiting Task Migrations") is a hierarchical scheme in which several tasks are bundled into a single "supertask." Such a supertask can easily have a weight exceeding $1/2$. Furthermore, many of the scheduling problems considered in Section 5.3.2 also involve establishing tardiness thresholds. We regard the problem of establishing EPDF tardiness as an important "bellwether" problem in this class.

5.3.2   Applicability Issues

We now present ideas for addressing the two assumptions of *uniform and aligned quanta* and *unconstrained migration*, which limit the applicability of Pfair-scheduling algorithms for packet processing in routers.

Allowing nonuniform and nonaligned quanta

Fixed-Length Quanta. Allowing only fixed-length quanta simplifies the analysis of multiprocessor schedulers; this, however, may result in lower

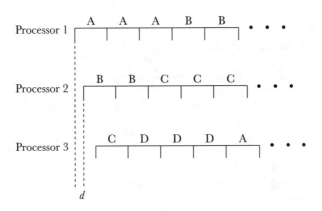

5.4

FIGURE

A partial schedule on three processors with staggered quantum allocations. This schedule is shown differently from those in other figures: each line shows quantum allocations on one processor. Four tasks, denoted A through D, of weight 3/4 each are scheduled. The tth quantum ($t \geq 0$) begins at time $t + d(i - 1)$ on processor i. (Note that it may not always be possible to migrate a task scheduled in two consecutive slots. Thus, we have additional restrictions.)

utilization due to partially wasted quanta. An obvious way to reduce the extent of waste is to use a smaller quantum size. Unfortunately, scheduling at a finer granularity in this way increases context-switching and scheduling overheads, and thereby reduces the amount of processor time available for tasks. Thus, there is a trade-off between system overheads and partially wasted quanta that needs to be carefully analyzed to determine an optimal quantum size.

Interconnect contention due to aligned quanta could possibly be avoided by staggering quantum allocations on each processor, as shown in Figure 5.4. The exact extent to which such staggering might impact the algorithms and techniques described in this chapter remains to be determined.

Variable-Length Quanta. A liberal quantum-allocation model is one in which quanta may vary in length (up to some threshold) and do not have to align. While allowing variable-length quanta would probably be disastrous if task deadlines were hard, we are somewhat optimistic that the impact may be acceptable if deadlines can be missed. We are currently analyzing EPDF for use in this model and are trying to derive corresponding tardiness thresholds.

Limiting task migrations

For systems with nonmigratory tasks, the hierarchical *supertask* approach proposed by Moir and Ramamurthy [31] can be used. In this approach, the

Tasks	Schedule
V 1/2	
W 1/3	
X 1/3	
Y 2/9	
S 2/9	
Within S	*Deadline miss*
T 1/5	
U 1/45	
Time	0 5 10

5.5

FIGURE

PD^2/EPDF schedule with a supertask S on two processors.

nonmigratory tasks bound to a specific processor are combined into a single "supertask," which is then scheduled as an ordinary Pfair task; when a supertask is scheduled, one of its component nonmigratory tasks is selected for execution. Unfortunately, while supertasking is a promising approach, the following example illustrates that nonmigratory tasks can actually miss their deadlines when supertasking is used in conjunction with PF, PD, or PD^2.

To see why supertasking can fail, consider the two-processor Pfair schedule shown in Figure 5.5. In this schedule, there are four normal tasks (V, W, X, and Y—with weights 1/2, 1/3, 1/3, and 2/9, respectively—and one supertask, S, which represents two component tasks T and U, with weights 1/5 and 1/45, respectively. S competes with a weight of $1/5 + 1/45 = 2/9$. The windows of each task are shown on alternating lines (e.g., S's first window spans $[0, 5)$), and a shaded box denotes the quantum allocated to each subtask. In the upper region of the figure, the PD^2 schedule for the task set is shown. In the lower region, allocations within S are shown. These allocations are based on EPDF priorities.

It can be seen that T misses a deadline at time 10. This is because no quantum is allocated to S in the interval $[5, 10)$. In general, component tasks may be misallocated if there exists an interval that contains more component-task windows than supertask windows. Observe that $[5, 10)$ is such an interval; it contains one component-task window and no supertask windows.

Holman and Anderson subsequently showed that such deadline misses can be avoided by inflating supertask weights [22, 23]. While such a scheme is necessarily suboptimal, experiments presented by them suggest that inflation factors should be small in practice.

In work on real-time systems, the fact that deadlines can be missed has been seen as a shortcoming of supertasking. However, as we have stressed before, deadline misses in routers are not a serious problem, provided reasonable tardiness thresholds can be established. Thus, supertasking may be a very viable approach in this setting. To determine if this is so, we are currently trying to derive tight tardiness thresholds for EPDF-scheduled systems in which supertasks are used.

5.3.3   Flexibility Issues

To reallocate spare capacity in a dynamic Pfair-scheduled system, tasks need to be *reweighted*. In particular, when spare capacity increases (for instance, when a flow becomes inactive or departs the network), the weights of all the active flows should be scaled *up* so that all processing capacity in the system is utilized. When spare capacity reduces due to the arrival of packets in a new or previously inactive flow, the weights of active flows should be scaled *down*, to accommodate the new flow (though no flow should be scaled below its minimum guaranteed share). When using PD^2, or one of the other optimal algorithms described in Section 5.1.2, weight changes can cause tie-breaking information to change, as shown in Figure 5.6. In the worst case, this may require completely re-sorting

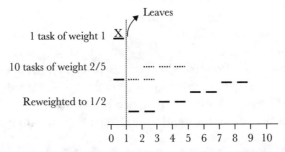

5.6

FIGURE

A reweighting example on five processors. At time 0, there are 10 tasks of weight 2/5 and 1 task of weight 1. At time 1, the latter task leaves. The excess capacity of 1 is redistributed among the remaining 10 tasks, giving each a new weight of 1/2. The dotted lines indicate the original windows of those tasks. The new windows can be aligned so that the new and old deadlines match. The b-bit of the first subtask of a task of weight 2/5 is 1, whereas a task of weight 1/2 has no subtask with a b-bit of 1. Thus, the PD^2 priorities of these subtasks differ.

the scheduler's priority queue at a $\Theta(N \log N)$ cost, where N is the number of flows. This cost might be incurred *every time a flow becomes active*. In the following sections, we discuss two approaches for avoiding this complexity.

Fast-reweighting approach

Under EPDF scheduling, a *fast-reweighting* procedure can be used in which each task's next deadline is preserved. In particular, suppose that task T needs to be reweighted at time t. Let T_i be the subtask of T that is eligible at t. A task T can be reweighted by simply replacing it by a new task U with the new weight and by aligning U_1's window so that $d(U_1) = d(T_i)$ and $e(U_1) \leq t$. (In practice, T's weight can simply be redefined, instead of creating a new task.) This ability to perform fast reweighting is another key virtue of EPDF. The fast-reweighting approach, however, requires $\Theta(N)$ time, which may be unacceptable in high-speed routers that handle a large number of flows.

Virtual-time approach

The concept of *virtual time* is central to many previously proposed fair-link- and uniprocessor-scheduling schemes. Such schemes typically associate a virtual-time function with the shared resource (processor/link): at each "real" time instant t, the virtual-time value $V(t)$ reflects the amount of load upon the resource thus far. For instance, if the current load is half the resource's capacity, then $V(t)$ increases at twice the rate of "real" time: $(d/dt)V(t) = 2$. Using virtual time, these uniprocessor-scheduling schemes are able to achieve exactly the effect of the fast-reweighting procedure, discussed previously, by merely varying the rate of change of $V(t)$. Hence, when a connection/task enters or leaves the system, reweighting is mimicked in *constant* time rather than the $\Theta(N)$ time required for explicit reweighting.

For various reasons (some of which are discussed in [5]), the concept of virtual time does not generalize directly to multiprocessor systems. The main problem here is that different task weights may need to be scaled by different factors,[5] due to the fact that no task's weight may exceed unity. A heuristic for dealing

5. If quanta of variable length are allowed (as discussed in Section 5.3.2), then additional problems arise. Allowing variable-length quanta is equivalent to allowing subtasks with different execution costs. Because task weights may be scaled by different factors, the order in which such subtasks complete execution in the ideal GPS schedule may change. For example, consider a two-processor system that has three tasks T, U, and V of weights 1/4, 3/4, and 1, respectively. If T and U have subtasks of length 1 and 2, respectively, then the initial finishing times in the GPS schedule will be 4 and 8/3, respectively. However, if V leaves, then the weights of both T and U are increased to 1 in order to fully utilize the two processors. The finishing times of the subtasks of T and U now become 1 and 2, respectively, thus resulting in a change in the order of finishing times. Since tardiness bounds

with this problem that requires $\Theta(M)$ time is given in [13]. We are currently trying to develop a notion of virtual time that can be used to mimic the effect of reweighting in only constant time.

5.3.4   Performance Issues

As mentioned earlier, deadline-based scheduling algorithms require routers to maintain a sorted queue of tasks, the complexity of which is a function of the number of packets (or flows). The use of nontrivial tie-breaking mechanisms increases this complexity. The overhead due to tie-breaks is much greater if flows are allowed to utilize idle capacity, as this may introduce the need to reorder sorted task lists (see Section 5.3.3). To enable routers to operate efficiently in high-speed networks, the complexity associated with sorting packets needs to be reduced.

One option is to employ an *approximate* constant-time priority queue implementation that does not sort packets in the exact order of their deadlines, but according to the intervals in which deadlines fall [17, 30]. However, there is no evidence that suggests that meaningful deadline guarantees can be provided with such implementations. Nevertheless, we plan to analyze such implementations as part of our future research.

5.3.5   Scalability Issues

A number of end-to-end link-scheduling frameworks have recently been proposed that enable networks to provide end-to-end per-flow guarantees with respect to shared-link access, without requiring per-flow state in core routers [27, 37, 40]. Over the past year, we have implemented routers from core-stateful and core-stateless networks on Intel's IXP1200-based router platform and compared their performance with that of conventional IP routers [21]. We have found that core routers in stateful networks may be able to process packets at less than 50% of the processing rates of current IP routers, whereas those in core-stateless networks can operate within 75% of these routers. Thus, core-stateless link-scheduling frameworks significantly improve the link speeds at which core routers can operate. This concept has not yet been applied to the problem of processor scheduling in routers.

To see the need for per-flow state in Pfair-based multiprocessor scheduling algorithms, observe that the deadline for processing a packet (or a subtask, in

---

for the actual schedule are determined based on these GPS finishing times, it is not clear whether reasonable bounds can be obtained.

Pfair terminology) depends on its eligibility time, which in turn is a function of the deadline of the *previous* packet of the same flow. Thus, the latest deadline used within each flow must be stored (per-flow state).

As shown by Kaur and Vin [28], *upper bounds* on these latest deadlines can be computed based on the state of the *same* packet at the first node on the end-to-end path of the flow. Since the first node is an edge router of the network, it maintains per-flow state, and can compute deadlines. The edge router can communicate these deadlines to core routers by encoding them in packet headers. Kaur and Vin showed that when core routers use such upper bounds, instead of actual deadlines, guarantees on end-to-end delays remain unchanged. They also showed that core-stateless networks can be designed to provide end-to-end throughput and fairness guarantees as well [27, 29]. We believe that the need for per-flow state in processor scheduling can also be eliminated by using similar state-encoding and deadline-computation techniques. We are currently trying to obtain various end-to-end guarantees that are applicable to packet processing and analyze the guarantees that can be provided in a core-stateless network.

5.3.6   Other Issues

Recent advances have provided architecture designers with the ability to implement simultaneous multithreading (SMT) in a single superscalar processor [15]. SMT is a technique that allows several independent threads to issue instructions to different functional units in a single cycle. An SMT processor can thus dynamically partition its resources among several simultaneously active threads on a cycle-by-cycle basis. The maximum number of simultaneously active threads is determined by the number of available hardware contexts.

SMT-based systems benefit from schedulers that take into account the various functional units accessed by threads, when trying to schedule threads. Recent results by Jain et al. suggest that deadline-based algorithms are capable of making effective use of SMT [24]. However, more research is needed to determine the best approach for allocating resources in combination with our scheduling algorithms, which may need to be adapted to take advantage of SMT.

5.4   EXPERIMENTAL EVALUATION

The techniques presented in Section 5.3 represent our efforts toward designing multiprocessor scheduling schemes that can provide strong assertions about service guarantees. To assess the performance and scalability of these techniques,

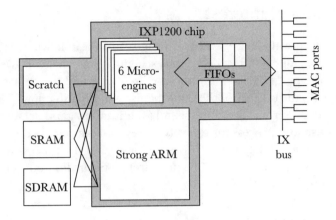

5.7
FIGURE

Block diagram of the IXP1200 [34].

a real prototype is required. We plan to use Intel's IXP1200 [1]—a platform with six RISC-based *microengines*, each with four hardware contexts (see Figure 5.7)—to instantiate our techniques.

5.4.1 Implementation Challenges

Over the past year, we have used the IXP1200-based router platform to conduct a preliminary investigation of the implementation of router building blocks—specifically, IP routing, flow classification, and priority queue maintenance—in popular network architectures. While we expect to leverage from this prior router implementation for instantiating new multiprocessor scheduling mechanisms, we need to address new implementation challenges. The most relevant is the lack of explicit software support for thread scheduling within a microengine. In the software reference design provided with the IXP1200 platform, new threads can run on a microengine only when the current thread voluntarily gives up control of that microengine. To address this challenge, we plan to explore two different scheduling approaches: (1) using explicit instructions in the code of each thread that force it to give up control after a certain number of instructions, and to select the next thread to run, and (2) devoting one of the threads within each microengine to perform all scheduling functions on that microengine. While the former approach will result in less fine-grained control over quantum durations, the latter will result in greater complexity and overheads due to the need for inter-thread communication.

5.4.2   Metrics of Interest

We plan to use the router testbed to measure the following: (1) the processing speeds supported by the various scheduling mechanisms we develop and those of the past (e.g., EPDF without reweighting and the heuristic schemes of [13, 14]), (2) the efficacy of these mechanisms in isolating flows from each other and providing service guarantees, and (3) utilization gains achieved by allowing flows to use idle processing capacity. These measurements depend on several factors, such as traffic load, network topology, and the processing architectures of routers. We plan to repeat our measurements for different settings for these parameters.

5.5   CONCLUSIONS

Two important trends are expected to guide the design of next-generation networks. First, with the commercialization of the Internet, providers will use value-added services to differentiate their service offerings from other providers. Such services require the use of sophisticated resource-scheduling mechanisms in routers. Second, to enable extensibility and the deployment of new services in a rapid and cost-effective manner, routers will be instantiated using programmable network processors. In this chapter, we have focused on the problem of scheduling processing capacity on programmable multiprocessor router platforms. Our contributions are twofold. First, we have identified several issues that arise if existing multiprocessor scheduling schemes are used on routers. Existing fair multiprocessor scheduling techniques have considerable promise in this setting, but need to be refined to address performance, scalability, flexibility, and applicability concerns. Second, we have presented new ideas and planned research directions to address these concerns.

ACKNOWLEDGMENTS

The work represented in this chapter was supported by NSF grants CCR 9972211, CCR 9988327, ITR 0082866, and CCR 0204312.

REFERENCES

[1]   Intel IXP1200 network processor. *www.intel.com/design/network/products/npfamily/ixp1200.htm*.

[2]   Intel IXP2400 network processor. *www.intel.com/design/network/products/npfamily/ixp2400.htm*.

[3]   Intel IXP2800 network processor. *www.intel.com/design/network/products/npfamily/ixp2800.htm*.

[4]   V. Agarwal, M. Hrishikesh, S. Keckler, and D. Burger, "Clock Rate Versus IPC: The End of the Road for Conventional Microarchitectures," *Proceedings of the 27th International Symposium on Computer Architecture*, June 2000, pp. 248–259.

[5]   J. Anderson, S. Baruah, and K. Jeffay, "Parallel Switching in Connection-Oriented Networks," *Proceedings of the 20th IEEE Real-Time Systems Symposium*, Dec. 1999, pp. 200–209.

[6]   J. Anderson and A. Srinivasan, "Early-Release Fair Scheduling," *Proceedings of the 12th Euromicro Conference on Real-Time Systems*, June 2000, pp. 35–43.

[7]   J. Anderson and A. Srinivasan, "Pfair Scheduling: Beyond Periodic Task Systems," *Proceedings of the 7th International Conference on Real-Time Computing Systems and Applications*, Dec. 2000, pp. 297–306.

[8]   J. Anderson and A. Srinivasan, "Mixed Pfair/ERfair Scheduling of Asynchronous Periodic Tasks," *Proceedings of the 13th Euromicro Conference on Real-Time Systems*, June 2001, pp. 76–85.

[9]   S. Baruah, N. Cohen, C. G. Plaxton, and D. Varvel, "Proportionate Progress: A Notion of Fairness in Resource Allocation," *Algorithmica*, 15:600–625, 1996.

[10]   S. Baruah, J. Gehrke, and C. G. Plaxton, "Fast Scheduling of Periodic Tasks on Multiple Resources," *Proceedings of the 9th International Parallel Processing Symposium*, Apr. 1995, pp. 280–288.

[11]   J. Bennett and H. Zhang, "WF^{2}Q: Worst-Case Fair Queueing," *Proceedings of IEEE INFOCOM*, Mar. 1996, pp. 120–128.

[12]   J. Bennett and H. Zhang, "Hierarchical Packet Fair Queueing Algorithms," *IEEE/ACM Transactions on Networking*, 5(5):675–689, Oct. 1997.

[13]   A. Chandra, M. Adler, P. Goyal, and P. Shenoy, "Surplus Fair Scheduling: A Proportional-Share CPU Scheduling Algorithm for Symmetric Multiprocessors," *Proceedings of the 4th Symposium on Operating System Design and Implementation*, Oct. 2000, pp. 45–58.

[14]   A. Chandra, M. Adler, and P. Shenoy, "Deadline Fair Scheduling: Bridging the Theory and Practice of Proportionate-Fair Scheduling in Multiprocessor Servers," *Proceedings of the 7th IEEE Real-Time Technology and Applications Symposium*, May 2001, pp. 3–14.

[15]   CNP810SP, "Network Services Processor: Key Feature Summary," *www.clearwaternetworks.com/product_summary_snp8101.html*.

[16]   K. Coffman and A. Odlyzko, "The Size and Growth Rate of the Internet," Mar. 2001, *www.firstmonday.dk/issues/issue3_10/coffman/*.

[17]   T. Cormen, C. Leiserson, and R. Rivest, *Introduction to Algorithms*, New York, NY: McGraw-Hill, 1996.

[18]   A. Demers, S. Keshav, and S. Shenkar, "Analysis and Simulation of a Fair Queueing Algorithm," *Journal of Internetworking Research and Experience*, 1(1):3–12, Oct. 1990.

[19]   S. Golestani, "A Self-Clocked Fair Queueing Scheme for High-Speed Applications," *Proceedings of IEEE INFOCOM*, Apr. 1994, pp. 636–646.

[20]   P. Goyal, H. Vin, and H. Cheng, "Start-Time Fair Queuing: A Scheduling Algorithm for Integrated Services Packet Switching Networks," *Proceedings of ACM SIGCOMM*, Aug. 1996, pp. 157–168.

[21]   B. Hardekopf et al., "Scalability Analysis of Software-Based Service-Differentiating Routers Using Network Processors," Technical Report, Department of Computer Sciences, University of Texas at Austin, May 2001.

[22]   P. Holman and J. Anderson, "Guaranteeing Pfair Supertasks by Reweighting," *Proceedings of the 22nd IEEE Real-Time Systems Symposium*, Dec. 2001, pp. 203–212.

[23]   P. Holman and J. Anderson, "Using Supertasks to Improve Processor Utilization in Multiprocessor Real-Time Systems," *Proceedings of the 15th Euromicro Conference on Real-Time Systems*, July 2003.

[24]   R. Jain, C. Hughes, and S. Adve, "Soft Real-Time Scheduling on Simultaneous Multithreaded Processors," *Proceedings of the 23rd IEEE Real-Time Systems Symposium*, Dec. 2002, pp. 134–145.

[25]   M. Jones and J. Regehr, "CPU Reservations and Time Constraints: Experience on Windows NT," *Proceedings of the 3rd USENIX Windows NT Symposium*, July 1999, pp. 93–102.

[26]   P. Kaiser, "A (R)evolutionary Technology Roadmap Beyond Today's OE Industry," *NSF Workshop on the Future Revolution in Optical Communications and Networking*, Dec. 2000.

[27]   J. Kaur, "Scalable Network Architectures for Providing Per-flow Service Guarantees," Ph.D. thesis, Department of Computer Sciences, University of Texas at Austin, Aug. 2002.

[28]   J. Kaur and H. M. Vin, "Core-Stateless Guaranteed Rate Scheduling Algorithms," *Proceedings of IEEE INFOCOM*, Apr. 2001, pp. 1484–1492.

[29]   J. Kaur and H. M. Vin, "Core-Stateless Guaranteed Throughput Networks," *Proceedings of IEEE INFOCOM*, Apr. 2003.

[30]   J. Liebeherr and D. E. Wrege, "Priority Queueing Schedulers with Approximate Sorting in Output Buffered Switches," *IEEE Journal on Selected Areas in Communications*, 17:1127–1145, June 1999.

[31]   M. Moir and S. Ramamurthy, "Pfair Scheduling of Fixed and Migrating Periodic Tasks on Multiple Resources," *Proceedings of the 20th IEEE Real-Time Systems Symposium*, Dec. 1999, pp. 294–303.

[32]   A. K. Parekh, "A Generalized Processor Sharing Approach to Flow Control in Integrated Services Networks," Ph.D. thesis, Department of Electrical Engineering and Computer Science, MIT, 1992.

[33]   T. Spalink, S. Karlin, L. Peterson, and Y. Gottlieb, "Building a Robust Software-Based Router Using Network Processors," *Proceedings of the 18th ACM Symposium on Operating Systems Principles*, Oct. 2001, pp. 216–229.

[34]   T. Spalink, S. Karlin, and L. Peterson, "Evaluating Network Processors in IP Forwarding," Technical Report TR-626-00, Department of Computer Science, Princeton University, Nov. 2000.

[35]   A. Srinivasan and J. Anderson, "Efficient Scheduling of Soft Real-Time Applications on Multiprocessors," *Proceedings of the 15th Euromicro Conference on Real-Time Systems*, July 2003.

[36]   A. Srinivasan and J. Anderson, "Optimal Rate-Based Scheduling on Multiprocessors," *Proceedings of the 34th ACM Symposium on Theory of Computing*, May 2002, pp. 189–198.

[37]   I. Stoica, "Stateless Core: A Scalable Approach for Quality of Service in the Internet," Ph.D. thesis, Department of Computer Science, Carnegie Mellon University, Dec. 2000.

[38]   I. Stoica, H. Zhang, and T. Ng, "A Hierarchical Fair Service Curve Algorithm for Link-Sharing, Real-Time and Priority Service," *Proceedings of ACM SIGCOMM*, Aug. 1997, pp. 249–262.

[39]   L. Zhang, "Virtual Clock: A New Traffic Control Algorithm for Packet-Switched Networks," *ACM Transactions on Computer Systems*, 9(2):101–124, May 1991.

[40]   Z. Zhang, Z. Duan, and Y. Hou, "Virtual Time Reference System: A Unifying Scheduling Framework for Scalable Support of Guaranteed Services," *IEEE Journal on Selected Areas in Communication, Special Issue on Internet QoS*, 18(12):2684–2695, Dec. 2000.

A Massively Multithreaded Packet Processor

Steve Melvin
O'Melveny & Myers LLP

**Mario Nemirovsky, Enric Musoll, Jeff Huynh, Rodolfo Milito,
Hector Urdaneta, Koroush Saraf**
Kayamba, Inc.

There are increasing numbers of emerging applications for packet-processing devices in IP-based networks that are *stateful applications*. In a stateful application, memory is updated with each packet that is processed, and a large amount of memory must be maintained. Thus, unlike applications in which packets can be processed relying on tables that change infrequently (such as layer 2 packet forwarding), stateful applications require the network device to maintain state related to which packets have been processed and in what order, and to update that state with each packet. This state is typically flow based, and in cases that there are a large number of simultaneous flows (for example, 1 million or more), there can potentially be a large amount of memory that must be maintained (hundreds of megabytes or more). Stateful applications include quality-of-service enforcement, intrusion detection, sophisticated billing, and monitoring, among others. Many of these applications reside not in the core or at the edge but at an enterprise gateway or data center connection point. Data rates between 1 Gb/s and 10 Gb/s are currently the biggest challenge. Rarely are these types of applications needed at higher data rates, and at lower data rates conventional solutions are practical.

One characteristic of many stateful applications, especially at data rates where many flows are aggregated on a single link, is the lack of memory locality. There is little temporal locality, since the data being accessed by one packet is not needed again until a related packet is processed, which could be after a large number of intervening packets. There is also little spatial locality, since often data structures are sparse, with reads and writes only to small pieces of memory at a time. It is also the case that often a large memory footprint is needed, more than will fit on-chip, even using advanced embedded DRAM techniques.

A consequence of these application requirements is that data caches improve performance little, if at all. In fact, data caches can often lower performance by forcing large blocks of memory (i.e., cache lines) to be read from and written to external memory, tying up this valuable resource longer than necessary. The only significant value of a data cache in these scenarios is to capture the working set locality of a single packet workload (i.e., the stack operations used to perform local computation). Our analysis has shown that the working sets for stateful applications of interest are in the range of 200 to 400 bytes. Thus, this amount of memory can easily be buffered on-chip, eliminating the need for a data cache and freeing up the external data memory to perform a larger number of randomly addressed memory operations.

The random address rate, or the rate at which nonsequential pieces of memory can be accessed, is a critical underlying performance metric that often governs overall performance. To achieve high random address rates in processors with low spatial locality, narrow buses using short bursts are desirable. Memory devices and access mechanisms optimized for large block transfers (such as are needed for graphics applications) are often very inefficient in these applications, except where packet DMA is involved.

Our analysis of applications of interest has shown that overall workloads range from 100 to 10,000 instructions, with 10 to 20% of all instructions making external memory accesses. Thus, there are a significant number (up to several thousand) of external memory accesses required to process a single packet. Given best-case DRAM latencies and packet transmission times for short packets, it is clear that a high degree of packet overlap (on the order of hundreds of packets simultaneously being processed) is necessary to cover this latency. Multithreading at some level is the only practical way to implement this high degree of parallelism, since to fit in a reasonable silicon area there must be a high level of sharing of resources. Most threads are waiting for memory most of the time, and these waiting threads should consume as few resources as possible.

To satisfy these application requirements, we have designed a packet processor code-named *Porthos*, a block diagram of which is shown in Figure 6.1. We refer to Porthos as a "massively multithreaded" packet processor. Porthos has multiple memory ports, multiple multithreaded processing engines, and other special features that emphasize efficiency over single-threaded performance to achieve its design goal. The processing engines are each associated with an independent port to memory. Each processing engine, called a *tribe*, can execute up to 32 threads simultaneously. A tribe is itself a multithreaded

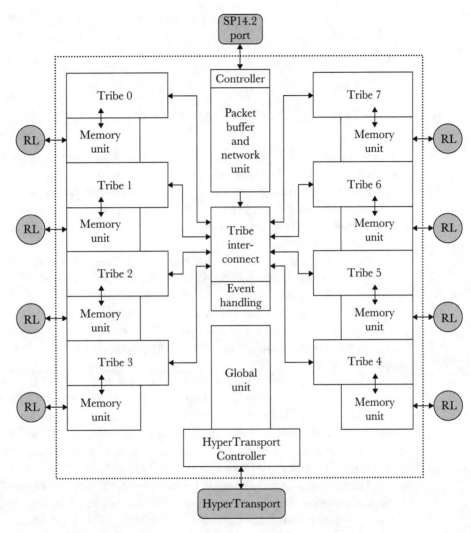

6.1   Porthos block diagram.

FIGURE

processor with two memory ports, one to external memory and one to the packet buffer.

In this chapter we will first explore the concept of random external accesses to memory and compare Porthos to other processors. Then we will discuss different memory/processor architectures. In Section 6.3 we describe the microarchitecture of each multithreaded processing unit of Porthos in detail.

Section 6.4 describes the special-purpose network block, and Section 6.5 provides details on the interconnect block. Finally, we summarize with conclusions in Section 6.7.

6.1 RANDOM EXTERNAL MEMORY ACCESSES

As mentioned in the previous section, the rate of random external accesses is often a more important constraint than the total amount of memory bandwidth. We introduce a term, *REAPS*, for *random external accesses per second*. The number of REAPS necessary for a given application can be compared against the maximum number a given processor is capable of. REAPS are orthogonal to memory bandwidth as a design parameter.

We have extensively studied a number of applications in terms of their requirements for MIPS and REAPS. A summary of our analysis is shown in Table 6.1. The applications shown are Cisco Express Forwarding (CEF), packet classification, packet reassembly, a monitoring application (Argus [1]), and an intrusion detection application (Bro [2]). The second column in Table 6.1 shows the average number of instructions per packet we measured for these applications.

The number of MIPS required is shown for OC48 (2.5 Gb/s, full-duplex) with 500-byte packets. The last column illustrates the number of REAPS needed in billions (that is, GREAPS or giga REAPS) per second. This data is based on our observed numbers of load and store instructions per workload, which ranges from 25 to 46%, and the simulated fraction of those that would miss in an internal cache, which ranges from 35 to 40%.

The bottom section of Table 6.1 illustrates MIPS and REAPS capabilities for three processors: a Pentium running at 2 GHz, a Sibyte 1250, and Porthos using realistic assumptions on IPC. This table indicates that the Pentium and Sibyte processors are much closer to handling these applications in terms of MIPS than in terms of REAPS. This is mainly due to the different design goals between processors running large single-threaded applications (that have high temporal and spatial memory locality) and those of packet processors, as discussed previously. As Table 6.1 indicates, the GREAPS/GIPS ratio in the applications we have studied is on the order of 1/10. While the Sibyte has a GIPS/GREAPS ratio of 1/15, and the Pentium has a ratio of barely 1/40, Porthos is designed to accommodate a peak GREAPS rate of 1/4 of its sustained GIPS rate. Processors such as the Pentium are optimized for transferring large blocks of memory externally rather than a higher number of small transfers.

Application requirements at OC48, 500-byte packets

Applications	Instructions/packet	GIPS	GREAPS
CEF	70	0.09	0.01
Classification	400	0.50	0.05
Reassembly	400	0.50	0.08
Monitoring	2500	3.13	0.38
IDS	3500	4.38	0.51
Processor capabilities			
Intel, 2 GHz		3.0	0.08
SB1250		2.4	0.16
Porthos		9.6	2.40

6.1

TABLE

MIPS/REAPS requirements and capabilities.

6.2   PROCESSOR/MEMORY ARCHITECTURES

Given the REAPS requirements of applications of interest at the rates of interest, it quickly becomes clear that multiple memory ports are required. Even the fastest external DRAM with the shortest burst length cannot deliver enough independent accesses. Our analysis has shown that eight RL-DRAM ports running at 300 MHz, each 32 bits in width, are sufficient to meet the overall design requirements. A 32-bit bus width with a burst length of 2 yields 64 bits every DRAM clock cycle. With enough buffering to keep all banks busy, an independent access can be started every DRAM cycle to keep the number of random external accesses high.

Given these multiple memory ports, a significant issue is whether each memory port should be coupled to a particular processing engine, or whether there should be a decoupled arrangement where memory ports and processing engines are connected via an internal network. We have performed extensive modeling of these architecture choices and shown that higher memory utilizations are possible with a coupled architecture. This result is intuitively clear when one considers that a coupled architecture suffers less contention. A coupled architecture exposes a memory arrangement to the software/application level, which allows best-case utilization to increase.

The disadvantage of a coupled architecture is that the programmer and/or compiler now must partition the application such that workloads and/or flows are

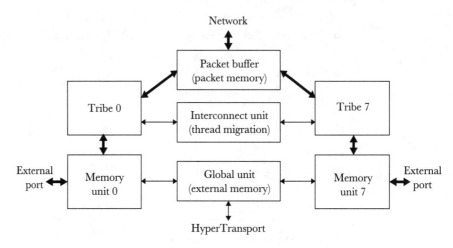

Network

Packet buffer
(packet memory)

Tribe 0

Interconnect unit
(thread migration)

Tribe 7

External
port

Memory
unit 0

Global unit
(external memory)

Memory
unit 7

External
port

HyperTransport

6.2   Loosely coupled architecture.

FIGURE

split across the multiple processing elements. Exposing this detail to software had advantages in performance, but can only be taken advantage of if the applications can be fit into this model. In Porthos, we have chosen a hybrid approach, which could be called "loosely coupled," as shown in Figure 6.2.

While there is a coupling of a tribe to a memory port, there is also an internal switch in which each memory unit is connected to every other memory unit. This permits software running on any tribe to access any memory in any tribe, with a preferential access to the local memory port. This is possible, since each port represents a distinct region of the physical address space. In Figure 6.2, two tribes are shown, but the same connections exist for all tribes. The heavy arrows illustrate the high-bandwidth paths. It is anticipated that the vast majority of all memory accesses made within a tribe are directed either to the packet buffer or to the external memory that is local.

The partitioning of the memory space into distinct regions for each of the tribes is a key design detail of the Porthos chip. Partitioning is based on the assumption that a large number (at least 90%) of memory accesses for threads within a given tribe are destined for the local memory associated with that tribe. Partitioning reduces the interconnect cost, since the global interconnect is needed for only a small fraction of the total memory accesses. Partitioning also reduces contention, thereby reducing queuing delay and/or allowing a higher efficiency of external memory accesses. As discussed previously, the key to this reduction in contention is that a preferential memory region is exposed to software so that partitioning can be addressed statically.

Memory partitioning does represent software challenges. It will be necessary to have compiler and linker support to insulate this detail as much as possible from the programmer. It is also necessary to have hardware support to move threads between processing engines. Thus, it is more efficient to move a thread to run on a particular processing engine that is closer to the data it is operating on than to move the data to a particular tribe. More details on the manner in which threads are moved between processing engines is discussed in material to follow. It is important to note that because of this loosely coupled architecture memory partitioning has been moved from a correctness issue to one of performance.

6.3   THE TRIBE MICROARCHITECTURE

Figure 6.1 illustrates the major blocks of Porthos. A full-duplex network interface of 10 Gb/s is provided that may be channelized into 4 OC48 ports (2.5 Gb/s each) or 10 1-Gb/s Ethernet ports. The packet buffer is a FIFO that stores the packet data until it is determined if the packet should be dropped, forwarded (with modifications if necessary), or transferred off-chip for later processing. Packets may be transmitted from data stored externally and may be created by software and transmitted. The processing on packets that are resident in the chip occurs within the tribes. A block diagram of the microarchitecture of each tribe is shown in Figure 6.3, which illustrates the modules that implement the tribe and the major data path connections between those modules. A software thread would typically execute on a single packet in one tribe at a time, and may jump from one tribe to another. A hypertransport interface is used to communicate with host processors, co-processors, or other Porthos chips.

6.3.1   ISA Specification

Each tribe executes instructions to accomplish the necessary workload for each packet. The ISA implemented by Porthos is similar to the 64-bit MIPS-IV ISA with a few omissions and a few additions. The main differences between the Porthos ISA and MIPS-IV are summarized as follows. The Porthos ISA contains 64-bit registers, and utilizes 32-bit addresses with no TLB. There is no 32-bit mode, and thus all instructions that operate on registers operate on all 64 bits. This functionality is the same as a MIPS R4000 in 64-bit mode. All memory is treated

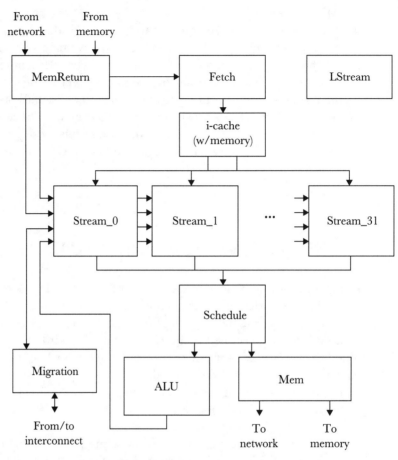

Tribe block diagram.

FIGURE

as big-endian and there is no mode bit that controls endianness. Since there
is no TLB, there is no address translation and there are no protection modes
implemented. This means that all code has access to all regions of memory. The
physical address space of Porthos is 32 bits, so the upper 32 bits of a generated
64-bit virtual address are ignored and no translation takes place. There are no
TLB-related CP0 registers and no TLB instructions.

There is no floating-point unit and therefore no floating-point instructions.
However, the floating-point registers are implemented as well as 2 co-processor
registers. This allows additional registers (up to 95) to be used by integer codes
in a way that fits within the standard MIPS ISA. Instructions that load, store,

and move data between the regular registers and the floating-point registers (CP1 registers) are implemented. The SC, SCD, LL, and LLD instructions are implemented. Additionally, there is an *ADDM* instruction that atomically adds a value to a memory location and returns the result. In addition, there is a *GATE* instruction that stalls a thread to preserve packet dependencies (this is described in more detail in material to follow).

External events and timer interrupts are treated such that new threads are launched. Thus, a thread has no way to enable or disable these events itself, since they are configured globally. This is explained in more detail in material to follow. There are four new CP0 registers: *SequenceNumber*, *Tribe/Stream Number*, *FlowID*, and *GateVector*. There are also three new thread control instructions: *DONE*, *FORK*, and *NEXT*.

Support for string search, including multiple parallel byte comparison, has been provided for in new instructions. In addition there are bit field extract and insert instructions. Finally, an optimized 1's-complement add is provided for TCP checksum acceleration.

Events can be categorized into three groups: triggers from external events, timer interrupts, and thread-to-thread communication. In the first two groups, the events are not specific to any physical thread. In the third group, software can signal between two specific physical threads.

6.3.2   Thread Migration

The process by which a thread executing on a stream in one tribe is transferred to a stream in another tribe is called *migration*. We use the term *thread* to refer to a software construct, and *stream* to refer to the particular physical resources used by a thread when active. When migration occurs, a variable amount of context follows the thread. The CPU registers that are not transferred are lost and are initialized to 0 in the new tribe. Migration may occur out of order, but it is guaranteed to preserve thread priority as defined by the *SequenceNumber* register. Note, however, that a lower-priority thread may migrate ahead of a high-priority thread if it has a different destination tribe. Threads may migrate to the tribe they are already in. A thread may change its priority by writing to the *SequenceNumber* register. The thread migration instruction *NEXT* specifies the destination tribe and an immediate that contains the amount of thread context to preserve. More details on thread migration, including deadlock avoidance, are discussed in the section on the Interconnect block.

Thread migration is a key feature of Porthos, and it is important to understand how thread migration interacts with the loosely coupled processor/memory architecture. Since the memory map is not overlapped, every thread running in each tribe has access to all memory. Thus, from the standpoint of software correctness, migration is not strictly required. However, the ability to move the context and the processing to an engine that is closer to the state the processing is operating on allows a flexible topology to be implemented. A given packet may do all of its processing in a specific tribe, or may follow a sequence of tribes. Furthermore, this decision can be made on a packet-by-packet basis.

The thread migration module is responsible for migrating threads into the Tribe block and out of the Tribe block. A thread can only be participating in migration if it is not actively executing instructions. During migration, a single register read or write per cycle is processed by the Stream module and sent to the Interconnect block. A migration may contain any number of registers. When an inactive stream is migrated in, all registers that are not explicitly initialized are set invalid. An invalid register will always return 0 if read. A single valid bit per register allows the register file to behave as if all registers were initialized to 0 when a thread is initialized.

Note that code can be written that is tribe-aware, since the current tribe and thread number can be read from a control register. It is also possible to execute an indirect migration by loading a memory address and using one version of the *NEXT* instruction to migrate to the tribe associated with that address. This allows code to be written that does not need to know specifically which tribe to migrate to, just which data it wants to be close to.

6.3.3   Flow Gating

The efficient handling of packet dependencies is an important design element to any packet processor. Many workloads we have studied have the property that most packets can be processed completely independently, but a nontrivial fraction, and sometimes even back-to-back packets, requires serialization. Furthermore, packet dependencies are difficult to predict or model. A hardware mechanism to enforce packet dependencies with no changes to software is discussed in [3]. Porthos uses a different technique, known as "flow gating," which requires software changes, but fairly modest ones.

Flow gating is a mechanism in which packet seniority is enforced by hardware through the use of a *GATE* instruction inserted into the packet-processing workload. When a *GATE* instruction is encountered, the instruction execution for that packet is stalled until all older packets of the same flow have made progress past the same point. Software manually advances a packet through a gate by updating the *GateVector* register. Multiple gates may be specified for a given packet workload, and serialization occurs for each gate individually.

Packets are given a sequence number by the packet buffer controller when they are received, and this sequence number is maintained during the processing of the packet. A configurable hardware preclassifier is used to combine specified bytes from the packet and generate a *FlowID* number from the packet itself. The *FlowID* is initialized by hardware based on the hardware hash function, but may be modified by software. The configurable hash function is also used to select which tribe a packet is sent to. Afterward, tribe-to-tribe migration is under software control.

A new instruction is utilized that operates in conjunction with three internal registers. In addition to the *FlowID* register and the *PacketSequence* register (discussed previously), each thread contains a *GateVector* register. Software may set and clear this register arbitrarily, but it is initialized to 0 when a new thread is created for a new packet. A new instruction, named *GATE*, is implemented. The *GATE* instruction causes execution to stall until there is no thread with the same *FlowID*, a *PacketSequence* number that is lower, and a *GateVector* in which any of the same bits are 0. This logic serializes all packets within the same flow at that point such that seniority is enforced.

Software is responsible for setting a bit in the *GateVector* when it leaves the critical section. This will allow other packets to enter the critical section. The *GateVector* register represents progress through the workload of a packet. Software is responsible for setting bits in this register manually if a certain packet skips a certain gate, to prevent younger packets from unnecessarily stalling. If the *GateVector* is set to all 1s, this will disable flow gating for that packet, since no younger packets will wait for that packet. Note that forward progress is guaranteed, since the oldest packet in the processing system will never be stalled and when it completes another packet will be the oldest packet.

A seniority scheduling policy is implemented such that older packets are always given priority for execution resources within a processing element. One characteristic of this strictly implemented seniority scheduling policy is that if two packets are executing the exact same sequence of instructions a younger packet will never be able to overtake an older packet. In certain cases, the characteristic of no-overtaking may simplify handling of packet dependencies in software. This is because a no-overtaking processing element enforces a pipelined implementation of packet workloads, so the oldest packet is always guaranteed to be ahead of all younger packets. However, a seniority-based instruction scheduler and seniority-based cache replacement can only behave with no-overtaking if packets are executing the exact same sequence of instructions. If conditional branches cause packets to take different paths, a flow gate would be necessary. Flow gating in conjunction with no-overtaking processing elements allows a clean programming model to be presented that is efficient to implement in hardware.

6.3.4   Tribe Pipeline

The Tribe block contains an instruction cache and register files for 32 threads. The Tribe block interfaces with the Network block (for handling packet buffer reads and writes), the Interconnect block (for handling thread migration), and the Memory block (for handling local memory reads and writes). An overview of the pipeline structure of the tribe is shown in Figure 6.4.

The Tribe block consists of three decoupled pipelines: a Fetch pipeline, a Stream pipeline, and an Execute pipeline. These pipelines can generally be categorized as SMT (simultaneous multithreading), SMP (symmetric multiprocessing), and SMT, respectively.

The fetch logic and instruction cache form a fetch unit, which will fetch from two threads per cycle according to thread priority among the threads that have a fetch available to be performed. The Stream blocks within the tribe contain their own state machines that sequence reads and writes to the register file and execute certain instructions. These state machines operate independently in the absence of thread synchronization events. Finally, the global ALU and ports to external memory and the packet buffer form an execute unit. The execute unit schedules operations based on global priority among the set of threads that have an instruction available for scheduling. At most, one instruction per cycle is scheduled from any given thread.

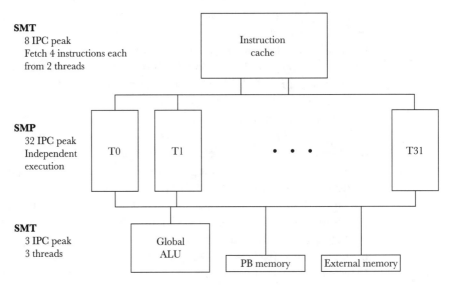

SMT
8 IPC peak
Fetch 4 instructions each
from 2 threads

SMP
32 IPC peak
Independent
execution

SMT
3 IPC peak
3 threads

6.4   Tribe pipelines.

FIGURE

Globally, up to three instructions can be scheduled in a single cycle (one ALU, one packet buffer memory, and one external memory). Many instructions can be fully executed within the Stream block, not requiring global scheduling. Thus, the peak instantaneous instruction execution rate is 32. Practically, the maximum rate of instruction execution is limited by the fetch unit, which can fetch up to eight instructions each cycle. A sustained execution rate of four to five instructions per cycle has been simulated under typical workload conditions.

Instruction fetch

The instruction fetch mechanism fetches four instructions from two threads for a total fetch bandwidth of eight instructions. The fetch unit includes decoders so that eight decoded instructions are delivered to two different stream modules in each cycle. There is a 16-KB instruction cache shared by all threads that is organized as 1024 lines of 16 bytes each, separated into four ways of 256 lines. The fetch mechanism is pipelined, with the tags accessed in the same cycle as the data. The fetch pipeline is illustrated in Figure 6.5.

Fetch priority is based on the seniority scheduling mechanism, described in material to follow. This gives priority to the oldest two packets that have a fetch request pending. The instruction cache is a two-read/one-write design so that writes can take place without interfering with instruction fetches. Porthos does not implement any speculative fetch, so a thread will not be a candidate for fetch until all pending branches have been resolved. In the case of straight-line code, a Stream block can detect that there are no branches in cycle F4 (corresponding to cycle S1, discussed next) and thus can in the following cycle become a candidate for fetching another four instructions. This means that a single thread could theoretically request four instructions every four cycles, but in most cases a Stream block could not execute instructions at this rate.

Stream modules

The Stream modules (one per stream for a total of 32 within the Tribe block) are responsible for sequencing reads and writes to the register files, executing branch instructions, and handling certain other arithmetic and logic operations. A Stream module receives four decoded instructions at a time from the fetch mechanism and saves them for later processing. One instruction is processed at a time, with some instructions taking multiple cycles to process. Since there is only a single port to the register file, all reads and writes must be sequenced by the Stream block. The basic pipeline of the Stream module is shown in Figure 6.6.

Note that in cases where only a single operand needs to be read from the register file, the instruction would be available for global scheduling with only a

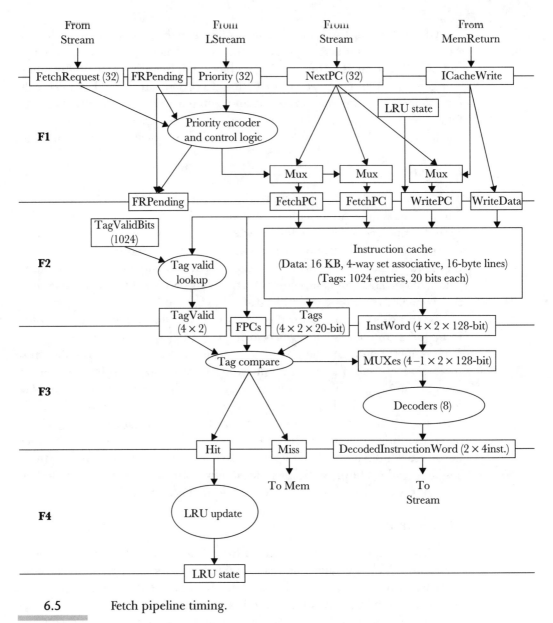

Fetch pipeline timing.

FIGURE

single RF read stage. Each register contains a ready bit that is used to determine if the most recent version of a register is in the register file, or it will be written by an outstanding memory load or ALU instruction. In spite of the fact that MIPS is a three-operand architecture, requiring up to three cycles to process

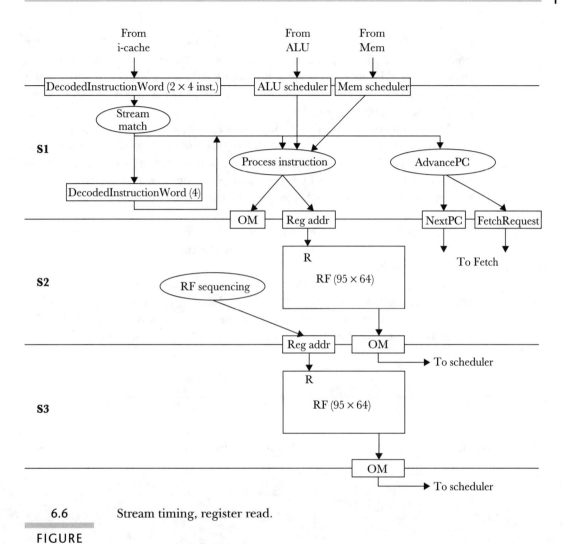

6.6
Stream timing, register read.

FIGURE

each instruction, in practice the number of register cycles is only slightly more than one. This is due to the fact that many instructions use only one or two operands, and many operands are in flight (requiring a write, but not a read). Since single-threaded performance can be sacrificed to a small degree without impacting overall performance, it is sufficient to supply only a single register port for each thread and suffer the additional latency when multiple cycles are required to sequence the register file. Single-ported register files are far smaller and lower in power consumption than multiported register files. Extending this concept, it would be possible to combine two Stream blocks and utilize only a single register file between them. This would have effectively 1/2 of a register port per thread. This option has higher power efficiency and area efficiency, since the reduction in performance due to the added latency per thread is small compared to the reduction in area and power. This concept is explored in more detail in Section 6.7, Conclusions.

Writes returning from the Network block and the Memory block must also be sequenced to the register file. The register write sequencing pipeline of the Stream block is shown in Figure 6.7. When a memory instruction (or an instruction for the global ALU) is encountered, the operation matrix, or *OM*, register is updated to reflect a request to the global scheduling and execute mechanism.

Branch instructions are executed within the Stream module, as illustrated in Figure 6.8. Branch operands can come from the register file, or can come from outstanding memory or ALU instructions.

The branch operand registers are updated in the same cycle in which the write to the register file is scheduled. This allows the execution of the branch to take place in the following cycle. Since branches are delayed in the MIPS ISA, the instruction after the branch instruction must be processed before the target

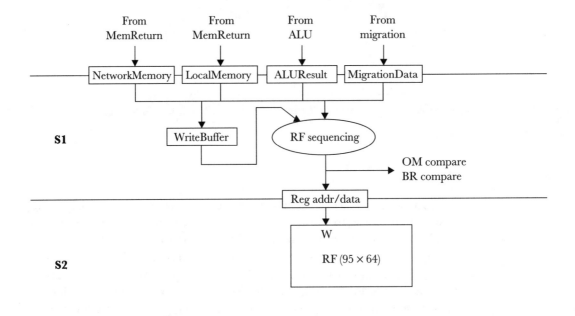

6.7   Stream timing, register write.

FIGURE

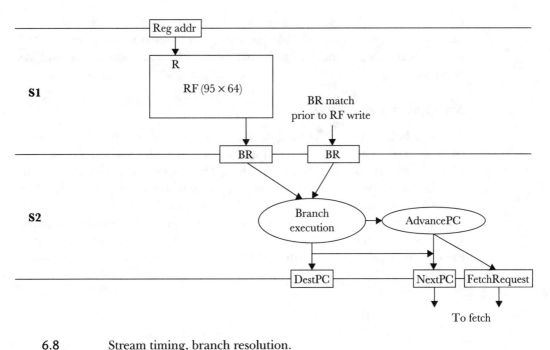

6.8   Stream timing, branch resolution.

FIGURE

of the branch can be fetched. The earliest that a branch delay slot instruction can
be processed is the same cycle that a branch is executed. Thus, a fetch request
can be made at the end of this cycle at the earliest. The processing of the delay
slot instruction would occur later than this if it were not yet available from the
fetch pipeline.

The ALU operations that are local to a Stream block are a small set of logical
operations. These are needed to execute branches and the *ADDIU* instruction.
This instruction adds a 16-bit immediate to a 32-bit register and generates a
32-bit result. This is the only arithmetic operation implemented by the Stream
block. The *ADDIU* instruction is one of the most frequently executed instructions,
accounting for over 20% of the dynamic frequency in some applications. It is used
for *for* loops and in array indexing.

In spite of the focus on overall performance over single-threaded performance, there are a few enhancements made within the Stream block, since they
are low in complexity. One is a no-branch detector, which will look at a group of
four instructions, and if there is no branch will request another four instructions by the end of that cycle. This is part of the AdvancePC block, shown
in Figure 6.6. This requires that a Stream block be able to store up to eight

instructions. Another enhancement is that if the target of a branch lies within the group of instructions already buffered, a new fetch is not required. This allows short forward branches to be executed with the minimum wasted fetch bandwidth.

Scheduling and execute

The scheduling and execute modules schedule up to three instructions per cycle from three separate streams, and handle register writes back to the Stream modules. The execute pipeline is shown in Figure 6.9. Streams are selected based on what instruction is available for execution (only one instruction per stream is considered a candidate) and on the overall stream priority. Since there is no data cache, all memory instructions executed will be directed to either the packet buffer or the external memory. However, it should be noted that the implementation of the floating-point and CP2 registers minimizes stack operations.

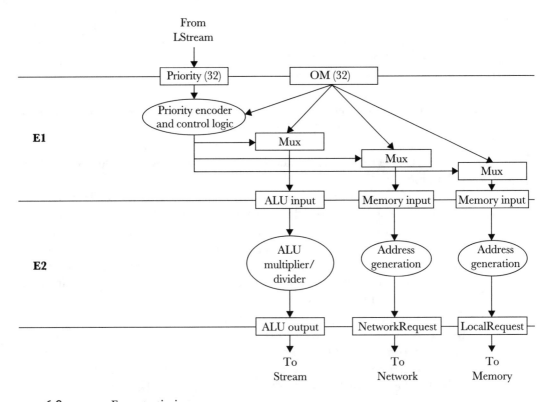

6.9   Execute timing.

FIGURE

Additionally, the use of temporary space in the packet buffer can be used to direct some stack operations to the packet buffer rather than to external memory. On average, our simulations show that approximately 20% of all instructions constitute packet buffer memory operations, and approximately 20% of all instructions constitute external memory operations.

Once selected, a stream will not be able to be selected in the following cycle, since there is a minimum two-cycle feedback to the Stream block for preparing another instruction for execution. This means that the maximum instruction rate per thread is 0.5 IPC. In practice, a higher IPC could be achieved, since some instructions are executed within the Stream block. However, given expected memory latencies and realistic workloads, an IPC per thread of 0.1 to 0.2 is expected.

Thread priority

Thread priority (used for fetch scheduling and execute scheduling) is maintained by the LStream module. This module also maintains a gateability vector used to implement flow gating. The LStream module is responsible for determining for each thread whether or not it should stall upon the execution of a *GATE* instruction, or can continue. This single bit per thread is exported to each Stream block. Anytime a change is made to any CP0 register that can potentially affect gateability, the LStream module will export all 0s on its gateability vector (indicating no thread can proceed past a *GATE*) until a new gateability vector is computed.

Changes that affect gateability are rare. They are as follows:

✦ A new thread is created, which will be migrated in with its own sequence number, gate vector, and flow ID register.

✦ An existing thread is deactivated, due to either a *DONE* instruction or a *NEXT* instruction (migration out to another tribe).

✦ A thread explicitly updates one of its gateability CP0 registers (sequence number, gate vector, flow ID) using the *MTC0* instruction.

Thread priority is based on a seniority concept, where older packets have priority over younger packets. Packet age is determined by the sequence number that represents order of arrival and is generated by the Network block. This means that when a packet first migrates to a tribe it may get very little execution resources until older packets finish or are migrated out. In most cases this is the desirable behavior, since the packet buffer represents a FIFO where packets must be either processed or moved off-chip to avoid head-of-line blocking.

In some cases, other thread priority schemes are needed, so thread priority can be overridden by software when necessary. One example of a special-case thread would be a background thread not associated with a packet. It may need a guaranteed minimum level of service, with the minimal impact to other threads. Another example is a thread operating on a packet that is no longer in the packet buffer. In these cases, a non-starved priority level is established by using a software-accessible configuration register.

6.4   NETWORK BLOCK

The Network block contains a packet buffer as well as a variety of other control logic and data structures. A block diagram of the Network block is shown in Figure 6.10. The packet buffer is an on-chip 256-KB memory that holds packets while they are being worked on. The packet buffer is a flexible FIFO that keeps all packet data in the order it was received. Thus, unless a packet is discarded, or consumed by the chip (by transfer into a local memory), the packet will be transmitted in the order it was received. The packet buffer architecture allows for an efficient combination of "pass-through" and "reassembly" scenarios.

In a pass-through scenario, packets are not substantially changed; they are only marked, or modified only slightly before being transmitted. The payload of the packets remains substantially the same. Pass-through scenarios occur in TCP splicing, monitoring, and traffic management applications. In a reassembly scenario, packets must be consumed by the chip and buffered into memory, where they are reassembled. After reassembly, processing occurs on the reliable data stream and then retransmission may occur. Reassembly scenarios occur in firewalls and load balancing. Many applications call for a combination of pass-through and reassembly scenarios.

The Packet Buffer module interacts with software in the following ways:

✦ Providing the initial values of some GPRs and CP0 registers at the time a thread is scheduled to start executing its workload

✦ Satisfying the requests to the packet buffer memory

✦ Satisfying the requests to the configuration registers, for instance
  • Hash function configuration
  • Packet table read requests
  • Packet status changes (packet to be dropped, packet to be transmitted out)
  • Allocating space in the packet buffer for software to construct packets

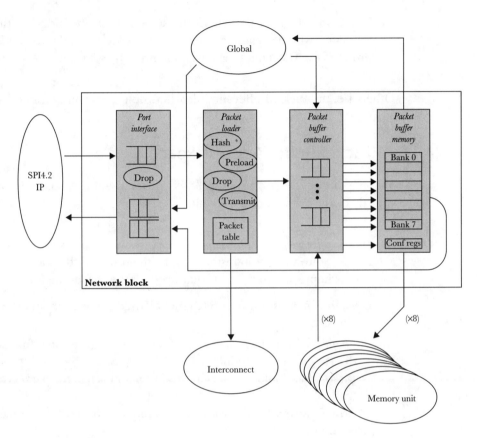

6.10   Network block overview.

FIGURE

Frames of packets arrive to the Packet Buffer module through a configurable number of ingress ports and leave the Packet Buffer module through the same number of egress ports. The maximum ingress/egress interleave degree depends on the number and type of ports, but it does not exceed four.

Software is responsible for completing the processing of the oldest packets. This is done in the Packet Buffer module, which keeps track of packets in a timely manner; namely, before:

◆ The subsequent newest packets fill up the packet buffer so that no more packets can be fit into it. At the 300-MHz core frequency, the peak rate of ingress data of 10 Gb/s, and a packet buffer size of 256 KB, this will occur in approximately 200 microseconds.

♦ There are 512 total packets in the system, from the oldest to the newest, no matter whether packets in between the oldest and the newest have been dropped (or DMA out to external memory) by software.

Otherwise, the Packet Buffer module will drop the incoming frames.

6.4.1   Packet Buffer Address Space

Two regions of the Porthos chip 32-bit physical address space are controlled directly by the Packet Buffer module.

♦ *Packet buffer memory.* 256 KB of memory where the packets are stored as they arrive. Software is responsible to take them out of this memory if needed (for example, in applications that need reassembly of the frames)

♦ *Configuration register space.* 16 KB (not all used), which contains the following sections:
  • *Configuration registers themselves.* Used to configure some functionality of the Packet Buffer module.
  • *Packet table.* Contains status information for each of the packets being kept track of.
  • *Get room space.* Used for software to request consecutive chunks of space within the packet buffer.

Software can perform any byte read/write, half-word (2-byte) read/write, word (4-byte) read/write, or double-word (8-byte) read/write to the packet buffer.

Even though the size of the packet buffer memory is 256 KB, it actually occupies 512 KB in the logical address space of the streams. This has been done to help minimize the memory fragmentation that occurs when incoming packets are stored in the packet buffer. This mapping is performed by hardware and, as a consequence, from the software viewpoint, packets are always stored consecutively into the 512 KB space.

Software should only use the packet buffer to read the packets that have been stored by the Packet Buffer module, and to modify these packets. Allocating portions of the 512-KB logical address space (for scratchpad purposes, for example) other than by means of the GetRoom command (explained later on) can lead to undefined results. The requests from the eight tribes are treated fairly; all tribes have the same priority in accessing the packet buffer.

6.4.2   Completing and Dropping Packets

Software eventually has to decide what to do with a packet that sits in the packet buffer, and it has two options:

+ *Complete the packet*. The packet will be transmitted out whenever the packet becomes the oldest packet in the packet buffer.

+ *Drop the packet*. The packet will be eventually removed from the packet buffer.

In both cases, the memory the packet occupies in the packet buffer and the entry in the packet table will be made available to other incoming packets as soon as the packet is fully transmitted out or dropped. Also, in both cases, the Packet Buffer module does not guarantee that the packet will be either transmitted or dropped right away. Software completes and drops packets by writing into the *done* and *drop* configuration registers, respectively. The information provided in both cases is the sequence number of the packet. For the completing of packets, the following information is also provided:

+ *Header growth offset*. A 10-bit value that specifies how many bytes the start of the packet has either grown (positive value less than or equal to 511 bytes) or shrunk (negative value less than or equal to 512 bytes) with respect to the original packet. The value is encoded in 2's complement, and negative values cannot exceed the original packet size. If software does not move the start of the packet, this value should be 0.

+ *Encoded egress channel*.

+ *Encoded egress port*.

6.4.3   GetRoom Command

Software can transmit a packet it has generated through the *GetRoom* mechanism. This mechanism works as follows:

+ Software requests some space to be set aside in the packet buffer. This is done through a regular read to the *GetRoom* space of the configuration space. The address of the load is computed by adding the requested size in bytes to the base of the *GetRoom* configuration space.

+ The Packet Buffer module will reply to the load in either of the following ways.

  • *Unsuccessfully*. It will return a 1 in the MSB bit and 0 in the rest of the bits.

- *Successfully*. It will return in the 32 LSB bits the physical address of the start of the space that has been allocated, and in bits [47...32] the corresponding sequence number associated with that space.

✦ Software, upon the successful *GetRoom* command, will construct the packet into the requested space.

✦ When the packet is fully constructed, software will complete it through the packet complete mechanism (explained previously).

6.4.4   Initial Migration

When the packets have been fully received by the Packet Buffer module and have been fully stored into the packet buffer memory, the first migration of those packets into one of the tribes will be initiated. The migration process consists of a request of a migration to a tribe, waiting for the tribe to accept the migration, and providing some control information of the packet to the tribe. This information will be stored by the tribe in some software-visible registers of one of the available streams.

The Packet Buffer module assigns to each packet a flow identification number and a tribe number using configurable hashing hardware. The packets will be migrated to the corresponding initial tribes in exactly the same order of arrival. This order of arrival is across all ingress ports and, if applicable, all channels. If a packet has to be migrated to a tribe that has all its streams active, the tribe will not accept the migration. The Packet Buffer module will keep requesting the migration until the tribe accepts it.

After the migration has taken place, the following registers are initialized in one of the streams of the tribe: the PC will be initialized with a configurable vector; CP0 registers will be initialized with an initial *FlowID* number obtained by the hashing hardware and a *SequenceNumber* that contains the order of arrival of the packet; and two GPRs will be initialized with the ingress port/channel of the packet and the 32-bit logical address where the packet resides.

6.5   INTERCONNECT

The Interconnect block consists of three modules: Event, Arbiter, and Crossbar. A block diagram of the Interconnect block is shown in Figure 6.11, and more detail of the Interconnect crossbar is shown in Figure 6.12. The Event module collects event information and activates a new stream to process the event. The Arbiter

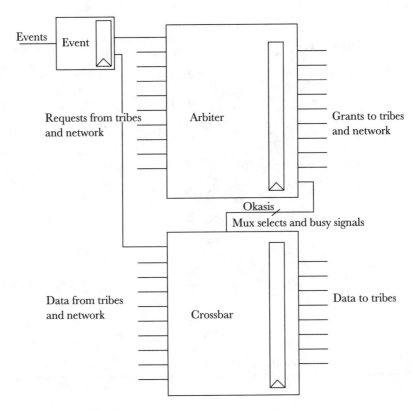

6.11   Interconnect overview.

FIGURE

module performs arbitration between sources and destinations. The Crossbar module directs data from sources to destinations.

6.5.1   Arbiter

The Arbiter of Figure 6.11 has 11 sources of requests; the eight tribes, the Network block, the event-handling module, and the transient buffers. Each source tribe can make up to seven requests, one for each destination tribe. The Network block, event-handling module, and transient buffers each can make one request to one of the eight tribes. If there is a request from transient buffers to a tribe, that request has the highest priority and no arbitration is necessary for that tribe. If transient buffers are not making a request, then arbitration is necessary.

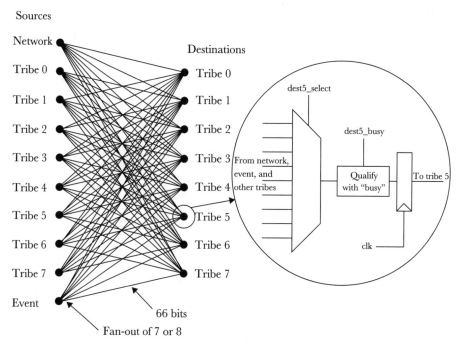

6.12   Interconnect crossbar.

FIGURE

The arbiter needs to match the requester to the destination in such a way as to maximize utilization of the interconnect, while also preventing starvation. We use a round-robin prioritizing scheme. There are two stages. The first stage selects one non-busy source for a given non-busy destination. The second stage resolves cases where the same source was selected for multiple destinations. Each source and each destination has a round-robin pointer. This points to the source or destination with the highest priority. The round-robin prioritization logic begins searching for the first available source or destination, beginning at the pointer and moving in one direction.

The arbitration scheme described previously is "greedy," meaning it attempts to pick the requests that can proceed, skipping sources and destinations that are busy. In other words, when a connection is set up between a source and a destination, the source and destination are locked out from later arbitration. With this scheme, there are cases when the arbiter starves certain context. It could happen that two repeated requests, with overlapping transaction times, can prevent other requests from being processed.

To prevent this, the arbitration operates in two modes. The first mode is "greedy" mode, as described previously. For each request that cannot proceed, there is a counter that keeps track of the number of times that request has been skipped. When the counter reaches a threshold, the arbitration will not skip over this request, but rather wait at the request until the source and destination become available. If multiple requests reach this priority for the same source or destination, then one-by-one will be allowed to proceed in a strict round-robin fashion. The threshold can be set via the Greedy Threshold configuration register.

6.5.2 Deadlock Resolution

Deadlock occurs when the tribes in migration loops are all full; that is, when tribe 1 requests migration to tribe 2, and vice versa, and both tribes are full. The loops can have up to eight tribes. To break a deadlock, Porthos uses two transient buffers in the interconnect, with each buffer capable of storing an entire migration (66 bits times maximum migration cycles). The migration request with both source and destination full (with destination wanting to migrate out) can be sent to a transient buffer. The transient stream becomes the highest priority and initiates a migration to the destination, while at the same time the destination redirects a migration to the second transient buffer. Both of these transfers need to be atomic, meaning no other transfer is allowed to the destination tribe and the tribe is not allowed to spawn a new stream within itself. The migrations into and out of transient buffers use the same protocol as tribe-tribe migrations.

This method begins by detecting only the possibility of deadlock and not the actual deadlock condition. It allows forward progress while looking for the actual deadlock, although there may be cases where no deadlock is found. It also substantially reduces the hardware complexity with minimal impact on performance.

A migration that uses the transient buffers will incur an average of two migration delays (a migration delay is the number of cycles needed to complete a migrate). The delays do not impact performance significantly, since the migration is already waiting for the destination to free up.

Using transient buffers will suffice in all deadlock situations involving migration, including simple deadlock loops involving two to eight tribes, multiple deadlock loops with one or more shared tribes, multiple deadlock loops with no shared tribe, and multiple deadlock loops that are connected. In the case of multiple loops, the transient buffers will break one loop at a time. The loop is broken when the transient buffers are emptied.

Hardware deadlock resolution cannot solve the deadlock situation that involves software dependency. For example, a tribe in one deadlock loop waits for some result from a tribe in another deadlock loop that has no tribe in common with the first loop. Transient buffers will service the first deadlock loop and can never break that loop.

6.5.3   Event Module

Upon hardware reset, the Event module spawns a new stream in tribe 0 to process reset events. This reset event comes from the Global block. The Event module spawns a new stream via the interconnect logic based on external and timer interrupts.

Each interrupt is maskable by writing to *Interrupt Mask* configuration registers in configuration space. There are two methods by which an interrupt can be directed. In the first method, the interrupt is directed to any tribe that is not empty. This is accomplished by the Event module making requests to all eight destination tribes. When there is a grant to one tribe, the Event module stops making requests to the other tribes and starts a migration for the interrupt-handling stream. In the second method, the interrupt is being directed to a particular tribe. The tribe number for the second method and the method to be used are specified using *Interrupt Method* configuration registers.

The Event module has a 32-bit timer, which increments every cycle. When this timer matches the *Count* configuration register, it activates a new stream via the migration interconnect.

6.5.4   Crossbar Module

The Crossbar module of Figure 6.12 has 10 inputs and 8 outputs. Each input consists of a "valid" bit, 64-bit data, and a "last" bit. Each output consists of the same. For each output, there is a corresponding 4-bit select input that selects one of 10 inputs for that particular output. Also, for each output there is a 1-bit input that indicates whether the output port is being selected or busy. This "busy" bit is ANDed with the selected "valid" and "last" so that those signals are valid only when the port is busy. The output is registered before being sent to the destination tribe.

6.6   PROJECT STATUS

Porthos was projected at a size of 120 mm^2, a frequency of 300 MHz, and a power consumption of 12 W implemented in a 0.15-micron process. Assuming a sustained IPC of four per tribe, this represents a performance of 9.6 GIPS and equates to a performance/area ratio of 80 MIPS/mm^2. We believe this is a conservative estimate. Sustained IPCs of five per tribe have been simulated, the area estimates are conservative, and we believe the design could achieve a frequency of 500 MHz or greater. Also, because the tribe and memory unit combination are only projected at approximately 10 mm^2, an IPC of five and a clock frequency of 500 MHz would yield a performance/area ratio of 250 MIPS/mm^2 for a single tribe and memory unit.

Porthos was designed and developed by the authors of this chapter while at the company FlowStorm, Inc. FlowStorm was founded in July 2001 as a venture-funded start-up. Development continued for a year and a half and included over 90% of the register transfer language (RTL) coding and substantial verification of the major functionality. Partial synthesis and timing evaluation were also performed. Performance modeling, software development, and system engineering were extensive. Alas, FlowStorm was dissolved in December 2002.

Some of the authors, as identified on the title page, are continuing development of a packet processor in a new company, Kayamba, Inc. The first author is a technical advisor with the law firm of O'Melveny & Myers, LLP.

6.7 CONCLUSIONS

In this chapter we have presented *Porthos*, a new packet processor designed for stateful applications. The design of Porthos is derived from fundamental observations about stateful networking applications: that a significant number of off-chip accesses with little locality need to be supported for each packet. To efficiently implement the requisite large number of parallel packets, Porthos implements a massively multithreaded processor with a strong bias toward efficiency over single-threaded performance.

Multithreaded processors have a long history as commercial projects—including the HEP-1 [4], Horizon [5], and Tera [6]—and as academic research [7, 8]. More recent commercial designs have included the Compaq Alpha EV-8 [9], the Clearwater Networks CNP810SP [10], Intel [11], and announced development by Sun Microsystems, among others. Porthos differs from most of this previous work in several important ways, and it is for this reason that we refer to it as "massive multithreading," or MMT. We define an MMT processor as one with most (but perhaps not all) of the following characteristics:

✦ General-purpose ISA (not microengines)

✦ Hardware support for large numbers of threads

  • On the order of 100s, rather than 2 to 8

✦ Single-threaded performance has been sacrificed:
  • No branch prediction
  • No speculative fetch or execution
  • One port (or less) per register file per thread
  • No ALU bypass
  • Maximum of one operation per thread per cycle

This results in a design that can practically implement 256 threads in a reasonable silicon area (projected at 120 square millimeters), at a reasonable power (projected at 12 watts). It is also the case that since the applications tend to be limited by external memory device access time, internal clock frequency is not a strong performance factor. At a projected clock frequency of 300 MHz using 0.15-micron technology, the design well exceeds other processor designs operating at 1 GHz and above.

One way to measure designs of this nature is in terms of power efficiency. By mapping an exponential power function to a few design points, we have come up with a model of power as a function of single-threaded performance. Figure 6.13 illustrates this result, where we utilize models for memory latency and locality and where 20% of all instructions are directed at the packet buffer and 20% are directed to external memory. Due to the high latency of these accesses (10 to 20 cycles), the performance impact of increasing the latency of non-memory instructions is relatively small.

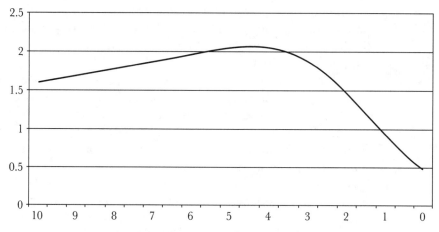

6.13   GIPS/watt versus single-thread CPI.

FIGURE

As this figure illustrates, the best performance-to-power ratio is achieved at a design point well below what can be achieved utilizing aggressive single-threaded techniques. Under these assumptions, the maximum GIPS-to-watt ratio occurred at a single-thread CPI of about 4.5. In Porthos, we designed for a single-thread CPI of around 2, as packet dependencies limit the parallelism available and thus push the maximum design point further to the right. It should be noted that the design trade-offs that Porthos has optimized for are not exclusive to packet processing. There are other applications where power and area efficiency are more important than single-threaded performance. In particular, data center environments, in which application servers are providing services to large numbers of connected users, could potentially benefit from MMT processors. If additional latency can be tolerated (for example, if the computation time is small compared to the overall transaction time) and if there are enough independent tasks, an MMT processor may be a better solution.

Besides providing an MMT packet processor, another key innovation in Porthos is the implementation of a loosely coupled processor/memory architecture. This allows performance to be optimized by software and provides topological flexibility (through the use of thread migration) and a uniform software model (so that code will still work if memory partitioning issues are ignored). Finally, the use of flow gating allows efficient memory synchronization with minimal software porting issues.

REFERENCES

[1]   Argus—The All Seeing System and Network Monitoring Software, *www.tcp4me.com*.

[2]   V. Paxson, "Bro: A System for Detecting Network Intruders in Real-Time," *7th Annual USENIX Security Symposium*, Jan. 1998.

[3]   S. Melvin and Y. Patt, "Handling of Packet Dependencies: A Critical Issue for Highly Parallel Network Processors," *International Conference on Compiler, Architecture, and Synthesis for Embedded Systems (CASES)*, Oct. 2002.

[4]   B. Smith, "Architecture and Applications of the HEP Multiprocessor Computer System," *Proceedings, SPIE Real-Time Signal Processing IV,* Aug. 1981.

[5]   J. Kuehn and B. Smith, "The Horizon Supercomputing System: Architecture and Software," *Proceedings, Supercomputing 1988*, Nov. 1988.

[6]   R. Alverson et al., "The Tera Computer System," *Proceedings, 1990 International Conference on Supercomputing,* June 1990.

[7]   W. Yamamoto and M. Nemirovsky, "Performance Estimation of Multistreamed, Superscalar Processors," *27th Hawaii International Conference on System Sciences*, Jan. 1994.

[8]   D. Tullsen, S. Eggers, and H. Levy, "Simultaneous Multithreading: Maximizing On-Chip Parallelism," *Proceedings of the 22nd Annual International Symposium on Computer Architecture*, June 1995.

[9]   J. Emer, "Simultaneous Multithreading: Multiplying Alpha Performance," *Microprocessor Forum*, 1999.

[10]   M. Nemirovsky, "XStream Logic's Optical Network Processor," *Microprocessor Forum*, 2000.

[11]   G. Hinton and J. Shen, "Intel's Multi-Threading Technology," *Microprocessor Forum*, 2001.

Exploring Trade-Offs in Performance and Programmability of Processing Element Topologies for Network Processors

Matthias Gries[1], Chidamber Kulkarni[1], Christian Sauer[2], Kurt Keutzer[1]
[1]University of California, Berkeley
[2]Infineon Technologies, Corporate Research, Munich

Contemporary network processor units (NPUs) exhibit a wide range of architectures for performing similar tasks: from simple RISC cores with dedicated peripherals, in pipelined and/or parallel organization, to heterogeneous multiprocessors based on complex multithreaded cores with customized instruction sets [13]. Although so diverse, all NPUs exploit task-level concurrency in applications by means of parallel programmable processing elements (PEs) to meet line-speed requirements. Thus, the inter-PE communication and the topology of PEs are performance-critical aspects of any NPU architecture.

Programming such concurrent systems still remains an art. The programmer is required to partition and balance the load of the application manually among multiple PEs and to implement each task often in assembly, to obtain a reliable performance estimation. Hence, a robust application-mapping strategy for such architectures requires a balance among thread partitioning, scheduling, memory accesses, and I/O. With current tools this task becomes time consuming and error prone, due to trial-and-error methods employed by system implementers based on simulation runs. Therefore, topology, inter-PE communication, and the ease of mapping are likely to be key aspects of the quest for a natural programming model.

For the next generation of NP-based system implementations, we strongly believe that a considerable emphasis will be placed on performance-per-cost (for example, power consumption) aspects and on support of appropriate programming models. Therefore, it is essential to identify and investigate limitations and bottlenecks in system implementation without going all the way down to complete implementations, as is the current practice. Hence, the use of high-level design space exploration tools is required that support a wide range of heterogeneous architectures and enable precise reasoning about different implementation styles and their performance.

The main goal of this chapter is to clearly understand the performance/cost trade-offs for different network processor topologies and their influence on programmability. To avoid time-consuming implementation we adapt and deploy an analytical framework [5]. In addition, we implement two differently mapped versions of our IPv4 benchmark [11] on IXP1200 to gain detailed insight into programmability of existing NPU architectures. In the process, we also verify the preciseness and usefulness of such an analytical framework compared to a detailed simulation of the system.

7.1   PROBLEM IDENTIFICATION

Before describing our methodology for exploring the trade-offs for different PE topologies for network processors, it is first necessary to define the axes of the design space. It is worth noting that a description of the complete design space for a network processor is beyond the scope of this chapter. However, based on our earlier work [14], we have identified a few axes of the architectural space for network processors, such as the degree of parallel processing, special-purpose hardware employed, on-chip communication mechanisms, memory architectures, and integration of peripherals. We recognize that in practice all of these choices are interrelated.

In this chapter, we restrict our study to the exploration of different interconnection topologies between PEs for performance and programmability constraints. Both the achievable performance and the ease of programmability are coupled to the way different PEs are connected. Thus, investigating different trade-offs involved in such a design is fundamental to understanding both performance and programmability.

In our study, the explored design space comprises the different interconnection topologies between PEs. We characterize our design space using two axes; namely, the number of PEs per stage of the pipeline and the number of pipeline stages. The two extremes of our design space are indeed a fully pipelined

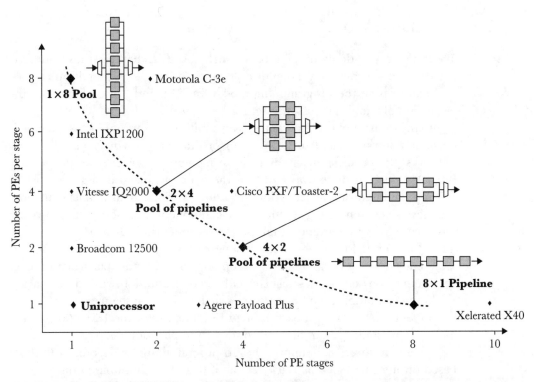

7.1

FIGURE

Design space for PE topologies annotated with existing NPUs.

solution and a fully pooled solution. Figure 7.1 illustrates the different design points in this space annotated with existing NPs[1]. In this study, the number and type of PEs, throughput (line rate), different external interfaces (such as memory), media access control (MAC), and the application are specified up front and are kept constant. Thus, only the connections between the PEs and the partitioning of tasks onto PEs vary for the particular setup.

The metrics used to determine the usefulness of a particular design point are utilization of the PE, required bus bandwidth, latency experienced by each packet, and memory consumption. In addition to evaluating each topology using the metrics previously cited, we consider the impact of scalability and programmability of a given topology, although qualitatively. In particular, we are interested in understanding the interrelation between scaling per flow as compared to number of flows and the PE topology.

1. "Pipeline-of-pools" architectures, such as that of EzChip Inc., can be modeled using a hierarchical approach. This is not the focus of this chapter.

7.1.1   Related Work

There are three domains of related work for this chapter: those addressing the trade-off between different topologies for single-chip multiprocessors, those addressing the programming model for NPs, and works addressing the evaluation of a multiprocessor system.

In the domain of trade-off analysis for multiprocessor topologies, we mostly encounter works related to exploration of different on-chip communication networks [2] and different approaches to memory consistency and coherency [20, 21]. Much of these works address the issue of how to design an efficient on-chip communication network or techniques to avoid invalidated memory accesses, given remaining architectural components. In addition, past work has focused on fine-grained multiprocessor systems, such as systolic arrays, and coarse-grained loosely coupled supercomputers (such as Cray). To our knowledge, the interrelation between topology of PEs and a particular on-chip communication network has not been addressed. In addition, we find approaches exploring communication networks for switches [18]. Lakshamanamurthy et al. [4] present an ad-hoc approach limited to modeling of the IXP2400 NP that allows for reasoning about different trade-offs in partitioning.

There are three main approaches to programming models for NPs: those based on libraries, such as Click [15] and Teja [16]; those based on domain-specific languages [19]; and those based on dynamic scheduling of tasks, such as Calisto [17]. Library-based approaches are limited by the fact that any scaling of the architecture invariably results in recoding most of the library components. The dynamic scheduling of tasks as implemented in [17] requires additional hardware overhead, such as control and status registers. Thus, very little work exists on supporting the partitioning and scheduling of tasks on NPs.

There are three approaches for system evaluation; namely, simulation, trace analysis, and analytical models. Simulation-based approaches, such as [1], require application specifications in a high-level language or assembly, compiled to the particular architecture, and a cycle-precise simulator. In addition, different workloads need to be specified or generated for both the simulation- and trace-based analyses. Trace-based analysis (such as [2]) is limited by the fact that it captures details of a single execution for the particular workload. Thus, for event-driven systems with varying workloads a large amount of traces need to be generated for any useful analysis, and hence the gap between simulation and trace is no longer that large. In contrast, analytical models promise a fast evaluation that allows for a larger design space to be explored. In the packet-processing domain, [3] presents an approach to explore different cache configurations based on general-purpose computing elements.

Thiele et al. [5] present a generic approach to modeling applications and architectures in this domain. The framework used in this work is based on [5, 12].

This chapter is organized as follows. First, we introduce the methodology and the analytical framework used for performance modeling and exploring trade-offs. This follows with a brief introduction to our benchmark and a comparison with simulation. Second, we explore different topologies from a performance point of view and provide a brief discussion of the results. Third, we compare the different topologies from a programmability and scalability point of view. We provide some conclusions based on our work at the end.

7.2   PERFORMANCE MODELING AND EVALUATION

In the following we will briefly introduce task and architecture models, service and arrival curves, and the network calculus used to model and determine the workload, application, architecture, and performance of a given mapping of the application onto the architecture.

Our approach to design space exploration, as used in Section 7.3 for evaluating topologies, is based on the Y-Chart approach [22] (see Figure 7.2). Separate descriptions of the application (workload) and the microarchitecture are bound to each other in an explicit mapping step, describing bindings of tasks and communication onto microarchitecture building blocks. The following evaluation of the system may manually or automatically trigger adaptations of the workload, the allocation of architecture building blocks, or the mapping of the application onto the architecture.

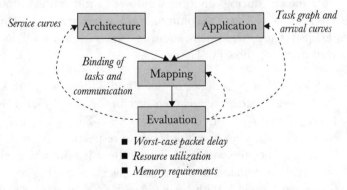

7.2   Design space exploration using Y-Chart.

FIGURE

We restrict the description of the network calculus to the basics and refer the reader to [5, 6] for a more refined description, providing tighter bounds by using upper and lower arrival and service curves. We have extended the analytical framework described in [5] to incorporate bus models, as well as round-robin and generalized processor sharing scheduling, to enable modeling and evaluating a network processor such as IXP1200. We continue this section with a comparison of abstract benchmarking results using this analytical approach with results from simulation in order to underpin the usefulness of the model for evaluating different topologies.

7.2.1   Workload Description

A workload on the network processor is defined by arrival curves of the incoming network traffic and the task model associated with network traffic flows. Arrival curves describe a kind of worst-case envelope by which traffic patterns are restricted in terms of, for instance, burstiness and average rate. Arrival curves are used in the context of integrated services [7] and thus provide a natural abstraction of network traffic in the application domain of network processing.

+ *Arrival function x.* The arrival function $x(t)$ of a network flow is equal to the number of packets seen on the flow within the time interval $[0, t]$ at a defined place in the NP's microarchitecture.

+ *Arrival curve α.* Given a non-decreasing function $\alpha(t)$ defined for $t \geq 0$, a flow with arrival function x is constrained by the arrival curve α if and only if for all $s \leq t : x(t) - x(s) \leq \alpha(t - s)$.

That means, during any time window of width τ the amount of traffic for the flow is limited by $\alpha(\tau)$. A common traffic specification is defined by the IETF (TSPEC [8]) that restricts peak p and average rates r, as well as the burstiness b of a traffic flow, as shown in Figure 7.3.

+ *Task model.* Let F be a set of flows and T be a set of tasks. To each flow $f \in F$ there is one directed acyclic graph $G(f) = (V(f), E(f))$ with task nodes $V(f) \subseteq T$ and communication edges $E(f)$. The tasks $v \in V(f)$ must be executed for each packet of flow f while respecting the precedence relations in $E(f)$. Associated with each task v there is a weight $w(v)$ describing the computation demand of task v on a given computing resource (e.g., specified in clock cycles). With each edge $e \in E(f)$ there is a weight $w(e)$ defining

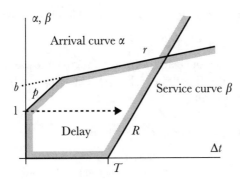

7.3

FIGURE

Arrival and service curves.

the communication demand between the two connected tasks (e.g., given in units of bytes).

7.2.2   Microarchitecture

+ *Architecture components.* The microarchitecture consists of computation (CPU cores, special units, and so on) and communication components (buses), as well as separate RAMs. Associated with each architecture component there is one service curve describing the service capabilities of the component.

+ *Service curve β.* Given a component S and a flow through S with arrival function $x(t)$ at the input of S and arrival function $y(t)$ after processing at the output of S, S offers a service curve β to the traffic flow if and only if for all $t \geq 0$ there is some $t_0 \leq t$ such that $y(t) - x(t_0) \geq \beta(t - t_0)$.

That means in particular that a flow backlogged during any time interval τ receives at least a flow-through of $\beta(\tau)$ (e.g., specified in clock cycles/sec or bytes/sec). A curve representing round-robin (RR) scheduling with average rate R is sketched in Figure 7.3. Parameter T is derived from the RR frame length.

7.2.3   Performance Properties

Worst-case bounds for a flow's backlog at component S, as well as the delay experienced by a packet arriving at the component, can now be determined.

We only show a formula for the delay, since the backlog bound is not used in this chapter.

✦ *Bounded delay d.* A flow constrained by arrival curve α passes a component offering service β to the flow. The delay $d(t)$ experienced by a packet in the component satisfies for all t:

$$d(t) \leq \sup_{s \geq 0}(\inf\{\tau : \tau \geq 0 \text{ and } \alpha(s) \leq \beta(s+t)\}).$$

Since arrival curves are specified in units of packets/second, either the arrival or the service curve must be normalized to the unit of the other curve by using the corresponding computation or communication demand w. For all arrival and service curves used in this case study, determining delay bounds reduces to the calculation of the maximum horizontal distance between corresponding $\alpha(t)$ and $\beta(t)$ curves (see Figure 7.3).

To determine delay properties as well as the utilization of the entire network processor, the accumulated service curve offered by the NPU to a flow, as well as the arrival curves of processed flows, can be calculated by iterating through all service curves offered to the flows on different components [5, 6]. As an example we give the formula for the calculation of the remaining service $\beta'(t)$.

✦ *Remaining service β'.* The remaining service $\beta'(t)$ of a component offering a service β to a flow f (which is constrained by $\alpha(t)$) after processing one task v with demand $w(v)$ for all packets of flow f is given by $\beta'(t) = \sup_{0 \leq u \leq t}(\beta(u) - w(v) \cdot \alpha(u))$.

Finally, the utilization of an architectural component is an inherent characteristic of the remaining service curve of that component and can be determined as follows.

✦ *Utilization u of an architecture component.* Given an architecture component S with the initial service curve $\beta(t)$ and the remaining service curve $\beta'(t)$ after processing a set of tasks $\varsigma \subseteq T$, the utilization of S due to the processing of ς is

$$u = \lim_{t \to \infty} \frac{\beta(t) - \beta'(t)}{\beta(t)}.$$

For our evaluation in this chapter, the utilization of architecture components can easily be calculated from the slopes of the right-most segments of $\beta(t)$ and $\beta'(t)$, which are both described by piecewise linear service curves.

7.2.4   Capabilities and Limitations

Since the calculus approach using service curves is derived from the traffic and service model used in the quality-of-service framework for the Internet [7], this method is in particular suited to describe workloads and performance properties in the packet-processing domain. Some inherent features include the following:

+ *Multithreading can be captured.* If several tasks from different traffic flows are mapped to the same computation component, each flow usually requires its own thread of execution. If more tasks were mapped to a component than it can support using separate thread contexts, any additional tasks could be punished by an increase in its computation demand to account for the required thread context swap.

+ *Heterogeneous microarchitectures can be considered.* Besides different types of computation components, such as general-purpose computation cores or dedicated hardware units, several concurrent communication buses and single-port memory interfaces can be modeled.

+ *Pipelining of processing elements is possible.* Tasks of the execution path of a flow may be mapped to different computation components that are connected by point-to-point connections.

+ *Shared resource arbitration is considered.* The order by which service curves are processed, as well as the shape of the curves, determine the thread scheduling and access arbitration scheme used by computation and communication components, respectively. In [5], examples for fixed priority scheduling and generalized processor sharing are shown.

Due to their accumulative nature, service curves cannot express any locality of accesses. This is not a drawback for most applications in the packet-processing domain. The incorporation of caches would require the interplay with other analytical models.

It should be noted that the service curve approach is in particular suited to determine worst-case corner cases of a design, since its foundations are in the real-time domain. Simulation is better suited to capture sporadic and arbitrary dynamic effects during the runtime of the system. The analytical approach only needs per-packet processing and communication demands, which could, for instance, be determined by analysis of pseudocode or some other estimation technique. A simulation framework, however, always requires an executable model of the design.

7.2.5   Modeling IPv4 Forwarding Application

The application used in this work is an IPv4 forwarding switch with 16 Fast
Ethernet ports. Our functional specification of the application is based on
RFC 1812 [9]. Figure 7.4 illustrates the main components in the functionality
of our benchmark, annotated with cycle counts for 64-byte packet size. A more
detailed description can be found in [12].

It is important to note that in addition to the core functionality a number
of steps are required to receive the packets from the external MAC unit into the
IXP1200 and extract the packet header, on which the previously stated operations are performed. Finally, the modified packet header and the packet payload
need to be written back into the external MAC unit via the IX bus unit. These
additional operations, in fact, result in most of the programming effort for our
application. For example, 14 detailed tasks are required to perform the core

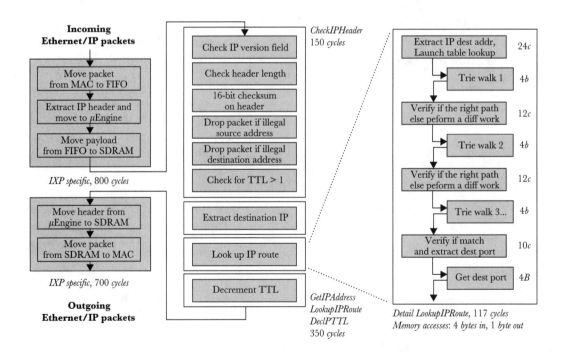

7.4   Instance of annotated IPv4 task graph derived from the application for analysis.

FIGURE

functionality of our benchmark, whereas we need 42 detailed tasks to perform the ingress and egress operations on each packet.

7.2.6   Modeling IXP1200 Architecture

The Intel IXP1200 network processor [10] is targeted for applications performing packet forwarding and classification at layer 3 and below of the OSI model. In this chapter, we introduce only the main components of the IXP1200 utilized by our application as needed for modeling.

The IXP1200 comprises six microengines, with four threads on every microengine, for computation. There are four unidirectional on-chip buses connecting both the off-chip memories (SRAM and SDRAM) to the microengines. External media access control (MAC) units are connected to the IXP1200 via the IX bus. The IX bus interface unit has the required logic and memories to receive and transmit packets from/to the external MAC unit. The IX bus unit has a scratch-pad memory (SRAM) and two FIFO memories, with each having 16 entries of size 64 bytes. In addition, the SDRAM unit is connected to the IX bus unit via a separate on-chip bus, used to transfer packet payloads directly based on microengine commands. Finally, an on-chip command bus carries events and signals between microengine and the IX bus unit.

In this chapter, we focus only on the data plane of the IXP1200 network processor. Hence, aspects related to the StrongARM processor are not modeled. Also, we have not modeled the PCI bus interface or the hash engine, since we do not utilize these peripherals. A typical packet flow through the IXP1200 follows the steps shown in Figure 7.4.

7.2.7   Comparing Results from Analysis and Simulation

We have first implemented the application on IXP1200 and then derived a task model as an input to the analytical framework. The analytical model only requires ideal, per-packet computation and communication demands. The calculus inherently considers delay effects due to resource arbitration and utilization based on the workload.

Experimental setup

In our case study, we first developed the application in microengine C, following the previously cited specification based on the Intel reference code. We did a few modifications to the transmit threads for improving the performance.

The application was partitioned so that 16 threads on four microengines were assigned one port each on the receive (and forwarding) part. The transmit part of the application was assigned eight threads on two microengines. This partitioning holds, since the end-to-end delay for a packet on the receive part is more than twice that on the transmit part. This implementation was used to derive the per-packet profiling information used to build the task graph for the network calculus-based approach.

Performance on the IXP1200 was measured using version 2.01 of the Developer Workbench assuming a clock frequency of 200 MHz; the IX bus is 64 bits wide and has a clock frequency of 80 MHz. Two IXF440 external media access control units (with eight duplex Fast Ethernet ports each) are connected to the IX bus, and Ethernet IP packets are streamed from this unit to the IXP1200 and back. The packets for the application contain destination addresses evenly distributed across the IPv4 32-bit address space. We employ different packet sizes; namely, from 40 bytes to 256 bytes. There is a single packet source for each input port that generates an evenly distributed load. Also, the range of destination addresses and associated next-hop destinations provides an evenly distributed load on every output port.

For the analytical model, the processing of 16 ports has been split into 16 separate flows. Each flow sees the same kind of task graph as sketched in Figure 7.4, where part of the annotation with per-packet cycle counts and byte transfers for computation and communication tasks, respectively, are shown on the right. Connectors are annotated with the amount of bytes transferred between corresponding tasks (not shown). Trie-walk tasks are mapped to SRAM, where the lookup table resides, whereas the computation tasks are mapped onto a microengine. Consequently, connectors are mapped to SRAM read and write buses in this example. The actual mapping of tasks onto microengines determines the service curves offered to a flow. As an example we consider one of the receive microengines that has to process the workload of four ports. Since a microengine is scheduled round-robin (RR), each of the flows will only get one-fourth of the capacity of the engine in the worst case. Moreover, although a task may be ready for processing, in the worst case it has to wait up to three times the processing time of a task, since all other flows may be serviced before, following the RR order. Those two properties are expressed by the parameters R and T (see Figure 7.3) of the initial service curve offered by the microengine to a flow. Accordingly, the capabilities of buses are derived from the task mapping. Finally, the arrival curve of the traffic seen at each port is described by burstiness of one packet and Fast Ethernet rate in the worst case.

The following properties are determined for comparing simulation with the analytical approach: end-to-end delay for individual packets with different sizes, throughput for different packet sizes, and utilization for each microengine.

Results and analysis

To have a reference set of design points we have determined the maximum possible throughput for IPv4 forwarding without packet loss by simulation. We varied the packet length to account for payload storage versus header processing trade-offs. We approach line speed only for larger packet sizes, where the microengines can keep up with the processing demand of the reduced number of packet arrivals (compared with small packet lengths). We can also recognize the influence of the 64-byte receive and transmit FIFOs in the IX bus unit. As soon as an additional 64-byte segment is needed, there is a drop in the throughput, due to the basic unit of data transfer between SDRAM and FIFOs being 64 bytes. Thus, for a given delay of two 64-byte transfers we are transferring only 65 bytes (instead of 128 bytes).

Given these throughput numbers, we compare the results from simulation with the performance values calculated with the analytical model of IP forwarding on the IXP microarchitecture by matching the corresponding throughput values. Differences in the accuracy of the approaches thus become apparent by looking at delay values experienced by packets and the load generated by packet processing on the microarchitecture components. Figure 7.5a compares the end-to-end delay experienced by packets for different packet lengths, and Figure 7.5b compares the load of microengines responsible for the receive threads.

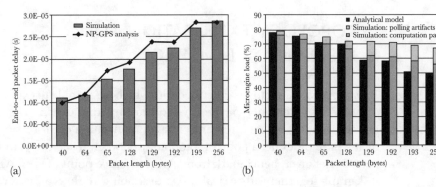

(a)   (b)

7.5

FIGURE

(a) End-to-end delay experienced by packets and (b) load of the receive μEngines.

The worst-case assumption for the arbitration penalty to equal the service time of an RR frame is too pessimistic. The results from analysis, shown in Figure 7.5a, are therefore based on non-preemptive generalized processor sharing (NP-GPS). This choice reduces the arbitration penalty to one task length only (parameter T in Figure 7.3), whereas the service rate remains unchanged compared with RR. Close examination by simulation indeed confirms that the average waiting time of a task is only on the order of one task length. The results shown in Figure 7.5b are subdivided into polling effects and the load generated by the actual computation. Polling artifacts are not included in the analytical model.

Both figures show a deviation of less than 15% between the cycle-accurate simulation and the analytical model. Moreover, the values obtained by simulation and by analysis show the same increasing or decreasing trends in the same order of magnitude. For instance, the end-to-end delay sharply increases as soon as the processing of an additional 64-byte segment is required.

In our case study we have shown that the evaluation of a challenging real-world example showed only minor differences between simulation-based and analytical-model-based approaches. Since we had to perform a reverse engineering of the IXP to perform the comparison in such detail, some uncertainties remain, such as the rotating-priority-based arbitration scheme of the command bus, which cannot be accurately modeled in the current framework. More important than matching exact numbers, however, is the matching of trends when modifying parameters. This is why we believe that the service curve approach is indeed a reasonable candidate for evaluating different PE topologies where the main goal is to find a ranking among those designs.

7.3 TOPOLOGY EXPLORATION FOR PERFORMANCE METRICS

In the following, a setup is described with which we are able to explore topologies of processing elements for the IPv4 forwarding application. The main goal of this analysis is to reveal whether a certain organization of processing elements—be it a pure pipeline, a pool, or a topology between those two extreme cases—is best for the given benchmark from a performance point of view. Again, an IPv4 task graph together with arrival curves describing 16 flows at peak rate using 64-byte packets is used as an abstract benchmark to drive the exploration using the network calculus to determine resource utilization and the end-to-end delay of packets. For this setup, we reuse the I/O infrastructure of the IXP configuration;

namely, the 16 bidirectional networking ports and the single SDRAM using separate buses for read and write accesses.

7.3.1   Configurations

The simulation and analysis results of the IXP have revealed that given a computation requirement of about 400 clock cycles at least seven microengines are required to support IPv4 forwarding at line speed. For the following investigation we assume an allocation of eight microengine-like processing elements to ease a fair comparison between pipelined and pooled topologies for a given set of 16 traffic flows. Since we do not elaborate on the allocation of different kinds of processing elements in our study, we can be sure that for the IPv4 benchmark computational requirements can always be met by the microengines if communication between processing elements is not the bottleneck. That means, differences in performance among topologies are in particular based on the properties of interconnections and arbitration/scheduling effects.

For our analysis, the original IPv4 task graph has been subdivided for each flow into a balanced sequence of eight computation segments with a requirement of about 50 clock cycles each. We have enabled the underlying communication scheme to support direct communication between two microengines (this feature has recently been added to new generations of the IXP). The task graph has been changed to reflect this feature by always passing a constant amount of context data between computation tasks (header fields, payload descriptors, and so on; arbitrarily set to 20 bytes in this case). Thus, for our analysis, we do not depend on SRAM or scratchpad memory, since the described communication between tasks is either mapped to direct connections between two engines or processed internally if the corresponding tasks are mapped to the same engine. The surrounding I/O infrastructure of the original IXP configuration remains constant for the analysis; that is, the number of bidirectional ports is 16, one traffic flow is associated with each input port, and the single SDRAM uses separate buses for read and write accesses. Topologies using eight processing elements are listed in Table 7.1 together with static design characteristics.

The first four topologies (I through IV) are also shown in Figure 7.1. We distinguish five different topologies, where the last two (IV and V) model different variants of a pooled configuration. Topology V uses a single shared bus for communication between engines, whereas IV has two separate unidirectional buses for the same purpose. Configuration (I) represents a pure pipeline, where all flows are handled by all engines in sequence. The pure pipeline relies on point-to-point connections (P-2-P) only. However, it may have to support the maximum amount of 16 threads per engine to utilize the computing resources

| Config. | Allocation [number of items] | | | | | Memory requirements [number of data fields] | | | |
| | | | | | | Lower bound | | Upper bound | |
	Cores/ stage	Stages	Threads per core (max.)	Buses	Bus interfaces	P-2-P connect	Thread context	Packet descriptor	Thread context	Packet descriptor
I (pipe)	1	8	16	0		9	8	15 + 8	8 * 16	15 + 8 * 16
II	2	4	8	2	3	6	8	15 + 8	8 * 8	15 + 8 * 8
III	4	2	4	2	5	4	8	15 + 8	8 * 4	15 + 8 * 4
IV (pool)	8	1	2	2	9	0	8	15 + 8	8 * 2	15 + 8 * 2
V (pool)	8	1	2	1	18	0	8	15 + 8	8 * 2	15 + 8 * 2

7.1   Topology configurations and characteristics.

TABLE

most by hiding memory latency with context switches. Depending on the ratio of communication to computation latencies, the actual number of threads required for the pipeline may vary from eight (one thread per engine) to $8 * 16 = 128$ threads (16 threads per engine). Moreover, memory requirements for packet descriptors that point to the location of the corresponding packet in SDRAM are considered separately. The underlying assumption is that we do not allow a backlog of more than one packet (the packet in process) per thread and engine. A larger backlog due to the burstiness of packet arrivals could, however, be absorbed by the global SDRAM. In our case, where we assume packet arrivals at constant peak rate, the maximum backlog external to the engines could rise to 15 packets.

The other configurations can be interpreted accordingly. Configuration III, for instance, comprises four concurrent pipelines, with two stages each. Bundles of four flows are mapped to each pipeline. One bus is needed to distribute packet information to different pipes at the beginning, and another bus is needed at the end of the pipeline. Between stages, point-to-point connections are used.

7.3.2   Results from Analysis

Given the topology configurations in Table 7.1, analysis results from abstract benchmarking are given in Figure 7.6. The arrival rate of packets is fixed to the point where the modeled SDRAM reaches saturation in utilization. This is the case for a line rate that is by a factor of 1.25 higher than in the original IXP. That means, 64-byte packets arrive every four μs on every input port. This operation point coincides quite well with the saturation of the engines, which show a utilization of 98%. We vary the throughput settings of the interconnecting buses and point-to-point (P-2-P) connections. For the simplicity of the representation, the throughput is set to the same value for buses and P-2-P connections, although the communication demands may be different, looking at the same topology. The initial throughput setting of 400 MB/sec represents the capability of buses used in the IXP1200, organized in 32 bits at 100 MHz. We further throttle the throughput of the interconnections to reach an operation point where the communication infrastructure is saturated as well.

Under ideal assumptions that the task graph can be well balanced and a static, synchronized schedule can be imposed on all resources, lower bounds on the packet latency are given in the figure. Further latency values consider the cases that we employ service curves based on non-preemptive generalized processor sharing (NP-GPS), as done in Section 7.2.7, and worst-case RR service curves for all resources, respectively. The latter configurations more realistically model runtime jitter and arbitration effects, as well as effects due to slightly

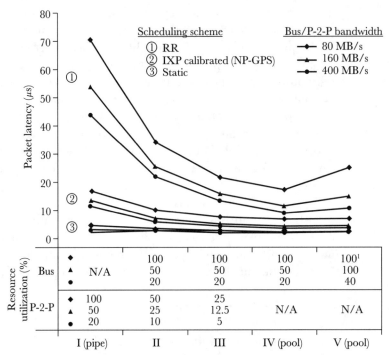

			I (pipe)	II	III	IV (pool)	V (pool)
Resource utilization (%)	Bus	◆	N/A	100	100	100	100[1]
		▲		50	50	50	100
		●		20	20	20	40
	P-2-P	◆	100	50	25	N/A	N/A
		▲	50	25	12.5		
		●	20	10	5		

[1] For this particular design point, line speed cannot be maintained, but the packet throughput halves.

7.6

FIGURE

Latency and utilization results for different topologies.

unbalanced task graphs, since a fully synchronous design is not feasible in our application domain. Note that the worst-case memory bounds given in Table 7.1 for packet descriptors do not hold in the plain RR case in Figure 7.6. We would consider those designs unbalanced for our application scenario since, for instance, in the pure pipeline case up to 18 packets per flow could be in the network processor concurrently (as opposed to up to nine packets in Table 7.1).

Only under ideal assumptions is the pure pipeline [configuration I] able to match latency values with pool configurations (configurations IV and V) by overprovisioning the throughput of point-to-point (P-2-P) connections and thereby decreasing the transport delay. Under practical assumption, however, the pipeline always falls behind the pooled topology. This effect is in particular emphasized in our configurations, since the pool topologies employ an optimized mapping of tasks to processing elements so that the full processing of a packet occurs on the same processing element, thus minimizing communication overhead. Consequently, the dynamic range between lower and upper latency bounds for a pipeline must be larger than for a pool in our case. If we tried to map pipelined processing onto a pool, the results for a pool would degrade, as an example in Section 7.4.2 reveals.

On the other hand, since P-2-P connections are always available, the latency experienced along the pipeline is relatively less affected by higher utilizations of P-2-P connections as compared to a pool by higher bus utilizations (causing higher arbitration penalties). The crossover point, however, is not visible in our analysis and would only be apparent using more than eight computing cores.

Note that the bus load for the topologies II, III, and IV must be the same, since the buses are used to distribute the traffic from 16 ports to the corresponding number of pipelines. The implementation costs for those topologies would, however, be quite different, since the buses require a varying number of bus interfaces (see Table 7.1).

7.3.3   Concluding Remarks on Topology Exploration

From a performance point of view, all indications are that a pooled topology will always outperform a pipelined version for the configurations under consideration in this chapter. Apart from the performance indications revealed by using the network calculus, the following inherent issues may further narrow and guide design decisions.

+ A processing element must eventually be pipelined as soon as the computation requirement of a task is above the interarrival time of a packet.

+ Topologies toward a pure pipeline could possibly support more parallel threads of execution and enable higher resource utilization if the nature of the task graphs showed a beneficial ratio of computation to communication latency to hide memory access latencies.

The design decision about choosing a particular processing element topology, however, is not as straightforward when we look from the programming model point of view. We also recognize that given an application task graph automatic refinement of the task graph needs to be performed for mapping applications to architectures in general. This is, however, not the focus of this chapter. In the literature there are many approaches for performing refinements. See [23] for one such instance.

In the following section we discuss the interrelation between programmability and processing element topologies. In particular, we focus on the influence of partitioning, scheduling, communication cost, scalability, and determination of performance on programmability of the chosen topology.

7.4 INTERRELATION BETWEEN PROGRAMMABILITY AND TOPOLOGIES

Programming a network processor comprises partitioning of the application onto potentially multiple processing elements (or threads therein) and scheduling those tasks according to the order of packet flow and with respect to resource utilization. Partitioning and scheduling need to be performed by the programmer in a manual way due to the absence of any automated support for multiprocessor programming. Thus, the architecture should be kept as simple and predictable as possible, in order to ease programmability.

Since parallelism is essential to achieve performance, the ease of programmability of any network processor heavily depends on the chosen topology of PEs. In addition, issues related to determination of performance and scalability, such as bus arbitration, also influence the programmability to a certain extent. Hence, we need to classify different topologies with respect to programmability-related issues; namely, partitioning, scheduling, and communication cost, as well scalability and determination of performance. In addition, we also study two different partitionings of our benchmark on IXP1200 to understand the programming efforts for the two implementations.

7.4.1 Comparison of Topologies

Table 7.2 compares the different topologies with respect to partitioning, scheduling, communication costs, scalability issues, and determination of performance. We observe that it is easy to partition an application for a pool organization as compared to a pipelined one, since for a pipelined organization we need to ensure equal latency for each pipeline stage per flow. Also, the number of flows does not impact the partitioning on a pool organization, but has an indirect impact on the pipelined organization, since the amount of available cycles reduces when the number of flows per pipeline increases. In this work we have considered only parallel flows with no feedback. However, if we have applications that have dependencies between flows, a pipelined topology may become more beneficial. In addition, if the requirement for program memory is a serious concern, a pipeline may be the better solution, although balancing pipeline stages may introduce some coding overhead. However, a processing element in a pool must store the complete program in order to process a flow, whereas a pipeline stage only requires a fraction of it.

There are two types of scheduling that influence the programmability of a particular PE topology. The intra-PE scheduling has very little impact on almost

Design issue	Pool	Pipeline	Mixed versions
Partitioning # tasks per flow	Depends on PE performance; multiple solutions possible.	Needs to equal the number of stages and to be equal in latency.	Depends on total pipe performance and number of stages.
# flows	Replicate the single flow onto remaining PEs.	Does not matter directly, but influences the cycle budget per task.	Replication is possible between pipes, but pipe needs to be balanced.
Scheduling Intra-PE	Any scheme possible; data driven.	Any scheme possible; data driven.	Any scheme possible; data driven.
Inter-PE	Only necessary if used in pipelined fashion, in addition to bus arbitration.	Handshake between stages for synchronization, fully synchronous pipeline otherwise.	Handshake between stages, in addition to bus arbitration.
Cost of communication	All PEs connected to expensive shared common buses.	Only inexpensive point-to-point connections between PEs	Mixed communication. Trade-offs possible (bus length, # buses).
Scalability # tasks/flow	If a PE is fully utilized, a flow needs to be spread over PEs in a pipelined fashion. This requires communication overhead.	Simply add another PE to the chain, but a repartitioning of task flow is likely.	Add another stage to all chains and repartition as needed.
# flows	Simply add another PE and run the same program.	Add more PEs to the pipe and repartition every task.	Add more chains, as done in pool case.
Determination of performance	Performance heavily depends on bus arbitration. Data-dependent effects.	Performance more deterministic, because of sequential execution. There are, however, data-dependent effects.	Depends on the number of parallel pipelines.

7.2 Comparing topologies with respect to programmability and scalability.

TABLE

all organizations from a programmability perspective, and will most likely be data driven. The inter-PE scheduling, however, impacts the pipelined organizations in the general case, since some sort of handshake between different stages needs to be implemented for synchronization. It is important to note that such an overhead due to synchronization is a complex function of the balancing between pipeline stages (and potentially partitioning of the original application) and application-given data dependencies. In addition, the inter-PE scheduling is influenced by any bus arbitration, and this impacts all PE topologies. The cost of communication for pool topologies is clearly much larger as compared to pipelined ones. The mixed topologies incur somewhat lesser penalty compared to pool topologies, depending upon the degree of pipelining for a given number of PEs, and this involves trade-offs.

We note that scaling in our context is scaling of an existing implementation with new requirements. Scaling an application per flow results in increased computation requirements. Thus, if the increase in computational requirements cannot be met by the PE, then additional PEs need to be added. For a pool topology, this results in a pipelined style of mapping, along with communication overhead. However, for a pipelined topology this not only adds a stage to the existing pipeline but results in repartitioning of the code. For a mixed version, this involves addition of a PE to all pipelines. In contrast, if the number of flows increases, then for a pool topology we only need to add a new PE and map the existing code, whereas for a pipelined topology we will have to add a PE to the pipeline and repartition the code. In the mixed version, if the existing pipelines cannot handle a new flow, then we need to add a complete new pipeline to handle the increase in flow(s). Determination in performance becomes crucial for exploring different alternatives in mapping a given application and has a significant impact on the productivity. A pooled topology does not exhibit good determination due to the bus arbitration effects apart from the data dependencies given by the application. A pipelined topology is limited mostly by application-given data dependencies only, and hence allows for better estimation. A mixed topology, however, is limited by the number of parallel pipelines it has, since more parallel pipelines will reduce the amount of determination it can exhibit.

In our experiments in Section 7.3, we have found the pool topology to perform better than pipelined or mixed topologies for our application and the chosen environment for the given metrics. However, we recognize that in practice there are many other considerations (as outlined in Table 7.2) that influence the choice of a particular topology.

7.4.2   Study of Different Partitionings

Two different versions of our IPv4 forwarding application have been implemented on the IXP1200 to understand the programming requirements of both a parallel and pipelined topology. In the first case, we took the Intel reference code for layer 3 forwarding. This code was mapped to the IXP1200 so that 16 threads on four microengines performed the receive and forwarding functions, and eight threads on the remaining two microengines performed the transmit operation. For 64-byte Ethernet/IP packets we obtained a throughput of 55% for a line rate of 1600 Mb/s (same configuration as in Section 7.2.7). In the second implementation, we repartitioned the code on receive microengines to separate receive, header check, route lookup, and packet descriptor write functions. We now mapped four input ports to one thread each, and the remaining three functions were mapped to three different threads in a pipelined fashion. Thus, we now have a completely pipelined implementation of the receive functionality on four microengines supporting 16 ports. The transmit part remained the same as the original implementation. We observe that the pipelined implementation required two times more registers and thus we had to implement this communication using SRAM, since the backlog of packets prevented us from using scratchpad memory. This resulted in a drop of throughput to 35% of the line rate. In fact, when we evaluated the latter mapping with our analytical framework we understood that the pipelined implementation we have is unbalanced and some of the receive stages are underutilized (utilization of 27% only). Simulations do not provide complete utilization information, since polling effects hide the true utilization. This indeed shows that balancing pipelined implementations is a difficult and cumbersome task. A future work is to use the analytical framework to explore different mappings for network processors.

7.5   CONCLUSIONS

In this chapter, we have explored different trade-offs for processing element topologies based on an analytical framework and our IPv4 benchmark. Also, we have implemented different partitioning for our benchmark on the IXP1200.

The main conclusions from this work are:

+ The employed analytical performance modeling is suited to exploring design space for network processors, since it is quite accurate, within 15%, compared to full system simulation—apart from alleviating the need for detailed executable models and packet traces.

+ For performance metrics, we found pipelined topologies to be consuming more local data memory and causing more end-to-end delay, although they have only point-to-point connections. Even overprovisioning these connections cannot alleviate the increase in end-to-end delay compared to a bus-arbitrated pooled topology for our configurations.

+ Based on our task partitioning, the pooled version does not require any intermediate communication apart from the initial load distribution and the final output arbitration, thus favoring the pooled topology.

+ Programming pooled architectures is simpler than pipelined ones, since the effort in balancing and partitioning pipeline stages is higher. Reasoning about cycle budgets and achievable performance on every processing element requires more effort for a pipelined topology.

+ Our practical implementations underpin our observations, based on earlier experiments, that balancing a pipeline is not trivial and that exploration of different partitioning and scheduling is time consuming and error prone. Some automated support for exploring different alternatives is needed. We observe that if scalability is an afterthought, it makes programmability difficult (requiring recoding in most cases) and, even worse, the communication overhead quickly dominates the initial architecture.

We believe the value of our study is twofold: our results (1) will help in reasoning of and comparing existing architectures and (2) provide insights into the cost-driven development of architectures.

In summary, we believe that for forwarding applications pool topology is the best, since we found it to be most flexible from a programmability and scalability point of view, as well as best-performing for our metrics.

ACKNOWLEDGMENTS

This work was supported, in part, by the Microelectronics Advanced Research Consortium (MARCO) and Infineon Technologies, and is part of the efforts of the Gigascale Silicon Research Center (GSRC).

REFERENCES

[1] P. Crowley, M. Fiuczynski, J. Baer, and B. Bershad, "Characterizing Processor Architectures for Programmable Network Interfaces," *Proceedings of the 2000 International Conference on Supercomputing*, Santa Fe, NM, May 2000.

[2] K. Lahiri, A. Raghunathan, and S. Dey, "System-Level Performance Analysis for Designing On-Chip Communication Architectures," *IEEE Transactions on Computer Aided Design of Integrated Circuits and Systems*, vol. 20(6):768–783, June 2001.

[3] M. Franklin and T. Wolf, "A Network Processor Performance and Design Model with Benchmark Parameterization," *First Workshop on Network Processors* at the 8th International Symposium on High Performance Computer Architecture (HPCA8), Cambridge, MA, Feb. 2002.

[4] S. Lakshmanamurthy, K.-Y. Liu, Y. Pun, L. Huston, and U. Naik, "Network Processor Performance Analysis Methodology," *Intel Technology Journal*, vol. 6(3):19–28, Aug. 2002.

[5] L. Thiele, S. Chakraborty, M. Gries, and S. Künzli, "Design Space Exploration of Network Processor Architectures," *First Workshop on Network Processors* at the 8th International Symposium on High Performance Computer Architecture (HPCA8), Cambridge, MA, Feb. 2002.

[6] J.-Y. Le Boudec and P. Thiran, "Network Calculus: A Theory of Deterministic Queuing Systems for the Internet," *LNCS 2050*, Springer-Verlag, New York, 2001.

[7] B. Braden, D. Clark, and S. Shenker, "Integrated Services in the Internet Architecture: An Overview," *RFC1633*, Internet Engineering Task Force (IETF), June 1994.

[8] S. Shenker and J. Wroclawski, "General Characterization Parameters for Integrated Service Network Elements," *RFC2215*, Internet Engineering Task Force (IETF), Sept. 1997.

[9] F. Baker, "Requirements for IP Version 4 Routers," *RFC1812*, Internet Engineering Task Force (IETF), June 1995.

[10] Intel Corporation, *Intel IXP1200 Network Processor Family: Hardware Reference Manual*, Rev. 8, Aug. 2001, pp. 225–228.

[11] M. Tsai, C. Kulkarni, C. Sauer, N. Shah, and K. Keutzer, "A Benchmarking Methodology for Network Processors," *First Workshop on Network Processors* at the 8th International Symposium on High Performance Computer Architecture (HPCA8), Cambridge, MA, Feb. 2002.

[12] M. Gries, C. Kulkarni, C. Sauer, and K. Keutzer, "Comparing Analytical Modeling with Simulation for Network Processors: A Case Study," *Design Automation and Test in Europe (DATE)*, Munich, Germany, Mar. 2003.

[13] N. Shah, "Understanding Network Processors," master's thesis, Department of Electrical Engineering and Computer Sciences, University of California, Berkeley, Sept. 2001.

[14] A. Mihal et al., "Developing Architectural Platforms: A Disciplined Approach," *IEEE Design and Test of Computers*, vol. 19(6):6–16, Nov./Dec. 2002.

[15]   E. Kohler, R. Morris, B. Chen, J. Jannotti, and M. Kaashoek, "The Click Modular Router," *ACM Transactions on Computer Systems*, vol. (18)3:263–297, Aug. 2000.

[16]   Teja Technologies, "IPv4 Forwarding Application Performance," white paper, July 2002.

[17]   J. Nickolls et al., "Broadcom Calisto: A Multi-channel Multi-service Communication Platform," *Hot-Chips Symposium*, 2002.

[18]   F. Karim, A. Nguyen, S. Dey, and R. Rao, "On-Chip Communication Architecture for OC-768 Network Processors," *Design Automation Conference*, Las Vegas, June 2001, pp. 678–683.

[19]   A. Tillmann, "A Case for Using a Specialized Language for NPU Design," *EE Times*, Aug. 5, 2002.

[20]   D. Lenoski et al., "The Stanford DASH Multiprocessor," *IEEE Computer*, vol. 25(3): 63–79, Mar. 1992.

[21]   M. D. Hill, J. R. Larus, and D. A. Wood, "Parallel Computer Research in the Wisconsin Wind Tunnel Project," *NSF Conference on Experimental Research in Computer Systems*, June 1996.

[22]   B. Kienhuis, E. Deprettere, K. A. Vissers, and P. Van Der Wolf, "An Approach for Quantitative Analysis of Application-Specific Dataflow Architectures," *Proceedings of the International Conference on Application-Specific Systems, Architectures and Processors (ASAP'97)*, 1997, pp. 338–349.

[23]   J. Peng and D. Gajski, "Automatic Model Refinement for Fast Architecture Exploration," *Asia South Pacific Design Automation Conference (ASP-DAC 2002)*, Bangalore, India, Jan. 2002, 332–337.

Packet Classification and Termination in a Protocol Processor

Ulf Nordqvist, Dake Liu
Department of Electrical Engineering, Linköping University, Sweden

Both computer and human communication networks use protocols with ever-increasing demands on speed, cost, and flexibility. There is also a strong development toward an increased use of network protocols for applications that traditionally used other implementation techniques (e.g., voice and video). One reason is that packet-based network protocols can normally handle a mixture of any kind of traffic. For network node components such as routers, switches, and bridges, the performance needs have been fulfilled using application-specific integrated circuits (ASICs) or application-specific standard products (ASSPs), since these applications have traditionally made quite moderate demands on programmability. These traditional approaches will probably continue to coexist with more programmable solutions, such as network processors (NP), in the future, due to their relatively cost-insensitive and performance-demanding consumers. Having said this, it is clear that the networking industry is requesting more programmable devices in tomorrow's network.

To let end users take advantage of the bandwidth enhancement in today's networks, tomorrow's network terminal (NT) hardware must support transmission speeds of Gb/s. Hardware for such NT components is, on the other hand, sold on a cost-sensitive market share with high demands on flexibility and usability. Traditionally NT has been implemented using ASICs situated on the network interface card, processing the lower layers in the OSI Reference Model [1] and a CPU-RISC-based SW implementation of the upper layers. Usage of standard general-purpose CPUs is expensive in terms of cost, space, and power due to their lack of dedicated hardware. There is also an upper capacity limit, set by the I/O capacity and the instruction rate of the CPU. Today it is easy to find a network interface card (NIC) supporting multi-gigabit networks, but such bandwidth cannot be utilized by the host, since it requires the host to be fully loaded, processing layer 3 and 4 protocols, leaving nothing for the application and system processing. The research focus has mainly been on router and switching applications so far, but in the future the terminals will also require offloading using programmable high-speed solutions.

To meet these new requirements, a new area of communication-handling hardware platforms has emerged. These are commonly denoted as TCP offload engines (TOEs). One of these TOE solutions is called programmable protocol processor (PPP), introduced in [1] and [2] in 1999. Most of the TOE consists of programmable parts that can accelerate and offload a terminal host processor by handling the communication protocol processing. The protocol processor platform is a domain-specific processor solution with superior performance over a general-purpose CPU, which still provides flexibility through programmability within the limited-application domain. The proposed architecture cannot handle fragmented packets. This chapter introduces a cost function and discussion around the processing of fragmented packets. The protocol processor hardware platform is discussed in Section 8.1. In Section 8.2, a novel methodology and architecture for handling and distributing control flow information to and from our protocol processor is introduced. The proposed architecture enables the protocol processor to be used in networks with fragmented packets. In Section 8.3, a discussion on system performance based on behavioral models is included.

8.1   PROGRAMMABLE PROTOCOL PROCESSOR

The main task of the protocol processor (see Figure 8.1) is to process the packets transferred between the application on the host processor and the network, so that a secure and reliable connection is provided between the sender and transmitting function. The protocol-processing architecture (and the research project behind it) discussed in this chapter deals with the reception of packets only. Since the transmission of packets is limited by the application's construction of packets, we have chosen to concentrate our research on the packet reception problem before discussing packet creation acceleration. The goal of this research project is to process as much of the protocol stack as possible before storing the data payload to the system's main memory. By reducing the memory access and buffering, illustrated in Figure 8.2, both memory bottleneck problems and power consumption can be reduced. To achieve this, the protocols must be processed at network speed and multiple layers must be processed simultaneously, as proposed in [7].

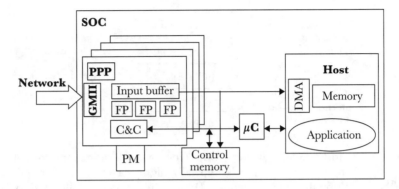

8.1

FIGURE
The PPP together with a general-purpose microcontroller handles the communication of one network port. In a system-on-a-chip (SOC), many PPPs can be
used as port processors in order to provide high bandwidth between the application and the network. A control memory is used for storage of inter-packet
control variables.

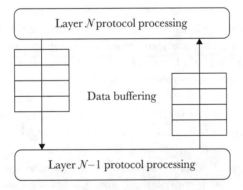

8.2

FIGURE
Using inter-layer processing, the power consumption and required memory
usage in the protocol processor can be reduced, since all buffering of data
between different protocol layers can be eliminated.

To deal with the fact that a protocol processor must deal with a variety
of processing tasks, the hardware platform has been divided into two parts.
This is illustrated in Figure 8.1. The first part is the PPP, which is dedicated
to data-intensive protocol processing tasks mainly originating from the lower-
level protocols in the OSI protocol stack standard. Examples of such tasks are
checksum calculations, address checks [3], and length counters. Normally they

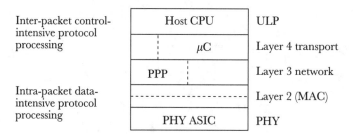

Inter-packet control-intensive protocol processing	Host CPU	ULP
	μC	Layer 4 transport
	PPP	Layer 3 network
Intra-packet data-intensive protocol processing		Layer 2 (MAC)
	PHY ASIC	PHY

8.3

FIGURE

Host offloading using various types of accelerators for different types of processing tasks and protocols. Typically, higher-layer protocols require more flexibility through programmability. Hence, these tasks are allocated to the host CPU or the flexible microcontroller.

are intra-packet processing tasks that have to be performed even if the protocols covered are very simple. The other part of the platform is a general-purpose microcontroller (μC) that deals with control-intensive protocol-processing tasks such as connection-state handling and other inter-packet processing tasks. The microcontroller is also used for the configuration of the PPP for different types of protocols, as well as for updates. (See Figure 8.3.) Further, the microcontroller handles the control communication with the host processor and the DMA (e.g., setting up and closing sockets). Using DMA communication between the PPP and the host reduces the interrupts compared to bus communication [6]. In the NP research community there is today a clear trend toward a separation of the processing in slow and fast paths similar to our approach. Figure 8.4 is an illustration showing how different layers in the protocol stack are distributed to different processing resources.

The microcontroller is suitable for implementation of the various finite-state machines (FSMs), which contribute a large part of the control processing. Nevertheless, there are other tasks within the inter-packet processing domain, which the microcontroller efficiently can be offloaded from. One of the main operations is a search and access of control data based on header information in a receiving packet. This operation is comparable to the *bind* and *in_pcblookup* C functions used in software implementations. In a receiving situation, the PPP will process the packet and then discard it or hand it over to the microcontroller.

The proposed platform, including a PPP together with the μC, is essentially a TOE dedicated to network terminals. A TOE for NT does not make any routing decisions. It only discards packets or accepts them before they are passed on to the correct host memory buffers. Further, the number of connections is much less than in a layer 4 router. Hence, the architectural design of such an offloading

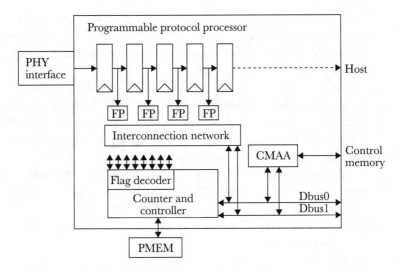

The programmable packet processor includes four parts: the counter and controller (C&C), the input buffer chain, accelerating functional pages, and a control memory access accelerator (CMAA).

device has other goals and requirements. Consequently, the research on such devices must divert from the network processor research area.

As illustrated in Figure 8.4, the PPP hardware architecture for protocol processing consists of four main parts. One is the input buffer chain that provides the data to the accelerating functional pages (FPs). By using a 32-bit-wide chain of flip-flops, the fan-out from the flip-flops can be kept on a tolerable level, even if the number of FPs increases with new protocols and an increased protocol coverage. Using a RAM-based FIFO buffer instead of flip-flops would decrease the activity, but the fan-out would be a huge problem. As long as the fan-out is kept low, it is still possible to replace the last flip-flops in the chain with a minimal RAM-based FIFO. The total buffer size is dependent on the decision latency of the PPP. The decision answer is normally to either discard or send a packet to memory for further processing. Some payloads should be sent to the host memory and some to the control memory.

The control of the various accelerators (FP) in the PPP mainly consists of start and stop flags. These flags are provided from the counter and controller (C&C). The flags are generated based on an internal program in the C&C, and result flags from the FPs and counter values are generated in the C&C. The C&C is responsible for scheduling the start of the processing in the FPs at the correct clock cycle as the data stream through the register chain. Based on the result from the FPs, the C&C can either discard the packet or continue the processing by configuring and starting new FPs. If a packet is discarded (e.g., because the destination address was erroneous), all FPs are immediately shut down in order to save power.

Since the processor operates on streaming data, instead of stored data in memory, decisions on which program flow to execute require minimal latency. Different protocol configurations use different program flows. Hence, program flow selection is dependent on the type and content of the receiving packet. The C&C includes a special assist for acceleration of multi-choice conditional jump instructions in order to provide maximum system performance. The payload of received packets of TCP or UDP type will be sent to the host, while the payload of control-oriented protocols such as ARP, RARP, ICMP, and IGMP will be stored in the control memory. The control memory acceleration part is further discussed in Section 8.2.

8.1.1   Functional Pages

The FPs must operate at wire speed. FPs are configured from the microcontroller during setup for a specific set of protocols or a single protocol. Each of the FPs is dedicated ASIC with a limited configurability. Together, the microcontroller and the C&C support a high degree of programmability. To better understand the nature of the FP, a common set of network protocols has been used. The protocols are TCP, UDP, ICMP, IGMP, IPv4, IPv6, ARP, RARP, and Ethernet (Fast E and GigE). To support processing of these protocols, the following FPs have been implemented:

✦ One CRC FP, described in [4].

✦ Two extract and Compare (XAC) FPs responsible for checking address numbers and port numbers against the actual host address. Further, they are used to extract and compare checksums.

✦ Two length-counting adders.

✦ Two checksum calculation adders.

✦ One generic adder.

Other possible processing tasks suitable for acceleration in an FP are various types of decoding and decryption algorithms. They are, however, not used, since such algorithms are not included in the selected protocol suite.

As mentioned previously, the FPs are self-contained dedicated ASICs. After configuration, the control needed for their operation is very limited. Actually, most of the control signaling can be reduced to only start and stop flags, since most control is distributed to the individual FPs.

8.2 CONTROL MEMORY ACCESS ACCELERATOR

As mentioned previously, the microcontroller is responsible for the communication control (signaling) handling. Using a general microcontroller is a straightforward method, similar to the traditional way of slow-path processing in a GP CPU. The problem with this solution is that the control information must be transferred among the microcontroller, the PPP, and the control memory with low latency in order for the PPP to process its part at wire speed and make the decision if the packet should be discarded. This is needed because of the use of fragmentation. Further, acceleration of slow-path processing offloads the microprocessor. Hence, a platform including an accelerating-hardware assist and a control interface dedicated to packet recognition and control memory access have been developed. The control memory access accelerator (CMAA) presented in this chapter uses two lookup engines (LUE) in order to recognize and classify the incoming packet. These LUE essentially consist of content-addressable memories (CAM), which are well known and commonly used in routing and switching applications. One of the early works in this area is [5].

8.2.1 Header Data

The purpose of storing control information is to ensure that connection-oriented protocols (e.g., TCP) can perform protocol processing on the payload, which can be divided or segmented into many lower-layer packets. These packets can arrive out of order, and in case of connection-oriented protocols the routing information is not included in all packets. Hence, it is obvious that some information on the current status of a connection must be stored in order to be able to continue the processing when the next packet arrives. In the case of the protocol set discussed earlier in the chapter, the following information is normally needed.

+ Protocol type
+ Length (received so far)
+ Total length (included in the last fragment)

The length field(s) is provided to the length-counting adder in the PPP, which updates the number and finally sends the updated value to one of the XAC FPs.

There it is compared to the total length value, which is stored in the control memory. If they are equal, the microcontroller is notified that all packet fragments have been received, and this entry will be removed from the search list. If unequal, the new length value is written back to the control memory.

+ Accumulated checksum results

The checksum result is provided to one of the checksum-calculating adders, which adds it to the recent packets checksum using a 1's-complement addition that produces a new checksum. If the length is equal to the total length (which means that the entire payload message has arrived), the updated checksum is sent to one of the XAC FPs for comparison with the received checksum.

+ IP source and destination address

The source address is extracted from the data stream by the PPP. The address value is then used to construct a pseudoheader. The pseudoheader is used in the checksum calculation. Normally, only one destination address is used for unicast packets in a terminal. This means it does not need to be stored in the control memory.

+ TCP source and destination ports

The type, ports, and addresses identify a specific connection. To see if an incoming packet should be discarded or accepted, these fields must be checked. They are also used to identify which application the payload should be directed to.

+ Identification number

The IP identification number is used to find the correct memory buffer in the control memory.

+ Pointers to the memory position of preceding and successive packets/ segments

To provide all of the services stipulated by the TCP standard, more connection-related information than listed previously needs to be stored. On the other hand, the only information needed for the PPP to perform its processing is the information highlighted in bulleted text. The information stored in the control memory can also be used to calculate the host memory address. An algorithm for this type of memory address calculation remains to be implemented for the general case, even if it is simple for special applications (e.g., VoIP). A general algorithm for in-order data buffering in the host memory would significantly reduce the host processor interrupts. This type of algorithm would benefit from an accelerated access to the control memory. This issue will not be further discussed in this chapter.

8.2.2   Accelerator Interface

The CMAA interface to the rest of the PPP and the microcontroller is illustrated in Figure 8.5. The input to the CMAA consists of flags and an instruction generated in the C&C. In Table 8.1, the simple instruction set (six instructions) is listed.

As output, the CMAA generates a number of flags. The two data buses are being used for data transport.

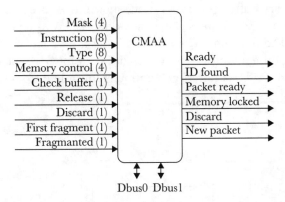

8.5   Accelerator interface.

FIGURE

New packet	Protocol type
Load register	Port or address word
PLUE operation	Write, read, or remove
SLUE operation	Write, read, or remove
Release to microcontroller	
Set memory buffer pointer	Protocol type

8.1   Lightweight instruction set.

TABLE

8.2.3   Data Path

An overview of the CMAA architecture is illustrated in Figure 8.6. The CMAA data path includes two LUEs, a buffer pointer generator, and a simple memory access selector. The primary LUE (PLUE) includes just one CAM with M 16-bit entries, and the result memory is W bits wide. The purpose of this unit is to check if we have already received a fragment of the incoming packet. This is checked using the IP identification field (IP ID). If an arriving packet is fragmented, the fragmented flag will be produced in the C&C and provided to the CMAA. Then the fragment is checked in the PLUE to see if a packet buffer exists in the control memory. If the CAM in the PLUE does not have a matching identification field entry, a new packet buffer will be created and the IP ID will be written to the PLUE CAM. In the packet buffer, inter-packet variables such as length and checksums will be stored. If the packet is non-fragmented, there is no need to store its IP ID, so the packet buffer is created directly on the control memory address provided from the memory buffer generation unit, shown in Figure 8.6. The secondary LUE (SLUE) is a classification engine, including six CAMs, and its purpose is to check for valid connections. The two data buses are 32 bits wide. The memory buffer generation generates new buffer addresses for both packet buffers and connection buffers. The address generation is controlled from the μC.

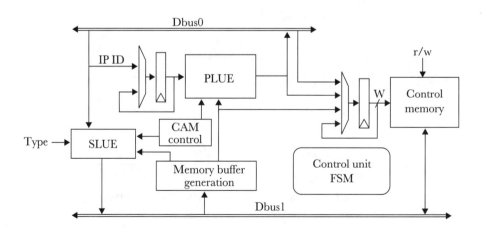

8.6

FIGURE

The CMAA architecture, an accelerating hardware architecture for control memory access in the protocol processor. Based on traditional packet classification techniques, it supports low-latency access to stored connection variables in the control memory.

As with the other accelerating devices in our protocol processor (e.g., FPs), the CMAA remains in idle mode while not in operation. Power-up will be performed when a new packet arrives. This reduces the power dissipation significantly in a network terminal, due to the uneven time distribution of the packet reception.

In this chapter we leave the final CAM design and implementation to be further investigated and optimized. The reason behind this is that they are extremely important for the overall performance and require different design techniques, tools, and expertise than the rest of the PPP. Final implementation of the LUE will of course have a huge impact on the performance of the CMAA. A layout of the CMAA, excluding the two LUEs and the buses, has been produced. The number of standard cells and the area of the CMAA, excluding the input registers and the two LUEs, are 716 and 0.105 mm^2, respectively. This part of the CMAA has been simulated, using static timing analysis on the layout, to run at almost 300 MHz. This means that it is not included in the critical path of the PPP. Since we use registered inputs and outputs in the CAMs, it is the SLUE that will be the critical path of the CMAA.

8.2.4   Control Procedure

The normal packet reception procedure of operation in the CMAA is illustrated in Figure 8.7. The procedure is controlled by the control unit finite-state machine (FSM) in the CMAA.

If an arriving packet is fragmented, the PPP provides CMAA with the IP identification number and gives a new-packet instruction to the CMAA. The IP ID is then stored in the input registers to the PLUE. In the next two clock cycles, the CMAA continues to load ports and IP addresses while the PLUE checks if a fragment of this payload has already been received. If there is a match in the PLUE search, the corresponding address pointer to the buffer in the control memory, which is stored in the PLUE result memory, is stored in the input register to the control memory. While the PPP continues the packet processing, it can then access the control memory directly. If the new fragment contains the layer 4 header, the port, source, and type fields are loaded from the PPP and then checked in the SLUE. If this loading is completed after the PLUE search (i.e., it is an IPv4 packet), the SLUE can immediately check the connection information. Otherwise, the control unit remains in the check connection state while the loading continues. Based on the SLUE result, either the packet is discarded or the matching-connections address pointer is provided to data bus 1. In the next clock cycle, the data bus 1 value will be stored at the packet buffer address, which is already stored in the input register to the control memory.

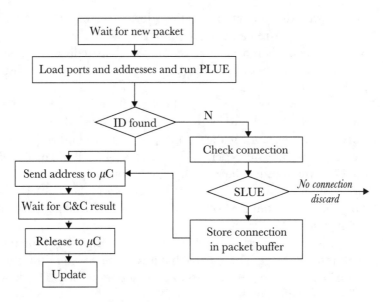

Control-handling procedure within the CMAA.

FIGURE

This means that the μC can easily access the connection information. Then the CMAA hands over to the PPP using the packet-ready flag. After the PPP has received the packet-ready flag, it continues to process the packet and updates the control memory.

After successful packet processing, the PPP releases the packet to the CMAA. In the next clock cycle, the CMAA releases the lock of the control memory, starts buffer pointer updating, and sends the new-packet flag to the μC. During the update state, the CMAA also updates the write address for new entries to the two LUEs. This is only done if a write operation has been performed. During the write address search, the CMAA uses one of the generic adders in the PPP to search for empty entries. When the pointer updating and the CAM write search are finished, the CMAA returns to the wait-for-new-packet state.

8.2.5   Control Memory Organization

The control memory is organized according to Figure 8.8. As illustrated, the control memory consists of a number of different buffers storing inter-packet information. Further, the memory includes all control-oriented packets to be processed in the microcontroller software. Since these protocols are completely

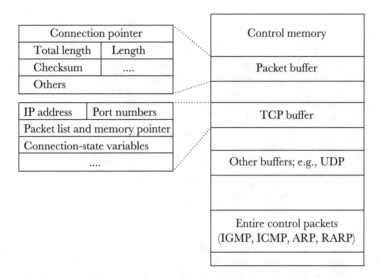

Connection pointer	
Total length	Length
Checksum	....
Others	

IP address	Port numbers
Packet list and memory pointer	
Connection-state variables	
....	

Control memory
Packet buffer
TCP buffer
Other buffers; e.g., UDP
Entire control packets (IGMP, ICMP, ARP, RARP)

8.8   Memory organization in the control memory.

FIGURE

processed by the microcontroller, the payload of these packets is also stored in the control memory. For TCP and UDP packets, only preprocessed header information is stored. In the packet buffers, layer 3 information needed for reassembly is stored. Each packet buffer is deleted when all fragments have arrived.

8.2.6   Lookup Engine Architectures

The SLUE consists of six CAMs, as illustrated by Figure 8.9. The outputs generated by the CAMs are vectors containing 0s or 1s describing table matches. These are used to select the address pointer in the result memory; that is, the control memory address for the received packet.

The seven different CAMs we propose to be used in the CMAA architecture will have a huge impact on the performance, size, and power figures of the entire design. Therefore, they require a thorough investigation and optimization procedure, in order to obtain the optimal system performance. Even if the optimization of these CAMs is not in the scope of this chapter, some characteristics and requirements on the CAMs can be noted. First, we propose that CAMs should be used instead of TCAMs (ternary content-addressable memory) ([8] and [9]). This reduces the cell size and power dissipation. The primary LUE is a

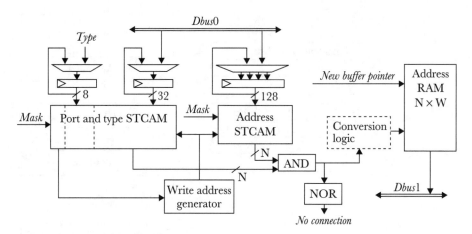

Secondary lookup engine (SLUE) architecture. Note that the conversion logic that converts the matching vector to a result memory address can be eliminated if the matching vector is used directly as word lines in the memory. This, however, requires that the RAM must be implemented in the same manufacturing process.

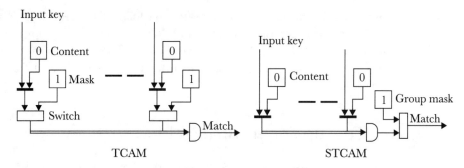

Simplified TCAM principle.

standard CAM memory of 16-bit content and M entries. The result memory is M times the length of the control memory address W.

To provide flexibility for different protocols, we use a concept we call simplified TCAM (STCAM), illustrated in Figure 8.10. Instead of using ternary bit comparisons, as in TCAMs, we provide a wildcard function to the entire CAM. Figure 8.11 shows how the secondary LUE uses the STCAM principle. The mask input enables a wildcard functionality for different fields when recognizing an incoming packet according to Table 8.2. The table shows that the

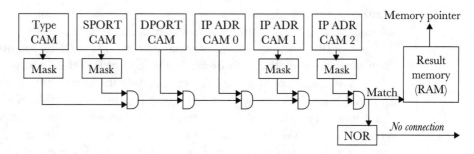

Each of the two STCAMs in the SLUE consists of three ordinary CAMs and masking functions. Each of the CAMs uses N entries.

Protocol examples	Type	Source port	Destination port	Source address	Destination address
IPv6 unicasting	Optional	Optional	16	128	*
IPv6 broad- or multicasting	Optional	Optional	16	*	128
IPv6 alt	Optional	Optional	16	64	64
IPv4	Optional	Optional	16	32	32
IPv4	Optional	Optional	16	32	*
UDP	Optional	16	16		32

Configuration technique using masking.

proposed SLUE architecture can be used for various types of protocols. A careful use of these wildcards is needed in order to avoid multiple matches. By using the type field, which is an internal type, it is possible to avoid multiple matches, which means that the priority logic in the SLUE can be eliminated. Further, it enables the connections to be written in the CAM in an arbitrary order.

It can always be discussed how much the IP version 6 (IPv6) protocol will be used in the future. We have chosen to include it because the penalty is not as severe in network terminals as it is in routers. The reason for this is that in network terminals we have only one destination address to check for unicasting. This can be done in other parts of the PPP. Hence, 128 bits can be excluded from the CAMs entries. For broad- and multicasting packets, a different type field is generated and only the destination is checked (instead of the source address). This reduces the penalty we have to pay in the form of larger CAMs when including IPv6. There exist, however, routers where only 64 bits out of the 128 in the IPv6 address are used for packet classification. The reason is that in such networks the other 64 bits are just a copy of the MAC address. If such a method would be applied, the CAMs can reduce the word length of the content by an additional 64 bits by eliminating the IP address 2, shown in Figure 8.11. Since this architecture will be used in a network terminal, the activity will not be as high in the CAMs as it would be in a router. The reason is that we only do a load and search operation when a new packet arrives, not every clock cycle. The low activity significantly reduces the power consumption in the CAMs.

8.2.7   CAM Implementation Issues

The total size of the seven CAMs and their result memories will be a major part of the system chip area. It is very difficult to make predictions on the sizes of these CAMs, since that is a matter of optimization effort and implementation strategy. Further, the complex placement and routing requires a full custom approach, even for standard cell-based designs. Even without a final layout, a lower bound on the chip area can be estimated. Using standard cells from our design process (AMS 0.35 μm 3.3 V 3-M), an optimized bit-slice cell in a CAM is approximately 350 μm^2, which results in a lower bound on the combined CAM area, according to Equation 8.1. The result memories must store M + N times W bits, using approximately 180 mm^2 each.

$$A_{CAM} = 350 \times (16 \times M + (128 + 40) \times N) + (M + N) \times W \times 18 \,[\mu m^2] \quad (8.1)$$

As an example, M = 16, N = 64, and W = 20 can be considered. The chip area for the two LUEs would then be at least 4 mm^2. This figure is acceptable, but if more entries are to be considered a process migration to smaller geometries is natural. The number of entries to implement is a matter of optimization. This optimization procedure requires a careful analysis of application requirements and network traffic. Nevertheless, it is clear that in NT the required number of network links is not as great as in routers. Hence, M and N do not need to be very large for most applications and networks. To examine our architectural performance, it is crucial to know how many clock cycles each search operation in the two LUEs requires. We expect the system clock to have a period of maximally 7.5 ns in a 0.35-micron process, based on timing analysis on other parts of the PPP. Hence, the maximum network speed is 4.3 Gb/s, using the specified 32-bit-wide input buffers. Since we are sure that there is only one packet being processed at any given time, we do not necessarily need the LUEs to be pipelined; that is, we do not need any internal intermediate results to be stored. Instead, a multicycle-path design technique can be used. To use pipeline stages or not is an implementation issue for CAM designers. Simulations show that the small PLUE will not require more than two clock cycles to complete one search; that is, it has a critical path shorter than 15 ns. Then we assume M is maximally 64. The number of clock cycles required for a search operation in the SLUE is equal to the critical path divided by 7.5 ns. The critical path consists of circuit delays and wire delays. If the SLUEs are being implemented using standard cells, the logic delay is simple to calculate. For N = 64, there will be approximately 15 logic cells in the critical path, which leads us into believing that two clock cycles is enough. The problem is that in larger CAMs a big part of the critical path is wire delay. In our research design (N = 256), we have used synthesis and place and route (P&R) tools from Cadence. The resulting implementation result is very far from optimal and does not meet a requirement of three clock cycles. The design is simply too large, and hence the P&R problem is too complex. Therefore, the conclusion is that the design strategy must be changed to something more custom-oriented, even if the CAM is rather small compared to the one used in routers. Clearly, a bit-slice manipulating placement strategy has to be used for efficient CAM design, regardless of the size. The conclusion after studies of other comparable CAM designs and discussion with industry CAM designers is that for N less than or equal to 256, a search operation will require maximally four clock cycles (or pipeline stages). For N = 64, three clock cycles is definitely enough. These figures apply to standard cell-based designs.

Even with a pessimistic feature size projection, there is no reason to believe that scaling cannot support the CMAA to run at clock periods around 3 ns using three clock cycles for one search operation. Hence, the CMAA could be used in a 10-Gb/s network such as 10-Gigabit Ethernet, using already available processes (e.g., 0.13 micron). The resulting latency for CMAA operations is further discussed in the next section.

The latency, critical path, and power consumption in the LUE are of course dependent on M, N, and W. To optimize these variables, simulation on real-world network traffic is required. Until this optimization phase is completed, the numbers M = 16, N = 64, and W = 20 will be considered for further architectural development.

8.2.8   Latency

The proposed control memory architecture has an access latency of a few clock cycles. The fast-path latency determines how large the input buffer chain has to

Layer 3 protocol	Number of clock cycles for CMAA operation, three-stage SLUE	Number of clock cycles for CMAA operation, four-stage SLUE
IPv4; new packet	9	10
IPv4; old packet, new fragment	4	4
IPv6; new packet	11	12
IPv6; old packet, new fragment	4	4

8.3

TABLE

Memory access latency for various packets received (PLUE requires two clock cycles to perform a search).

be. The latency of the CMAA must be added to the latency of the PPP in order to calculate the total fast-path latency. We propose that the SLUE should use three clock cycles to perform a search. A three-clock-cycle type of SLUE would give a maximum memory access latency of 11, according to Table 8.3, when a new packet has been received. Further, the table shows that a four-cycle type of CAM architecture will give a maximum memory access latency of 12 clock cycles. This of course has an impact on the pipeline register chain in the PPP and the total latency for a packet reception and delivery to the microcontroller.

The PPP can start the processing of an incoming packet before the control data has been accessed from the control memory. Therefore, this latency only sets a lower limit on the latency of the total packet reception. The total latency is, however, mainly dependent on the processing activities, including interrupts and stalls, in the microcontroller.

8.2.9   Enabling Flow-Based QoS

Using the fast-control memory access, it is possible to enable quality of service (QoS) to the reception. Any kind of priority parameters or flow parameters can be stored in the different buffers in the control memory. These can then be used for multiplexing of the incoming data stream, if a flow-based operation is demanded.

8.2.10   Shared Control Memory

The motivation for separating the protocol processing into one PPP part and one μC part is of course to use the programmability of the μC when processing control-intensive tasks, and still have high performance and low power implementation of the data-intensive processing. This distributed architecture, however, requires an interface, and that interface is the control memory unit together with control flags to and from the C&C. As mentioned previously, the PPP need only access the memory when a new packet is received, and then only a limited part of the control information is used. Since the latency of this access directly affects the length of the input buffer chain, the PPP must have priority over the μC when it comes to memory access. In fact, the μC has access to the control memory only when the CMAA resides in the update or wait-for-new-packet state, according to Figure 8.7.

8.3   SYSTEM PERFORMANCE

Each hardware acceleration block in the PPP has been separately implemented and simulated using static timing analysis. The conclusion is that they can operate at network speeds of more than 170 MHz. Since all parts of the fast path operate on streaming data, the network can run at this clock frequency. The fast-path architecture processes each packet, delivers data and control signals to the microcontroller, and then returns to idle mode. When the fast path (i.e., the C&C) has returned to idle mode, it can start processing the next packets. Hence, the proposed fast-path architecture can operate in high-speed networks as long as the gap between the incoming packets is sufficient for the processor to return to idle mode. This must be supported by the network protocol. Hence, better solutions are to use either an input packet buffer or multiple protocol processors that are hardware multiplexed.

The slow path consists of the microcontroller, which is flexible enough to fully offload the TCP and protocols alike. The microcontroller is not capable of processing the packets at wire speed. This may limit the performance of the entire system for extreme traffic situations. The fast path does, however, offload some of the tasks traditionally processed on general-purpose hardware. This will relax the slow path. The amount of offloading depends on the traffic flow and requires further simulations. To verify the functionality of the CMAA block used as proposed in a fast path, a cycle-true and bit-true behavioral model has been simulated. The simulation model covers the fast-path packet reception. In the model, the C&C has been modeled as a simple version of the architecture presented in [10]. The principle is represented in Figure 8.12. The C&C is modeled as a program counter (PC), which selects instructions in the program memory. These instructions are then decoded to produce all control signals in the PPP. To make conditional jumps without losing any clock cycles, a programmable

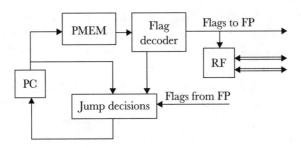

Conceptual model of the counter and controller.

jump decision block calculates the next PC value based on the current PC value and result flags from the rest of the PPP. This architecture supports wire-speed processing of non-fragmented packets.

The model includes a GMII network interface (32-bit-wide input). Further, a behavioral model of the CMAA (including 16-entry, three-stage pipeline CAMs) has been used.

So far, the only protocols simulated are TCP and IPv4. Fast-path tasks simulated include CRC, IP reassembly, checksum calculation, and data stream demultiplexing. The C&C is programmed to cover these protocols using the program memory in the C&C model. The network traffic simulated is random.

The simulations verify that the proposed CMAA architecture can be used in the protocol processor environment. Further, they show that when programmed for TCP the minimal distance allowed between two packets is 23 clock cycles (the ideal is none). In addition to this limitation, the simulations also show that the minimal number of clock cycles required per received Ethernet packet processed is 38. The decision latency in the CMAA contributes to this figure. These architectural limitations strongly affect the performance compared to an ideal solution, especially for small packets, which represent the worst case. The overall system performance is, on the other hand, largely dependent on network traffic. If the traffic does not include many fragmented packets, the CMAA may not be worth using due to performance degradation. In that case, a PPP without CMAA acceleration should be used.

To illustrate how much processing is offloaded from the slow path using a CMAA, we can count microcode instructions needed for an address check using a general-purpose RISC machine. Assume that there are N possible addresses we have to check against a received address. The setup requires four instructions for loading addresses and a loop variable. Then 6N instructions are needed for a comparison loop. With N = 16 entries, 100 instructions are needed in the worst case. Thirty-two of them are conditional jumps. This processing is performed on every received packet, which is just a small part of the CMAA processing.

8.4   CONCLUSIONS

A novel architecture for acceleration of control memory access in a protocol processor for network terminals was presented. The architecture uses classification engines and concepts that have traditionally been used for network infrastructure components. The proposed architecture enables low-latency access to connection-state variables, partial checksum results, and any other control information stored in the shared control memory. Hence, inter-packet processing, such as reassembly, has been accelerated using the proposed architecture in network terminals. This enables efficient processing of fragmented packets in a network terminal. Further, the architecture offloads the slow path, which is very important in high-speed networks. The proposed architecture can process the fast path in a multi-gigabit network, implemented in a mature standard cell process such as AMS 0.35 μm. Simulations do, however, show that the protocol processor requires increased packet gaps, input buffering, or the use of multiple hardware-multiplexed port processors in order to manage fragmented packets. This increased hardware and complexity cost has to be compared to the benefits of accepting fragmented packets.

8.5   FURTHER WORK

To complete the specification of the protocol processor, three main research areas remain. The first one is to specify the interface between the μC and the host system and its DMA. Second, the C&C unit is not finally implemented and programmed. The third issue regards the configuration method of the protocol processor. What does the programming and reconfiguration interface look like from the μC?

ACKNOWLEDGMENTS

This research was funded by the ECSEL Graduate Research School and TFF, the Swedish Scientific Research Foundation.

REFERENCES

[1]   D. Liu, U. Nordqvist, and C. Svensson, "Configuration-Based Architecture for High-Speed and General-Purpose Protocol-Processing," *Proceedings of IEEE Signal Processing Systems*, 1999, Taipei, Taiwan, pp. 540–547.

[2]   T. Henrikson, U. Nordqvist, and D. Liu, "Specification of a Configurable General-Purpose Protocol-Processor," *Proceedings of CSNDSP 2000*, Bournemouth, England.

[3]   A. S. Tannenbaum, *Computer Networks*. 3d. ed., ISBN 0-13-349945-6, Prentice Hall PRT, 1996.

[4]   U. Nordqvist, T. Henriksson, and D. Liu, "CRC Generation for Protocol Processing," *NORCHIP 2000*, Turku, Finland.

[5]   A. McAuley et al., "Fast Routing Table Lookup Using CAMs," *IEEE INFOCOM '93*, Mar. 1993.

[6]   P. Steenkiste, "A Systematic Approach to Host Interface Design for High-Speed Networks," *IEEE Computer*, vol. 27, no. 3: 47–57, Mar. 1994.

[7]   M. B. Abbott and L. L. Peterson, "Increasing Network Throughput by Integrating Protocol Layers," *IEEE/ACM Transactions on Networking*, vol. 1, 1993, pp. 600–610.

[8]   J. van Lunteren and A. P. J. Engbersen, "Multi-field Packet Classification Using Ternary CAM," *Electronics Letters*, vol. 38 no. 1, Jan. 3, 2002, pp. 21–23.

[9]   N-F. Huang et al., "Design of Multi-field IPv6 Packet Classifiers Using Ternary CAMs," *GLOBECOM'01. IEEE*, vol. 3, 2001, pp. 1877–1881.

[10]   T. Henriksson, U. Nordqvist, and D. Liu, "Embedded Protocol Processor for Fast and Efficient Packet Reception," *Proceedings of the International Conference on Computer Design*, Sep. 16–18, 2002, Freiburg, Germany, pp. 414–419.

9 | NP-Click: A Programming Model for the Intel IXP1200

Niraj Shah, William Plishker, Kurt Keutzer
University of California, Berkeley

The past five years have witnessed over 30 attempts at programmable solutions for packet processing [1]. With these architectures, network processor designers have employed a large variety of hardware techniques to accelerate packet processing, including parallel processing, special-purpose hardware, heterogeneous memory architectures, on-chip communication mechanisms, and the use of peripherals [2]. However, despite this architectural innovation, relatively little effort has been made to make these architectures easily programmable. In fact, these architectures are very difficult to program [3].

The current practice of programming network processors is to use assembly language or a subset of C. This low-level approach to programming places a large burden on the programmer to understand fine details of the architecture simply to implement a packet-processing application, let alone optimize it. We believe the programmer should be able to implement an application using a natural interface, such as a domain-specific language. To accomplish this, we need an *abstraction* of the underlying hardware that exposes enough architectural detail to write efficient code for that platform, while hiding less essential architectural complexity. We call this abstraction a *programming model*.

Our goal is to create an abstraction that enables the programmer to realize the full computational power of the underlying hardware. We realize our programming model will initially introduce some implementation inefficiencies versus a hand-coded approach. However, our programming model offers a compelling design flow that produces implementations that are within 10% of the performance of a hand-coded approach (for a realistic packet mix) at a fraction of the design time.

Further, we believe network processors are just one example of a broader trend of the search for application-specific solutions with fast time-to-market. This trend is drawing system designers away from the time-consuming and risky process of designing application-specific integrated circuits (ASICs) and toward programming application-specific instruction processors (ASIPs). As system designers increasingly adopt programmable platforms, we believe the *programming model* will be a key aspect to harnessing the power of these new architectures and allowing system designers to make the transition away from ASICs.

This chapter describes NP-Click, a programming model for a common network processor, the Intel IXP1200. We illustrate our approach by using NP-Click to implement an IPv4 packet forwarder.

The chapter is organized as follows. Section 9.1 describes some background. Section 9.2 introduces and motivates the notion of a programming model. Section 9.3 describes our programming model for the Intel IXP1200. We report our results in Section 9.4. Finally, we summarize and comment on future research directions in Sections 9.5 and 9.6, respectively.

9.1   BACKGROUND

In this section, we describe some relevant background to our work. We first give an overview of Click, a domain-specific language and infrastructure for developing networking applications, upon which our programming model is based. Next, we describe the Intel IXP1200, the target architecture for our application.

9.1.1   Click

Click is a domain-specific language designed for describing networking applications [4]. It is based on a set of simple principles tailored for the networking community. Applications in Click are built by composing computational tasks, or elements, which correspond to common networking operations like classification, route table lookup, and header verification. Elements have input and output ports that define communication with other elements. Ports are connected via edges that represent packet flow between elements.

In Click, there are two types of communication between ports: push and pull. Push communication is initiated by the source element and effectively models the arrival packets into the system. Pull communication is initiated by the sink and often models space available in hardware resources for egress packet flow. Click designs are often composed of paths of push elements and paths of pull elements. Push paths and pull paths connect through special elements that have input and output ports of different types. The *Queue* element, for example, has

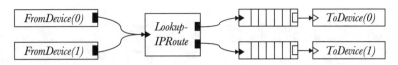

9.1   Click diagram of a two-port packet forwarder.

FIGURE

a push input but a pull output, while the *Unqueue* element has a pull input but a push output.

Figure 9.1 shows a Click diagram of a simple two-port packet forwarder. The boxes represent elements. The small triangles and rectangles within elements represent input and output ports, respectively. Filled ports are push ports, while empty ports are pull ports. The arrows between ports represent packet flow.

Click is implemented on Linux using C++ classes to define elements. Element communication is implemented with virtual function calls to neighboring elements. To execute a Click description, a task scheduler is synthesized to run all push (pull) paths by firing their sources (sinks), called schedulable elements.

A natural extension of this Click implementation is to multiprocessor architectures that may take advantage of the inherent parallelism in processing packet flows. A multithreaded version of Click targets a Linux implementation and uses worklists to schedule computation [5]. Two pertinent conclusions can be drawn from this work. First, significant concurrency may be gleaned from Click designs in which the application designer has made no special effort to express it. Since packet streams are generally independent, ingress packets may be processed by separate threads with very little interaction. Second, a Click configuration may easily be altered to express additional concurrency without changing the application's functionality.

9.1.2   Intel IXP1200

The IXP1200 [6] family is one of Intel's recent network processor product lines based on their Internet Exchange Architecture. It has six RISC processors, called microengines, plus a StrongARM processor (see Figure 9.2). The microengines are geared for data plane processing and have hardware support for four threads that share a program memory. The StrongARM is mostly used to handle control and management plane operations. The memory architecture is divided into several regions: large off-chip SDRAM, faster external SRAM, internal scratchpad, and local register files for each microengine. Each of these areas is under

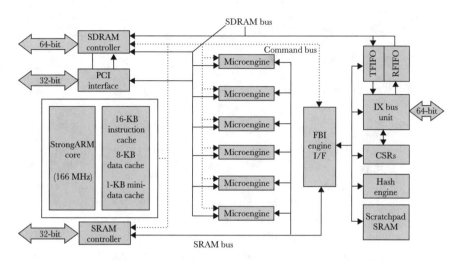

Intel IXP1200 architecture.

software control and there is no hardware support for caching data from slower memory into smaller, faster memory (except for the small cache accessible only to the StrongARM). The IX bus (an Intel proprietary bus) is the main interface for receiving and transmitting data with external devices such as MACs and other IXP1200s. It is 64 bits wide and runs up to 104 MHz, allowing for a maximum throughput of 6.6 Gb/s. The microengines can directly interact with the IX bus through an IX bus unit, so a thread running on a microengine may receive or transmit data on any port without StrongARM intervention. This interaction is performed via transmit and receive FIFOs, which are circular buffers that allow data transfers directly to/from SDRAM. For the microengines to interact with peripherals (e.g., to determine their state), they need to query or write to control status registers (CSRs). Accessing control status registers requires issuing commands across the command bus, which is also used for issuing hash engine, scratchpad memory, and transmit and receive FIFO commands.

Initially, the programming interface provided with the IXP1200 was an assembler. This was later augmented with a subset of the C language (which we refer to as IXP-C) [7]. IXP-C supports loops, conditionals, functions, types, and intrinsics (function calls using C syntax that call assembler instructions). However, it has several notable deficiencies: it does not support function pointers, it lacks recursion, and it forces the user to control thread swapping. In addition, for practical implementations, the programmer must effectively allocate data to the multiple-memory regions (SDRAM, SRAM, scratchpad, data registers, transfer registers), arbitrate access to shared resources by multiple threads, divide code among threads, interact with peripherals, and take advantage of the concurrency inherent in the application. We believe this places undue burden on the programmer to generate even a functional implementation of an application, let alone an efficient one. It is this concern that motivates our own new layer to sit atop IXP-C.

9.2   PROGRAMMING MODELS

There is currently a large gap between domain-specific languages that provide programmers a natural interface, such as Click, and the complex programmable architectures used for implementation, such as Intel's IXP1200. In this section, we introduce and define the concept of a *programming model* to assist in bridging this gap.

9.2.1   Implementation Gap

We believe Click to be a natural environment for describing packet-processing applications. Ideally, we would like to map applications described in Click directly to the Intel IXP1200. However, there is currently a large gap between Click and the low-level programming interface the IXP1200 exposes. The simple, yet powerful, concept of push and pull communication between elements that communicate only via passing packets, coupled with the rich library of elements of Click, provides a natural abstraction that aids designers in creating a functional description of their application. This is in stark contrast to the main concepts required to program the IXP1200. When implementing an application on this device, the programmer must carefully determine how to effectively partition his application across the six microengines, make use of special-purpose hardware, effectively arbitrate shared resources, and communicate with peripherals. We call this mismatch of concerns between the application model and target architecture the *implementation gap* (see Figure 9.3). To facilitate bridging this gap, we propose an intermediate layer, called a *programming model*, which presents a powerful abstraction of the underlying architecture while still providing a natural way of describing applications.

9.2.2   What Is a Programming Model?

A programming model presents an abstraction that exposes only the relevant details of the architecture necessary for a programmer to efficiently implement

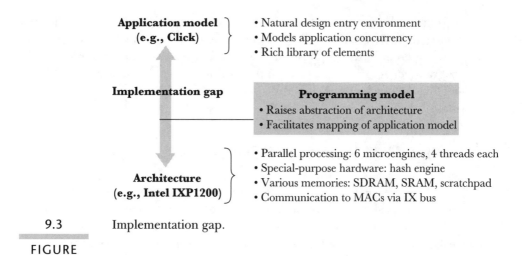

Application model
(e.g., Click)
• Natural design entry environment
• Models application concurrency
• Rich library of elements

Implementation gap

Programming model
• Raises abstraction of architecture
• Facilitates mapping of application model

Architecture
(e.g., Intel IXP1200)
• Parallel processing: 6 microengines, 4 threads each
• Special-purpose hardware: hash engine
• Various memories: SDRAM, SRAM, scratchpad
• Communication to MACs via IX bus

9.3   Implementation gap.

FIGURE

an application. It is a programmer's view of the architecture that balances opacity and visibility, described in the following.

+ *Opacity: Abstract the underlying architecture*. This obviates the need for the programmer to learn intricate details of architecture just to begin programming the device.

+ *Visibility: Enable design space exploration of implementations*. This allows the programmer to improve the efficiency of their implementation by trading off different design parameters (e.g., thread boundaries, data locality, and implementation of elements). Our goal is that the full computational power of a target device should always be realizable through the programming model.

In summary, a programming model supplies an approach to harvesting the power of the platform. It is a more productive way of harvesting that power. A programming model will inevitably balance between a programmer's two competing needs: desire for ease of programming and the requirement for efficient implementation. Further, we believe the programming model is a necessary, but not sufficient, condition of closing the implementation gap.

9.2.3   Possible Approaches to Solving the Implementation Gap

There are many different approaches to solving the implementation gap. We classify prior works in this area into four major areas: library of application components, programming-language approach, refinement from formal models of computation (MOCs), and runtime systems. In this section, we describe and evaluate these alternatives.

The *library of application components approach* exports a collection of manually designed blocks to the application programmer, who stitches these together to create her application. The advantage of such an approach is a better mapping to the underlying hardware, since the components are hand-coded. In addition, these components implement an abstraction that is natural for an application writer, as the components are often similar to application model primitives. The disadvantage of this approach is the need to implement every element of the library by hand. If only a limited number of library elements are needed, this approach may be successful. However, in practice we suspect a large number of elements are needed as application diversity grows. This problem is further compounded when a number of variants of each library element are needed [8].

A *programming-language approach* utilizes a programming language that can be compiled to the target architecture. With this approach, a compiler needs to be written only once for the target architecture and all compiler optimizations can be applied to all applications written for the architecture. The principal difficulty with this approach is the requirement to compile to heterogeneous architectures with multiple processors, special-purpose hardware, numerous task-specific memories, and various buses. In addition, the programming abstraction required to effectively create a compiler for such architectures would likely force the programming language to include many architectural concepts that would be unnatural for the application programmer. Examples of this alternative include the numerous projects that have altered the C programming language by exposing architectural features [7, 9].

Another class of approaches uses *refinement from formal MOCs* to implement applications. Models of computation define formal semantics for communication and concurrency. Examples of common MOCs include Kahn Process Networks [10], synchronous data flow [11], and discrete event. Because they require applications to be described in an MOC, these approaches are able to prove properties of the application (such as maximum queue sizes required and static schedules that satisfy timing constraints). This class of solutions also emphasizes application modeling and simulation [12]. The disadvantage of this method is that implementation on heterogeneous architectures is inefficient because most implementation paths require significant compiler support. As an example, Edwards has written a compiler to implement designs described in Esterel, a language that implements the synchronous/reactive MOC [13]. However, his work generates C code and relies on a C compiler for implementation on target architectures [14]. In addition, the MOCs used by these approaches may not be natural design entry environments. For example, POLIS requires all applications to be expressed in co-design finite-state machines [12].

Runtime systems offer another category of solutions to the implementation gap. Runtime systems introduce dynamic operation (e.g., thread scheduling) that enables additional freedom in implementation. Dynamic operation can also be used to present the programmer with an abstraction of the underlying architecture (e.g., a view of infinite resources). While runtime systems are necessary for general-purpose computation, for many data-oriented embedded applications (such as data plane processing) they introduce additional overhead at runtime. Additionally, some ASIP architectures have included hardware constructs to subsume simple runtime system tasks such as thread scheduling on the IXP1200 and inter-processor communication (ring buffers on the Intel IXP2800 [15]). Examples of this approach include VxWorks [16] and the programming interface for the Broadcom Calisto [17].

Based on the trade-offs between the previously cited approaches, we propose a programming model that is a hybrid of the application component library and programming-language approaches. We describe our approach in the next section.

9.3   DESCRIPTION OF NP-CLICK

In this section, we describe NP-Click, our programming model as implemented on the Intel IXP1200. NP-Click combines an efficient abstraction of the target architecture with features of a domain-specific language for networking. The result is a natural abstraction that enables programmers to quickly write efficient code. The model is designed to ease three major difficulties of programming network processors: taking advantage of hardware parallelism, arbitration of shared resources, and efficient data layout. This section describes the main components of the programming model: elements and their communication, threading, and arbitration of shared resources. We also give hints for using NP-Click to arrive at an efficient implementation.

9.3.1   Overview of the Model

Our programming model integrates concepts from Click to provide a natural design entry environment and an abstraction of the IXP1200 architecture in order to leverage the computational power of the device.

To describe applications, we borrow Click's simple yet powerful abstraction of elements communicating by passing packets via push and pull semantics. Since our initial studies of the IXP1200 architecture showed the importance of multithreading to hide memory and communication latency, we chose to export thread boundaries directly to the application programmer.

Unlike Click's implementation, elements in our programming model are implemented in IXP-C, the subset of C the IXP1200 supports. In addition, due to the performance impact of data layout on the target architecture (between registers, scratchpad, SRAM, and SDRAM), our implementation enables the programmer to effectively use these memories. Since the IXP1200 has separate program memories for each microengine, we allow multiple implementations of the same element of a design to exploit additional application concurrency. However, since most data memory is shared among microengines, the programmer must specify which data are shared among these instances and which data can be duplicated. We also provide the programmer with a machine API that hides pitfalls of the architecture and exports a more natural abstraction for unique memory features and co-processors. In addition, we provide a library that abstracts shared resources to separate the problem of arbitration from computation.

9.3.2 Elements

Computation in our programming model is described in a fashion similar to Click, with modular blocks, called elements, which are sequential blocks of code that generally encapsulate particular packet-processing functions. However, in our model elements are defined using IXP-C, keywords for memory layout, and a machine API that provides key abstractions of low-level architectural details of the IXP1200.

Before describing the details of our programming model, it is important to understand the distinction among *elements*, *types*, and, *instances*. An *element* is a defined functional block within a design that has a *type*, which defines its functionality and the semantics of its ports. There may be multiple elements of the same type in a design. An *instance* is an implementation of an element. Depending on an application's mapping onto the target architecture, an element may have multiple instances to exploit parallelism.

Figure 9.4 shows a small Click network that illustrates the difference among type, element, and instance. The boxes in the diagram represent elements. *FromDevice(0)* and *FromDevice(1)* are multiple elements of the same type. *LookupIPRoute* is a single element with multiple instances (i.e., it is implemented by thread 0 and thread 1).

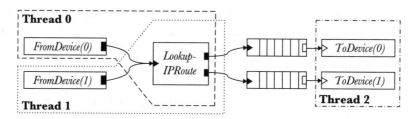

9.4

FIGURE
Example packet forwarder with thread boundaries.

Data layout

As a significant portion of implementation speed is due to memory access latency, we provide some mechanisms when describing an element to guide memory layout.

To separate memory layout concerns from computation, we supply a facility to describe data by its scope. We provide four data descriptors:

+ *Universal*: Data shared among all types.

+ *Global*: Data shared among all elements of a specific type.

+ *Regional*: Data shared among all instances of a specific element.

+ *Local*: Data local to an instance.

The *universal* data descriptor describes data that needs to be accessible by all elements. Since this descriptor breaks the element abstraction, we aim to minimize the use of this descriptor. To date, we have not encountered applications that require this construct. We suspect it will mostly be used as an optimization.

Global data descriptors are used for data that must be shared across all elements of a given type. It could be used for a shared hardware resource that all elements of a particular type must use. For example, metering elements need to access a clock to determine the rate of packet flow.

Since elements in a Click design may be instantiated multiple times for performance reasons, the *regional* modifier describes data within an element that must be shared across instantiations. For example, a *LookupIPRoute* element, which looks up the destination port of a packet, requires a large amount of storage for the routing table. As a result, to implement multiple threads that contain instances of the *LookupIPRoute* element without duplicating the entire routing table in memory, as shown in Figure 9.4, the lookup table must be shared among the instances but not different *LookupIPRoute* elements.

The *local* data descriptor is used for the state local to an element that need not be shared across multiple instantiations of an element. Examples of this type include temporary variables and loop counters.

Our abstraction is built on top of the *declspec* construct used in IXP-C to bind data to a particular memory (e.g., SRAM, SDRAM, and scratchpad) at compile time. This may be used by the programmer for additional visibility into the memory architecture to improve performance of the implementation by specifying, for example, that certain large data structures, such as routing tables, be placed in a large memory.

Machine API

In addition to data descriptors, our programming model hides some of the nuances of the Intel IXP1200 architecture. These abstractions are used in conjunction with IXP-C to describe computation within an element.

The IXP1200 implements special-purpose hardware for tasks that are commonly executed in software. To shield the programmer from the details of interacting with these hardware blocks, we export an application-level abstraction that encapsulates common uses of the hardware. For example, the IXP1200 has eight LIFO (last-in, first-out) registers that implement the common stack operations (*push* and *pop*) in a single atomic operation. However, these operations do not, for example, perform bounds checking or thread safety checks. We implement a lightweight memory management system that exposes a natural interface—namely, *malloc()* and *free()*—which makes use of the LIFO registers to implement a thread-safe freelist that performs bounds checking. These abstractions enable the programmer to reap the performance advantage of special-purpose hardware without understanding particulars of their implementation.

9.3.3 Communication

Our programming model borrows the communication abstraction from Click [4]: elements communicate only by passing packets with push or pull semantics. However, our implementation of this abstraction is quite different from that of the Click software.

We define a common packet data layout that all elements use. We use a packet descriptor, allocated to SRAM, which stores the destination port and the size of the packet. The packet itself is stored in SDRAM. We define methods for reading and writing packet-header fields and packet bodies, so these implementation details are hidden from the user.

As an optimization, we implement the packet communication by function calls that pass a pointer to the packet descriptor and not the packet itself. We enforce that compute elements not send the same packet to multiple output ports, to ensure that only one element is processing a particular packet at any given time. The packet data layout provides an abstraction that efficiently communicates packets among elements, but shields the programmer from the specifics of the IXP1200's memory architecture.

9.3.4   Threading

Arriving at the right allocation of elements to threads is another key aspect to achieving higher performance. Thus, we enable the programmer to easily explore different mappings of elements to threads on the IXP1200. While we believe this task may be automated in the future, given the great performance impact of properly utilizing threads, we make thread boundaries visible to the programmer.

As observed in [5], paths of push (pull) elements can be executed in the same thread by simply calling the source (sink). We implement a similar mechanism, however, because of the fixed number of threads on the IXP1200. We also allow the programmer to map multiple paths to a single thread. To implement this, we synthesize a scheduler that fires each path within that thread. For example, to implement the design shown in Figure 9.4, we would synthesize a round-robin scheduler for the schedulable elements in thread 2 (*ToDevice(0)* and *ToDevice(1)*). We hide the details of how to implement multiple schedulable elements within a thread from the user, but still give them the power to define thread boundaries at the element level.

9.3.5   Arbitration of Shared Resources

The amount of parallelism present in the target architecture places pressure on shared resources. For example, the IXP1200 has 24 threads that may each simultaneously request a control status register. Such situations lead to potential hazards that necessitate arbitration schemes for sharing resources. To recognize the importance of sharing common resources, we separate arbitration schemes from computation and present them as interfaces to the elements. The two main resources that require arbitration on the IXP1200 are control status registers and the transmit FIFO.

Control status registers are used to communicate with the MACs (e.g., determining which ingress ports have new data, or which egress ports have space).

Our experiments have shown access times to the control status registers ranging from 9 to >200 clock cycles, with multiple simultaneous accesses sometimes leading to deadlock. The variability is due to contention on a common bus (the command bus) used for issuing SDRAM, SRAM, scratchpad, IX bus, and control status register commands. This bus quickly saturates with multiple threads checking the status of the MAC at the same time. This variability is a critical factor in determining performance, and is one of the major difficulties of programming the IXP1200. To eliminate the need for the programmer to cope with this variability, we implement a per-microengine restriction on the number of concurrent control status register accesses. If a thread attempts to access a control status register while the maximum threshold of accesses is outstanding, a context swap is performed and another thread is loaded. While this may reduce overall microengine computational efficiency, it significantly reduces the variability in control status register access times. This abstraction wraps all reads and writes to the control status registers and is transparent to the programmer. This gives the user enough visibility to interact with peripherals efficiently while not allowing him to saturate the command bus.

The transmit FIFO (TFIFO) is the principal mechanism for sending data off-chip that is shared by all threads. It is a 16-entry buffer used to queue data to be sent to the MAC. Each entry in the buffer has a flag that indicates whether that entry contains valid data. Microengines send data to the MAC by loading data into a TFIFO buffer entry and then setting the valid flag. A hardware state machine in the IX bus interface steps through the TFIFO as a circular buffer, waiting at each entry for the valid flag to be set. Once the valid flag is set for the current entry, the data in the entry is sent to the MAC and the state machine steps to the next entry. Microengines may query the valid flags and the entry the state machine is currently pointing to. Due to the unique nature of the TFIFO and the numerous threads that may be accessing it, managing the arbitration to this resource is a difficult problem. Perhaps the simplest arbitration scheme is to map *a priori* each port to one entry in the TFIFO. This eliminates the overhead associated with runtime coordination between elements but does not scale to applications with more than 16 ports. In addition, this scheme only performs well on an evenly distributed packet mix, as the state machine will wait at a TFIFO entry even if there are no data to be sent on that port, thereby slowing the entire system. A slightly more complicated scheme that avoids these limitations is to allow threads to check out any entry in the TFIFO. This requires a variable in shared memory to coordinate the free locations and mutex locking and unlocking. While this is able to scale functionally and can better handle a burst of data on a port, it imposes significant runtime overhead. To allow different arbitration schemes, we present an interface of the TFIFO to the elements.

The implementation of this interface can be customized by the user without modifying the elements themselves.

9.3.6   Hints for Efficient Implementation

While NP-Click uses modularity to provide a productive method to implement networking applications, this incurs some performance overhead. In this section, we describe some hints for using NP-Click to achieve efficient implementations.

First, an element may exist in a thread that has multiple push paths or pull paths to service. To ensure the thread is making progress, elements should yield control when waiting on a long-latency activity to complete or an intermittent event to occur. This is a coarser version of swapping threads on a multithreaded processor to hide memory access latency. For example, *ToDevice* often polls the MAC to determine whether to send more data. In this case, it is better for a thread if *ToDevice* checks the MAC once, then (if false) moves to another schedulable element. Whereas a multithreaded processor may implement thread swapping with multiple program counters and a partitioned memory space, swapping at the element level may be performed with static variables in an element instance.

While the programming model as presented may be sufficient for some applications, we concede it will fall short for others. As part of the path to final implementation, we provide facilities to further improve performance. These may include configuration-specific enhancements that might be encapsulated in a single element or optimizations across elements (such as a specific scheduler for a set of schedulable elements). The enhancements we have used to date are minor changes to a single element or small modifications of arbitration schemes that greatly improve performance. By using NP-Click, the programmer is able to quickly pinpoint performance bottlenecks in the implementation.

9.4   RESULTS

We explore the effectiveness of our programming model by using it to describe the data plane of an IPv4 router and implementing this application on an Intel IXP1200. This section describes the application we implemented, the experimental setup used to gather data, and our results for maximum data rates for numerous packet mixes.

9.4.1   Application Description

To test our programming model, we used it to implement the data plane of a 16-port Fast Ethernet IP version 4 router [18]. This application is based on the network processor benchmark specified in [19]. The major requirements of our application are as follows:

+ A packet arriving on port P is to be examined and forwarded on a different port P'. The next-hop location that implies P' is determined through a longest prefix match (LPM) on the IPv4 destination address field.

+ The packet header and payload are checked for validity, and packet header fields checksum and TTL (time to live) are updated.

+ Packet queue sizes and buffers can be optimally configured for the network processor architecture unless large buffer sizes interfere with the ability to measure sustained performance.

+ The network processor must maintain all non-fixed tables (i.e., tables for route lookup) in memory that can be updated with minimal intrusion to the application.

+ Routing tables should be able to address any valid IPv4 destination address and should support next-hop information for up to 64,000 destinations simultaneously.

Figure 9.5 shows a graphical representation of the Click description of the router. We allocate 16 threads (four microengines) for receiving packets and eight threads (two microengines) for transmitting packets.

9.4.2   Testing Procedure

To test our implementation, we used a software architecture simulator of the IXP1200 assuming a microengine clock rate of 200 MHz and an IX bus clock rate of 100 MHz. Our simulation environment also modeled two 8-port Fast Ethernet MACs (Intel IXF440s) connected to the IX bus. For each port, the IXF440 has 256-byte internal buffers for both ingress and egress traffic.

For measuring performance, we strived to create a realistic testing environment. We tested the router with a 1000-entry routing table whose entries were chosen at random. The destinations of the input packet streams are randomly distributed evenly across output ports. We tested performance with packet streams composed of a single packet size (64, 128, 256, 512, 1024, 1280, and 1518 bytes) and the IETF Benchmarking Methodology Workgroup mix [20].

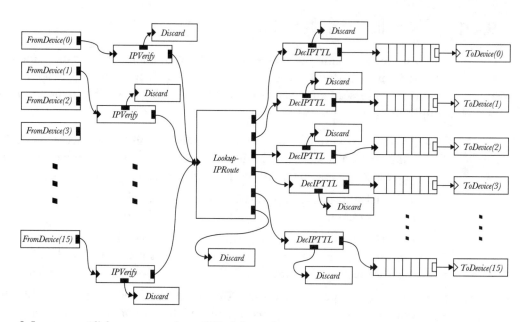

9.5

Click representation of IPv4 data plane.

FIGURE

We considered the router to be functional at a certain data rate if it had a steady-state transmit rate that was within 1% of the receive rate without dropping any packets. We defined *steady state* to be a long interval of time at which data were being constantly received on all ports and data were always ready to be sent on all ports (i.e., no output port was starved).

For each input packet stream, we measured the maximum sustainable data rate. We tested two different implementations of the router: one that includes a hand-coded optimization and one that does not. The optimization was a better arbitration scheme for the transmit FIFO that did not use shared memory. Our results are shown in Figure 9.6.

9.4.3 Interpretation of Results

As Figure 9.6 shows, our packet-forwarding implementation without optimizations achieves the same performance regardless of packet size. For this implementation, packet processing is not the bottleneck. Rather, the limitation is a result of the simple arbitration scheme used for the transmit FIFO. The scheme uses a shared variable among all *ToDevice* elements, which requires a locking mechanism to access and update. As a result, the transmit threads spend

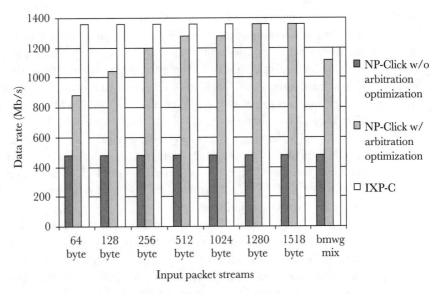

9.6   IPv4 packet-forwarding results.

FIGURE

the majority of their time attempting to acquire this lock. To alleviate this contention, we wrote a configuration-specific arbitration scheme that uses an *a priori* partitioning of the transmit FIFO, which obviates the need for the global variable to be shared across all *ToDevice* elements. Because of NP-Click's separation of computation and arbitration, this hand-coded optimization was simple to implement, as it was fully contained within the transmit FIFO library and thus no change to the *ToDevice* element was necessary.

This new scheme results in a much higher maximum data rate across all packet sizes. We believe this illustrates a typical usage of the programming model: NP-Click will be used to quickly gain functional correctness. Performance bottlenecks in the NP-Click implementation are identified, and where needed, hand-coded optimizations will be resorted to. In our experience, these optimizations are easy to implement and localized to an element or a thread.

Comparison of our implementation to published results is difficult because relatively few are available for the Intel IXP1200. Of those results, little information is given about their experimental setup (e.g., IXP1200 and IX bus clock speed, peripherals used, size of routing table, and data rate measurement methodology). These details can have an enormous impact on the reported performance. Hence, for comparison to another implementation we hand-coded the entire application in IXP-C based on the reference design supplied by

Intel [21]. The results of this implementation are also given in Figure 9.6. The
NP-Click implementation (with the arbitration optimization) is able to match
the performance of the hand-coded IXP-C implementation for larger packets.
For smaller packets, NP-Click is able to achieve 65 to 88% of the data rate of the
IXP-C implementation. For the IETF Benchmarking Methodology Workgroup
packet mix, a representative packet mix, the NP-Click version performs within
7% of the IXP-C version.

The NP-Click version achieves this performance by using a more natural
abstraction of the architecture that greatly reduces design time. We estimate
NP-Click reduces design time fourfold versus IXP-C. Moreover, NP-Click provides a fast path to initial implementation and produces code that is easier to
debug, improve, maintain, and reuse.

We believe our programming model is effective for implementing applications on the IXP1200 and trying different functional partitions across microengines. The modularity and architectural abstraction, however, is responsible
for some performance overhead. In particular, the execution time spent in
receiving packets and header processing is worse in the NP-Click version due to
redundant memory accesses. Given the initial results, we are confident we will be
able to further close the performance gap by focusing on NP-Click's processing
of smaller packets.

9.5   SUMMARY AND CONCLUSIONS

As application complexity increases, the current practice of programming network processors in assembly language or a subset of C will not scale. Ideally, we
would like to program network processors with a network application model,
such as Click. However, the *implementation gap* between Click and network
processor architectures prevents this. In this chapter, we define NP-Click, a
programming model that bridges this gap by coupling the natural expressive-
ness of Click with an abstraction of the target architecture that enables efficient
implementation.

Initial experiments show that our programming model greatly reduces the
development time to implement a networking application on the Intel IXP1200
versus current practices. Additional performance tuning is also made significantly easier due to the modularity of the design and the visibility into relevant
architectural details.

We used this programming model to implement the data plane of an IPv4
router. Initial results indicate that this approach is quite promising, achieving
93% of the performance of a hand-coded 16-port packet forwarder with the IETF

Benchmarking Methodology Workgroup packet mix, a realistic set of Internet traffic. Though our approach currently incurs some performance overhead when compared to a hand-coded implementation, we believe we can close this gap in the near future.

As a result, we believe our programming model combines application developer productivity with efficient implementation, which results in a powerful paradigm for programming network processors.

9.6 FUTURE WORK

We aim to generalize and improve this work in a number of ways. The first is to quantify the trade-offs in productivity and quality of results for different programming models. We plan to compare our work to other approaches to programming network processors, including assembler, Teja Technologies' Teja NP, and Consystant's StrataNP. This will give us a relative measure of effectiveness for a variety of programming paradigms. A challenge with this project will be properly quantifying productivity.

The second direction is to implement additional networking applications with our programming model. We are currently considering network address translation (NAT), a label edge router/label switch router for multiprotocol label switching (MPLS), and a quality-of-service (QoS) application.

We also plan to further ease the pain of programming network processors through automation. We aim to provide the programmer with additional automation in the programming flow. Tools could be written to determine thread boundaries, lay out data, synthesize scheduling schemes, and perform optimizations based on network topology—similar to optimizations presented in [22].

Finally, we seek to broaden this work by applying NP-Click to other network processors, such as the latest Intel IXP architectures (2400, 28xx) and Motorola's DCP C-5. We expect this to be relatively easy for the new IXP architectures, as many of the architectural abstractions can be ported. Generalizing this work to other network processors will have its challenges, but we believe we have identified the key problems in programming network processors: parallelism, arbitration of shared resources, and data layout. The IXP1200 is representative of network processor architectures, as it demonstrates a majority of the common features: multiple processing elements, hardware multithreading, special-purpose hardware, exposed memory regions, and use of peripherals.

ACKNOWLEDGMENTS

This work was supported in part by a grant from the Micro-electronics Advanced Research Consortium (MARCO). The authors would like to thank Eddie Kohler, Scott Weber, Andrew Mihal, and the rest of the MESCAL team for their help in developing NP-Click. We would also like to thank the anonymous reviewers for their feedback on the paper.

REFERENCES

[1]   N. Shah, "Understanding Network Processors," master's thesis, Dept. of Electrical Engineering and Computer Science, University of California, Berkeley, 2001.

[2]   N. Shah and K. Keutzer, "Network Processors: Origin of Species," *Proceedings of ISCIS XVII, the Seventeenth International Symposium on Computer and Information Sciences*, 2002.

[3]   C. Matsumoto, "Net Processors Face Programming Trade-Offs," *EE Times*, Aug. 30, 2002, *www.eetimes.com/story/OEG20020830S0061*.

[4]   E. Kohler et al., "The Click Modular Router," *ACM Transactions on Computer Systems*, 18(3): 263–297, Aug. 2000.

[5]   B. Chen and R. Morris, "Flexible Control of Parallelism in a Multiprocessor PC Router," *Proceedings of the 2001 USENIX Annual Technical Conference (USENIX '01)*, Boston, Mass., June 2001, pp. 333–346.

[6]   Intel Corp., "Intel IXP1200 Network Processor," Product Datasheet, Dec. 2001.

[7]   Intel Corp., *Intel Microengine C Compiler Support: Reference Manual*, Mar. 2002.

[8]   J. L. Pino, S. Ha, E. A. Lee, and J. T. Buck, "Software Synthesis for DSP Using Ptolemy," *Journal on VLSI Signal Processing*, vol. 9, no. 1, Jan. 1995, pp. 7–21.

[9]   K. Leary and W. Waddington, "DSP/C: A Standard High-Level Language for DSP and Numeric Processing," *Proceedings of the International Conference on Acoustics, Speech and Signal Processing*, 1990, pp. 1065–1068.

[10]   G. Kahn, "The Semantics of a Simple Language for Parallel Programming," *Proceedings of the IFIP Congress 74*, 1974, North-Holland Publishing Co., Amsterdam, the Netherlands.

[11]   E. A. Lee and D. G. Messerschmitt, "Synchronous Data Flow," *IEEE Proceedings*, Sept. 1987.

[12]   F. Balarin et al., *Hardware-Software Co-Design of Embedded Systems: The POLIS Approach*, Kluwer Academic Publishers, Norwell, MA, 1997.

[13]   G. Berry and G. Gonthier, "The Esterel Synchronous Programming Language: Design, Semantics, Implementation," *Science of Computer Programming*, 19(2):87–152, Nov. 1992.

[14]   S. Edwards, "Compiling Esterel into Sequential Code," *Proceedings of the 37th Design Automation Conference (DAC 2000)*, Los Angeles, CA, June 5–9, 2000, pp. 322–327.

[15]   Intel Corp., "Intel IXP2800 Network Processor," product brief, 2002.

[16]   Wind River Systems, Inc., *VxWorks Reference Manual*, May 1999.

[17]   J. Nickolls et al., "Broadcom Calisto: A Multi-channel Multi-service Communications Platform," *Hot Chips* 14, Aug. 2002.

[18]   F. Baker, "Requirements for IP Version 4 Routers," *Request for Comments-1812*, Network Working Group, June 1995.

[19]   M. Tsai, C. Kulkarni, C. Sauer, N. Shah, and K. Keutzer, "A Benchmarking Methodology for Network Processors," *1st Network Processor Workshop, 8th Int. Symposium on High Performance Architectures*, 2002.

[20]   S. Bradner and J. McQuaid, "A Benchmarking Methodology for Network Interconnect Devices," *Request for Comments-2544*, Internet Engineering Task Force (IETF), Mar. 1999.

[21]   Intel Corp., "IXP1200 Network Processor Microengine C RFC1812 Layer 3 Forwarding Example Design," application note, Sept. 2001.

[22]   E. Kohler, R. Morris, and B. Chen, "Programming Language Optimizations for Modular Router Configurations," *Proceedings of the 10th International Conference on Architectural Support for Programming Languages and Operating Systems (ASPLOS-X)*, San Jose, CA, Oct. 2002, pp. 251–263.

NEPAL: A Framework for Efficiently Structuring Applications for Network Processors

Gokhan Memik, William H. Mangione-Smith
Department of Electrical Engineering,
University of California, Los Angeles

Networking components constitute one of the biggest sections of the semi-conductor industry. Traditionally, these systems are built either using general-purpose processors or ASICs (application-specific integrated circuits). ASIC solutions generally have better performance, but lack the flexibility of the general-purpose processors. With the recent increase in the number of applications and protocols, this rigidity is becoming a major limitation for systems using ASICs. High link speeds, on the other hand, leave the general-purpose processors underpowered for many networking tasks. Network-processing units (NPUs) are optimized for networking applications and attempt to combine the advantages of ASIC and general-purpose processors. By utilizing application-specific hardware units, these processors achieve performance comparable to ASIC solutions. Since they are software programmable, they have flexibility comparable to general-purpose processors. Their advantages over existing solutions made the NPU market one of the fastest-growing segments of the microprocessor industry. Currently there are more than 40 companies with a variety of NPU designs [9].

Two important properties of networking applications are utilized by the NPU designers. First, these applications consume and produce well-defined data segments (network packets). This property leads the designers to utilize intelligent memory controllers specifically designed to move packet data to/from and within the processor. Second, for many of the networking applications, though not all, these packets can be processed independently. Therefore, there is a large

Processor	No. of exec. cores	Par. technique
Agere PayloadPlus	3	MT, VLIW
AMMC (MMC) nP7510	6	MT
Broadcom SB-1250	2	Superscalar
Cisco Toaster	16	VLIW
Clearspeed (Pixelfusion)	4	MT
Clearwater CNP810SP	1	MT
EZChip	~40	MT
IBM Rainier	16	MT
Intel IXP2800	16	MT
Intel IXP1200	6	MT
Lexra NetVortex	16	MT
Motorola C-5	16	MT
PMC-Sierra RM9000	2	Superscalar
Vitesse (Sitera) IQ1200	4	MT

10.1

TABLE

Important characteristics of representative network processor designs: *exec. cores* is the number of execution cores, and *par. technique* is the technique(s) used for task- or instruction-level parallelism (MT: multi-threading, VLIW: very long instruction word) in the execution cores.

amount of data-level parallelism available in the applications. The designers take advantage of this fact with the use of multithreading and with multiple execution cores. Almost all of the available NPUs in the market today use a variation of multithreading and have several execution cores. Table 10.1 presents some characteristics of the representative NPUs, that is, the number of execution cores and the parallelism technique (data- or instruction-level parallelism) employed in these processors. Another important property of these applications that is mostly overlooked is their modular nature. Most of the networking applications implement a set of tasks that have to be performed on each packet. In many cases, these tasks are defined by international standardization organizations. Hence, it is easier for a designer to visualize the application as a set of tasks (or modules) instead of a traditional program implemented in a high-level program such as C. In this work, we develop techniques that take advantage of this modular[1] nature of the networking applications. Particularly, we present the NEPAL (NEtwork Processor Application Language) design environment,

---

1. In this chapter, a module represents a distinct task that has to be performed on the packet. Section 10.1 presents a detailed description of a module.

where the users define the modules needed by the application and the relation between these modules. These modules can be implemented as separate threads if the target machine supports threaded execution (software or hardware), or they can be combined efficiently to generate binaries for processors with no thread support.

There has been a significant amount of activity for designing efficient NPU architectures. Such activities resulted in complex processors that are relatively difficult to program. This complexity and the lack of sophisticated design environments force the designers to implement low-level issues, such as allocating the tasks to each of the execution core and coordinating the communication between these tasks. Compiler support for implementing applications is available for several NPUs. However, a programmer usually has to learn a proprietary language and in addition has to have a deep knowledge about the processor to implement efficient code.

Each new generation of NPUs employs more execution cores than its predecessors. Therefore, traditional communication structures between these execution cores (global buses or crossbar-based fabrics) become less effective. Many of the newer NPUs employ special neighbor-to-neighbor communication or enhanced interconnection networks to reduce the need for accessing global structures. In such systems, effective task allocation becomes particularly difficult, even for the most experienced programmers. In this chapter, we present runtime mechanisms that perform such tasks and hence relieve the responsibilities from the designer. The NEPAL design environment can also modify existing sequential binaries to take advantage of these runtime mechanisms. This approach allows a variety of applications implemented for general-purpose processors to be mapped to the NPUs efficiently and helps generate a larger pool of applications. The ease of programming also reduces the complexity of maintaining or upgrading the applications.

The NEPAL environment generates the modules and a module tree that will be used during runtime. A dynamic control environment (dynamic module manager) uses this high-level information about the modules to efficiently schedule the tasks. Since the tasks are scheduled dynamically, designing processors with backward compatibility becomes easier. In this chapter, we propose and evaluate runtime mechanisms and a design environment that is crucial for next-generation NPUs. Specifically, we make the following contributions:

+ We propose a programming framework where the code for the applications can be generated efficiently.

+ We show that there is significant task-level parallelism in the networking applications, and modularization can take advantage of this parallelism to improve the performance of the applications significantly.

✦ We propose a runtime environment that has an overall view of the module tree.

✦ We show how this runtime environment can be modified for different underlying architectures.

✦ We present simulation numbers of a generic chip-multiprocessor (CMP) architecture that takes advantage of this overall view and moves the modules dynamically within the execution cores to increase the efficiency of the processor.

✦ We show that a CMP with a systolic array of execution cores can be efficiently employed by the designers with the help of the dynamic movement of modules within the cores.

In the next section, we give examples of application modules and present simulation results motivating the usage of modules as the building blocks of an application. Section 10.2 gives an overview of the NEPAL design environment. In Section 10.3, we present techniques for generating modules from sequential binaries and discuss the advantages and disadvantages of the granularity of the modules. Section 10.4 explains the Dynamic Module Manager (DMM). Section 10.5 lists the advantages and disadvantages of the modular execution. In Section 10.6, we present the experimental results. We discuss the related work in Section 10.7. Section 10.8 summarizes our approach and contributions.

10.1 MODULES

In the remainder of this chapter, each application is viewed as a set of interrelated modules. A module is a distinct task that has to be performed on a packet; it can implement functions such as queuing, scheduling, and interfacing with devices. These functions might be simple, such as decrementing the time-to-live (TTL) value of the packet, or might be complex, such as performing a signature calculation for the packet. Specifically, a module is the smallest implementation-independent section of a networking application that conceptually accomplishes a complete task. For example, consider the tasks defined in RFC 1812 [1]. The author defines the requirements that an IP router has to comply with. Each requirement is given as a task. Each of these tasks conforms to the module definition: they are not implementation dependent and each task corresponds to a separate activity the router has to complete. According to this definition, while verifying the header checksum is a module, reading the header is not a module, because it is a part of the conceptual task of verifying the header checksum.

Application	No. of modules	Speedup
route	16	3.28
url	17	2.98
nat	19	3.05
drr	19	3.36

10.2

TABLE

Experiments for modules with Intel IXP1200.

Depending on its complexity, a module might be a portion of a procedure or it might span several procedures. For example, the IPv4 routing application implemented for our experiments consists of 16 different modules that perform tasks such as IP header checking, performing a routing table lookup, and verifying the header checksum. In the next section, we discuss the advantages and disadvantages of this modular view of the applications. We compare the granularity of the modules to the granularity of procedures and show that the modules are an efficient method for partitioning the networking applications.

The relation between the modules dictates the order in which the modules can be executed. In most applications considered here, there is little dependency between the modules, and hence there is a significant amount of parallelism that can be exploited. To evaluate the advantages of modules, we have implemented different networking applications on the Intel IXP1200 [3]. Each module is implemented as a separate thread, and we use all six microengines. The improvement over a naive solution, where each thread is the complete application (i.e., there are four copies of the same application running in each core processing different packets), is presented in Table 10.2. Since each thread corresponds to a section of the application, the applications can be executed faster because the tasks are executed in parallel for a single application. Then, each packet starts in one module, traversing the modules similar to traditional pipelining. Figure 10.1 illustrates how the execution time is improved. In this figure, A, B, C, and D correspond to different tasks (either different applications or the same application with different input). For example, A, B, C, and D might correspond to performing routing for four different packets. In Figure 10.1a, the processor switches between different applications to increase the overall throughput. Hence, the processing of a single packet is delayed. In Figure 10.1b, the processor switches to other tasks within the application. This reduces the execution time of the packet compared to the naive approach. The improvement for this configuration is in terms of processing time of a packet, not in throughput. Eventually, all packets (four of them) will be processed in the same amount of time,

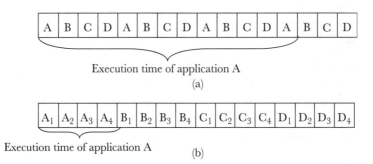

Overview of modular execution: in (a), each thread is an application; in (b), the application is divided into modules, which are implemented as separate threads.

and hence the throughput will not be affected. However, the modular execution requires significantly less time to complete the processing of the packet. Therefore, the modularization is likely to improve the packet loss ratio: since the packets have to be kept shorter in memory, the overall memory requirement reduces, which should affect the loss ratio positively. Note that other advantages of modularization, such as reduced footprint, cannot be observed for this framework, because both the modular and nonmodular applications have to bring the entire application to each execution core.

10.2   NEPAL DESIGN FLOW

We now present the NEPAL design environment, which generates efficient code for a variety of NPU systems. The NEPAL design environment uses information about the modules in the networking applications to generate the code segments. There are predefined modules the user can utilize (e.g., decrement *TTL*, queue) or he/she can define new module templates. After all of the necessary templates are defined, the user defines the relation between these modules. Getting this input, NEPAL generates the corresponding code according to the target processor. The generated code is compiled by the native compiler. The overall flow is shown in Figure 10.2. As depicted in Figure 10.2, NEPAL can process existing sequential binaries to generate the module tree. This process is explained in Section 10.3. The programs in C, as well as the binaries, should be processed by the NEPAL converter to generate a format the optimizer can process. The NEPAL optimizer also accepts application configuration generated by the NEPAL API, as explained previously. The NEPAL API generates a graph showing the dependencies between the modules. This graph corresponds to a

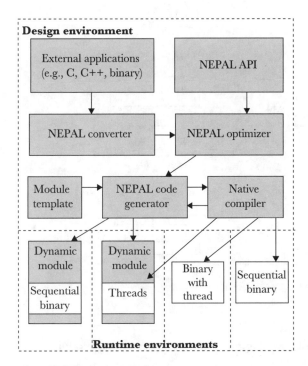

10.2

FIGURE

The NEPAL design environment.

module tree. Given the graph and the module templates, NEPAL generates the code and the module tree and passes it to the NEPAL optimizer. The optimizer checks the memory accesses and removes the links between the modules that can be executed in parallel. The generated module codes are compiled by the native compiler, and the module tree is provided to the DMM if the target processor supports dynamic modules.

10.3   MODULE EXTRACTION FROM SEQUENTIAL BINARIES

To find the modules from a sequential binary, we first build a control-data flow diagram of the application. Then, the memory operations that are accessing packet data (e.g., performing a load or store operation to the memory position containing the packet) are marked. A basic block that contains a load to a packet is called a *load block*, and a basic block that contains a store operation to the

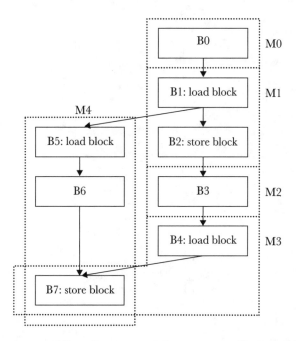

10.3   A control flow diagram and the corresponding modules.

FIGURE

packet is called a *store block*. Load blocks mark the start of the modules. Starting from a load block, all successor basic blocks are added to the module until either a store block or another load block is reached. A new module is started if a load block is reached, whereas a store block ends the current module. New modules start with the basic blocks following the store blocks, even if they are not load blocks. If a basic block contains both a load and a store operation to the packet data, a module is formed containing just the single basic block, and module formation is continued as if the block were a store block. Due to the formation of the modules, each module has a single entrance point, but might contain several exit points. Some basic blocks have to be included in more than one module, possibly resulting in code expansion. We propose an extended module definition to prevent code expansion. In extended module formation, artificial modules are generated when two modules intersect. The intersection basic block is the start of the artificial module. Note that the extended modules also have a single entry and possibly multiple exit points. Figure 10.3 presents a control flow diagram and the corresponding modules. The corresponding module tree is shown in Figure 10.4a. The corresponding extended module tree is shown in Figure 10.4b. M5 in Figure 10.4b corresponds to the artificial module containing

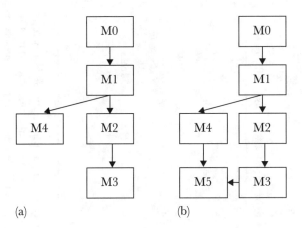

The module (a) and the extended module (b) trees.

B7 of Figure 10.3. *Note that forming modules by observing accesses to the packet data is only an approximation of the definition of the module presented in Section 10.1. NEPAL API should be used to generate the modules precisely.*

A significant amount of research has been conducted in the area of speculative parallelization of sequential binaries utilizing multithreading support. In these studies, potential procedure calls, loops, or basic blocks are speculatively executed [4, 8, 11, 12, 16, 17]. These techniques are designed for general-purpose applications. Hence, they do not take advantage of any application-specific information. The forming of the threads in our work, on the other hand, depends on a property of the networking applications; namely, the modularity. Similar to these studies, procedure call graphs or basic block call trees can also be used as a representation of the application. We have generated such representations along with the module and extended module trees of the applications. Table 10.3 presents the number of blocks required by each application and the total amount of communication required between the blocks (or clusters). When the amount of communication between the clusters increases, the number of predictions that have to be made also increases. Our experimental results reveal that clustering basic blocks within modules is more efficient both in terms of space and inter-block communication than a clustering based on procedure boundaries. On average, the module representation requires 6.1 times fewer clusters (hence, space to represent the application), and 105.7 times less communication is required between the clusters.

NetBench application code	Basic blocks		Procedures		Modules			Extended modules	
	# blocks	Total com. (Mbyte)	# blocks	Total com. (Mbyte)	# blocks	Total com. (Mbyte)	Code expans. (%)	# blocks	Total com. (Mbyte)
crc	501	619	30	288	10	421	8.8	14	537
rou	791	766	90	423	16	6	51.2	66	19
drr	1289	257	131	131	24	4	41.8	80	47
md5	540	960	46	498	13	51	24.8	36	479
nat	899	779	108	429	15	5	69.6	67	24
ipchains	810	903	97	495	19	101	34.0	65	167
ssl	3434	141942	397	75375	54	8	61.9	212	34898
url	746	743	85	411	12	3	88.1	63	7
tl	905	1128	114	610	17	146	68.6	83	573
mean	1101.7	16444.1	121.8	8740.0	20.0	82.7	49.9	76.1	4094.6

Comparison of basic blocks, procedures, modules, and extended modules for representing applications: *# blocks* represents the number of entities required to represent the entire application, *Total com.* is the total amount of data (in number in million bytes) communicated between the entities during the execution, and *Code expans.* is the increase in the binary size.

10.4 DYNAMIC MODULE MANAGER

As we have mentioned in the previous sections, the applications are represented as a set of modules. The DMM controls module activation. It also decides the execution core where the module will be activated.

Each execution core implements a local manager (LM). The LM is responsible for gathering and storing information about the local modules (modules that are activated in the specific execution core) and the successors of the local modules. The inter-module communication is achieved with the help of the LMs. When a local module generates data for one of its successors, it sends a message to the LM. If the location of the destination module is known by the LM, the LM allocates the necessary registers to store the communication data. If the location is not known, the LM communicates with the DMM to locate the destination module and stores the information about it. If the destination module is local, then the LM starts the module and execution continues. If the destination module is activated in another execution core, the LM sends a message to the corresponding LM, indicating the availability of data. The destination LM performs a remote read operation, copying the necessary data to the local registers, and then starts the destination module. The inter-module communication is viewed as a *port* to each of the modules. Ports are virtual entities mapped to physical registers (or communication registers) dynamically at runtime. Modules read data from, and write data to, ports without having any information of the destination module. The LM locates the destination module with the help of the DMM. The destination module also does not have any information about the producer of the data. Therefore, dynamic movement of modules (moving modules from one execution core to another) can be performed efficiently. Once data are read from a port, the module is responsible for moving the data to one of the registers. Therefore, each port is written and read once, generating an automatic producer-consumer relation.

Although the overall activation of the modules is controlled by the DMM, modules are responsible for initiating the activation. For each application, the modules are statically labeled with a unique ID. If a module wants to send data to another module, it sends the ID of the new module to the LM. If the consuming module is not active, the LM communicates to the DMM for the specific module and gathers information about the location of the module. If an active module is initiated by another module, the LM will send a message to the corresponding LM, indicating that the module is activated.[2]

---

2. The message is useful when modules are speculatively executed. After the message is sent, the corresponding LM changes the status of the destination module from speculative to active.

The module tree (as a control-data flow diagram) is provided to the DMM. We assume that the DMM also has information about the approximate execution time of each module. This might be achieved through offline profiling, static estimation, or by observing the execution time in the previous activations of the modules. Since the DMM has information about the module tree, the data communication between modules, and the execution time of the modules, it can efficiently distribute the load between the execution cores.

We have used two different heuristics to assign the locations of each module. The first heuristic (heuristic 1) considers the execution time of the modules only, and tries to achieve a balanced load among the execution cores. Once the initial distribution is made, the DMM monitors the load in each execution core. This is achieved with the help of the LM. The LM gathers information about the local modules by observing the port read/write operations. The delay of each module is estimated by the difference in port writes and reads. Then, using this estimation it finds the sum of the execution times of all the modules assigned to the execution core. The DMM monitors the total execution time provided by the LM. Then, if the load variance is above the average module execution time, it moves a module from the core with the highest load (src with load L_{src}). The decision of which module to move is based on the processor architecture. If the architecture employs only a global connection, then the core with the lowest load (dst with load L_{dst}) is selected as the destination. If the processor employs a neighbor-to-neighbor communication, the neighbor of the src with the lower load is selected as the destination (dst with load L_{dst}). The module with load closest to $((L_{src} - L_{dst})/2)$ is moved from the src to dst. The second heuristic (heuristic 2) considers the amount of data communicated between the modules and tries to assign the modules with large communication in the same core, reducing inter-core communication. This goal is achieved by first finding the highest amount of communication between any two modules and assigning the modules to the same core. Then, the couple with the next highest communication is found and assigned to another core. This process continues until all cores have approximately the same number of modules assigned. Similar to heuristic 1, heuristic 2 monitors the amount of data communication between the execution cores and moves the modules to minimize the communication. Section 10.6 presents results for both heuristics.

The DMM can be extended to implement additional optimizations, such as speculative execution. Since the DMM controls which modules are activated, it can implement control speculation by speculatively invoking modules that are successors of the active modules. Then, by observing the speculation success it increases or reduces the speculation level. To achieve this, the LM is extended to check whether a module is speculative or active. Speculative modules are not allowed to perform store or port write operations, or to perform speculative reads on the ports.[3] In Section 10.6, we present simulations showing that speculative execution is much more effective using the module tree instead of a basic block or procedure tree.

Network packet arrival times vary among different systems and different times of the day. The DMM controls where the threads are initialized, and hence has control over the overall performance parameters. If the packet arrival times are below a certain level, it can remove modules from certain execution cores and turn these cores off, thereby reducing the overall energy without affecting the packet drop rates.

Another advantage of dynamic task distribution is flexibility. For example, if a specific module becomes a bottleneck (the execution time of each thread may vary according to the data processed), the DMM might create multiple versions of the same module, increasing the overall performance. Similarly, the system can transparently provide fault tolerance.

10.4.1   Memory Disambiguation

Arguably, the most important problem with parallelizing sequential binaries is the memory disambiguation problem; that is, guaranteeing for any load-store pair that their destination addresses will be disjoint so that the execution order can be changed. The DMM solves this problem with a restricted snoop algorithm. Note that at any time there is only one active module with possibly multiple speculatively executing modules. The DMM stores information about each of these modules. Hence, the destination addresses of the store instructions from the active module can be efficiently forwarded to the speculative modules. Speculative modules check this address against the load addresses and halt the execution if the address matches. The stores from the speculative threads are not executed until the module becomes active, but are instead kept in a store buffer in the execution core.

10.5   DISCUSSION

In this section, we discuss the advantages and disadvantages of the modular representation of the applications. The next section presents the experimental results showing the effectiveness of modular execution.

3. A speculative read is a prediction based on the previous values at the port. We use a stride-based prediction in Section 10.6.

Below, we list the advantages of the modular representation of applications:

+ *Explicit parallelism.* Since the application is represented as a control-data flow diagram, the DMM can efficiently start execution of modules that do not depend on any other modules. Therefore, the representation forms explicit parallelism that can be used at runtime.

+ *Ease of programming.* The networking applications are in nature modular. Therefore, it is easier for a programmer to see the application as a set of modules.

+ *Reusability.* Many of the modules appear in more than one application. For example, modules that interface devices with the processor are common in almost all applications. Therefore, representing the application as a set of modules helps the designers reuse existing implementations.

+ *Portability.* Once an application is implemented for a processor, it is easy to generate code for different systems, only the module templates have to be changed. In addition, a new generation of a processor can efficiently execute a binary generated for a processor with a smaller number of cores or different communication structure because the tasks are allocated at runtime to specific execution cores.

+ *Flexibility.* The DMM controls the overall processor parameters. Therefore, according to the load of the processor it might switch between low-power and high-performance mode efficiently by activating or deactivating modules.

There are some disadvantages of modular execution of the applications:

+ *Overhead.* If the processor cannot utilize the modular information efficiently due to a small number of execution cores or a very high number of concurrent applications, overhead of communication between the modules can degrade the performance. We have also shown that the modules can increase the code size, possibly increasing cost.

+ *Hardware complexities.* To execute the applications in a modular way, several hardware enhancements are necessary. This might increase the processor area and degrade the performance.

10.6 EXPERIMENTS

We have performed several experiments to measure the effectiveness of the proposed mechanisms. In the first set of experiments, we measure the performance of chip multiprocessors with different communication systems employing the DMM structure. Our goal in these experiments is to see how partitioning the application affects the overall performance. In the second set of experiments, the potential performance improvements through speculative execution are measured.

In all experiments, we measure the maximum throughput achieved by the processor. Throughput is the number of packets the NPU can process within a given time and hence is an important measure of the performance of the processor. Note that NEPAL reduces the processing time of the applications. Hence, the loss-free throughput will also be improved. However, due to the limitations of the simulation environment, we cannot measure this property.

10.6.1   Simulation Parameters

In all experiments, the base processor is a chip multiprocessor with each execution core similar to StrongARM SA-110 [6]. We have modified some parameters of the StrongARM to model cores similar to the execution cores in the NPUs. First, the cores use in-order execution, with an issue width of 2. Second, they have 4-KB direct-mapped L1 data and instruction caches, and the processor has a 128-KB, four-way set-associative unified L2 cache shared between the cores. The latency for all L1 caches is set to one cycle, and the L2 cache latency is set to 12 cycles. We use the SimpleScalar/ARM [15] simulator to simulate the events in each core. We have implemented a trace-driven multicore simulator (SimpleCMP) that processes the single-core events and simulates a multicore processor with varying communication structures and number of execution cores. We simulate two different systems: a shared-memory chip multiprocessor similar to Intel IXP1200 [3] (System 1) as depicted in Figure 10.5, and a chip multiprocessor with neighbor-to-neighbor communication (System 2)—as depicted in

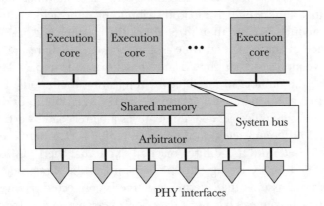

10.5   System 1: Execution cores are connected through a global system bus.

FIGURE

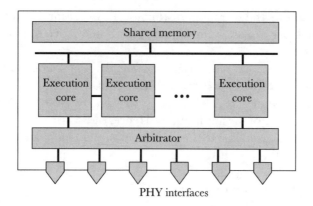

PHY interfaces

10.6

FIGURE

System 2: Execution cores with neighbor-to-neighbor communication. Shared memory is mostly used for global data structures.

Figure 10.6—which resembles Cisco Toaster [2]. In System 1, the shared data and the packet data are placed into the shared memory. The execution cores read the necessary positions of the packet from the shared memory into their local memory. In System 2, the packet data is read by the first execution core and passed to the neighboring cores, each executing the appropriate tasks on the packet. In this system, the execution cores access the shared bus to read the shared data and to communicate to the execution cores that are not their neighbors. We simulate the NetBench applications [10]. Table 10.4 presents the properties of the simulated applications for a processor with a single execution core.

We have performed simulations with 4 and 16 execution cores for both systems. Note that for some applications the number of modules in the application is less than 16. Even for applications with more modules, our simulations revealed that a more effective load distribution can be achieved if the number of active modules is more than three times the number of cores. The reason is the variance in the execution time of the modules. If there are a small number of active modules, then the variance has a dramatic impact. However, when we increase the number of modules (by replicating the module tree and treating each tree as a separate application), the DMM is able to find a number of short and long modules. The DMM achieves a better load by activating several modules (of different execution time) in the same core. Therefore, the module tree is replicated until this limit is reached. Note that the DMM does not have to be modified for executing multiple versions of the same module tree. The DMM does not assume that the module tree is connected. Hence, an application with two disconnected control-data flow diagrams is executed the same way as a replicated module tree.

Application	Arguments	# inst (M)	# cycle (M)	# IL1 acc (M)	# DL1 acc (M)	# L2 acc (M)
crc	crc 10000	145.8	262.0	219.0	59.8	0.6
drr	drr 128 10000	12.9	33.5	22.8	7.9	1.1
Ipchains	ipchains 10 10000	61.7	160.2	103.9	26.2	3.6
md5	md5 10000	209.1	474.7	296.8	73.2	11.0
nat	nat 128 10000	11.4	26.7	17.3	5.6	1.2
rou	route 128 10000	14.2	32.0	23.3	7.1	0.9
ssl	openssl NetBench strong 10000	3616.1	8727.5	4453.4	1383.3	426.8
tl	tl 128 10000	6.9	15.7	11.8	3.9	0.7
url	url small_inputs 10000	497.0	956.7	768.9	249.1	10.0
average		508.3	1187.7	657.5	201.8	50.7

10.4

TABLE

NetBench applications and their properties: *arguments* are the execution arguments, *# inst* is the number of instructions executed, *# cycle* is the number of cycles required, *# IL1 acc* (*# DL1 acc*) is the number of accesses to the level 1 instruction (data) cache, and *# L2 acc* is the level 2 cache accesses.

We simulate with the DMM mechanisms using the module tree (*mod*) and the extended module tree (*ext*) representations. We also simulate two different heuristics to make the task assignments to the cores: heuristic 1 (*heu1*) and heuristic 2 (*heu2*) as explained in Section 10.4. The simulations consist of two parts: a warm-up period and the execution period. For the warm-up period, we process 5000 packets and invoke the DMM for every 200 packets. The DMM is allowed to move one module at a time if necessary. After the warm-up period, we process 5000 packets without invoking the DMM. For each simulated system, we measure the delay for processing the last 5000 packets. For the inter-module communication we assumed a two-cycle delay if the destination module is in the same execution core. If the destination module is activated in a different execution core, the delay is four cycles added to the delay of inter-core communication. The first port read/write operations take an extra five cycles (to simulate the delay of the LM to locate the port). The delay for activating the modules does not have any effect on the simulation results because we measure the delay for the last 5000 packets.

We also report simulation numbers for a system, where the tasks are statically assigned to the execution cores using profiling information (*prof*). To find the static distribution, we first executed the same NetBench applications using a different trace. During the execution, we measured the average time spent in each basic block. Then the basic blocks were assigned to the execution cores, distributing the load as much as possible.

For each system, we report the improvement over a base system, which does not partition the application (i.e., each core executes the same application, processing different packets).

10.6.2   Effects of Program Modularization

The first set of experiments is conducted to measure the effects of modular execution of the applications on the performance of the network processors. The throughput effects of modular execution on System 1 with four cores are presented in Figure 10.7. The throughput increase is due to fewer local data and instruction cache misses. Note that these misses have to perform global memory accesses, reducing the overall performance. Since the application is modularized, the instruction cache footprint and the amount of data read is significantly reduced, improving the overall efficiency of the processor. The modular representation with the DMM implementing heuristic 1 improves the performance by 18.3% on average. For the application *crc*, on the other hand, modularization reduces the efficiency of the processor. This application has a very small code size, and most of the execution time is spent in a single module. Therefore, the load distribution has a large variance reducing the throughput. The simulation results reveal that the modular representation performs better than the extended module representation in spite of the larger code size. The reason is the

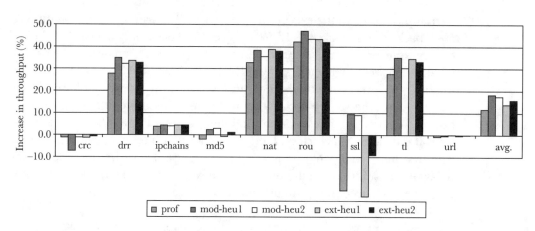

10.7   Improvement in the throughput for System 1 with four execution cores.

FIGURE

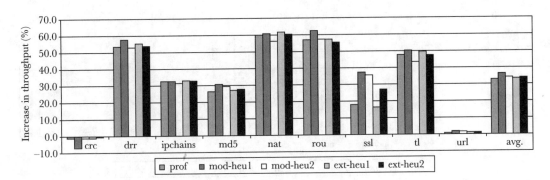

10.8
Improvement in the throughput for System 1 with 16 execution cores.

FIGURE

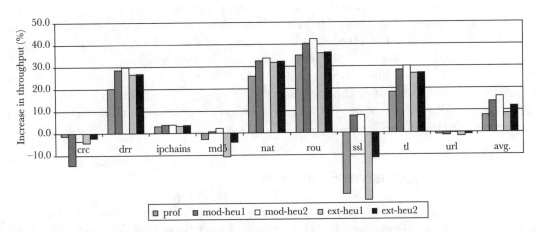

10.9
Improvement in the throughput for System 2 with four execution cores.

FIGURE

significantly larger amount of communication that has to be performed between the extended modules. Therefore, heuristic 2, which minimizes the communication, performs better for the extended module than heuristic 1. The results for System 1 with 16 execution cores are presented in Figure 10.8. As the number of cores is increased, the number of bus accesses also increases. Therefore, reducing the bus accesses has a more dramatic effect on the performance of the processor. The modular representation with the DMM implementing heuristic 1 improves the performance by 36.2% on average.

Results for System 2 with 4 and 16 execution cores are presented in Figures 10.9 and 10.10, respectively. On average, we see that the effect of

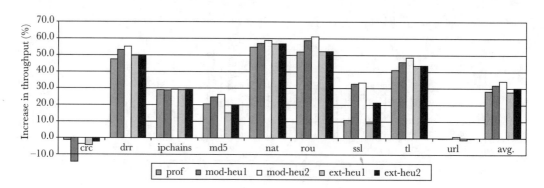

Improvement in the throughput for System 2 with 16 execution cores.

modularization is slightly less compared to System 1. This is due to the reduced number of accesses to the shared bus. Fewer accesses to the shared bus result in less bus stalls for System 2. On average, the modular representation with the DMM implementing heuristic 2 improves the throughput by 16.3% for System 2 with 4 execution cores and 34.4% for System 2 with 16 execution cores. On average, heuristic 2 performs better for System 2 than System 1, due to better utilization of the neighbor-to-neighbor communication for reducing the accesses to the shared bus.

10.6.3   Speculative Execution

Besides partitioning of the applications, the modular representation can be used for speculative execution, as explained in Section 10.4. We have performed experiments for a single-core processor to measure the limitations of speculative execution for different representations of the applications. We use a two-level prediction. In other words, if a block (or module) is activated, its successors and the children of the successors are speculatively executed. We assume no resource constraint (i.e., unlimited number of blocks or modules can be speculatively executed without affecting the execution time of the active modules). The speculation is limited with the value prediction. In other words, when a module is speculatively executed, the port read operations on the modules have to be predicted. If the prediction is incorrect, the module is squashed and restarted when the port is written. If the value written is equal to the predicted value, the execution of the module continues.[4] The prediction mechanism we used is stride

---

4. If the prediction is correct, the state of the module is changed to active from speculative by the LM.

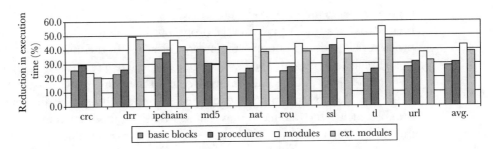

Improvement in the execution cycles by speculative execution.

based. Specifically, if the last two values written to a port are n_i and n_{i-1} the prediction made is $(2*n_i - n_{i-1})$.

The results are summarized in Figure 10.11. The basic block representation is an upper limit for a speculation using loops. Similarly, the results for procedure representation correspond to the upper limit on speculation using speculative procedure calls. The results reveal that the module representation is the most efficient among the simulated representations. The performance is improved by 43.1% on average for the module representation.

10.6.4 Discussion

The experiments in the previous sections have shown that modular execution of the networking applications is an attractive method. The performance improvements mostly resulted due to an increased efficiency of resources: better instruction and data cache utilization as well as reduced inter-core communication. We have also seen that similar improvements can be achieved by extensive static optimizations (e.g., profiling). However, such optimizations have to be performed on an application basis, and NEPAL offers an easier implementation compared to such optimizations.

10.7 RELATED WORK

Modularizing the network applications has been studied before. The Click environment [7] allows a designer to implement an application as a set of tasks similar to the modules in our work. In the Click environment, on the other hand, this modularization is done to increase the programmability without any performance consideration. In addition, the module definition of the user is not used to generate efficient code, but instead is interpreted by a runtime environment dynamically. This runtime environment is designed for general-purpose processors and does not perform any optimization on the tasks.

Thread-level speculation has been one of the active research areas in the last few years [4, 11, 17]. These techniques try to take advantage of the free resources in the processor by spawning threads speculatively. Although we did not directly propose such a technique, we have shown that the modular representation of the application improves the benefits of speculative execution.

Software-distributed shared-memory (SDSM) machines are distributed memory machines, where the data are moved between the cores to give the illusion of a shared-memory processor. Shasta [13] from Compaq is a representative of these processors. In our approach, a runtime system moves the tasks to achieve application partitioning. Howard and Lowenthal [5] present an integrated compiler/runtime environment for efficient execution of the programs. However, their goal is data distribution instead of task distribution. In addition, the distribution decisions are made by the compiler.

Static and dynamic load balancing has been one of the important research areas for multiprocessor systems [14]. Xirogiannis and Taylor [21] propose dynamic task scheduling for logic programs by executing different sections of the Boolean logic in parallel. Unsal et al. [18] propose techniques to increase the parallelism of real-time systems using quality constraints. To our best knowledge, we are not aware of any technique that is similar to our proposed system (a runtime system moving tasks formed using application-specific information).

Recently, studies have been conducted for implementing efficient compilers for NPUs. Wagner and Leupers [19] discuss a compiler tuned for NPUs. Wuytack et al. [20] discuss a memory-oriented synthesis methodology and use embedded network applications as an example. These studies do not assume any hardware support such as the one we propose.

10.8   CONCLUSIONS

In this chapter, we have proposed a runtime system, the Dynamic Module Manager (DMM), which controls the overall execution of the applications in network processors. The runtime system has information of the overall execution precedence of the tasks in the application. This is achieved through representing the applications as a control-data flow diagram consisting of modules. A module is a distinct task that has to be performed on the packet. By using the module diagram, the runtime system controls which modules to activate. It also selects where to activate the selected module. By performing these tasks dynamically, the designer is relieved from complex responsibilities such as task allocation and synchronization. We have shown that there is usually a very small amount of data communication between the modules, increasing the parallelism during execution. We have also shown that the DMM can efficiently partition the application and execute the parts in different execution cores, increasing the overall efficiency of a variety of network processor designs. Specifically, we have shown that the performance of a chip multiprocessor with 16 execution cores connected by a global communication bus can be improved by as much as 62.4% (36.2% on average). The tasks can also be scheduled efficiently on a processor with 16 execution cores that utilizes neighbor-to-neighbor communication, increasing the performance by as much as 61.1% and 34.4% on average). We have also shown that speculative execution can be efficiently governed by the DMM, and the module representation is most suitable for speculative execution. On average, the performance of a single-core processor is increased by 43.1% using speculative execution.

REFERENCES

[1]   F. Baker, "Requirements for IP Version 4 Routers," RFC-1812, Network Working Group, June 1995.

[2]   Cisco Inc., "Cisco's Toaster 2 Chip Receives the Microprocessor Report Analyst's Choice 2001 Award for Best Network Processor," *www.cisco.com*.

[3]   T. R. Halfhill, "Intel Network Processor Targets Routers," *Microprocessor Report*, Sept. 13, 1999.

[4]   L. Hammond, M. Willey, and K. Olukotun, "Data Speculation Support for a Chip-Multiprocessor," *Proceedings of ACM Conference on Architectural Support for Programming Languages and Operating Systems (ASPLOS)*, Oct. 1998, San Jose, CA.

[5]   G. M. S. Howard and D. K. Lowenthal, "An Integrated Compiler/Run-Time System for Global Data Distribution in Shared Memory Systems," *Second Workshop on Software Distributed Shared Memory*, May 2000.

[6]   Intel Corp. *SA-110 Microprocessor Technical Reference Manual*.

[7]   E. Kohler, R. Morris, B. Chen, J. Jannotti, and M. H. Kaashoek, "The Click Modular Router," *ACM Transactions on Computer Systems*, vol. 18, 2000, pp. 263–297.

[8]   V. Krishnan and J. Torrellas, "A Chip-Multiprocessor with Speculative Multithreading," *IEEE Transactions on Computers*, vol. 48, 1999, pp. 866–880.

[9]   W. H. Mangione-Smith and G. Memik, "Network Processing: Applications, Architectures and Examples," tutorial at *International Symposium on Microarchitecture*, Austin, TX, Dec. 2001.

[10]   G. Memik, W. H. Mangione-Smith, and W. Hu, "NetBench: A Benchmarking Suite for Network Processors," *Proceedings of International Conference on Computer-Aided Design (ICCAD)*, Nov. 2001, San Jose, CA, pp. 39–42.

[11]   J. Oplinger et al., "Software and Hardware for Exploiting Speculative Parallelism with a Multiprocessor," CSL-TR-97–715, Feb. 1997.

[12]   J. Oplinger, D. L. Heine, and M. S. Lam, "In Search of Speculative Thread-Level Parallelism," *Proceedings of International Conference on Parallel Architectures and Compilation Techniques (PACT)*, 1999, Newport Beach, CA.

[13]   D. J. Scales, K. Gharachorloo, and C. A. Thekkath, "Shasta: A Low-Overhead Software-Only Approach to Fine-Grain Shared Memory," *Proceedings of the 7th International Conference on Architectural Support for Programming Languages and Operating Systems (ASPLOS-VII)*, Oct. 1996, pp. 174–185.

[14]   B. A. Shirazi, A. R. Hurson, and K. M. Kavi, *Scheduling and Load Balancing in Parallel Distributed Systems*, ISBN 0-8186-6587-4, Computer Society Press, 1995.

[15]   "SimpleScalar LLC," SimpleScalar Home Page, *www.simplescalar.com*.

[16]   G. S. Sohi, S. E. Breach, and T. N. Vijaykumar, "Multiscalar Processors," *25 Years {ISCA}: Retrospectives and Reprints*, 1998, pp. 521–532.

[17]   J. G. Steffan and T. C. Mowry, "The Potential for Using Thread-Level Data Speculation to Facilitate Automatic Parallelization," *Proceedings of International Symposium on High Performance Computer Architecture*, Feb. 1998, Las Vegas, NV.

[18]   O. S. Unsal, I. Koren, and C. M. Krishna, "Application Level Power-Reduction Heuristics in Large Scalar Real-Time Systems," *Proceedings of IEEE International Workshop on Real-Time Systems*, Sept. 2000.

[19]   J. Wagner and R. Leupers, "C Compiler Design for an Industrial Network Processor," *ACM Workshop on Languages, Compilers, and Tools for Embedded Systems*, Snowbird, UT, June 2001.

[20]   S. Wuytack, J. L. da Silva, F. Cathoor, G. de Jong, and C. Ykman, "Memory Management for Embedded Network Applications," *IEEE Transactions on Computer-Aided Design*, vol. 18, no. 5, May 1999, pp. 533–544.

[21]   G. Xirogiannis and H. Taylor, "A Dynamic Task Distribution and Engine Allocation Strategy for Distributed Execution of Logic Programs," *Proceedings of International Conference on High Performance Computing*, April 1998, pp. 294–304.

Efficient and Faithful Performance Modeling for Network-Processor-Based System Designs

Prashant Pradhan, Indira Nair, Sambit Sahu
IBM T. J. Watson Research Center

Wen Xu
Department of Computer Science, Princeton University

To design new system architectures or optimize existing ones, a designer needs to quantify the performance impacts of various design choices. A performance model of the system is thus an essential tool for a system designer. While microbenchmarking of individual system components (e.g., network processors) is important in many cases, ultimately the performance of a complete system design is of interest. The performance of a complete system is determined not only by the raw capabilities of each system component but by the interaction between them. This interaction is primarily driven by the application running on the system, which in turn is driven by the workload the application is handling.

Take for example a web server system that uses a network-processor-based adapter to offload TCP/IP processing. The metric of interest is the performance benefit, in terms of increased number of transactions per second, the server can derive from using the intelligent adapter. Clearly, the performance will depend on hardware capabilities, such as the host and network processor speeds, cache sizes, memory bus, and I/O bus characteristics. However, to a large extent the performance would be dictated by the interaction between these components, which is driven by the web server and TCP/IP processing. For instance, a web server employing zero-copy optimizations would generate different interactions than one that does not employ these optimizations and would result in very different performance. The web server's behavior is also significantly impacted by its workload's characteristics. For instance, depending on the distribution of static file requests and dynamic script requests, or the profile of file sizes, the performance implications of a design choice will be vastly different.

Apart from quantifying the benefits of a given design choice, it is also important that the designer be able to try alternative choices easily to find the optimum solution. While a part of trying new design choices involves trying new hardware parameters, in many cases the key performance wins lie in optimizing the system software. For example, zero-copy optimizations can significantly impact server performance. The designer thus also needs to be able to try application modifications or different function placements. For example, one may want to compare performance differences between full, partial, or no offload of TCP processing to the network processor in a server.

The key point in this discussion is that a performance modeling framework that does not capture application behavior faithfully has limited utility for complete system simulation. In this chapter, we present *Countach*, a performance-modeling framework that integrates application and workload behavior tightly within the performance model of the system. The key idea is to derive the processor models from the application itself. Since the applications execute natively with the system model, the approach is efficient. However, even with native execution Countach captures the application's memory reference behavior and enforces tight time synchronization between the application and the simulator. Countach also allows modeling of multiple processors running different applications.

The rest of the chapter is organized as follows. We first start by presenting some broad approaches to performance modeling and highlight their important limitations in Section 11.1. Section 11.2 then describes some basics of discrete-event simulation, which is utilized by our approach. Section 11.3 describes how the interface between system software and the hardware is modified to convert applications into Countach processor models. Section 11.4 describes how memory performance is captured, and Section 11.5 describes how tight timing control is achieved between the simulator and the natively executing processor models. Section 11.6 describes how multiple processors (or SMT hardware execution contexts) are modeled. Section 11.7 describes how we use Countach to model a network server with a network-processor-based adapter. Section 11.8 presents a performance evaluation of Countach, highlighting its slowdowns over native application execution, when the modeled application is a web server using a TCP stack. Finally, Section 11.9 concludes with a description of ongoing work.

11.1 APPROACHES TO PERFORMANCE MODELING

Given the requirement of accurately capturing application and workload characteristics, some advocate a purely measurement-based approach, where an existing system and software implementation are extensively profiled to understand system performance. A limitation of this approach is that it can only work for existing hardware. For example, this approach would not work for system-on-a-chip designs, which need to be thoroughly analyzed before they are produced. Further, this approach limits a performance analyst to work with "packaged" hardware settings that typical systems are configured with. For example, one cannot easily work with modified cache or bus parameters unless a system with the desired configuration is available.

A more important limitation of this approach is that profiling does not expose important component interactions. For example, cache size determines access behavior over the memory bus. This, in turn, determines contention for the memory bus between the processor and the DMA engine on a network adapter. Now, if profiling tells us that the CPU is fully utilized, we do not know whether it is because the application is compute intensive or whether instructions are just stalled for memory. If the I/O bus is fully utilized, we do not know whether the application is doing a lot of I/O or the adapter DMA engine is stalled for memory due to the contention generated by CPU cache misses. Lower-level instrumentation with bus analyzers may expose such factors, but such techniques provide a fairly nonportable analysis method. Essentially, by hiding detailed component interactions this method does not accurately tell us what to fix.

Analytical modeling of the system is another approach. However, application behavior is too complex to abstract out in an analytical model, without introducing extremely coarse-grained parameterization of the models. Moreover, some important performance aspects of the application cannot be captured by a crisp analytical formula. An example is cache performance, where the behavior can really only be inferred by playing a memory reference trace to a simulated cache.

The limitations of measurement-based or analytical approaches suggest that a simulation approach is the most sound approach to performance modeling for a system. Here, we capture the behavior and performance of each system component in a model and place all of these models in a discrete-event simulator. Work flows through the system in the form of events, which allows us to take into account the interaction of all components and derive the resulting performance. Data on the overhead and utilization of each component is easily available and tells us what to fix to improve performance. However, to capture application behavior, modeling of processors becomes the key challenge. A processor model must capture the behavior of the application running on it. There are two broad options to model a processor. The first one, which is fairly common, is to create a relatively abstract processor model parameterized by offline measurement. This technique works well for simple applications; for example, modeling packet forwarding in a router [2]. However, this approach starts to quickly become impractical with an increase in application complexity. For example, instead of IP processing if we were modeling TCP processing the abstract model would need to mimic the TCP state machine completely. Further, for applications such as web servers, this technique becomes completely impractical.

An alternative is emulation, which is the approach taken by SimOS [8]. The processor is modeled by a fetch-decode-execute loop, which interprets an unmodified application binary. The trade-off is in simulation performance, which may be orders of magnitude slower than the native execution speed. SimOS supports two efficient simulation modes as well. In the most efficient mode, the application is executed natively. However, there is no simulation of cache performance or timing control. In a more detailed mode, cache performance is modeled, but still each instruction is translated to an equivalent set of instructions of a SimOS abstract machine. Further, a practical limitation with using SimOS is that the emulation as well as translation modes work with MIPS binaries, since both the emulator and translator understand the MIPS instruction set.

The approach taken by Countach is to use the application directly as the processor model. Actual application code is executed whenever the simulator gives control to the processor model. Further, this code is executed natively on the machine that runs the simulator. The difference in the speeds of the actual and modeled processors is incorporated by scaling. Countach does not model details of the processor's pipeline implementation or superscalarity. If needed, averaged CPI measurements may be taken offline to feed into Countach (see Section 11.5). A key reason for this design choice is that our domain of interest is network processing, where the inherent ILP is very low. However, as we will demonstrate in Section 11.6, Countach can model simultaneous multithreading (SMT) architectures [1], which are more appropriate for network processing [3].

The challenge with native application execution is to capture memory reference behavior and to enforce time synchronization between the simulator and the processor model. The following sections describe how these requirements are met. We start by discussing the relevant aspects of the basic discrete-event simulator used by Countach.

11.2 DISCRETE-EVENT SIMULATION

Discrete-event simulation is a useful method that is often used to gain insight into the operation and performance of a system. The system is modeled as a set of components, each with an associated behavioral and performance model. The flow of work through the system is modeled as a flow of events between its components. These events may be triggered by external stimuli or by the actions of various components. Figure 11.1 illustrates a physical network server system with an intelligent adapter and its corresponding representation in a discrete-event simulator.

Events are associated with timestamps to indicate when they should be fired in terms of simulated time. Events posted to a component are processed by its model, which may generate events for other components. A component's performance is captured by the delay after which its output event is scheduled. The events are discrete in that nothing happens between the execution of successive events.

Correct event scheduling is critical to ensuring correct concurrent behavior and the proper chronology in processing events. We achieve accurate scheduling by using a single system clock and by requiring that all intercomponent communication be via a single event queue, in which events are ordered by their activation time. Each component is modeled as a finite-state machine that

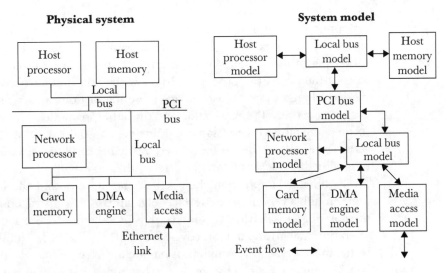

11.1 A physical network server system and its model.

FIGURE

processes events. To ensure that events received when a component is in a busy state are not lost, each component uses a private event backlog queue to defer these events until it is free to process them.

A key consideration in developing performance models for predesigned hardware components (cores) is the right level of abstraction for the model. A desirable level of abstraction is one that is detailed enough to expose key performance issues while being high-level enough to allow for quick analysis. As an example, consider data transfer over a bus. One approach is to simulate the bus protocol as faithfully as possible, requiring several bus cycles, each involving multiple operations corresponding to setting the control signals and the data transfer operations. An alternative approach we favor is including both data transfer information (size, destination, and so on) and control-and-scheduling information in a single event, resulting in far better simulation performance while having the same impact on the performance numbers of the system that is being evaluated. Thus, we create simple, efficient performance models for cores by abstracting out their functionality and by extracting their performance impact alone.

The following sections describe how the processor models are created within the discrete-event simulator.

11.3   APPLICATION-HARDWARE INTERFACE

An application running on a processor interacts with the system hardware in various ways. For example, an interaction with the bus happens when the application performs I/O. Similarly, an interaction with a hardware device occurs when it interrupts the processor. To allow the application to interact with the modeled hardware, we must replace these interactions with a simulated event exchange between the application and the hardware model. This event is passed to the simulator with the same parameters as would be passed to the hardware. For example, the packet created by the networking stack would be passed unmodified to the simulator, packaged within an event.

Fortunately, interactions between the application and the hardware happen through a very narrow interface (e.g., an IN/OUT instruction or a mapped memory region). Further, this interface is used by the system software (i.e., the operating system) and not directly by the application. The key implication of this is that most applications would not require any change to make them ready for hybrid simulation. The changes would be required at a small number of places in the system software.

Another key point to note is that we have complete freedom in choosing the level of abstraction at which a hardware interaction is replaced with a simulated event exchange. For instance, we do not have to worry about going through the parts of the device driver code that do not add much value to the performance estimation. Instead, we can simply replace a lot of driver-specific detail with a single event that can be passed to the simulator. This flexibility is very useful because we only need to worry about a relevant subset of the system software. In contrast, SimOS provides "packaged" levels of abstraction, where the designer does not exercise control over replacing parts of the application with an equivalent simulated action. In SimOS, hardware interactions would be modeled by replacing them at the lowest level, say, by replacing an IN/OUT instruction.

In Section 11.7, we will present a concrete example of this process where the application is a web server and the system software is the networking stack. In the rest of this chapter, unless explicitly specified, the "application" means the combination of the application and the modified system software.

11.4   MODELING MEMORY REFERENCE BEHAVIOR

Once an application has been prepared for simulation as described previously, in principle we are ready to replace the processor model in our discrete-event simulator with the application. However, native execution would not expose the memory reference behavior of the application for a given cache size. In network-intensive applications, copying behavior is often a very important performance determinator, and hence must be modeled.

To capture memory performance, we post-process the application with a binary annotation tool. We modified an existing tool called *cacheprof* [5] to suit our purpose. *cacheprof* takes an application binary and places glue code around its load and store instructions. This glue code plays the address to a simulated cache. We modified *cacheprof* to also annotate the application binary to send events to the memory model when a miss occurs. This allows us to correctly capture memory bus contention between the processor and the hardware DMA engines, and the true cache performance for a given application/workload combination. Figure 11.2 demonstrates a sample *cacheprof* annotation. The left column shows the original code, and the right one shows the annotated code. The load operation is replaced by a call to a hook that would play the address to a simulated cache and send an event to the memory model if it is a miss. The address is passed as a parameter to the hook function. In this example, it is the address of the local variable *var*.

Once the application has been annotated for capturing cache behavior, it can be natively executed with the simulator. The overhead on top of native application execution is that of the glue code, which depends on the number of loads

```
movl $var, %edx            movl $var, %edx
                           pushl %eax
                           leal -4(%ebp), %eax
                           call Rd_hook
                           popl %eax
addl -4(%ebp), %eax        addl -4(%ebp), %eax
```

11.2   A sample *cacheprof* annotation.

FIGURE

and stores in the application. Note that this is the bare minimum extra overhead needed to capture an application's memory performance.

The binary annotation currently identifies x86 memory instructions. To annotate applications on other architectures, we only need to understand the memory opcodes in the instruction set. This is a minor architecture dependency of Countach. This is in contrast to binary-translation-based approaches (such as SimOS's intermediate and detailed modes), which need to understand the entire instruction set of the modeled architecture.

11.5   TIME SYNCHRONIZATION

An important issue with native application execution is time synchronization between the application and the simulator. When the simulator gives control to the application to process an event, the simulated time taken by the processing may extend past the time at which the next event in the simulator's event queue is supposed to fire. This would lead to incorrect modeling of interrupts, for example. Native execution also means that applications that never block and execute infinite loops waiting for events would need special handling.

Fortunately, there is an elegant solution to this problem. Compiled applications typically take the form of a set of "basic blocks," which are blocks of instructions that do not have a branch into or out of them. Basic blocks are often no more than 10 to 15 instructions in size. Thus, basic blocks provide us a natural, fine-grained synchronization boundary at which the application can synchronize time with the simulator.

We modified *cacheprof* further to insert time synchronization code at basic block boundaries. This code checks if the time since the processor model got control has proceeded past the scheduling time of the next event in the simulator's event queue. If it has, it yields control to the simulator; otherwise, it continues execution. Note that this avoids unnecessary switching between the application and the simulator. To identify and annotate basic blocks, *cacheprof* needs to identify branch instructions, which again is a minor architecture dependency.

As the application processes an event, elapsed time is counted by multiplying the number of instructions with the cycle time of the modeled processor. Instruction counting is done for each basic block at the time when *cacheprof* parses the application binary for basic blocks. At basic block boundaries, these counts are used to advance elapsed time.

We mentioned earlier that superscalarity is not modeled. Note that the CPI of an application depends only on the application code and the CPU it runs on. Hence, if the modeled CPU is available, a CPI measurement of the application may be done on this CPU offline. This measurement can then be used to scale the elapsed time appropriately.

11.6   MODELING MULTIPLE PROCESSORS

The processor model is different from other hardware component models because it has execution state. This state needs to be saved when the processor yields control to the simulator, and resumed when it gets control back from the simulator. If we are modeling only one processor, then the simulator invocation can be thought of as a "function call" made by the application. Hence, the saving and restoring of state is done automatically on the application's stack. However, when multiple processors are being modeled, this still poses a problem. In our system of interest, there are at least two processors: a host processor and a network processor. Hence, this simplification was not possible.

We extended the basic discrete-event simulator to have multiple execution contexts, one corresponding to each modeled processor or hardware context (for SMT architectures). When the simulator starts, it allocates a stack for each modeled processor. When a processor model yields control to the simulator, all the registers and flags being used by its application are saved onto its stack. When the simulator returns control to some processor, it switches the stack pointer to that processor's stack, restores the state, and resumes the application.

Note that this functionality could have been implemented using a threads package, such as GNU pthreads. However, since the application itself may be using such a threads package, linking all components would be a problem. For example, the scheduling of threads would be across all threads, and not just application threads. Hence, we developed a native implementation of stack switching.

11.7   USING COUNTACH FOR MODELING NETWORK SERVERS

We have completed the implementation of Countach with all of the pieces described previously. In our current implementation, Countach is a user-level program that runs on the Linux operating system.

In this section, we will describe a project for which Countach is being used. We are investigating the design of next-generation network servers that can scale with the trends in increasing I/O, network, and processing bandwidth. An important aspect of this work is the exploitation of intelligent network interfaces with network processors on them. The scope of the design includes new hardware architectures, new operating system primitives, and choices of the function split between the network processor and the host processor. We are interested in quantifying the performance benefits of various design choices to choose the best design for a given application/workload combination.

The system model we are simulating is shown in Figure 11.1. The key components we focus on here are the host and network processors. Our current study is on the benefits of offloading TCP/IP processing onto the network processor. Hence, the application running on the network processor is the TCP/IP stack, whereas the code running on the host processor is the Flash web server [4] and the socket layer of the operating system.

To derive the processor models, Countach needs the implementations of the applications that run on each processor. The Flash web server code is publicly available. The implementations of the socket layer and the TCP/IP stack are taken from a user-level TCP stack derived from the Linux 2.3.29 kernel. This user-level stack was originally developed at Cambridge [6] to work with a specific Alteon Gigabit network adapter. To create a system supporting TCP offload, we have modified their implementation significantly by making the implementation hardware independent, and by cleanly separating out the socket layer processing from TCP/IP protocol processing. This means that purely event-driven TCP protocol processing runs on the network processor, whereas multiple application process or thread contexts are understood only by the socket layer of the host processor.

In an offload design, the socket layer on the host and the TCP stack on the card need to define an API between them to communicate commands, data, and results. This is a more advanced equivalent of the interface between a typical device driver and a network interface. The socket layer writes requests to the adapter in the form of a queue of descriptors. Similarly, the adapter returns responses in the form of a queue of descriptors. Data are passed between the host and the interface via DMA, and the descriptors point to the data associated with a request or a response.

In our server modeling example, this API is essentially the narrow interface that we need to replace with simulator events. The Flash web server did not have to be changed, and in the system software (socket layer) we needed a replacement at exactly two places. The first was where command descriptors were being written to the card, and the second was where the socket layer was polling for responses from the card. This demonstrates that given the application's code the manual effort involved in converting it to a model is minimal. The rest of the steps, which annotate the application for timing and tracking memory behavior, are completely automated.

Figure 11.3 shows how various pieces of code go into creating two independent processor models, which are then implemented in separate execution contexts in the simulator.

To implement and quantify the benefits of various system software optimizations—such as zero-copy data transfers, interrupt avoidance, and batching—we are able to freely make changes to our code, and then quantify their performance impact. We play a workload to the model using *actual* workload generators, such as *httperf* [7]. This is possible because the simulator simply passes the actual packets received from the workload generator to the application, and those created by the application to the workload generator.

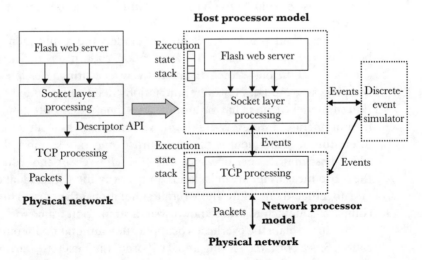

11.3
FIGURE

Converting a TCP offload implementation into host and network processor models.

Since the actual applications are implemented in the models, all packets are created and processed exactly as they would be in a real system. Note that since the system slowdown is much smaller than in emulation-based approaches, problems such as long delays causing timeouts in the workload generators are avoided.[1]

Since Countach is currently an entirely user-level tool, we utilized a user-level networking stack for the socket layer and TCP implementations. However, nothing in the design of Countach precludes working with actual operating system (OS) code. If OS code were to be used within a processor model, it would be desirable to have the simulator's core logic in the kernel so that it can directly process events from the OS without protection boundary crossings. In our case, since we already had a user-level stack to work with, the effort of doing a kernel implementation for the simulator was deemed unnecessary.

11.8   PERFORMANCE EVALUATION

In this section, we present a performance evaluation of Countach. We present results for the case when the sample modeled application is the Flash web server running over the Linux TCP stack and a simple Ethernet interface. Workload is generated using a separate client machine running *httperf* [7]. Recall that using actual application code to derive processor models allows us to use unmodified standard workload generators. We are currently in the process of conducting more extensive evaluations on the server implementation that supports full TCP offload.

As described previously, Countach models the application and workload behavior faithfully by using the application code itself to derive the processor model. Efficiency comes from natively executing the application within the processor model. However, annotations need to be added to the application to model cache behavior and enforce time synchronization. Hence, a key measurement of interest is the slowdown caused by these annotations. Another interesting measurement is the event-processing rate supported by Countach, which baselines the performance of the discrete-event simulator. We perform these two measurements in isolation to quantify their individual contributions, and together to quantify the overall simulation efficiency. This allows us to compare Countach to other known system simulation frameworks.

We first isolate the overheads of application annotation for our chosen application. Since both web serving and TCP processing exercise fairly complex code

---

1. Note that if needed even the workload generators could be modeled in the system using their actual implementations.

paths while serving web requests, and the measured file serving delays include network delays, computing the overall slowdown is trickier than simply timing the code through instrumentation. Instead, we must perform a server saturation experiment to figure out the overall effect of annotation. What this means is that we saturate the web server to full CPU utilization using *httperf* and measure the achieved connection rate.[2] Once we run the saturation experiment for the native application and the annotated application, the difference in the achieved connection rate in both cases exposes the annotation overhead.

To run the experiment, we used a 733-MHz Pentium III with 128-MB SDRAM running Linux 2.2.16. We used *httperf* to generate requests for a 300-byte file at a given request rate. This request rate is increased until we see a 100% saturated CPU. In our experiment, native Flash running over user-level TCP saturated at a connection rate of 563.9 connections per second, whereas the annotated server saturated at 75.8 connections per second. The annotated code included the Flash web server, the user-level TCP stack, and two libraries used by the user-level TCP stack (the thread library and the packet-capturing library). Through an independent kernel profiling experiment, we know that the overhead of kernel network processing that hands over a packet from the network to the packet-capturing library was quite small. The annotation thus introduces an aggregate slowdown factor of 7.44.

We also measured the event-processing overhead in isolation. We did this by running a simulation with all packet movement operations except processing, thus excluding the application overhead. Note that the packet size and content do not affect this measurement, since the overhead of the dicsrete-event simulation logic does not depend on the size or content of the packets. This experiment showed an event-processing rate of 159358.7 events per second, where there were about 363 events generated per packet. This gives us a packet-processing rate of 439 packets per second.

In a combined experiment, we include both application processing and event processing. Each TCP connection causes several packets to be exchanged for the connection setup, teardown, and data transfer, each incurring some event-processing overhead. Together, both overheads yield a connection rate of 37.23 connections per second in a saturation experiment. When compared to the connection rate of the native web server implementation, this yields an aggregate slowdown factor of 15.14.

In the absence of a setup in which we could run a SimOS experiment with a MIPS binary of the Flash web server and the Linux TCP stack, we were not

---

2. Note that here the fully utilized CPU is the physical CPU we run Countach on, not the modeled CPU.

able to compare Countach slowdowns with SimOS slowdowns on Flash running over TCP. However, one can use the slowdowns reported in [8] for some SPEC97 and compilation workloads, to get an approximate comparison. Slowdowns of a factor of 20 to 26 are reported for the positioning mode, where caches are not modeled. A 38 to 49 times slowdown is reported for the rough characterization mode, where caches are modeled and instruction execution time is tracked. The accurate mode, which models the details of the MIPS processor, sees a factor of 212 to 350 slowdown.

Some low-hanging optimizations are possible in Countach, which we have not yet implemented. *cacheprof*, for example, maintains detailed information on "charging" misses to appropriate instructions in the program's source code, to help the programmer identify cache performance problems. We do not need this feature, and can cut down the introduced annotation's size, thus reducing the overhead per memory access instruction. Similarly, for generality, most of the event-processing code has been written in C++, parts of which can be easily hand optimized, or the entire code can be run through an optimizing compiler.

11.9   CONCLUSIONS AND ONGOING WORK

We have presented the design, implementation, and initial performance evaluation of a hybrid performance modeling framework called Countach, which faithfully and efficiently captures application behavior while predicting system performance. After a small manual step of replacing hardware interactions in the system software with simulated events, a set of automated post-processing steps converts an application to a processor model that captures memory performance and enforces tight time synchronization with the simulator. Multiple processors or hardware execution contexts can be modeled in this framework. Actual workload generators can be used unmodified, to drive the performance analysis.

We are currently using Countach to model various kinds of network servers (e.g., web servers and storage servers) that utilize network-processor-based network interfaces. Countach is a very useful tool for our studies, since it has allowed us to experiment with the entire spectrum of design choices, including hardware design, a rich variety of operating system optimizations, and choices of function split between the host and the network processors.

REFERENCES

[1]   S. Eggers et al., "Simultaneous Multithreading: A Platform for Next-Generation Processors," *IEEE Micro*, Sept./Oct. 1997, pp. 12–18.

[2]   P. Crowley and J-L. Baer, "A Modeling Framework for Network Processor Systems," *Proceedings of the HPCA8 Workshop on Network Processors*, Cambridge, MA, Feb. 2002.

[3]   P. Crowley, M. Fiuczynski, J-L. Baer, and B. Bershad, "Characterizing Processor Architectures for Programmable Network Interfaces," *Proceedings of Supercomputing*, Santa Fe, NM, May 2000.

[4]   V. Pai, P. Druschel, and W. Zwaenepoel, "Flash: An Efficient and Portable Web Server," *Proceedings of USENIX Annual Technical Conference*, Monterey, CA, June 1999.

[5]   J. Seward, "The Cacheprof Home Page," *www.cacheprof.org*.

[6]   I. Pratt and K. Fraser, "Arsenic: A User-Accessible Gigabit Ethernet Interface," *Proceedings of IEEE INFOCOM*, Anchorage, AK, April 2001.

[7]   D. Mosberger and T. Jin, "*httperf*—A Tool for Measuring Web Server Performance," *Proceedings of the First Workshop on Internet Server Performance (WISP '98)*, Madison, WI, June 1998.

[8]   S. A. Herrod, "Using Complete Machine Simulation to Understand Computer System Behavior," Ph.D. thesis, Stanford University, Feb. 1998, *http://simos.stanford.edu/papers.html*.

High-Speed Legitimacy-Based DDoS Packet Filtering with Network Processors: A Case Study and Implementation on the Intel IXP1200

Roshan K. Thomas[1], Brian L. Mark[2], Tommy O. Johnson[1], James B. Croall[1]
[1]Network Associates Laboratories, Network Associates, Inc.
[2]Department of Electrical and Computer Engineering, George Mason University

Distributed denial of service (DDoS) attacks have presented a growing concern to the security and networking communities, as well as to the industry at large. These attacks first received wide attention in February of 2000, when some well-known web sites (such as Yahoo, Amazon, and CNN) and electronic commerce companies were attacked. The DDoS problem is considered by many to be one of the most difficult to solve, and the situation is exacerbated by the reality that these attacks are increasing in sophistication, with many hacker sites now distributing free attack toolkits.

In this chapter, we present the development of a high-speed packet filtering solution using network processors (NPs) so as to provide a defense against DDoS attacks. Collectively, our solution is referred to hereafter as NetBouncer. At its core, the DDoS problem is fundamentally an availability problem that arises from the illegitimate use of resources. Thus, central to the NetBouncer approach to DDoS mitigation is the ability to distinguish legitimate traffic from illegitimate traffic and the ability to prioritize processing of legitimate traffic in a manner that gives legitimate packets the highest priority for service. A successful NetBouncer solution is independent of individual DDoS attack and vulnerability specifics.

In its current form, NetBouncer technology consists of high-speed packet processing and filtering devices. From a high-level concept-of-operations standpoint, the working of a NetBouncer device is very simple. Upon receipt of an incoming packet, a device has to make one of three decisions: (1) accept and schedule transmission of the packet if it is determined to be legitimate, (2) discard the packet, or (3) challenge the sender of the packet to prove legitimacy of the packet. To enable filtering of incoming packets, a NetBouncer device maintains a large legitimacy list of identifiers of clients that have been proven to be legitimate. If packets are received from a client (source) not on the legitimacy list, a NetBouncer device will proceed to administer a variety of legitimacy tests to challenge the client to prove its legitimacy. If a client can pass these tests, it will be added to the legitimacy list and subsequent packets from the client will be accepted until a certain legitimacy window expires. Once accepted, the transmission of legitimate packets is controlled by a traffic management subsystem that applies various bandwidth allocation and rate-limiting schemes to ensure that legitimate clients do not abuse bandwidth consumption and that target servers cannot be overwhelmed even by what appears to be legitimate traffic.

In theory, the use of legitimacy tests on incoming packets allows us to prevent illegitimate use of network bandwidth. However, to be practical, NetBouncer has to operate in a manner that can meet the scalability and performance needs of high-bandwidth real-world commercial and military environments. In particular, our objective is to create a solution that is easy to integrate and has low technology insertion cost, is scalable in terms of network topology complexity and network speeds, imposes minimal administrative overhead, and requires minimal collaboration and information exchange across organizational network infrastructures and Internet service provider (ISP) networks.

Meeting these needs poses several research, design, and architecture challenges. As such, the NetBouncer approach and design incorporates several innovative elements, including:

+ Novel techniques to test for the legitimacy of network traffic using state-safe[1] legitimacy tests and the subsequent enforcement of access controls on traffic

+ Algorithms to enable efficient lookup and update of very large legitimacy lists

1. The concept of state safety can be informally defined as a property that guarantees that the consumption of state at a NetBouncer device cannot be directly induced by the proportion and rate of illegitimate traffic.

+ Quality-of-service (QoS) related traffic management schemes to provide rate limiting and bandwidth management for various classes of traffic based on client legitimacy and service priorities

+ Hardware-assisted high-speed packet-processing techniques and architectures using network processors to implement the previously cited functions, so as to achieve high performance

The focus of this chapter is on the design and implementation of a NetBouncer high-speed prototype device using the Intel IXP1200 network processor. A much broader overview of the NetBouncer research project, including research topics such as traffic management, are beyond the scope of this chapter, but are discussed in [23]. The use of programmable hardware such as the Intel IXP1200 network processor chip was motivated by several factors, including the promise of building a low-cost rapid prototype that can operate at high line rates. A Linux-based software prototype of NetBouncer implemented on conventional PC hardware and software could only sustain about 10 Mb/s of throughput.

It is our belief that the NetBouncer approach and its implementation using network processor technology represents a case study that highlights the benefits as well as the limitations of low-end network processors, which will be of interest to the broader NP research community. In particular, NetBouncer functionality places unique demands on packet processing that go beyond traditional packet-processing applications such as IP routing (as reported in [20]), packet switching and forwarding, as well as established security applications such as firewalls and virtual private networks (VPNs). For example, the use of legitimacy tests to challenge incoming packets introduces substantial complexity and additional data paths in the packet-processing architecture when compared to common IP routing and forwarding applications. Another complication is the use of cryptographic techniques to authenticate and validate messages exchanged to administer legitimacy tests.

The maintenance of large legitimacy lists is also complicated. It is not unrealistic to think of a large e-commerce site possibly utilizing a legitimacy list of about half a million entries. This is in contrast to routers where the routing tables are typically on the order of about 80,000 entries. Also, when compared to routing table entries that evolve slowly, the legitimacy list may be updated very frequently, on the order of several hundred updates every minute. Further, the amount of memory and CPU cycles available for list storage and manipulation may be limited on a network processor. Collectively, these represent interesting challenges and call for memory-efficient schemes for representing large tables and for algorithms that can simultaneously be efficient at processing lookups as well as table updates. Another challenge is the maintenance and tracking of legitimacy. This requires that we maintain legitimacy state at several levels of abstraction—including individual packets, flows, and application sessions—and understand how states at these different levels are related. Maintaining and consulting such state information introduces additional overhead on packet processing. Finally, the integration of traffic management schemes that incorporate legitimacy weights into service priorities and queuing disciplines presents interesting problems (although we do not cover this topic in this chapter).

The rest of this chapter is organized as follows. Section 12.1 discusses some background material on our approach to DDoS mitigation using legitimacy tests and the management of legitimacy lists. Section 12.2 elaborates on our prototype built using the Intel IXP1200 network processor. Sections 12.3 and 12.4 cover our performance-testing experiments. Section 12.5 discusses lessons learned and architectural directions we desire in network processors, and Section 12.6 concludes the chapter.

12.1   BACKGROUND: LEGITIMACY TESTS AND LEGITIMACY LIST MANAGEMENT

12.1.1   Client-Based Legitimacy Tests and DDoS Mitigation

In response to the growing DDoS problem, we have seen the emergence of a variety of vendor-supplied and research-oriented solutions. Typically, these are based on a variety of techniques, such as traffic sampling and analysis using statistical techniques and traffic profiles [2, 3, 4, 5, 6, 7, 8], use of DDoS attack signatures to provide DDoS-specific traffic diagnosis [2, 3], rate-limiting mechanisms [4], and better connection and timeout management and congestion control [15]. Other techniques use network-wide automated tracing and blocking of attacks as close to the attacker as possible [18, 19].

The NetBouncer approach differs from these solutions in that it is based on distinguishing legitimate traffic from illegitimate traffic. A NetBouncer device is intended to provide localized DDoS protection close to a potential victim but upstream of the local chokepoint. If we examine the issue of legitimacy more closely, we come to the realization that determining if traffic is legitimate, in turn, requires us to determine if the origin of the traffic (the client) itself is legitimate in relation to the target of the traffic (such as a server). In general, determining legitimacy may require us to abstract and analyze the traffic at one or more levels of the protocol stack. The NetBouncer approach relies on a series of legitimacy tests, with each test targeted for a particular type of traffic recognized at a specific protocol layer. The source of the traffic and the related notion of the client identity that is validated (also called the legitimacy identifier) will depend on the protocol layer (e.g., network or application) and the application or service (*ftp*, real video, and so on) for which a test is administered.

Thus, it makes sense for a legitimacy test at the network layer to determine the validity of a host or router as identified by its IP address. At the transport layer, the legitimacy tests may be aimed at validating TCP connections. At the application layer, our legitimacy tests will attempt to determine valid application sessions and user processes and identifiers. Depending on the circumstances and the application, we may apply in succession a combination of tests for various protocol layers and application-level notions such as sessions.

Our ongoing research has led us to identify at least three categories of legitimacy tests. Specifically, these include packet-based tests, flow-based tests, and service-based tests. Informally, a legitimacy test *t* is a tuple <*assertion, legit-id, pre-scope, pre-state, post-state, post-scope*>. The objective in administering a test is to examine a set of entities (called the pre-scope)—such as a packet, protocol flow, or application session—in a manner that can validate a legitimacy assertion for a given legitimacy identifier (*legit-id*) such as a source-IP address, session-id, etc. The pre-state is the state used to examine and validate the assertion, and the post-state is used to process legitimate packets after legitimacy has been established. The post-state specifies the set of entities with which legitimacy is to be associated.

The distinguishing characteristic of a packet-based legitimacy test is that the pre-state and post-state that need to be examined are fully self-contained in an individual packet. In other words, a decision as to whether a packet can be passed is made solely on examining the content of the packet. In particular, there is no information from previously seen packets that needs to be retained and consulted.

Now let us consider flow-based tests. We define a flow as a stream of packets from a particular protocol connection/session (at layer 4 in the network stack) and thus having the same (<*source-address, source-port*> and <*destination-address, destination-port*>) properties. In contrast to a packet-based test, for a flow-based test the post-state is not contained within individual packets and more significantly a single post-state applies to the entire stream of packets that belong to a flow.

In contrast to packet-based and flow-based tests, the category of service-based tests is relevant for higher-level (above layer 4) services and applications. In particular, these tests understand application-level abstractions and structures as well as session semantics. Testing for legitimacy requires an understanding of the structure and semantics at the application level. Thus, a packet-based and flow-based examination of traffic at the level of IP packets and flows will generally not provide conclusive evidence of the legitimacy of application traffic. In an application-level test, the pre-state may be spread across several IP packets and applying the post-state may require examination of application-level headers.

Packet-based tests

A simple example of a packet-based test is one that attempts to validate for every incoming packet the assertion: *There exists a valid and live host at the claimed source IP address of the incoming packet.* One way to realize such a test is through the creative use of ICMP echo messages (and hence referred to as the "ICMP Echo test"). This is useful in filtering DDoS traffic, as many DDoS attacks use spoofed and bogus source IP addresses so as to make attack tracing difficult. One way to implement such a test is for NetBouncer to intercept every incoming packet and look up its source IP address on the legitimacy list. If no match is found, NetBouncer can challenge the legitimacy of the source IP address by issuing an ICMP echo message. However, to avoid storing any state in NetBouncer so as to make the test state safe, the original incoming request packet is encapsulated in the payload of the outgoing ICMP echo request. If the original sender of the packet is a valid host, NetBouncer can expect to get back an ICMP echo reply packet. However, we need to authenticate such replies and verify their integrity. To enable this, the payload of the ICMP echo request also includes a hashed message authentication code (HMAC) computed using a keyed hash function and taking as input a packet tag, the incoming request packet, source IP address, payload length, expiration time, and a nonce (randomly generated number). If an ICMP echo reply is received and the HMAC can be verified, the authenticity and integrity of the ICMP echo reply is verified and the source IP address of the extracted incoming request packet is added to a legitimacy list consisting of validated source addresses. The HMAC is an example of the pre-state.

Flow-based tests

A good example of a flow-based test is one that can be used to validate TCP connection requests for their legitimacy. Such a test provides a defense against denial-of-service attacks based on TCP SYN floods, where an attacker repeatedly issues TCP connection requests but never responds to the handshaking sequence required to complete the connection request. This typically results in the overflow of the connection table at various hosts due to the state reserved for half-open connections, the dropping of existing TCP connections, and the inability of new legitimate TCP connection requests to complete. This DDoS condition can be attributed to the fact that in many traditional TCP implementations as soon as the first TCP SYN packet is received, state is allocated for the connection. This violates state safety.

We now describe a flow-based test to validate TCP connection requests, referred to hereafter as the TCP SYN Cookies test. This test adapts the idea of SYN Cookies described in [1]. To implement such a test, a NetBouncer device basically intercepts TCP connection establishment requests. To elaborate, Net-Bouncer intercepts SYN packets and generates SYN/ACK packets that store a cryptographic checksum (cookie) of private rotating keying material, various fields in the TCP/IP header, and a NetBouncer-generated sequence number (this cookie is effectively the pre-state). The SYN/ACK is then returned to the source address of the SYN packet. When the ACK (which is the response from the client to the SYN/ACK) arrives at the NetBouncer, if the cookie (pre-state) verifies, state is instantiated for the connection, and the original SYN along with a client-supplied sequence number is re-created based on the information in the SYN/ACK packet and the stored cookie and is forwarded to the original destination server. However, the original destination will then return a SYN/ACK server sequence number of its own, and NetBouncer will complete the three-way handshake. NetBouncer will also retain the offset between its sequence number and the server sequence number, allowing it to transform the sequence number on each packet on the TCP connection from and to the server through NetBouncer. This offset and related information form the post-state for the test.

Service-based tests

As mentioned previously, service-based tests apply to higher-level (above layer 4) services and applications. Service-based tests may be thought of as consisting of two subcategories. The first is what we call *structured composite services* (SCSs). These consist of services and protocols such as the real-time streaming protocol (RTSP). The structure of an RTSP session can be thought of as a composite one consisting of many underlying lower-level protocol sessions and connections (including TCP, UDP, and RTP). However, the exact structure is fixed by the RFCs and standards.

The second subcategory consists of *ad-hoc composite services* (ACSs). The structure of ACS services is also a composite one, but it varies from one environment to another rather than being defined by a standard. A simple example of an ACS service would be one where a user clicks on a URL at a web site and the server subsequently downloads one or more applets to the client machine. These applets may subsequently initiate additional network connections and services, depending on the application logic and transaction structure. Thus, the critical challenge here is to understand how legitimacy state is preserved and tracked through various component sessions and application interactions.

A simple example of a service-level test is one that tries to determine if a human user really exists at the client end when a service request is issued. The need for service-level tests arises from the observation that as validation methods and countermeasures against DDoS attacks become more powerful, it is only natural to expect attacks to move up from the protocol level (layers 3 and 4) to the application and service levels. During a DDoS attack, it is critical to distinguish attackers from nonthreatening users. Since most DDoS attacks are composed of a handler guiding a large number of automated attack agents [11], we can use the nonintelligence of the digital agents to distinguish them from intelligent human users.

The key idea is to interrupt an application/service session and challenge the client host with a question only a human user can answer. In our current hardware prototype of NetBouncer, we have completed an initial implementation of this test at the application level and integrated it with HTTP/HTML. In this implementation, a user (client) initiating an HTTP (web) request from a web browser is confronted with a question (i.e., a puzzle). If the user can supply the correct answer, he is added to the legitimacy list. The test works by NetBouncer intercepting the connection establishment TCP SYN packet from the client and completing the TCP three-way handshaking procedure. When the client subsequently follows up with an HTTP *get* request, NetBouncer will issue a challenge by posting a puzzle in an HTML form. However, the correct answer to the puzzle is cryptographically sealed and sent with the form so as to preserve state safety. If the client responds correctly, as verified by comparing the user-supplied answer with the cryptographically sealed and extracted answer, NetBouncer will then send an HTTP *refresh* request to the client's browser, and this will result in the client issuing a second HTTP *get* request that NetBouncer routes directly to the server.

Due to space constraints, we omit a full exposition of the details of the previously cited tests in terms of the various message exchanges and cryptographic operations, but details are given in [23]. We are currently developing a formal framework to model legitimacy tests and reason about their correctness and safety properties. We are currently investigating popular services and protocols such as FTP, RTSP, H.323, and so on in order to understand the complex structure of application sessions and more importantly to study how legitimacy can be tracked and traced so as to provide legitimacy-based filtering of application traffic.

12.1.2   Approaches to Legitimacy List Management

Having discussed legitimacy tests, we now turn our attention to the organization of legitimacy information.

Organizing legitimacy state information

Legitimacy state information serves two purposes. First, it is consulted to quickly determine if an incoming packet is legitimate. Second, it is used to provide any required processing on a legitimate packet, such as header modification and scheduling for traffic management purposes. Also, the need to support packet-based, flow-based, and service-based tests requires that we maintain several related pieces of information on the incoming traffic. Briefly, these include:

+ The identifier (IP address) of the source of the traffic

+ All incoming protocol-level flows originating from a host

+ All higher-level application sessions (services) emanating from a host

+ For each protocol-level flow, a link to the application-level information for the instantiated flow

To support fast lookups, we have divided the legitimacy information and the lookup problems into two parts. The first part consists of extracting the source address of the incoming packet and checking a host lookup table (HLT) of IP addresses to see if there is a match. The second part consists of traversing and checking a more elaborate structure, called a legitimacy state entry (LSE), for more specific information regarding flows and application sessions in relation to the matched host. The LSE in turn consists of two substructures. The first is called the flow tree (FT) and is basically a binary tree of nodes with each node representing a single flow from a host. The second substructure is a linked-list structure called the application list (AL), where each node represents a unique application or service. An application object serves to bind all individual flows for a single application session. The relationship between flow objects and application objects is many-to-one and is represented by a back pointer from every flow object to its application object.

Several alternate approaches can be used to provide fast lookups into the HLT. Figure 12.1 shows a representation of legitimacy state information with the lookup on the HLT based on a hash table. Thus, every bucket may lead to a linked list of host objects, with each host object supporting an LSE. The basic

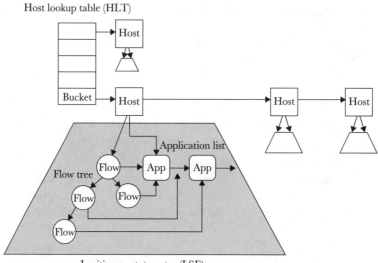

12.1 Organizing legitimacy state information with a hash table.

FIGURE

sequence for traversing legitimacy information is as follows:

+ Extract client's IP (source) address from the packet and find a match in the host lookup table.

+ Extract the flow tuple consisting of <*protocol, source address, source port, target IP address, target port*> and find a match in the flow tree.

Traversal of the flow tree is based on a binary search of a string representing the flow tuple. From every host node, we have a flow pointer that points to a tree of all flow nodes for that host. The links from the objects in the flow tree to objects in the application list are provided to implement higher-level service-based legitimacy tests, as well as QoS and traffic management on an application and per-host basis.

Efficient lookup and update strategies

The lookup function on the list of legitimate host IP addresses in NetBouncer differs from the table lookup function implemented in conventional IP routers in the following respects:

+ The lookup is based on the full source IP address, rather than a prefix of the destination IP address.

✦ New legitimate clients are added on a much faster time scale to the legitimacy list compared with typical IP routing tables.

Also, there is limited SRAM and SDRAM memory on a network processor such as the IXP1200, and thus the lookup schemes have to be space efficient. These requirements make the design and implementation of the legitimacy list a challenging task. A NetBouncer legitimacy list is expected to be significantly larger than typical IP routing tables (on the order of a few hundred thousand entries). On the other hand, we remark that longest prefix matching is not a required feature of the NetBouncer lookup function.

Current approaches to fast route table lookup include hardware-based solutions, software-based solutions, and hybrid solutions. Specialized CAM (content-addressable memory) hardware engines [16, 25] can achieve the best performance in terms of lookup speeds. However, large CAMs are very expensive and the cost grows significantly as the number of entries in the table increases, making them an infeasible approach for handling the large legitimacy list requirements of NetBouncer. Other approaches to table lookup include the use of hash tables [24] and variations on binary search trees, also called tries [12, 17, 21]. These structures do not require specialized hardware and are suitable for implementation on network processors such as the Intel IXP1200.

The hash table approach employs a hash function, which maps the host IP address into one of N hash buckets. Each bucket has an associated linked list containing host objects that have been hashed to the same bucket. In the trie approach, the computational complexity of a lookup or insert operation is generally logarithmic in the number of entries. Valid entries in the table correspond to leaf nodes in the trie. The non-leaf nodes of the trie, which are required in the search process, can incur a substantial memory space overhead. Paths in the tree that do not have branches can be compressed into single nodes, resulting in the so-called Patricia trees. The LC (level-compressed) trie proposed in [17] further employs "level compression," whereby the i highest complete levels of the trie are replaced by a single node with 2^i branches; this replacement is performed recursively on each subtree. LC tries generally have average depths that are significantly smaller than those of Patricia tries, resulting in smaller lookup times and less memory to store the lookup structure. On the other hand, the compact structure of the LC trie makes it comparatively difficult to perform insertions or deletions in an efficient manner. Doeringer et al. [12] propose a variant of a binary trie structure that accommodates dynamic updates but incurs a relatively large space overhead and does not exploit level compression.

Hash-trie structure

To meet the requirements of legitimacy list management, we are developing a novel structure called the hash trie, which combines features of hash tables and LC tries in order to perform efficient lookups and updates. Note that this has not yet been implemented on our prototype. The hash trie consists of a hash table in which collisions at each bucket are resolved by a variant of the trie stucture, which we call the LC-m trie. The hash trie allows us to exploit the efficient hash function provided by the IXP1200 and avoids the potentially time-consuming linear searches that may occur in the conventional hash table structure. The LC-m trie exploits path compression and up to m levels of level compression, but unlike the LC trie updates can be performed efficiently.

In the LC-m trie, a node contains pointers to up to 2^m child nodes. Each node contains a *skip* parameter for path compression and a *branch* parameter, where the value of *branch* can be at most m. Thus, up to m levels in an equivalent binary subtrie can be (level) compressed into a single node in the LC-m trie. To facilitate update operations, each node also contains a parameter *str*, which contains the actual bit sequence that was skipped in the path compression process. In the LC-m trie, the computational costs of lookups, insertions, and deletions are determined by the depth of the trie. Insertions and deletions incur a constant additional computational overhead compared to lookups.

A simple example of a hash-trie structure is illustrated in Figure 12.2. The hash table consists of $N = 11$ buckets, labeled 0 to 10. Bucket 5 in the hash table is highlighted to illustrate an example of an LC-2 trie. Each of the leaf nodes in the trie corresponds to a binary bit sequence indicated in the figure. The maximum number of child nodes of a given node is four, although some of the child pointers in a node may be null, as indicated in the figure by a downward arrow symbol. Nodes with non-zero skip values are labeled with the values of the *skip* and *str* parameters. Observe that nine entries are hashed to bucket 5 in this example, although the maximum depth of the corresponding LC-2 trie is only two.

12.2   PROTOTYPE ARCHITECTURE ON THE INTEL IXP1200 NETWORK PROCESSOR

12.2.1   Overview of the Intel IXP1200 Network Processor

The IXP1200 chip and network processor development system consists of a StrongARM processor and six microengines. The Intel StrongARM Core processor is a 32-bit RISC processor currently available at an operating frequency of

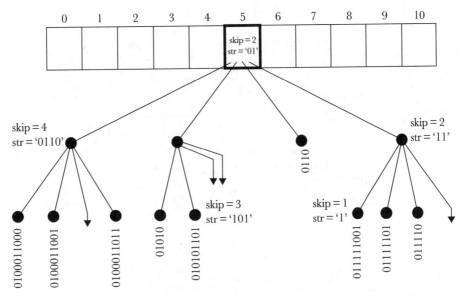

The hash-trie structure.

200 MHz. It acts as the master general-purpose processor and supports the control plane. It is responsible for performing the bulk of the signaling and network management functions comprising the control plane. The actual movement of data and packet-processing operations is performed by six 32-bit RISC microengines running at 200 MHz and acting as specialized slave processors. Each microengine can execute four parallel threads by means of four independent program counters, zero-overhead context switching, and hardware semaphores. In addition, the microengine contains an ALU and shifter, 4 KB of RAM control store, 128 32-bit general-purpose registers, and 128 32-bit transfer registers for accessing the SRAM and SDRAM units. The IXP1200 also contains a hash unit for generating 48- and 64-bit hash keys. The IXP1200 supports two Gigabit Ethernet ports and eight fast Ethernet (100-Mb/s) ports. For our current prototype, only the gigabit ports are used.

12.2.2   Prototype Architecture

Fast-path and test-path packet processing

The details of the architecture for our current hardware prototype are shown in Figure 12.3. Our prototype uses only the two gigabit ports. The path labeled 1

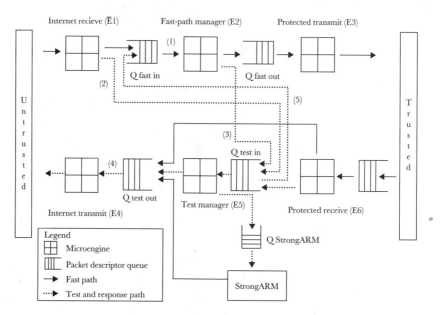

12.3   Architecture of the NetBouncer prototype.

FIGURE

and shown by thick arrows is the *fast path* in the architecture—the path through which legitimate packets are processed and transmitted. The paths labeled 2, 3, and 4 and as shown by dotted arrows are the *test paths*—the paths through which packets that failed legitimacy and test packets associated with sending legitimacy tests are processed and transmitted.

Figure 12.3 shows the careful allocation of various NetBouncer packet-filtering and legitimacy administration functions to the available microengines (labeled E1 through E6). This is basically a six-stage pipelined architecture. Packets are received from the media access control (MAC) layer, processed, and transmitted. To enable this, a variety of queues are used. As a packet is received from the MAC layer, it is stored in SRAM. However, vital information from the packet (such as critical header information) is extracted and stored in a structure called a *packet descriptor*. The packet descriptor also stores a pointer to the physical SRAM address where the packet is stored. The queues are used to pass the packet descriptors from one microengine to another as processing of the packet progresses in the pipeline. This is more efficient than passing the actual packet from one queue to another.

Let us look at the details of how packets are processed on the prototype. We start with the fast path in the architecture. Processing starts with the *Internet receive* microengine (E1) reading incoming packets from the MAC layer and depositing their packet descriptors into the queue labeled *Q fast in*. A second microengine, labeled *Fast-path manager*, (E2), dequeues these descriptors, extracts the source address, and checks the legitimacy list to see if the packet is coming from a legitimate source. If the source address is on the legitimacy list, we consider the packet to have passed the legitimacy test- and the corresponding packet descriptor is queued into the queue labeled *Q fast out*. A third microengine, labeled *Protected transmit* (E3), consumes descriptors from this queue and uses the pointer in the descriptor to extract the packet content and transmit it to the appropriate destination on the trusted side.

If a packet is not on the legitimacy list, its descriptor is queued into the queue labeled *Q test in*, and the packet is then processed through the test path. A micro-engine, labeled *Test manager* (E5), empties entries from this queue and issues one or more legitimacy tests. Each legitimacy test challenge packet is queued into the queue *Q test out*, from which the microengine *Internet transmit* (E4) transmits the challenge back to the client source on the untrusted (Internet) side of the network. Our design accommodates the scenario in which if a legitimacy test is too complicated for data plane processing in a microengine, the appropriate descriptor is forwarded to the StrongARM processor for further processing via the queue labeled *Q StrongARM*. The StrongARM may do more complex processing such as those involving very sophisticated legitimacy tests.

The microengine labeled *Protected receive* (E6) processes packets from the trusted side of the network, such as general traffic from server machines. It may forward packets directly to the queue *Q test out* for subsequent transmission by the *Internet transmit* microengine or alternatively send some packets to the *Test manager* microengine for further processing and tagging. The latter path is taken for some legitimacy tests (such as an anti-*smurf* test) that require certain outgoing packets, such as outgoing ICMP echo requests, to be cryptographically sealed and tagged so that subsequent ICMP echo replies can be verified for these tags. This can be used to defend against *smurf*-style amplification attacks that flood servers with ICMP echo replies (details are given in [23]).

Response-path packet processing

There also exist response data paths within the architecture. These are the data paths used for processing responses to challenges issued as part of legitimacy tests. Responses can be fed to the *Test manager* (E5) through one of two paths, also labeled (2) and (3) in Figure 12.3. The response path labeled (2) is taken if the *Internet receive* microengine (E1) receives a packet identified as a response from a client to a previously issued challenge and if it is determined that the challenge can be validated without consulting stored legitimacy state. In other words, the packet descriptor is put directly into the queue $Q\,test\,in$, thereby avoiding the *Fast-path manager* (E2) microengine. On the other hand, the second path, labeled (3), is taken when legitimacy information needs to be consulted with the help of microengine E2. Path 2 is basically an optimization to achieve speed-up response processing by exploiting certain properties of legitimacy tests, such as if the pre-state of the test is self-contained in a packet. Path 2 is generally possible for packet-based legitimacy tests such as the ICMP Ping test. The actual speedup is obtained by eliminating the *Fast-path manager* microengine from the processing pipeline. In either case, if legitimacy can be validated, the path labeled (5) is used by the *Test manager* microengine to send updates to the legitimacy table through the *Fast-path manager*.

Use of cryptography and digital signatures

As mentioned earlier, legitimacy challenges issued to clients are cryptographically sealed and responses from clients are cryptographically verified. Implementing cryptographic functions such as a hashed message authentication code (HMAC) function on the IXP1200 requires careful thought due to the limited instruction store and memory and other efficiency concerns. Common schemes, such as MD5 and SHA1, are too complex and inefficient. Thus, we have chosen to implement an alternative algorithm, called Michael [13], to generate HMACs for the various legitimacy test packets. Michael is simple to implement and offers acceptable trade-offs between performance and security strength, given NetBouncer's design intention to change keys frequently. By default, Michael generates 64-bit authentication tags. NetBouncer performs some modest post-processing of the Michael output by applying the XOR operation to the two 32-bit halves to generate a final 32-bit result that is encapsulated in outgoing legitimacy test packets.

12.3   PERFORMANCE ANALYSIS EXPERIMENTS

12.3.1   Test Configuration

Figure 12.4 shows our test configuration. The first component is a NetBouncer prototype based on the Intel IXP1200 network processor evaluation system with two 1-gigabit Ethernet ports, with each port capable of transmitting and receiving packets. The second component is an IXP1200 system configured to generate packets at 1 gigabit. The input stream, fast-path output, and test-path output

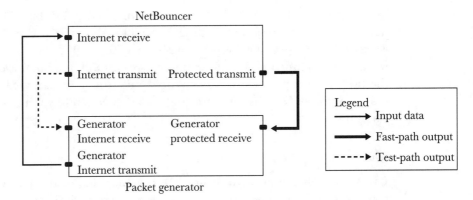

12.4

FIGURE

The test configuration consisting of NetBouncer and a packet generator.

were set up as shown in the figure. NetBouncer itself did not modify incoming or outgoing packets for the purpose of instrumentation with any information such as timestamps, as doing so would reduce the true throughput of the hardware. Instead, all instrumentation was done when packets were transmitted and received by the packet generator.

12.3.2 Test Methodology

We conducted two broad classes of experiments. The first set of experiments was aimed at getting bounds on throughput, latencies, and packet rates in our architecture. These experiments were thus conducted with the legitimacy list lookup function bypassed. In particular, we wanted to measure throughput and latency as a function of packet size, as packet sizes directly affect packet rates. Packet sizes were varied, starting at 64 bytes and going all the way to 1496 bytes in increments of 8 bytes. For each packet size, a set of three runs (trials) was conducted and plotted, where a run consisted of generating packets for a sample interval of 5 seconds. After the three runs at a packet size, the packet size was varied by 8 bytes and a "settling time" of 2 seconds was allowed, during which the flow of packets was not measured. The second set of experiments measured throughput and latency for 128-, 600-, and 1200-byte packets (referred to as small, medium, and large packets) in a configuration where every data packet resulted in a lookup on the legitimacy list. The experiment included the "all-good" configuration to test the fast path where every incoming packet was legitimate, and an "all-bad" configuration with only illegitimate packets so as to exercise the test path. Another parameter that was varied was the configuration of the legitimacy list. One used a hash-based host lookup table (HLT) with 256 buckets (called the small hash table), and the other used 4192 buckets (large hash table). The hash unit of the IXP1200 was used to implement the hash function. By comparing our results with the bounds obtained in the first set of experiments, we could compute the overhead incurred by the lookup function. Once again, three trials of 5-second samples were used for each variation.

Measuring latency

Latency was measured by inserting the current value of the IXP chip's cycle counter as a timestamp into the Ethernet addresses within the packets being sent by the packet generator. This avoided modifying the format of the packets sent, as well as any increase in the packet size due to our tests. After a packet was sent and eventually processed and transmitted by NetBouncer back to the packet generator's *Generator protected receive* port, the cycle counter was read again and the difference between the send and receive timestamps computed.

Measuring throughput

To measure throughput, we read a hardware counter on the Ethernet interface card of the packet generator at the end of each 5-second sample interval after having packets cycled through NetBouncer. It is to be noted that the throughput experiments did not have packets timestamped for latency measurements by the generator so as to avoid the overhead of reading the cycle counter when generating packets. Doing so would reduce the throughput of the generator.

12.4　PERFORMANCE RESULTS

12.4.1　Throughput on the Fast Path and Test Path

Figure 12.5a and b shows the throughput results for the first set of experiments where the lookup function was bypassed. The incoming throughput observed at the *Internet receive* port on NetBouncer ranged from about 990 Mb/s for packet sizes of 1496 bytes to about 707 Mb/s for small packet sizes of 64 bytes. The throughput observed on the fast path (*Protected transmit* port) very closely matched the incoming rate for packet sizes greater than 248 bytes. Below a packet size of 248 bytes there was a sharp drop in throughput, with the low end around 339 Mb/s for 64-byte packets. In general, the lower throughput for small

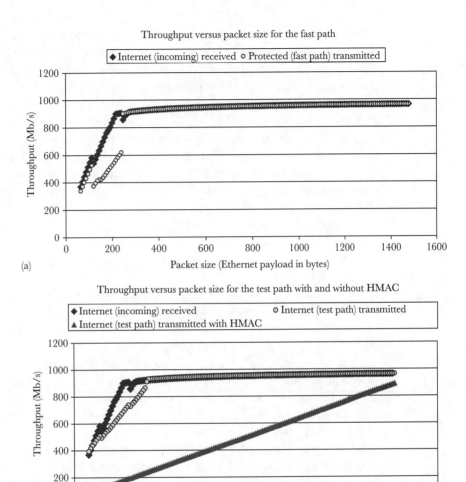

Throughput versus packet size for the fast path

◆ Internet (incoming) received   ○ Protected (fast path) transmitted

(a)

Throughput versus packet size for the test path with and without HMAC

◆ Internet (incoming) received   ○ Internet (test path) transmitted
▲ Internet (test path) transmitted with HMAC

(b)

12.5   Throughput for the (a) fast path and (b) test path with no lookup function.

FIGURE

packet sizes can be attributed to the fact that with smaller packet sizes the packet frequencies increase and the overhead per packet is thus greater. Depending on how much processing a packet incurs, NetBouncer can see packet rates ranging from about 64,000 to 166,622 packets per second for packet sizes of 1400 bytes, and rates ranging from 492,000 to 1,432,978 packets per second for a packet length of 64 bytes.

We next studied throughput as a function of packet size for the test path with and without the use of HMAC for the challenge packets (see Figure 12.5b). When HMACs are used, there is a significant reduction in throughput when compared to no HMACs being used, but this difference decreases steadily as packet sizes increase. This is an indication that the HMAC overhead is per packet and not per byte. At about 1400 bytes, the throughputs with and without HMACs are very close. When HMACs were not used and the packet size was below 305 bytes, the throughput degraded almost linearly and approached about 400 Mb/s. This is a reflection of the fact that the illegitimate packet rate exceeded the hardware's capability to issue test challenges. Further optimization of our code could improve this situation.

Figure 12.6a and b shows throughput results for our second set of experiments where the lookup function was incorporated. The figure shows throughput plotted as a function of the size of the legitimacy list. The size of the list was varied from about 100 entries to about 4200 entries, where the latter represents the maximum we could store given the memory constraints of the Intel IXP1200. Throughput was studied for 128-byte (small), 600-byte (medium), and 1200-byte (large) packets and for legitimacy list implementations of hash table configurations consisting of 256 (small) as well as 4192 (large) buckets. For the fast path, we see in Figure 12.6a that for the large packet size the throughput is steady, at an average rate of 990 Mb/s. The throughput characteristics for the medium packet size are nearly the same as for the large packet size. But with the small packet size of 128 bytes, throughput drops to an average rate of about 298 Mb/s. This can be attributed to the increased per-packet overhead at higher packet rates (as explained when we discuss latency in material to follow). In this case, NetBouncer is not able to keep up with the incoming packet rate, which is highest for the small packet size. The hash table configuration has very little impact on the throughput for the large and medium packet sizes. For the small packet size, a small gradual dip in throughput from about 325 Mb/s to about 285 Mb/s can be observed on the fast path when the small hash table is used. No such dip occurs when the large hash table is used.

To study the test path, NetBouncer was fed a set of addresses that were all illegitimate by subjecting it to the well-known TCP attack using SYN floods. Each incoming SYN packet was thus challenged with a legitimacy test. As shown in Figure 12.6b, we see that there is a dramatic reduction in overall throughput on the test path when compared to the fast path. Throughput is about 50 Mb/s for the large packet size, 98 Mb/s for the medium packet size, and about 140 Mb/s for the small packet size. Also notable is the inversion of throughput with respect to the packet size when compared to the fast path. In other words, smaller packet

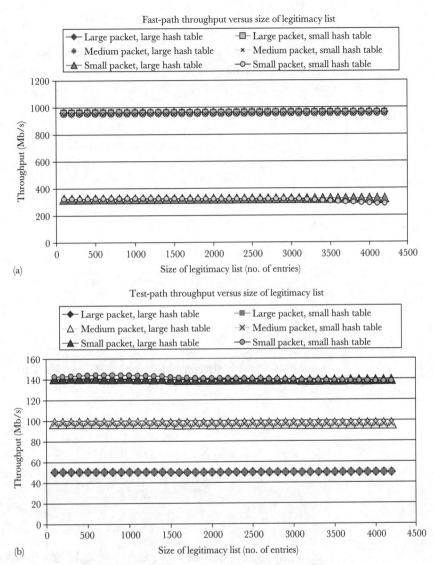

Throughput as a function of legitimacy list size for the (a) fast path and (b) test path.

sizes result in higher throughputs. This can be attributed to the fact that the larger the incoming packet the longer the duration the *Test manager* microengine has to wait to issue a challenge. This decreases the number of challenges issued per unit of time and thus lowers the throughput on the test path.

12.4.2   Latency on the Fast and Test Path

Figure 12.7a and b shows the packet latency through NetBouncer for the fast
and test paths. The latency numbers were obtained by first measuring the total
packet delay from the transmit to the receive ports of the packet generator with

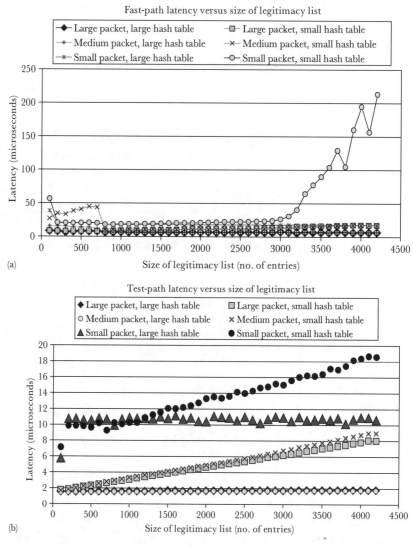

(a)

(b)

12.7   Latency as a function of legitimacy list size for the (a) fast path and (b) test path.

FIGURE

NetBouncer in the loop, and then subtracting the packet delay measured when NetBouncer was replaced by a short circuit. We observe two key facts. First, latency is largest for the trials with the small packet size (128 bytes) on both the fast and test paths. For the medium and large packet sizes, the latency numbers were markedly smaller. Second, one can observe the dependence of latency on the number of buckets used for the hash-based lookup, particularly for the small packets when the small hash table was used. On the fast path, the latency for small packets using the small hash table ranged from about 25 microseconds when the legitimacy list contained less than 3000 entries to over 200 microseconds when the list contained over 4000 entries. The dependence of latency on the legitimacy list for the small hash table can be clearly seen on the test-path results shown in Figure 12.7b. For the large packet sizes, the latency increases nearly linearly from about 2 to around 8 microseconds. The corresponding curve for the medium packet sizes is also approximately a line, with slightly higher slope. For the small packet sizes on the test path, the latency also shows an approximately linear growth from a latency of about 7 microseconds to about 19 microseconds. In Figure 12.7a and b, when the large hash table is used there is little or no dependence of the latency on the number of legitimate entries.

12.4.3 Analysis and Discussion

Focusing on the fast-path results with lookup, presented in Figures 12.6 and 12.7, we note that there was no packet loss within NetBouncer for the large- and medium-size packets. More precisely, the incoming and outgoing packet rate to NetBouncer for the large packets was about 99,000 packets per second (i.e., 99 Kpps), while the incoming/outgoing packet rates for the medium-size packets were 192 Kpps. For the small packets, the incoming rate was about 570 Kpps, while the outgoing rate was only about 275 Kpps (and actually slightly lower than this when the small hash table was used). Therefore, nearly 52% of the small packets are dropped by NetBouncer in this experiment. One can conclude from this that the maximum packet-processing rate of our NetBouncer prototype on the fast path is about 275 Kpps. On the test path, the maximum packet rate is slightly higher at 280 Kpps. This apparent contradiction is explained in the following.

The latency figures for the test path are markedly smaller than those for the fast path, which seems to contradict the nomenclature of "fast path" versus "test path." This can be explained as follows. The test that is being applied is the TCP SYN Cookies test (see Section 12.1.1), which requires relatively little processing to issue. More importantly, the size of the challenge packet is only

60 bytes (i.e., less than half the size of the small packet), which corresponds to the minimum Ethernet frame size. Therefore, the packet transmission time required for the challenge packet is significantly smaller than for the incoming packets of the three sizes considered. We found that in our experiments packet transmission time was a dominating factor in the latency of packet processing through NetBouncer.

In our NetBouncer prototype, the maximum number of entries on the legitimacy list was limited to less than 5000 entries. In a real implementation, we would expect NetBouncer to handle a list size about two orders of magnitude larger. In our experiments, the lookup time was not a factor when the large hash table was used. For the small hash table, however, the latency figures clearly showed a linear growth rate as the legitimacy list size was increased. For larger list sizes, the lookup time is expected to become a dominating factor in the packet-processing time. This strongly suggests the need for a more efficient lookup structure, such as the hash trie described previously, as a replacement for the hash and linked-list scheme we used.

The performance experiments we have conducted so far do not include measurements on updates to the legitimacy list. This is attributed to the fact that we found it difficult to set up tests that would generate steady-state conditions, since the maximum legitimacy table size of about 4000 entries would be populated in a fraction of a second at the incoming line rate of 900 Mb/s. To get reliable readings on metrics, such as the number of updates sustainable per second, we need to maintain steady state with legitimacy tests and response validations for some reasonable sample intervals. We hope to address this issue in the future, so that we can evaluate the time and space efficiency trade-offs of the hash-trie structure when the legitimacy list incurs a high rate of updates. Also, the tests that generated graphs in Figures 12.6 and 12.7 did not involve cryptographic operations for the HMAC function. Intuitively, combining HMAC along with the lookup function will lead to further throughput degradation on the test path. We hope to study this in the future.

12.5   LESSONS LEARNED ON ARCHITECTURAL DIRECTIONS FOR NETWORK PROCESSORS

In the course of developing the NetBouncer prototype on the IXP1200, we have seen the benefits, as well as the limitations, of low-end network processors. We now reflect on some of the lessons learned and discuss desirable features that would have simplified the implementation and increased efficiency and performance. We note that NetBouncer functionality goes significantly beyond pure IP routing and forwarding and represents a good case study of a complex and practical application that places unique demands on packet processing. These requirements can provide a set of guidelines for supporting advanced features in next-generation network processor technology. The complexity of NetBouncer-style packet filtering can be attributed to the fact that complex legitimacy state needs to be maintained, and challenge packets need to be sent back to the client machines. The administering and verification of legitimacy tests in real time introduces a variety of data paths and pipelines on the IXP1200 implementation.

A challenging aspect of programming the IXP1200 was constructing the pipeline of tasks and distributing them among the microengines. This is partly due to the programming model for the IXP family of network processors, which calls for the application designer to be aware of internal details such as the pipeline and queue structures, as well as the careful allocation of functionality across the various processors (microengines). The IXP1200 does not provide explicit mechanisms for queuing packets between the pipeline stages. Hence, we resorted to using the generic queue structures provided by a third-party application development environment for the IXP1200; namely, Teja [22]. If the queuing structures could support priority schemes, this would allow NetBouncer to make more efficient use of the IXP microengines. For example, we would like to sort the queue of challenge packets according to some service priority so that higher-priority challenges are issued more promptly.

Another limitation was the transfer register scheme of the IXP1200. It allows only eight 32-bit words of a packet to be read into the IXP at a time. This makes it rather cumbersome to access arbitrary fields in an entire packet and slows down packet classification and other packet-processing tasks. In particular, if the string to be searched is not aligned on a 32-bit word boundary, additional low-level bit manipulations are required to extract the string. The ability to efficiently perform "grep"-like or string-search operations would allow us to recognize application-specific messages. This would make the implementation of higher-level service-based legitimacy tests much more efficient.

The pipelined architecture of the IXP1200 can result in performance bottlenecks, as the computational loads incurred on the microengines can vary considerably based on the incoming traffic mix and DDoS attacks in progress. Mechanisms to perform dynamic load balancing across microengines could lead to significantly better performance by reallocating legitimacy testing and cryptographic operations across idle microengines so as to balance the microengine utilizations. On the other hand, dynamic load balancing would be difficult to implement on the current IXP architecture due to the lack of common register space and control stores across microengines. Moreover, load balancing would require an architecture that could dynamically monitor microengine utilization and allow relatively idle microengines to assume additional tasks with low overhead.

In implementing the NetBouncer architecture on the IXP1200, we found that several data-intensive tasks might be performed better by a co-processor or specialized hardware engine. NetBouncer performance could be greatly enhanced by a packet classifier that could parse incoming packets, extract the fields of interest, and hand these fields to the microengines further down the pipeline. This would avoid the need to move the entire packet into the IXP and would free up the microengines to perform other NetBouncer tasks. Moreover, a packet classifier could assign priorities to packets, and this could be used to reduce the burden on heavily loaded microengines during periods of congestion within the IXP.

General packet classification is cumbersome to implement on the IXP1200. Although classification of HTTP packets is relatively easy to perform on the IXP, parsing of more complex protocols is more difficult, especially when parameters such as UDP port numbers are dynamically assigned as in RTP. For the service-based legitimacy tests, it would be desirable to have a general packet classifier that could parse HTTP-style headers.

Another desirable function that could be implemented in hardware, or in a co-processor, is a generic checksum engine. For example, to rewrite a TCP header, NetBouncer would extract the TCP checksum, send the checksum engine the fields that were to be changed, change the fields, send the new values of the field, and finally query the new checksum value. A packet classifier and checksum engine could be combined to create a packet co-processor that would process packets at the ingress/egress of NetBouncer. Other common packet-processing functions that could be offloaded to the packet co-processor might include general hash functions and encryption/decryption operations. This is indeed the direction taken by more advanced network processors.

A general hardware lookup engine would also be a desirable feature that would simplify the NetBouncer architecture. While we devised an efficient lookup engine that could be implemented directly on the IXP, we feel that the resources of the IXP could be much better utilized to implement the NetBouncer functionality if the lookup function were offloaded to a specialized search engine. For flow lookup, such a search engine should allow an arbitrary block of data to be allocated to each flow. Other items on our hardware "wish list" that would simplify and improve the performance of a NetBouncer implementation on a network-processor-based system include a flow control engine and a TCP engine.

The flow control engine would provide flow management functionality such as packet buffering, packet dropping, and setting flow parameters.

A TCP engine would allow NetBouncer to effectively terminate and source a TCP connection. This would allow NetBouncer to see a stream of bytes arriving on a TCP flow rather than packets, which would simplify the implementation of service-based legitimacy tests such as the Turing test.

12.6   CONCLUSIONS AND FUTURE WORK

We have presented the results of the NetBouncer research effort to build a high-speed DDoS traffic-filtering appliance using the Intel IXP1200 network processor. The unique feature of the NetBouncer approach to DDoS mitigation is the use of legitimacy tests to distinguish and filter incoming illegitimate traffic. These tests exist at various levels of abstraction in the protocol stack and have to be administered on every incoming packet from untrusted clients in a manner that can maintain high line rates.

At this stage of our research project, we have seen the benefits, as well as the limitations, of low-end network processors. Our IXP1200 prototype has clearly outperformed earlier software (Linux-based) versions of NetBouncer implemented on mainstream PC processors. However, initial tests of the prototype have also exposed the limitations of low-end network processors, such as the IXP1200, in supporting functions beyond simple packet routing and forwarding. In a nutshell, the IXP1200 was not sufficient to implement the desired capabilities of NetBouncer.

The complexity of NetBouncer-style packet filtering can be attributed to many functions. First, NetBouncer functionality calls for packet content to be looked up in a legitimacy structure that is much more complex than IP routing tables. This structure is required to maintain and track legitimacy state across a variety of traffic-related abstractions and may incur a very high frequency of updates. We also failed to support the requirement to store at least a few hundred thousand entries in the legitimacy list due to memory constraints. Second, the administering and verification of legitimacy tests in real time introduces a variety of data paths and pipelines on a network processor architecture such as the IXP1200. In particular, this is required to support the sending of challenge packets back to client machines and the subsequent verification of client responses. This complexity is also partly due to the programming model for the IXP family of network processors, which calls for the application designer to be aware of internal details such as the pipeline and queue structures, as well as the careful allocation of functionality across the various processors (microengines).

From a security standpoint, we note that even a lightweight HMAC function for cryptography increased the per-packet overhead, resulting in considerably reduced throughputs and increased latencies.

A critical feature we desperately desired was the need to provide dynamic load balancing, as illegitimate and legitimate traffic loads vary considerably based on the incoming traffic mix and the DDoS attacks in progress. This could lead to better performance by reallocating legitimacy testing and cryptographic operations across idle microengines.

In the future, we hope to experiment with the more powerful IXP2400 or IXP2800 processor, as well as explore network processors with alternate programming models, such as the run-to-completion models (e.g., IBM and AMCC processors) that provide an abstract, single, and unified model to the application developer. These processors also provide cryptographic co-processors that should improve performance.

ACKNOWLEDGMENTS

The NetBouncer project is funded by the Defense Advanced Research Projects Agency (DARPA) under contract N66001-01-C-8046. We are grateful to Dr. Doug Maughan and the Fault Tolerant Networks program for their support. We are also grateful to Dr. Akash Deshpande and his colleagues at Teja Technologies for their assistance with the Teja development environment, and to our colleague Eric O'Brien at Network Associates for providing the initial inspiration for NetBouncer.

REFERENCES

[1]   D. J. Bernstein, SYN Cookies, *http://cr.yp.to/syncookies.html*.

[2]   Peakflow/DoS, Arbor Networks, *www.arbornetworks.com/up_media/up_files/Pflow _Enter_datasheet2.1.pdf*.

[3]   DDoS Enforcer, Mazu Networks, *www.mazunetworks.com/solutions/product _overview.html#300*.

[4]   S. Capshaw, "Minimizing the Effects of DoS Attacks," application note, Juniper Networks, Nov. 2000, *www.juniper.net/techcenter/app_note/350001.pdf*.

[5]   Cisco Systems, "Strategies to Protect Against Distributed Denial of Service (DDoS) Attacks," white paper, *www.cisco.com/warp/public/707/newsflash.html*.

[6]   Cisco Systems, "Characterizing and Tracing Packet Floods Using Cisco Routers,"
        technical note, July 1999, *www.cisco.com/warp/public/707/22.html*.

[7]   Cisco Systems, "Configuring TCP Intercept (Prevent Denial-of-Service Attacks),"
        www.cisco.com/univercd/cc/td/doc/product/software/ios113ed/113ed_cr/secur_c/scprt3/
        scdenial.htm.

[8]   Cisco Systems, "Cisco IOS Netflow," *www.cisco.com/warp/public/732/Tech/nmp/netflow*.

[9]   D. Dean and A. Stubblefield, "Using Client Puzzles to Protect TLS," *Proceedings of the*
        10th USENIX Security Symposium, Washington, D.C., Aug. 13–17, 2001.

[10]   M. Degermark, A. Brodnik, S. Carlsson, and S. Pink, "Small Forwarding Tables for
        Fast Routings Lookups, *ACM Computer Communication Review*, 27(4), Oct. 1997,
        pp. 3–14.

[11]   S. Dietrich, N. Long, and D. Dittrich, "Analyzing Distributed Denial of Service Tools:
        The Shaft Case," *Proceedings of the LISA XIV*, New Orleans, LA, Dec. 3–8, 2000.

[12]   W. Doeringer, G. Karjoth, and M. Nassehi, "Routing on Longest-Matching Prefixes,"
        IEEE/ACM Transactions on Networking, 4(1), Feb. 1996, pp. 86–97.

[13]   N. Ferguson, "Michael: An Improved MIC for 802.11 WEP," IEEE P802.11, *Wireless*
        LANs, Amsterdam, Netherlands, Jan. 17, 2002.

[14]   D. P. Morrison, "Practical Algorithm to Retrieve Information Coded in Alfanumeric,"
        Journal of ACM, 15(4), Oct. 1968, pp. 514–534.

[15]   R. Mahajan et al., "Controlling High Bandwidth Aggregates in the Network," AT&T
        Center for Internet Research at ICSI (ACIRI), draft, Feb. 5, 2001, *www.research*
        .att.com/~smb/papers/ddos-lacc.pdf.

[16]   A. McAuley and P. Francis, "Fast Routing Table Lookup Using CAMs," *Proceedings of*
        INFOCOM, Mar./Apr., 1993, pp. 1382–1391.

[17]   S. Nilsson and G. Karlsson, "Fast Address Lookup for Internet Routers," *Proceedings of*
        the International Conference on Broadband Communication, Apr. 1998.

[18]   K. Park and H. Lee, "On the Effectiveness of Route-Based Packet Filtering for
        Distributed DoS Attack Prevention in Power-Law Internets," *Proceedings of the ACM*
        SIGCOMM '01, pp. 15–26.

[19]   D. Schnackenberg, K. Djahandari, and D. Sterne, "Infrastructure for Intrusion
        Detection and Response," *Proceedings of the DARPA Information Survivability Conference*
        and Exposition, Hilton Head, SC, Jan. 2000.

[20]   T. Spalink, S. Karlin, L. Peterson, and Y. Gottlieb, "Building a Robust Software-Based
        Router Using Network Processors," *Proceedings of the Symposium on Operating Systems*
        Principles (SOSP), 2001.

[21]   D. E. Taylor et al., "Scalable IP Lookup for Programmable Routers," *Proceedings of the*
        IEEE Infocom'02, 2002, pp. 562–571.

[22]   Teja Technologies, "Software Development Platform for Network Processors,"
        http://teja.com/content/teja_np_datasheet.pdf.

[23]   R. Thomas, B. Mark, T. Johnson, and J. Croall, "NetBouncer: Client-Legitimacy-Based High-Performance DDoS Filtering," *Proceedings of the Third DARPA Information Survivability Conference and Exposition (DISCEX III)*, Washington, DC, April 22–24, 2003.

[24]   M. Waldvogel, G. Varghese, J. Turner, and B. Plattner, "Scalable High-Speed IP Routing Lookups," *ACM Computer Communication Review*, 27(4), Oct. 1997, pp. 25–36.

[25]   C. A. Zukowski and T. Pei, "Putting Routing Tables into Silicon," *IEEE Network*, Jan. 1992, pp. 42–50.

Directions in Packet Classification for Network Processors

**Michael E. Kounavis[1], Alok Kumar[2], Harrick Vin[3],
Raj Yavatkar[2], Andrew T. Campbell[1]**
[1]COMET Group, Columbia University
[2]Intel Corporation
[3]University of Texas at Austin

Packet classification involves identifying flows from among a stream of packets that arrive at routers. It is a fundamental building block that enables routers to support access control, quality-of-service differentiation, virtual private networks, and other value-added services. To be classified as belonging to a flow, each packet arriving at a router is compared against a set of rules. Each rule contains one or more fields and their associated values, a priority, and an action. The fields generally correspond to specific portions of the TCP/IP header, such as the source and destination IP addresses, port numbers, and protocol identifier. A packet is said to match a rule if it matches every field in that rule. Upon identification of the matching rules, actions associated with the rules are executed.

Packet classification is often the first packet-processing step in routers. It requires network systems to maintain and to navigate through search data structures. Since flows can be identified only after the classification step, to prevent performance interference across flows network systems must ensure that classification operates at line speeds. Unfortunately, the overhead of navigating through search data structures can often exceed the time budget enforced by the line-speed processing requirement. Thus, a key challenge is to design packet classification algorithms that impose low memory space and access overhead and hence can scale to high-bandwidth networks and large databases of classification rules.

In this chapter, we take a step in the direction of designing such efficient classification algorithms. In particular, we study the properties of packet classification rules. Our intent is to expose characteristics that can be exploited to design packet classifiers that can scale well with link bandwidths and the sizes of classification rule databases. Since access control is the most common application of packet classification today, we study four databases of classification rules collected from firewalls supported by large ISPs and corporate intranets. Our analysis yields the following key observations:

+ The fields contained in each rule in firewall databases can be partitioned into two logical entities: (1) distinct network paths characterized by source and destination IP address pairs, and (2) network applications characterized by a set of transport-level fields. In most cases, the number of distinct network paths far exceeds the number of network applications.

+ The IP address pairs define regions in the two-dimensional space that can overlap with each other. However, the number of overlaps is significantly smaller than the theoretical upper bound.

+ Many source-destination IP address pairs share the same set of transport-level fields. Hence, only a small number of transport-level fields are sufficient to characterize databases of different sizes.

We justify these observations based on standard network administration practices, and thereby argue that these findings, although derived from a small number of databases, are likely to hold for many firewall databases. Based on these findings, we provide the following guidelines for designing efficient classification algorithms.

+ The multidimensional classification problem should be split into two subproblems (or two stages): (1) finding a two-dimensional match based on source and destination IP addresses contained in the packet, and (2) finding an (n-2)-dimensional match based on transport-level fields. Whereas the first stage only involves prefix matching, the second stage involves the more general range matching.

+ Because of the overlap between IP address filters maintained in a database, each packet may match multiple filters. Identifying all matching filters is complex. Since the total number of overlaps observed in firewall databases is significantly smaller than the theoretical upper bound, a design that maintains all of the intersection filters and returns exactly a single filter is both feasible and desirable.

✦ Since each IP address filter is associated with multiple transport-level fields, identifying the highest-priority rule that matches a packet requires searching through all transport-level fields associated with the matching IP filter. Since the number of transport-level fields associated with most databases is rather small, it is possible to rely upon a small, special-purpose hardware unit (e.g., a TCAM unit) to perform the (n-2)-dimensional searches in parallel.

The chapter is structured as follows. In Section 13.1, we formulate the classification problem and discuss our methodology for studying access control lists (ACLs). We discuss our findings in Sections 13.2 and 13.3, and expose the implications of our findings in Section 13.4. Section 13.5 summarizes our contributions. Finally, the Appendix presents the derivation of a tighter upper bound on the number of partial filter overlaps.

13.1 PROBLEM FORMULATION

Since access control is the most common application of packet classification today, we focus on the problem of packet classification in firewalls. In a firewall rule database, each rule contains one or more fields and their associated values, a priority, and an action. The fields generally correspond to specific portions of the TCP/IP header, such as the source and destination IP addresses, port numbers, and protocol identifier. Because of the hierarchical nature of IP address allocation, source and destination IP addresses are often specified as prefixes. To accommodate a collection of user or network management applications, port numbers are often specified as ranges. Finally, other protocol attributes, such as the protocol identifier, are specified as exact values. Table 13.1 shows some examples of classification rules.

The first rule indicates that packets originating from the IP address 128.59.67.100 and destined to any host within the IP address domain beginning with 128 and port number 15 should be dropped. The priority level for

src. IP address	dest. IP address	src. port	dest. port	action	priority
128.59.67.100	128.*	*	15	drop	2
128.*	128.2.3.1	*	24	DSCP 2	1

13.1   Examples of classification rules.

TABLE

this rule is 2. The second rule states that packets originating from any host in the domain beginning with 128 and destined to the host 128.2.3.1 and port number 24 should be forwarded with the differentiated services code point (DSCP) set to 2. This rule has a priority level of 1.

In this context, the packet classification problem can be stated as follows: Given a set—often referred to as an ACL—of access control rules, determine the action A associated with the highest-priority rule that matches packet p. To reduce the overhead of identifying rules that may match each packet, most packet classification algorithms employ search data structures for organizing classification rules. These data structures occupy memory space. Furthermore, navigating on these data structures incurs several memory accesses. In what follows, we first discuss several existing packet classification algorithms and argue that they do not scale well with increase in network bandwidth or ACL sizes. We then argue that understanding the structure and properties of ACLs is crucial in designing efficient, scalable algorithms. Finally, we describe our methodology for studying the properties of ACLs.

13.1.1   State of the Art

Existing packet classification algorithms [1–14] can be grouped into four classes: trie-based algorithms, hash-based algorithms, parallel search algorithms, and heuristic algorithms. Throughout this discussion, we use n to denote the number of rules in a classification database, k to denote the number of fields (i.e., dimensions), and w to denote the maximum length of the fields (in bits).

✦ *Trie-based algorithms*. Trie-based algorithms [2, 3, 13, 14] build hierarchical radix tree structures where once a match is found in one dimension a search is performed in a separate tree linked into the node representing the match. Examples of such algorithms are the grid-of-tries [13] and area-based quad tree (AQT) [3] algorithms. Trie-based algorithms require, in the worst case, as many memory accesses as the number of bits in the fields used for classification. Multi-bit trie data structures are more efficient from the perspective of the number of memory accesses required. However, these data structures incur significantly higher memory space overhead. In general, trie-based schemes work well for single-dimensional searches. However, the memory requirement of these schemes increases significantly with an increase in the number of search dimensions.

✦ *Hash-based algorithms*. Hash-based algorithms [12] group rules according to the lengths of the prefixes specified in different fields. The groups formed in this manner are called tuples. Hash-based algorithms perform a series of hash lookups, (one for each tuple) to identify the highest-priority matching rule. Tuple space search has $O(n)$ storage and time complexity. Hash-based algorithms, in the worst case, require as many memory accesses as the number of hash tables, and the number of hash tables can be as large as the number of rules in a database. As a result, hash-based techniques do not scale well with the number of rules. An optimized hashing technique, referred to as rectangle search [12], reduces the lookup time complexity from $O(n)$ to $O(w)$ in two dimensions. However, to support lookups in more than two dimensions, the algorithm still requires a significant number of memory accesses.[1]

✦ *Parallel search algorithms*. These algorithms formulate the classification problem as an n-dimensional matching problem and search each dimension separately. In some algorithms [9], when a match is found in a dimension a bit vector is returned, identifying the matches. The logical *AND* of the bit vectors returned from all dimensions identifies the matching rules. Such bit-vector techniques are associated with $O(n)$ memory accesses in the lookup process. Fetching a single bit vector or an aggregate bit vector (as described in [1]) can be memory access intensive, especially in cases where the ACL contains more than a few thousand rules. Another parallel search technique, called the cross-producting table [13], reduces the lookup time complexity to $(O(kw))$, where k is the number of fields and w is the maximum length of the fields. However, this technique increases the worst-case storage complexity to $(O(n^k))$, making it impractical.

✦ *Heuristic algorithms*. A fourth category of algorithms includes heuristic algorithms that exploit the structure and redundancy in the rule set [6, 7]. The algorithms proposed to date are associated with very low lookup time complexity $(O(k))$; however, they impose significant memory space requirements $(O(n^k))$. Hence, these algorithms are suitable for single- or two-dimensional searches, but their space requirement makes them unsuited for the more common five-dimensional searches.

From the previous discussion, it is apparent that exploiting the structure and properties of ACLs is a promising direction for designing packet classification algorithms that can scale well with link bandwidth and ACL sizes. Unfortunately,

---

1. A lower bound on the complexity of rectangle search is discussed in [12]. It is proven that tuple probes can be at least $w(k-1)/k!$

the literature contains no detailed studies of ACL properties. This is in part because ISPs and enterprises, for privacy and security reasons, protect access to their rule databases. Recently, we have obtained access to four firewall databases from ISPs and corporate intranets. Hence, in this chapter we conduct a careful study to expose the structure and properties of these ACLs, and postulate how these properties can be used to design efficient classification algorithms. The design of specific packet classification algorithms, however, is beyond the scope of this chapter.

13.1.2   Experimental Methodology

We analyze four firewall databases. Three of these databases are from large ISPs, whereas one is from a corporate intranet. Table 13.2 summarizes the basic statistics of these ACLs.

As Table 13.2 indicates, the ISP ACLs are generally much larger than those of the enterprise intranets. Further, it shows that the fields specified in ACLs can be partitioned into two logical entities: (1) source and destination IP address pairs that characterize distinct network paths represented in ACLs, and (2) a set of transport-level fields (e.g., port numbers and protocol identifier) that characterize network applications. In most cases, the number of distinct network paths far exceeds the number of network applications represented in the ACLs.

In what follows, we first analyze IP address pairs and then study the characteristics of transport-level fields. We justify our findings based on standard practices for creating ACLs used by network administrators. Hence, we argue that although our observations are derived from a small number of rule databases our conclusions are likely to be valid across a large number of such rule databases.

	Type	Number of rules	Number of unique source-destination IP address fields	Protocol types	Unique port number fields
ACL1	ISP	754	426	4	140
ACL2	ISP	607	527	5	30
ACL3	ISP	2399	1588	5	192
ACL4	Intranet	157	98	4	36

13.2   Summary of ACLs.

TABLE

13.2   IP PREFIX PAIR ANALYSIS

Each rule in an ACL contains a specification of source and destination IP address pairs (also referred to as IP address filters). These addresses are specified as wildcards, prefixes, or exact values. Based on these specifications, the filters represent rectangles, lines, or points in the two-dimensional IP address space. Further, the filters may overlap with each other. In what follows, we first conduct a structural analysis of the filters. This allows us to characterize ACLs as a composition of different types of filters (i.e., filters that represent a different shape in the two-dimensional space). We find that only a small number of filters contain wildcards in the source or the destination dimensions in the ISP ACLs. Further, for most filters that do not contain any wildcards the destination field contains complete IP addresses (representing individual hosts), while the source field contains prefixes (representing IP address domains). Second, we analyze the overlaps among the filters. This allows us to characterize the number of filters that may match a packet, as well as the overhead of maintaining in the ACL a unique filter representing each of the overlaps. By maintaining a unique filter for each of the overlaps, the maximally matching filter can be uniquely identified for each packet. We find that overlaps are created mostly by filters that contain a wildcard in their source or destination fields. Since only a small number of filters contain wildcards, the actual number of overlaps observed in ACLs is significantly smaller than the theoretical upper bound.

13.2.1   Structural Analysis

The source-destination IP address pairs can be classified into two types: partially specified filters and fully specified filters. Partially specified filters contain at least one wildcard (*) in the source or in the destination IP address dimension. These filters capture traffic sent to/from designated servers or subnets of ISP networks. Fully specified filters, on the other hand, contain an IP address prefix in both the source and destination IP address dimensions. These filters identify the traffic exchanged between specific IP address domains of ISP networks. In most cases, the traffic handled by fully specified filters is exchanged between important servers (e.g., web, e-mail, NTP, or streaming servers) and clients.

Each IP address filter can be represented geometrically as a point, a line, or a rectangle in a two-dimensional IP address space. Whereas partially specified filters of the form (*,*) cover the entire two-dimensional address space, filters of the form (x, *) and (*, y) can be represented either as a line or a rectangle in the

	Partially specified filters	Fully specified filters	Total number of filters
ACL1	4 (1%)	421 (99%)	426
ACL2	68 (13%)	458 (87%)	527
ACL3	160 (10%)	1427 (90%)	1588
ACL4	83 (86%)	14 (14%)	98

13.3

TABLE

Partially and fully specified filters.

two-dimensional space, depending on the values of x and y. If x and y represent IP address domains (i.e., IP prefixes of length smaller than 32), then these filters are represented as rectangles. On the other hand, if x and y denote hosts (i.e., full 32-bit IP addresses), then the corresponding filters are represented as lines. Similarly, depending on the lengths of x and y, fully specified IP address filters of the form (x, y) represent lines, points, or rectangles in the two-dimensional space.

The first two columns of Table 13.3 show the breakdown of partially and fully specified filters in our firewall ACLs. The third column of Table 13.3 shows the total number of filters, which is equal to the sum of the number of partially and fully specified filters plus one more filter representing the wildcard pair (*, *). Table 13.3 illustrates that whereas partially specified filters represent a small percentage of the total number of filters in large ISP databases, they constitute a significant percentage of the relatively small-size enterprise intranet firewall ACL. This is because large ISPs often describe administrative policies between specific IP address domains within their network. Examples of such policies include the admission of all HTTP traffic between a server and a client subnet, or the blocking of all RTSP traffic between two specific IP address domains. In intranets, on the other hand, administrators do not specify cross-domain traffic management policies, since such policies are often enforced by their ISP. Instead, most of the rules in intranet firewalls refer to specific sources or destinations, but not both.

We further analyze the partially specified filters to determine the relative occurrence of the wildcard in the source or the destination IP address fields, as well as the lengths of specified IP addresses. We find that in the intranet ACL, which is the smallest in size, filters with the wildcard in the destination address are the majority. In the first two ACLs, which are of medium size, there is a balance between the filters that have the wildcard in the source and destination address fields. In the third ACL, which has the largest size, most filters have the wildcard in the source address field.

	Wildcard in source address	Wildcard in destination address
ACL1	2	2
ACL2	36	32
ACL3	112	48
ACL4	12	71

13.4

Breakdown of partially specified filters.

TABLE

From the results of Table 13.4, it appears as if there is a dependency between the size of an ACL and the numbers of filters that have the wildcard in the source or destination IP address fields. Typically, the smaller an ACL is the closer to client networks the firewall is located. The intranet ACL in our example describes policies that block the traffic from many specific client subnets of the intranet and thus contains many rules having the wildcard in the destination dimension. Larger ACLs, on the other hand, are closer to the Internet core and describe higher-level policies for connecting to important servers or networks. Such policies are typically expressed as rules having the wildcard in the source dimension.

Figure 13.1 shows the distribution of prefix lengths for partially specified filters. It shows that the source and destination IP address specifications are spread across the entire range of prefix lengths, with 8-bit, 16-bit, 24-bit, and 32-bit prefixes constituting the majority. Geometrically, this indicates that most partially specified filters represent lines or rectangles characterized by a few standard width values in the two-dimensional space.

There are four types of fully specified filters: (1) filters that characterize traffic exchanged between two domains, (2) filters that characterize traffic originating within a domain but destined to a host, (3) filters that characterize traffic originating from a host but destined to an IP domain, and (4) filters that characterize traffic exchanged between a specific pair of hosts. In these filters, a host is represented using a 32-bit address (IPv4 address), while a domain is represented by a shorter prefix. Table 13.5 shows the breakdown of these four types of filters in our ACLs. It shows that the majority of the fully specified filters in ISP databases represent communication where either the sender or the receiver is a host. In many cases, these hosts are servers representing important resources of large networks. On the other hand, in the intranet ACL the majority of fully specified filters represent domain-domain filters.

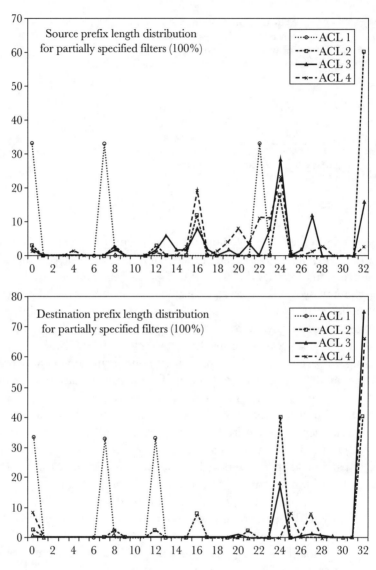

13.1

FIGURE

Distribution of prefix lengths for partially specified filters.

Figure 13.2 shows the distribution of source and destination prefix lengths for fully specified filters. Geometrically, this indicates that most fully specified filters represent lines or points in the two-dimensional space. The spatial distribution of IP prefixes is a very important property, especially to analyze

	Domain-domain filters	Host-domain filters	Domain-host filters	Host-host filters
ACL1	30	31	37	323
ACL2	124	99	154	81
ACL3	165	18	755	489
ACL4	9	0	2	3

13.5   Breakdown of fully specified filters.

TABLE

requirements to store the IP prefixes. We have created 4-bit trie data structures for both the source and destination IP addresses, measured the number of trie blocks required to store IP prefixes, and compared this number with the theoretical maximum for number of trie blocks. The results are shown in Table 13.6. We find that the total number of trie blocks needed to represent source and destination prefixes is much less than the theoretical upper bound in real-world databases.

From these analyses, we derive the following general conclusions:

✦ Filters in real-world ACLs are either fully specified or partially specified. Partially specified filters represent a small percentage of the total number of filters in medium and large ACLs.

✦ The breakdown of partially specified filters between filters having the wildcard in source and destination IP addresses may depend on the size of the ACL. Careful study of more ACLs would help in investigating the existence of such dependency.

✦ Most fully specified filters are segments of straight lines or points in medium and large ACLs.

✦ Trie data structures representing source and destination prefixes require many fewer blocks than the theoretical upper bound.

13.2.2   Overlap Analysis

The geometrical objects representing filters may overlay in the two-dimensional space. Since each packet represents a point in the two-dimensional space, it may be contained within the geometrical space defined by one or more filters in the ACL. In such an event, a packet may match multiple filters within the ACL.

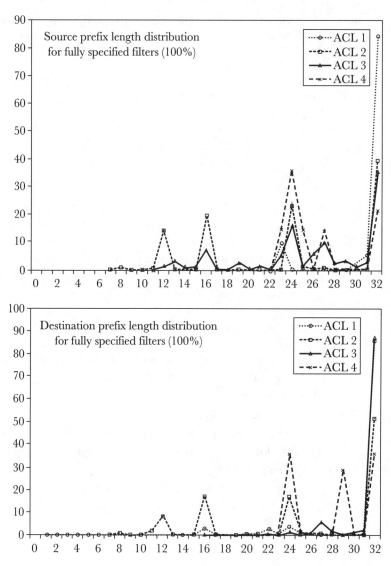

Distribution of source and destination prefix lengths for fully specified filters.

Hence, identifying the highest-priority rule requires comparing transport-level fields associated with all matching filters with the appropriate fields contained in the packet. Clearly, the larger the number of filters that a packet may match with, the greater is the complexity of identifying the highest-priority rule that

	Number of unique source prefixes	Observed number of source trie blocks	Theoretical bound on the number of source trie blocks
ACL1	97	29	759
ACL2	182	231	1439
ACL3	431	496	3256
ACL4	79	127	615
	Number of unique destination prefixes	Observed number of destination trie blocks	Theoretical bound on the number of destination trie blocks
ACL1	205	383	1623
ACL2	207	243	1639
ACL3	516	620	3855
ACL4	20	60	155

13.6 Trie block analysis.

TABLE

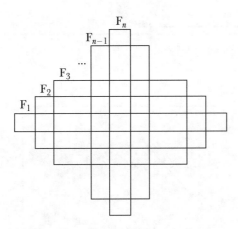

13.3 Worst-case filter structure.

FIGURE

matches the packet. In the worst case, if all filters within an ACL overlap with each other (as shown in Figure 13.3), then identifying the highest-priority rule for a packet that represents a point in the intersection of these filters may require a search on all filters. Thus, the complexity of packet classification depends on the amount of overlap between filters (which in turn determines the number of filters that may match a packet).

In what follows, we analyze our ACLs for their overlap properties. Table 13.7 and Figure 13.4 show the distribution of the number of filters that may match a packet. Figure 13.4 illustrates that for all ACLs, on average about four filters match every packet. Although this is not a very large number, identifying these filters imposes significant overhead. The navigation on the data structures that store two-dimensional filters (e.g., hierarchical single-bit or multi-bit tries) typically requires significantly more memory accesses than the number of filters matching a packet. For instance, the extended grid-of-tries (EGT) algorithm reported in [2] requires 137 accesses to classify packets from a database of 2799 rules.

	Average	Standard deviation	Maximum
ACL1	4.00	0.36	5.00
ACL2	3.96	0.73	7.00
ACL3	3.75	0.84	7.00
ACL4	3.71	0.90	7.00

13.7

TABLE

Number of filters that may match a packet.

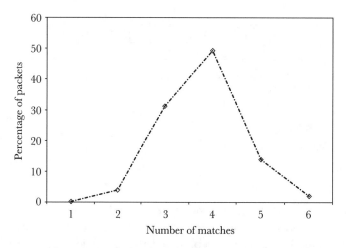

13.4

FIGURE

Distribution of the number of filters that may match a packet.

	Number of rules	Number of filters	Observed number of partial overlaps	Upper bound on the number of partial overlaps
ACL1	754	426	4	90,525
ACL2	607	527	2,249	138,601
ACL3	2,399	1,588	6,138	1,260,078
ACL4	157	98	852	4,753

13.8   Observed filter overlaps.

TABLE

An alternative architecture involves maintaining a filter that represents each overlap in the ACL. We observe that overlaps between filters can be complete or partial. In the event that one filter is completely contained in another, the overlap between the filters is represented exactly by the contained filter. In such a case, no additional filter needs to be stored. On the other hand, if filters overlap partially, then the overlap can be identified uniquely by a filter that represents the intersection region between the two filters. Hence, each partial overlap introduces a new filter in the ACL. If all such filters are maintained, then the classifier can determine the most refined filter for each packet. In the worst case, if each filter overlaps with all the other filters in the ACL, then maintaining all the intersection filters would incur an $O(n^2)$ overhead,[2] where n is the number of distinct IP prefix pairs in the ACL. However, as we have illustrated earlier, most ACLs contain filters that can be represented as points, lines, or small rectangles. Hence, we can expect the number of additional filters required for real ACLs to be much smaller than the theoretical worst case.

To validate this hypothesis, we determine the number of such overlaps observed in our ACLs. The results are shown in Table 13.8. Table 13.8 indicates that the number of filters representing intersections that may need to be stored is, in fact, several orders of magnitude smaller than the theoretical upper bound.

Our analyses of the ACLs show that the organization of filters in real-world ACLs is significantly different from the worst-case structure shown in Figure 13.3. A more realistic structure of filters is shown in Figure 13.5. The filters in the structure of Figure 13.5 are either fully specified or partially specified, as explained

2. The worst-case scenario is one where each filter in the ACL overlaps with all the other filters. In such a case, the number of filters that represents the overlaps can be bounded by $(n-1) + (n-2) + \ldots + 1 = n(n-1)/2$.

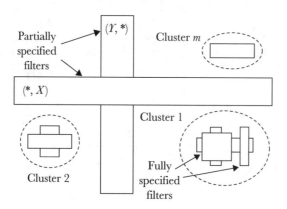

13.5

FIGURE

A realistic structure of filters in ACLs.

in the previous section. Some fully specified filters form clusters, as shown in Figure 13.5. A cluster is a set of filters where every filter overlaps either partially or completely with at least one other filter in the cluster. A closer analysis of the ACLs reveals that there are three cases that create partial overlap between filters.

- ✦ *Overlaps between partially specified filters.* Each filter having the wildcard in the source IP address dimension creates a unique partial overlap with all filters having a wildcard in the destination IP address dimension. Since IP addresses are specified as prefixes, filters with a wildcard in the same dimension do not create partial overlaps between each other; such filters are either disjoint or completely overlapping. The number of partial overlaps created only by partially specified filters is equal to the product of the number of partially specified filters in each of the two dimensions.

- ✦ *Overlaps between fully specified filters.* Fully specified filters may overlap with each other either fully or partially.

- ✦ *Overlaps between fully and partially specified filters.*

Table 13.9 shows the breakdown of the number of partial overlaps created in each of the four ACLs. It shows that the overlaps created by partially specified filters represent the majority in all ACLs, ranging from 51% in ACL 2 up to 100% in ACL 1 and ACL 4. We also observe that the overlaps created between partially and fully specified filters represent a significant percentage (45%) of the total number of overlaps in ACL 2. In all ACLs, fully specified filters create an insignificant number of overlaps (it turns out that most clusters have size

	Number of partial overlaps	Overlaps formed by partially specified filters only	Overlaps formed by fully specified filters only	Overlaps formed by between fully and partially specified filters
ACL 1	4	100%	0%	0%
ACL 2	2249	51%	4%	45%
ACL 3	6138	88%	1%	11%
ACL 4	852	100%	0%	0%

13.9   Breakdown of overlaps.

TABLE

equal to 1). These results indicate that partially specified filters are the main source of overlaps in all ACLs. Further, as we had demonstrated earlier, partially specified filters generally represent only a small percentage of the total number of filters in large databases. These two observations together justify why the total number of partial overlaps is significantly less than the theoretical upper bound. In Section 13.5, we derive a tighter upper bound on the number of partial overlaps.

13.3   TRANSPORT-LEVEL FIELD ANALYSIS

The Internet supports thousands of routes but relatively only a few, commonly used applications. Hence, as indicated in Table 13.2, only a small number of unique transport-level fields (consisting of port numbers and protocol types) are usually present in ACLs. Further, many source-destination pairs share the same transport-level fields. In what follows, we first analyze the transport-level fields associated with individual source-destination pairs (or IP address filters) and then expose the sharing of these transport-level fields across multiple IP filters.

13.3.1   Analysis of Transport-Level Fields for Individual IP Filters

ACLs generally contain several rules with the same IP address filter (i.e., source-destination IP address pair) but with different combinations of transport-level

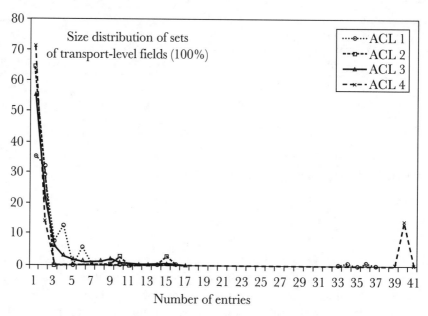

13.6   Distribution of sizes of transport-level field sets.

FIGURE

fields. To understand this phenomenon carefully, we analyzed the sets of such transport-level fields associated with the same IP filters.

Figure 13.6 depicts the distribution of the set sizes observed in the four ACLs under consideration. It shows that for all the ACLs most (about 90%) transport-level field sets are small (1 to 4 entries); the remaining 10% of the sets have sizes between 5 and 40. This is mainly because most ACLs contain rules that identify explicitly only a small number of the most popular applications. In today's Internet, the number of these applications is very small.

We observe that the highest percentage of transport-level fields in our ACLs specify TCP and UDP protocols. This is because most data traffic in today's Internet uses TCP, and a smaller percentage of traffic uses UDP. Further, most transport-level fields specify a destination port or port range. The source port field is generally unspecified (i.e., a wildcard specification). This is because most classification rules apply to packets that request the establishment of TCP connections. These packets are sent to servers that are listening to well-known nonephemeral or ephemeral ports. Table 13.10 depicts the distributions of the source and destination port numbers observed for the four ACLs.

	Number of unique transport-level fields	Source port number			Destination port number		
		Wildcard	Range	Exact value	Wildcard	Range	Exact value
ACL1	146	146	0	0	4	74	68
ACL2	40	40	0	0	8	29	3
ACL3	202	200	2	0	5	157	40
ACL4	43	42	1	0	8	32	3

13.10

TABLE

Distribution of source and destination port numbers in transport-level fields.

	Number of transport-level fields	Number of transport-level fields in unique sets	Number of unique transport-level fields
ACL1	754	316	146
ACL2	607	67	40
ACL3	2399	442	202
ACL4	157	48	43

13.11

TABLE

Sharing transport-level fields among IP filters.

13.3.2   Sharing Transport-Level Fields Across Multiple IP Filters

To analyze the sharing of transport-level fields across multiple IP filters, we derive the total number of transport-level field entries with and without any sharing across filters. Table 13.11 summarizes our findings. It shows that for all ACLs many source-destination IP prefix pairs share the same sets of transport-level fields. The relative priority and corresponding actions of fields are the same in different occurrences of each set. In addition, the number of unique entries characterizing the shared sets of transport-level fields is also small. This number is much smaller than the total number of entries in the unique sets.

13.4   IMPLICATIONS

Our evaluation of ACLs leads us to the following main conclusions.

✦ The fields contained in each rule in ACLs can be partitioned into two logical entities: (1) source and destination IP address pairs that characterize distinct network paths represented in ACLs, and (2) a set of transport-level fields (e.g., port numbers and protocol identifier) that characterize network applications. In most cases, the number of distinct network paths far exceeds the number of network applications.

✦ The IP address filters are either partially specified or fully specified. Partially specified filters represent a small percentage of the total number of filters in databases. Furthermore, most of the overlap between filters is caused by partially specified filters. Fully specified filters create only a few partial overlaps with each other. Thus, the total number of overlaps is significantly smaller than the theoretical bound.

✦ Many source-destination IP address pairs share the same set of transport-level fields. Hence, only a small number of transport-level fields are sufficient to characterize databases of different sizes.

Based on these findings, we provide the following guidelines for designing efficient classification algorithms.

✦ The multidimensional classification problem should be split into two subproblems (or two stages): (1) finding a two-dimensional match based on source and destination IP addresses contained in the packet, and (2) finding an (n-2)-dimension a match based on transport-level fields (see Figure 13.7). Whereas the first stage only involves prefix matching, the second stage involves the more general range matching.

✦ Because of the overlap between IP address filters maintained in an ACL, each packet may match multiple filters in stage 1. Identifying all matching filters is complex. Since the total number of overlaps observed for ACLs is significantly smaller than the theoretical upper bound, a design that maintains all of the intersection filters and returns exactly a single match from stage 1 is both feasible and desirable.

✦ Since each IP address filter is associated with multiple transport-level fields, identifying the highest-priority rule that matches a packet requires searching through all the transport-level fields associated with the matching IP filter. Since the number of transport-level fields associated with most ACLs

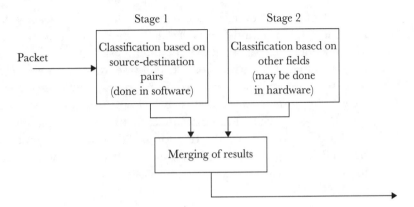

13.7

FIGURE
Two-stage classification architecture.

is rather small, it is possible to rely upon a small, special-purpose hardware unit (e.g., a TCAM unit) to perform the (n-2)-dimensional search in parallel.

The combination of a fast software algorithm for finding a two-dimensional match in stage 1 and a specialized hardware acceleration unit for performing an (n-2)-dimensional match in stage 2 can result in a classification system capable of meeting the stringent space/time constraints of network processors.

13.5   CONCLUSIONS

To classify a packet as belonging to a flow often requires network systems, such as routers and firewalls, to maintain large data structures and perform several memory accesses. Network processors, on the other hand, are generally configured with only a small amount of memory with limited access bandwidth. Hence, a key challenge is to design packet classification algorithms that can be implemented efficiently on network processor platforms. We argue that the design of such algorithms will need to exploit the structure and characteristics of packet classification rules.

In this chapter, we analyzed several databases of classification rules found in firewalls and derived their statistical properties. Our analysis yields three main conclusions: (1) the rules found in ACLs contain two types of fields (source-destination IP address pairs that identify network paths and transport-level fields that characterize network applications), and these rules refer to many more network paths than applications; (2) IP address pairs identify regions that overlap with each other (however, the number of overlaps is significantly smaller than the theoretical upper bound); and (3) only a small number of transport-level fields are sufficient to characterize ACLs of different sizes. We justify our findings based on several standard practices employed by network administrators, and thereby argue that although our findings are for specific databases the properties are likely to hold for most databases. Based on these findings, we suggest that a hybrid, two-stage classification architecture that combines a software scheme for matching in two dimensions (IP address pairs) with a hardware unit that performs efficient (n-2)-dimensional searches has the potential of scaling well with link speeds and ACL sizes.

APPENDIX: DERIVATION OF A TIGHTER BOUND ON THE NUMBER OF PARTIAL OVERLAPS

From the analyses of ACLs, we have shown that the number of overlaps between IP filters is significantly smaller than the theoretical upper bound of $n \cdot (n-1)/2$. In this appendix, we derive a tighter upper bound on the number of partial filter overlaps. The derivation of the upper bound is based on properties that characterize medium and large ISP ACLs. Therefore, the analysis presented in this appendix applies to the first three of our ACLs only.

There are three factors that produce intersections between IP filters in ACLs. First, partially specified filters create intersections with each other. The number of such overlaps O_1 is exactly equal to $S \cdot D$, where S is the number of partially specified filters that specify the source IP address dimension and D is the number of partially specified filters that specify the destination IP address dimension. Since partially specified filters represent a small percentage of the total number of filters in all databases (1 to 13%) we expect their overlaps to be bounded by the square of the number of filters divided by a large constant. In fact, the majority of partial overlaps (51 to 100%) are created by partially specified filters in databases.

Second, partial overlaps result from the intersections between fully specified filters in the same cluster. However, clusters with more than one element are only but a few in our ACLs. Fully specified filters form an insignificant amount of overlaps between each other. This happens mainly because server and client subnets are characterized by disjoint IP address domains in rules. As a result, the number of partial overlaps O_2 created by fully specified filters is also much less than the theoretical upper bound.

Third, partial overlaps are created between fully and partially specified filters. Each fully specified filter may create partial overlaps with one or more partially specified filters. In most medium and large ACLs the total number of servers specified per IP address domain is bounded. These servers represent the prefixes of partially specified filters. As a result, the total number of overlaps formed between fully and partially specified filters O_3 is bounded by the product of the number of filters times a constant. The detailed derivation of an upper bound is as follows:

$$O = O_1 + O_2 + O_3 \tag{A.1}$$

$$O_1 = S \cdot D \tag{A.2}$$

$$O_2 \leq \sum_{i=1}^{q} \frac{C_i \cdot (C_i - 1)}{2} \tag{A.3}$$

$$O_3 = \sum_{j=1}^{f} F_j \tag{A.4}$$

Equations 13.1 through 13.4 result in:

$$O \leq S \cdot D + \sum_{i=1}^{q} \frac{C_i \cdot (C_i - 1)}{2} + \sum_{j=1}^{f} F_j \tag{A.5}$$

S and D are the number of partially specified filters that specify the source and destination IP address dimensions (respectively), q is the number of clusters that contain more than one filter, C_i is the number of filters in cluster i, f is the number of fully specified filters that create partial overlaps with partially specified filters, and F_j is the number of partially specified filters that overlap with filter j. To complete the derivation of an upper bound we need to understand the relation between the parameters S, D, q, f, C_i, and F_j, and the number of filters in a database n.

Let r_1 be the ratio of the total number of filters in a database over the number of partially specified filters. Then $S + D = n/r_1$. The ratio r_1 is expected to be greater than one with very high probability in many different databases. The number of overlaps formed by partially specified filters O_1 is equal to the product $S \cdot D$. This product is maximized when $S = D = n/(2 \cdot r_1)$. Therefore:

$$O_1 \leq \frac{n^2}{4 \cdot r_1^2} \tag{A.6}$$

Let r_2 be the ratio between the number of fully specified filters in a database and the number of fully specified filters that create partial overlaps with each other. Such filters participate in clusters having more than one element. The ratio r_2 is also expected to be greater than one with very high probability. The number of fully specified filters that create partial overlaps with each other is equal to $(r_1 - 1) \cdot n/(r_1 \cdot r_2)$.

As a result:

$$O_2 \leq \frac{(r_1 - 1) \cdot n}{2 \cdot r_1 \cdot r_2} \left(\frac{(r_1 - 1) \cdot n}{r_1 \cdot r_2} - 1 \right) \tag{A.7}$$

The values of F_j refer to overlaps between partially and fully specified filters. The number of such overlaps per fully specified filter is independent of n as a property of a pair of IP address domains. As a result, we can consider that each F_j is bounded by some value F. Therefore:

$$O_3 \leq n \cdot F \tag{A.8}$$

Equations 13.1 and 13.6 through 13.8 result in:

$$O \leq \frac{n^2}{4 \cdot r_1^2} + \frac{(r_1 - 1) \cdot n}{2 \cdot r_1 \cdot r_2} \left(\frac{(r_1 - 1) \cdot n}{r_1 \cdot r_2} - 1 \right) + n \cdot F \tag{A.9}$$

Even though the result of Equation 13.9 is also $O(n^2)$, this bound is much tighter than the worst case. This happens because the number of filters n is divided by the parameters r_1 and r_2 in Equation 13.9. The parameters r_1 and r_2 are expected to be greater than 1. Another difference is that the worst-case bound is a deterministic bound, whereas the bound of Equation 13.9 is a stochastic bound, since the parameters r_1, r_2, and F are random variables.

The random variables r_1, r_2, and F have unknown distributions. However, we expect with very high probability that r_1 and r_2 are greater than 1 and F is a small number. Estimations on the upper bound of Equation 13.9 can be derived by selecting the values with the highest frequency from the limited number of databases we experimented with, for r_1, r_2, and F. The values for r_1, r_2, and F used in our calculations are $r_1 = 8.75$, $r_2 = 4.3$, and $F = 15$. More accurate results would require the parameters to be estimated from a greater number of samples. Our results are shown in Table 13.12. The worst-case estimations

Database number	Number of filters	Observed number of partial overlaps	Upper bound from Eq. 13.9	Worst-case upper bound
1	426	4	10,790	90,525
2	527	2,249	14,651	138,601
3	1,588	6,138	85,393	1,260,078

13.12

TABLE

Upper bounds on the number of partial filter overlaps.

derived from Equation 13.9 are compared against the worst-case estimations in this table.

REFERENCES

[1]   F. Baboescu and G. Varghese, "Scalable Packet Classification," *Proceedings of ACM SIGCOMM*, Aug. 2001, pp. 199–210.

[2]   F. Baboescu, S. Singh, and G. Varghese, "Packet Classification for Core Routers: Is There an Alternative to CAMs?," technical report, University of California, San Diego, 2003.

[3]   M. M. Buddhikot, S. Suri, and M. Waldvogel, "Space Decomposition Techniques for Fast Layer-4 Switching," *Proceedings of Conference on Protocols for High Speed Networks*, Aug. 1999, pp. 25–41.

[4]   M. Degermark, A. Brodnik, S. Carlsson, and S. Pink, "Small Forwarding Tables for Fast Routing Lookups," *Proceedings of ACM SIGCOMM*, Sept. 1997, pp. 3–14.

[5]   A. Feldman and S. Muthukrishnan, "Trade-Offs for Packet Classification," *Proceedings of Infocom*, vol. 3, Mar. 2000, pp. 1193–1202.

[6]   P. Gupta and N. McKeown, "Packet Classification on Multiple Fields," *Proceedings of SIGCOMM, Computer Communication Review*, vol. 29, no. 4, Sept. 1999, Harvard University, pp. 147–160.

[7]   P. Gupta and N. McKeown, "Packet Classification Using Hierarchical Intelligent Cuttings," *Proceedings of Hot Interconnects VII*, August 1999, Stanford, Palo Alto, CA. This paper is also available in *IEEE Micro*, vol. 20, no. 1, Jan./Feb. 2000, pp. 34–41.

[8]   P. Gupta and N. McKeown, "Algorithms for Packet Classification," *IEEE Network Magazine*, 2001.

[9]   T. V. Lakshman and D. Stiliadis, "High-Speed Policy-Based Packet Forwarding Using Efficient Multi-dimensional Range Matching," *Proceedings of ACM SIGCOMM*, Sept. 1998, pp. 191–202.

[10]   A. Prakash and A. Aziz, "OC-3072 Packet Classification Using BDDs and Pipelined SRAMs," *Hot Interconnects IX*, Aug. 2001, Stanford, CA.

[11]   F. Shafai, K. J. Schultz, G. F. R. Gibson, A. G. Bluschke, and D. E. Somppi, "Fully Parallel 30-MHz, 2.5-Mb CAM," *IEEE Journal of Solid-State Circuits*, vol. 33, no. 11, Nov. 1998.

[12]   V. Srinivasan, S. Suri, and G. Varghese, "Packet Classification Using Tuple Space Search," *Proceedings of ACM SIGCOMM*, Sept. 1999, pp. 135–146.

[13]   V. Srinivasan, S. Suri, G. Varghese, and M. Waldvogel, "Fast and Scalable Layer 4 Switching," *Proceedings of ACM SIGCOMM*, Sept. 1998, pp. 203–214.

[14]   P. Tsuchiya, "A Search Algorithm for Table Entries with Non-contiguous Wildcarding," unpublished report, Bellcore, Morristown, NJ.

PRACTICES

II

PART

Implementing High-Performance, High-Value Traffic Management Using Agere Network Processor Solutions

Jian-Guo Chen, David Sonnier, Robert Muñoz, Vinoj Kumar, Ambalavanar Arulambalam
Agere Systems

This chapter discusses differing design approaches for implementing a complete traffic management solution. A detailed discussion of how traffic management is implemented using the 10-G (APP750TM) and 5-G (APP550) Agere Systems network processors is provided to demonstrate real-world solutions to today's and tomorrow's networking challenges.

To provide a complete network processor solution for traffic processing requires the performance of many different functions: reassembly, classification, policing, statistics, state management, segmentation/fragmentation, packet/cell modification, and traffic management. Unfortunately, many network processor solutions do not deliver full traffic management functionality, leaving the implementation of these functions as an additional exercise for the system designer.

Traffic management functionality—the core of which includes queuing, buffer management, and scheduling/shaping—is key to delivering network efficiency and quality of service (QoS). Without effective traffic management, it is virtually impossible to deliver meaningful service guarantees in the face of any significant network congestion or overload. Service guarantees are required to offer high-value service-level agreements (SLAs) to enable network service providers to maximize the value of their network investments.

Although most markets demand that common traffic management functions be integrated in the network processor, many applications have additional requirements. For example, core routers impose stringent size and power constraints due to the cost of suitable floor space. Therefore, integrating traffic management into the same device that contains the other network processor functions is often advantageous. Integration reduces total system cost due to reduced board space and power. Lower power consumption means low heat dissipation, which reduces cooling costs and increases system reliability.

All traffic management functions share some common characteristics:

+ *Protocol independent and required by all types of traffic.* Regardless of the nature or content of traffic, packets must be buffered when congestion occurs, and a scheduling discipline must arbitrate the service of buffered traffic.

+ *Instantaneous state updates at line rate.* This can require a specialized hardware architecture at high data rates.

+ *Time critical.* Every function must be finished within a fixed time interval to meet throughput and delay requirements.

+ *Sequential processing.* Buffer management and scheduling operations are sequentially dependent, which makes parallel implementations difficult if not impractical.

+ *Customizing.* Functionality can be tailored to different applications by programming or configuring the device.

Implementing the required functions at high line-rates is simplified when using a hardware implementation built specifically for traffic management functions.

14.1 IMPLEMENTING TRAFFIC MANAGEMENT

There are three basic approaches to implementing the traffic management component of network processors: completely in software, completely in hardware, or a hybrid hardware/software solution. Each of these approaches has strengths and limitations in the following areas: performance (throughput, delay, QoS), programmability, scalability, and cost.

14.1.1 Software-Only Implementation

In a software-only approach, all traffic management algorithms are implemented through software programming. The network processor provides some basic primitives, such as lock/unlock and mutexes. The Network Equipment System

Designer implements the algorithms and all associated resource blocks, such as queues and tables in software. Although implementing traffic management in software can appear flexible, the resulting implementation is typically suitable only for the lowest-speed routers, where minimal traffic volumes do not stress the software implementation.

Software implementation requires the successive inspection of thousands of individual queues, resulting in poor performance, complex programming, and inaccurate provisioning of QoS. Consequently, since a hardware solution could search all or most queues in parallel, high-performance traffic management can be effectively implemented only in hardware.

14.1.2 Hardware-Only Implementation

Pure hardware-only solutions implement all traffic management functions in hardware. Typically, hardware solutions are configurable upon initialization but not programmable afterward. This approach is most suitable for applications where the algorithms undergo minimal change such as in the Internet core. High data rates are very challenging to accomplish, given the constraints imposed by process and memory technology. The Agere APP750TM network processor chipset is an example of a more hardware-centric solution for traffic management. Queuing, buffer management, and scheduling, which are all implemented on the APP750TM, are configurable rather than fully programmable. However, policing, classification, and statistics, which are implemented on the APP750NP, are fully programmable.

14.1.3 Hardware/Software Implementation

Hybrid solutions allow software programmability while maintaining the speed advantage of ASIC solutions by implementing certain blocks in hardware. This type of architecture implements key *functional blocks* in hardware (i.e., implements the *mechanism*), while the software determines the *policy* to be applied. The Agere APP500 family of network processors with integrated traffic management is an example of this approach.

Hardware primitives that aid traffic management include: timer support for differential services (*diffserv*) metering, policing, and rate shaping; a math unit (for QoS block policing and congestion management); schedulers; queue managers; and hierarchical port managers to implement shaping and scheduling algorithms.

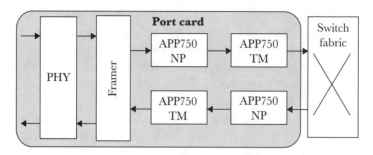

Agere 10-Gb/s packet-processing solution with APP750.

14.2   10-GB/S SYSTEM SOLUTION

This section describes the architecture of Agere Systems' 10-Gb/s traffic management product, the APP750TM. The APP750TM works with Agere's APP750NP to provide a two-chip complete 10-Gb/s network processor solution. The discussion focuses on the mechanisms that provide high performance and quality of service, with a special emphasis on buffer management, queuing, and scheduling. It also reveals some of the issues and challenges involved in implementing these schemes at full line rate with different packet sizes. A subsequent section describes the architecture of Agere Systems' APP550, which is a single-chip 5-Gb/s traffic-management-enabled network processor.

The APP750TM and the APP750NP provide a complete 10-Gb/s packet-processing solution. They are usually located on each line card of a chassis-based system, or on a main board in an integrated switching/routing system. Figure 14.1 shows a chassis-based system implemented with APP750NP and APP750TM.

In each switching or routing system implemented with Agere's 10-Gb/s chip sets, the APP750NP performs route lookup, packet classification, policing, and traffic statistics collection based on the program running on it. A simplified block diagram for APP750NP is shown in Figure 14.2.

14.2.1   APP750TM Architecture

The APP750TM is a simple 10-Gb/s traffic management chip. It operates at a clock frequency of 266 MHz. As in most designs, the APP750TM considers the time axis as slotted with a slot size (referred to as time slot) equal to the duration of transmitting a fixed-size data block.

Since traffic processing is performed on each packet (instead of on each bit), it is the packet rate rather than the bit rate that directly impacts the performance

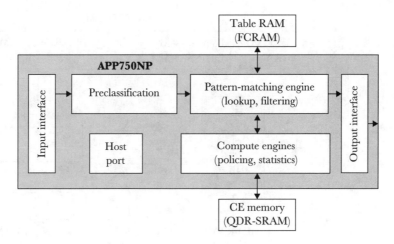

Agere APP750NP block diagram.

of a network switching system. However, for a fixed-bit rate, the packet rate varies with the packet size and the lower-layer protocol. In the case of packet over SONET, which results in the maximum packet rate performance of 10 Gb/s, one packet arrives approximately every 40 nanoseconds (ns). The APP750TM chooses a time slot duration of 37.5 ns to sustain the 10-Gb/s bit rate for all data protocols, even under worst-case conditions.

Within each time slot, the APP750TM dequeues one data block from memory and queues one data block into memory. The effective byte count in each data block is between 40 and 127 bytes. Depending on the size of the packet data unit (PDU), a data block can be either a portion of a PDU or a complete PDU.

Figure 14.3 shows the major functional blocks in an APP750TM. Among these blocks, the input/output interface, PDU assembly, destination ID (DID) manager, and PDU modification blocks are of less significance to the description of traffic management. They are briefly described in this section. Buffer-managing, queuing, and scheduling blocks are the core of traffic management, and are elaborated in great detail with a dedicated section for each block.

Input/output interface

The APP750TM supports one standard SPI-4.2 interface for the connection between a physical device (e.g., a framer) and an APP750TM (or between APP750NP and APP750TM). It also supports a SERDES interface (total bandwidth up to 25 Gb/s) for the connection between a fabric device and an APP750TM. Both interfaces can be configured as either input or output to allow the APP750TM to operate at either the ingress side or egress side of a line card.

APP750TM

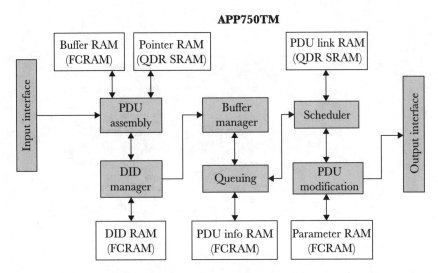

APP750TM block diagram.

The SERDES interface bandwidth is sufficient to sustain the 10-Gb/s data rate for any PDU size plus fabric overhead.

PDU assembly

Traffic data are stored as a complete packet in the PDU reassembly block after either:

+ Assembly from a physical device (PHY interface)
+ Reassembly from a fabric device

This procedure is necessary because partial data from a large packet is usually preempted by a small packet from other physical ports, or from other delay priorities and fabric ports, to reduce the switching delay.

The APP750TM supports up to 4096 assembly queues with eight priority classes. Each queue assembles the interleaved data blocks among physical ports or among fabric ports and classes. Error checking is also performed at this stage to ensure the integrity of an assembled packet. Only error-free packets are passed to the next stage.

DID manager

The DID manager keeps track of queue destinations with a preloaded DID table. The destination ID (DID), derived from the classifier, is used as an index into the

DID table. The DID manager performs lookups into the DID table to retrieve various information for other functional blocks. It is also responsible for computing the number of transmits for multiple-block PDUs to facilitate transmission of large PDUs.

PDU modification

The incoming and outgoing bit stream generally requires some modification as it is processed. This modification includes, but is not limited to, the following operations:

+ Decrements the time to live (TTL) in an IP header

+ Adjusts or inserts CRCs or checksums

+ Prepends or appends tags, labels, or other header/trailer information, possibly as part of encapsulating or tunneling a received packet through a network

+ Removes headers and trailers

+ Modifies data contained at arbitrary locations within the packet (e.g., translating addresses)

The complexity varies significantly, depending on the operation type. In the APP750TM, such modification functions are performed by programmable compute engines with specifically assigned parameter values and script instruction sequences. Packet modification can be programmed for each data flow. The APP750TM supports the following modifications to packets:

+ Adding or removing from the head of a PDU

+ Adding or removing from the tail of a PDU

+ Modifying the data anywhere in the PDU

+ Generating appropriate IP headers as part of IP fragmentation

+ Segmenting a PDU into different-size blocks

+ Adding programmable parameters or fabric information to each block

Packet modification processing is performed by compute engines that are programmable using C-NP, which Agere previously called the Agere Scripting Language. C-NP is a subset of C tailored for execution of concise algorithms and is the same programming language as used in Agere's 2.5-Gb/s routing switch processor (RSP). Four compute engines are implemented in parallel in the APP750TM to provide the computing power. Each compute engine is based on a bit-slice architecture and is used in a VLIW horizontally microcoded fashion.

Buffer management

A buffer management mechanism is employed to manage and protect the system buffer resources to provide low delay and low loss to diverse types of traffic—from steady-stream fixed-rate traffic to bursty low-long-term average-rate traffic. The APP750TM achieves such a goal by implementing both a threshold-based tail-drop scheme and a proactive *active* queue management scheme.

In the APP750TM, the entire buffer space is statically divided into two parts: the buffer space reserved for PDUs under assembly (reassembly buffer) and buffer space dedicated to PDUs after they have been assembled (PDU buffer). The division between the two buffers is configurable and they are managed separately.

Threshold-Based Scheme.   The threshold-based tail-drop scheme [1] applies to both the reassembly buffer space and PDU buffer space. Unlike a traditional implementation of a threshold-based tail-drop scheme, which sets a single maximum length for each buffer pool and accepts the packet until the maximum threshold is reached, the APP750TM threshold scheme allocates two thresholds for each buffer pool.

The first threshold is defined as the minimum guaranteed buffer space threshold; the second one is the maximum allowed buffer space threshold. In a traditional implementation, the entire buffer space is divided among all buffer pools exclusively. In the APP750TM threshold implementation, in addition to the minimum guaranteed buffer space allocated for each pool, a public shared buffer space is reserved with a size initialized to the total reassembly or PDU buffer space less the sum of the minimum guaranteed buffer space for each pool.

An incoming packet or data block, depending on whether it is for the reassembly or PDU buffer space, is accepted only when one of the following conditions are met:

✦ The queue length for the pool is below the minimum guaranteed threshold.

✦ The pool queue length does not exceed its maximum allowed threshold *and* there is enough space available in the public shared buffer.

Compared to the traditional, single-threshold scheme, the APP750TM threshold scheme has the advantage that the minimum guaranteed threshold provides isolation among the pools, while the maximum allocation threshold prevents a few traffic flows from unfairly dominating the usage of the shared buffer space. The public shared buffer among pools increases the effective buffer space for each pool by exploiting the bursty nature of traffic. This scheme allows for the dynamic sharing of the buffer space among pools.

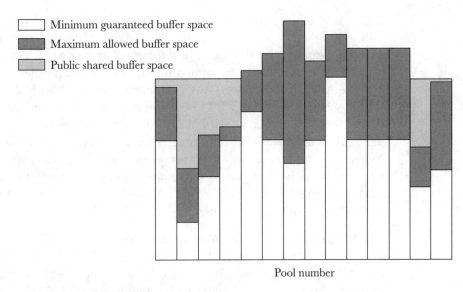

Minimum guaranteed buffer space

Maximum allowed buffer space

Public shared buffer space

Pool number

APP750TM threshold scheme.

With this threshold scheme, the reassembly buffer space is divided into nine disjointed buffer pools. Eight pools are dedicated to each traffic priority class, with the ninth buffer pool shared by traffic from all priority classes. Each priority assembly buffer pool is configured with a minimum guaranteed threshold, as well as with a maximum usable threshold.

The buffer space for assembled PDUs can be divided into disjointed buffer pools as well. The APP750TM can support up to 4096 dedicated buffer pools plus a public buffer space shared among all pools. Each buffer pool is configured with a minimum guaranteed allocation and a maximum allowable allocation. Figure 14.4 shows such a threshold scheme for the assembled packet.

Active Queue Management Scheme. Active queue management refers to the practice of managing queues in a "proactive" way in deciding which packets to discard and when to discard them. An active queue management scheme is regarded as a complement to a threshold-based tail-drop scheme. For example, random early detection (RED) has been singled out by the IETF as the recommended active queue management scheme, since RED reduces the possibility of tail drop by probabilistic packet dropping before the congestion occurs. The dropping probability in RED is usually set to be linearly proportional to average queue occupancy monitored. By dropping some packets early rather than waiting until the buffer is full, RED avoids dropping large numbers of packets all at once and minimizes the chances of global synchronization. A weighting factor is introduced into RED (thus, weighted random early discard) to provide differentiated treatment for the traffic of different characteristics. A WRED scheme usually implements more than one dropping probability profile.

The APP750TM supports a WRED scheme for the PDU buffer space. The WRED scheme can be applied to both individual buffer pools and the public shared buffer pool. Unlike most WRED implementations in which weights are determined only by packet-drop precedences, the weighting parameters in the APP750TM are both packet-drop precedence and traffic-flow specific. This is important when both responsive and nonresponsive flows coexist in the same network, making flow identification and isolation necessary to protect conforming traffic flows from aggressive ones.

Configurability of Buffer Management Scheme.   The effectiveness of combining the threshold and WRED schemes depends on the traffic protocol in use and the protocol implementation. Generally, a WRED scheme provides satisfactory performance for only a *responsive* flow, such as a TCP flow.

To achieve the desired behavior for all possible protocols, both the threshold scheme and the WRED scheme in the APP750TM can be enabled and disabled independently. In addition, the buffer management scheme is so flexible that it can be configured in various ways, from one big public shared pool to 4096 dedicated memory pools, from deterministic thresholding to random early dropping.

Queuing.   Queuing is one of the most fundamental operations in a routing or switching system. It has also become one of the most challenging issues in 10-Gb/s network processor designs. The queuing operation itself is simple and straightforward. The challenge comes solely from the physical limitations of memory bandwidth and access latency.

Memory is used in queuing operations to buffer traffic data, link the buffered data into queues according to certain criteria, and to hold various tables. There are some unique characteristics when memory is used in such applications:

+ Each memory access usually reads or writes a fixed-size data block to simplify the implementation.

+ The memory access sequence is neither predictable nor controllable.

+ The data have to be written into or read out within a fixed time to sustain the traffic throughput.

+ The memory bandwidth and size increase linearly with the traffic throughput. The memory bandwidth has to be at least equal to traffic throughput.

✦ A partially full data block requires even higher bandwidth. A partially full data block is created when storing a smaller-size packet or segmenting a large-size packet into multiple data blocks (internal fragmentation). A partially full data block is inevitable when a variable-size packet is segmented into fixed-size blocks.

Commercially available memory barely meets bandwidth and latency requirements when traffic throughput is at 10 Gb/s or beyond. Extensive effort has to be spent on how to meet throughput requirements with available memory.

Approaches that optimize memory bandwidth by packing multiple packets into memory blocks often have serious deficiencies. To support multicast, multiple copies of the packet must be written into memory. This both requires extra memory bandwidth and can create a serious performance bottleneck if many copies must be written. In addition, these schemes require partial buffers per queue on the write and read path to memory. This limits the number of queues that can be supported or requires large amounts of memory to store the partial blocks. Such schemes also require that all classification be completed prior to any data being written to memory. The approach taken by the APP750TM completely avoids these kinds of problems.

The APP750TM maintains a variety of queues for buffer management and scheduling purposes:

✦ *Page queue*. Traffic data in APP750TM is stored in buffer RAM (FCRAM) as fixed-size memory blocks, referred to as *pages*. Different pages belonging to one PDU are linked by a pointer in QDR SRAM.

✦ *PDU queue*. Different PDUs mapped to the same aggregate flow connection, referred to as a QID queue, are linked in PDU queues in QDR SRAM.

✦ *Port/class queue*. Different QIDs destined to the same port and mapped to the same class are linked as a port/class queue.

✦ *Multicast staging queue (MSQ)*. A set of multicast staging queues is provided as a holding area for multicast PDUs that are awaiting multicast linking. One queue is maintained for each of eight multicast classes. Arriving multicast PDUs are queued to the multicast staging queue corresponding to the multicast class the PDU belongs to. When the PDU comes to the head of the multicast staging queue and is selected for multicast linking, it is linked to all the branches of the multicast tree and dequeued from the staging queue.

✦ *Free buffer queue*. Data buffers not currently allocated to any PDU are linked as a single queue, referred to as the free buffer list (FBL).

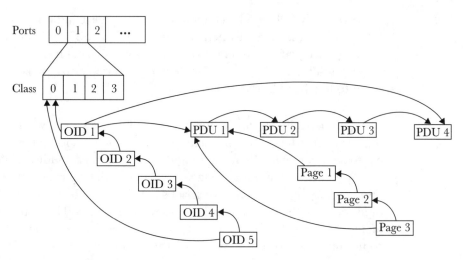

14.5 APP750TM queuing structure.

FIGURE

Different types of queues are organized based on their destination port and service class in a hierarchical structure, as shown in Figure 14.5.

The APP750TM implements different queuing mechanisms to address different requirements: a simple circular FIFO, a segmented linked list, FIFO-linked lists, and LIFO-linked lists with PDU link RAM and PDU info RAM. Among all these queuing mechanisms, the segmented linked list is of particular interest, since it is key to the ability to maintain full wire-speed operation with all workloads of interest.

To keep up with the line rate, a traffic manager must be able to perform one queue and one dequeue operation approximately every 40 ns. Each queue operation includes *at least* the following operations:

+ Writing the incoming traffic data into a buffer RAM addressed by a free buffer pointer
+ Obtaining the tail pointer of the queue assigned to the incoming PDU
+ Linking the incoming PDU to the queue
+ Reading the free-buffer-linked list to update the free buffer pointer

Each dequeue operation must include:

+ Obtaining the head pointer of the queue scheduled to be served
+ Reading out the PDU data from buffer RAM pointed to by a head queue pointer

✦ Reading the queue-linked list to update the head queue pointer

✦ Returning the freed buffer space to the free-buffer-linked list

These operations can be classified into three categories of memory operations: head and tail queue pointer access, PDU data access, and queue and PDU-linked list manipulation.

Head and tail pointers are usually stored in a per-queue table. Depending on the queue granularity and hardware architecture, a queue table can be stored in on-chip memory, SRAM, DRAM, or in an on-chip memory/cache combined with external memory. In general, supporting large numbers of queues provides finer-grained traffic management functionality but requires storing queue-state information in external memory. Whenever external memory is involved at 10-Gb/s line speeds, a hardware architectural approach such as pipelining or multithreading is required to mitigate the impact of memory access latency.

Some approaches that use on-chip memory as a cache only allow backlogging data in cached queues. Therefore, a key measure of effective traffic management granularity under worst-case traffic patterns is the number of queues that can be simultaneously backlogged. The APP750TM can have 16-K queues backlogged simultaneously.

Packet data are usually stored in DRAM due to the requirement to buffer many milliseconds of traffic during periods of congestion. The access latency of commercially available DRAM is several time slots. Pipelining and multithreading can be used to mitigate the impact of DRAM access latencies. Even more challenging, however, is the impact of DRAM random cycle time limitations (i.e., tRC is the required interval between random accesses to the same bank of memory). A naive packet buffer implementation using DDR SDRAM or RAMBUS can only support one access every 60+ ns, while buffering and retrieving packets from a 10-Gb/s link requires a read and a write access at sub-40 ns intervals. The APP750TM employs FCRAM (a low-cost, low-power DRAM with a much lower tRC than conventional DRAM) for packet buffering to help deliver a full 10-Gb/s line rate with any packet size regardless of the traffic pattern and scheduling policies chosen.

While packet data access can potentially tolerate large access latencies via pipelining and multithreading, linked-list access cannot. A queue ID and a buffer address must be available every 37.5 ns in the APP750TM design to sustain line rate. Linked-list memory access cannot start until the head/tail pointer is read out from the queue table. Therefore, two memory accesses must be performed within a 37.5-ns interval. Since SRAM could not directly provide such low latency for the desired memory density, the APP750TM uses a special queuing structure—a segmented linked list with prefetching—to achieve such low latency.

A segmented linked list is a linked list of FIFO segments. Each FIFO segment has a fixed number of entries. Addressing within a segment is the same as addressing in a regular FIFO. Only the addressing between two segments in a segmented linked list requires SRAM access, which is never required within two consecutive time slots. Therefore, its access latency can be hidden with prefetching. Setting the number of entries in each segment to the minimum value to cover the SRAM access latency provides the advantages of both low addressing latency and efficient usage. The segmented linked list structure dramatically reduces the pointer manipulation latency such that the APP750TM can perform one queue and one dequeue to any traffic queue and to any PDU within one time slot.

Scheduling

The performance offered by the scheduling scheme in a traffic manager has become one of the key differentiating factors in evaluating the overall performance of a network processor. Providing quality of service requires meeting bandwidth and delay guarantees, providing fair access to available resources, and providing isolation among traffic flows to protect well-behaving flows from malicious or misbehaving ones. A scheduler that controls the order in which packets are served therefore directly impacts the delivered service quality.

There are many scheduler mechanisms and combinations of mechanisms to choose from. There are significant differences in performance and capability as well as implementation cost and complexity between choices. Therefore, the design of the scheduler component of a traffic manager has a major influence on its performance, cost, reliability, and long-term viability.

The APP750TM device uses a hierarchical scheduling structure that provides true bandwidth guarantees, bounded and low delay, fair allocation of excess bandwidth, and traffic isolation at various levels. At the top level of the hierarchy, traffic destined to different fabric ports (ingress) or physical device subports (egress) is arbitrated by a subport-level scheduler. At the second level, service priorities among different scheduling classes within each subport are managed by a class-level scheduler. At the bottom level, traffic associated with a specific class and subport is further segregated into different queues or flows. A scheduler scheme is employed to control the service between different queues. Figure 14.6 depicts a simplified view of this scheduler hierarchy.

The algorithm used to schedule service depends on the hierarchy level to which a scheduler is allocated. Different scheduling algorithms are used at different levels based on the balanced consideration of quality-of-service guarantee requirements and implementation complexity.

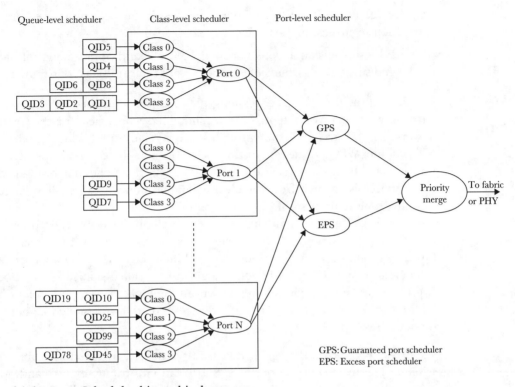

14.6   Scheduler hierarchical structure.

FIGURE

Port-level scheduler

At the top level, the subport scheduler is first divided into a guaranteed port scheduler (GPS) and an excess port scheduler (EPS). The GPS scheduler can provide guaranteed minimum latency as well as guaranteed bandwidth for each destination subport. The EPS scheduler provides fair excess bandwidth allocation among all competing subports. The GPS is implemented by using a shaped virtual-clock algorithm, while the EPS is implemented by a round-robin (RR) scheme.

Guaranteed Port Scheduler.   The GPS employs a shaped virtual-clock algorithm [2] as its scheduler scheme to manage service among different subports. This shaped virtual-clock scheme belongs to a class of scheduler algorithms called weighted fair queuing (WFQ) [3–6].

WFQ algorithms use a set of timestamps to denote when a packet of a session would start and finish in an idealized reference system. WFQ algorithms are proven to have two desirable properties:

◆ They guarantee end-to-end delay to a leaky-bucket constrained traffic session regardless of the behavior of other sessions.

◆ They ensure instantaneous fair allocation of bandwidth among all back-logged sessions regardless of whether or not their traffic is constrained.

To reset the timestamps of sessions that have previously been idle, a system virtual-time function or potential is also maintained, which measures the amount of work the system is performing for all sessions relative to this ideal model.

Different WFQ policies are distinguished by their choice of system potential functions and their service selection policy. The selection policy that results in the least service discrepancy from the ideal scheduler model is the smallest eligible finishing timestamp first (SEFF) selection policy.

A packet of a session is considered to be eligible if it has started service in the reference system. Of these eligible packets, the one with the smallest finishing timestamp is selected for service. When the system potential is equal to the real-time clock, the scheduling algorithm is called shaped virtual clock. It provides the least service discrepancy from the ideal reference model, with a built-in traffic-shaping ability that provides exactly the provisioned amount of service to sessions.

Excess Port Scheduler.   The EPS is implemented by a round-robin (RR) scheme. The main function of the EPS is to fairly distribute excess bandwidth among all competing subports. The excess bandwidth is the bandwidth left over by the GPS when it cannot serve any subport due either to back pressure or to bandwidth shaping. The EPS, when enabled, makes the entire APP750TM scheduler work-conserving.

Priority Merge.   At every time slot, all port-level schedulers can identify a candidate for service. Only one page of traffic data, however, can be served each time slot. When more than one candidate arises, arbitration is required. Based on the nature of each scheduler scheme, strict priority is used to arbitrate between them. Among these two schedulers, GPS has the highest priority.

Class-level scheduler

Within each subport, traffic is divided into four priority classes. The APP750TM can be configured to provide one of four different scheduling schemes to serve traffic among different classes:

◆ Unlimited strict priority among four classes

◆ Bandwidth-limited strict priority among four classes

✦ Smoothed deficit-weighted round-robin (SDWRR) among four classes

✦ One strict priority class plus three SDWRR classes

In addition, a class-level scheduler works in one of two modes: page mode or packet mode. Page mode is usually used on the ingress side, which allows the interleaving of pages from different traffic classes in order to avoid the delay caused by large packet transmission. Page mode requires that the egress queuing engine reassemble the complete packet. Packet mode, however, is usually used on the egress side, where the destination of traffic is a physical device. A physical device has to receive a complete data packet on each port. Packet mode is also required on ingress when the APP750TM is connected to a frame-based switch fabric.

Smoothed Deficit-Weighted Round-Robin. A traditional implementation of a deficit-weighted round-robin (DWRR) [7, 8] scheduler employs a single FIFO. The scheduler visits each queue only once per service frame and continues serving one session until its allocated per-frame share is exhausted. This results in extremely poor performance in terms of latency and service burstiness. In the APP750TM, a patented, smoothed version of DWRR is implemented that allows interleaving the transmission of packets from different queues while preserving the order of PDUs in one queue [9]. The SDWRR scheduler is implemented at both class and queue level to reduce latency and burstiness. In SDWRR, service to each session is distributed on a packet basis. Packets from different queues are served in round-robin fashion. The bandwidth share is fulfilled in a collective way, instead of in one shot, thereby eliminating the latency and burstiness problems traditionally associated with DWRR implementations.

Strict Priority. The strict priority configuration gives the highest priority to the desired traffic class, which is often necessary for delay-sensitive traffic. The priority order in a strict priority scheme is fixed; it is always from low class number to high class number.

In an unlimited-bandwidth strict priority configuration, the class with highest priority always gets serviced first, as long as it is backlogged and not back-pressured. This scheme produces the smallest delay for high-priority traffic.

In a bandwidth-limited strict priority configuration, the service priority given to each priority class within each service frame is limited to a certain bandwidth. When the service share is fulfilled for a high-priority class, the service opportunity is given to lower-priority traffic. This configuration achieves balance between providing minimum delays for high-priority traffic and not starving low-priority traffic.

In the one-priority-class-plus-three-SDWRR configuration, service priority is always given to one fixed class as long as it is backlogged and not back-pressured. The leftover bandwidth is distributed among the other three classes with a DWRR scheme. This scheme provides the smallest delay guarantee for one specific class and bandwidth guarantee for the other three classes when traffic from the strict priority class is regulated. This is suitable for IP *diffserv* support when traffic from an expedited forwarding class is given the highest priority and traffic from all other forwarding classes (including assured forwarding and best effort) is served by the SDWRR scheme.

It should be noted that the APP750TM can provide fairly tight delay bounds among traffic classes, even with the SDWRR scheme. The delay bound provided by SDWRR between classes is determined only by the maximum PDU size served by each class. In contrast, the delay bound provided by a conventional DWRR implementation is determined by both maximum PDU size and the traffic backlog situation in each class.

Queue-level scheduler

A queue-level scheduler manages the service among different queue sessions. A queue session in APP750TM is defined as a collection of virtual connections or IP flows, which is treated as an entry-from-traffic-scheduling perspective and addressed by a queue identifier (QID). In the queue-level scheduler, traffic with the same QID is queued in page-by-page fashion in a FIFO-linked list. Different queue sessions destined to the same subport and recognized as in the same scheduling class are organized into another FIFO-linked list, referred to as a flow. An SDWRR scheme is used to serve different queue sessions in each flow. The SDWRR scheduler used at queue level is similar to SDWRR used at class level.

External scheduling mode

Although the APP750TM has implemented a sophisticated scheduler scheme, the APP750TM also allows users to tailor the queuing structure to implement their own scheduler scheme. The APP750TM can be configured to allow an external device to schedule traffic through a special interface. In this mode, traffic is queued as it is with an internal scheduler, with the exception that the dequeue decision comes from an external device. Whenever a PDU is successfully queued, the APP750TM sends a signal to the external scheduler through the dedicated interface to indicate a PDU's arrival. The PDU resides in the

APP750TM buffer memory and waits for the external scheduler's notice. When an external scheduler presents an eligible dequeue decision, the APP750TM performs a dequeue operation. Each dequeue operation dispatches one page of data into the outgoing data stream.

Scheduling accuracy

Achieving bandwidth and delay guarantees depends heavily on the accuracy of the scheduler. Miscounting the packet size is one prominent factor that can cause inaccuracy in the scheduler.

Obviously, it is vital that the packet size gets accurately reflected in the amount of service offered to a queue. The packet size being served varies greatly, from 40 bytes to 64 KB. A packet, however, usually has to be segmented into fixed-size data blocks to be stored in memory. Since the packet size can be any value between minimum and maximum, some segments contain only partial data. For example, when a 65-byte packet is segmented into two 64-byte segments, the second segment contains only 1 byte. Therefore, when the second segment is read out from the memory only 1 byte should be counted for service. If a design uses 64-byte packet blocks to measure bandwidth rather than actual byte counts, the result is that a 65-byte packet and a 128-byte packet are treated the same (so the end user sending 65-byte packets would get almost half of the bandwidth they are paying for compared to the end user sending 128-byte packets).

Due to its low implementation complexity, a popular scheduler design for a high data rate is to use table lookup. In this scheme, one or more tables are maintained with each entry in the table storing the session index to be served. The number of entries allocated to a session's index in the table depends on the subscribed bandwidth of the session. Usually, more entries are allocated to a high-speed session. The table size is determined by the bandwidth range of sessions supported and the granularity of the scheduler. Every time slot, a traffic manager identifies a session to service by scanning the table. The service bandwidth to each session is determined completely by the number of session index entries in the table.

However, due to the unpredictable nature of the real byte count in each service data block and the static allocation of the service table, the real service amount cannot be reflected in the table even though the dequeued byte count is available. Therefore, these schemes always assume that a full block of data is being served. This approach clearly will not guarantee accurate bandwidth allocation.

In contrast, each session's bandwidth in the APP750TM's scheduler is controlled by the relation between a timestamp for each competing session and the system potential. Both timestamp and system potential are evolving dynamically with the service amount delivered. While the APP750 scheduling scheme sends out a block's worth of data in each dequeue operation, the real byte count served in each service is recorded and used to update the timestamp instantaneously. Therefore, APP750TM schedulers are able to track the outgoing traffic bandwidth with byte-level accuracy.

Another common practice in high-speed traffic manager design is to lengthen the scheduling decision interval by sending out more data at each scheduling decision. Although this approach can simplify maintaining full traffic throughput by sending out multiple minimum-size PDUs in one shot, it results in much more bursty traffic, resulting in an adverse impact on end-to-end delay and jitter bounds.

The APP750TM scheduler employs a special hardware design that allows instantaneous updating of scheduling state information. This design enables the APP750TM to perform one scheduling decision every 37.5 ns (one time slot), which is the exact time required to serve one minimum-size PDU. With such a design, the APP750TM is able to smoothly schedule traffic from different QIDs, different classes, and different ports based on the scheduler decision from time slot to time slot.

Other factors that impact the accuracy of a scheduler include the representation accuracy of the bandwidth desired and algorithm performance. These issues have been addressed in the APP750TM by implementing a high-performance scheduling scheme and allocating adequate bits to represent rate and timestamp information.

14.3   5-GB/S APP550 SOLUTION

The APP550 is a network processor with integrated traffic management functions that performs classification, traffic management, scheduling, and PDU modifications in a single, high-performance package. In addition, the APP550 features a co-processor interface to allow additional custom processing, such as encryption and compression.

The APP550 is both programmable and configurable to support multiple applications. For example, the APP550 supports multiple memory configurations, allowing designers to match the memory requirements to specific application needs. Figure 14.7 illustrates a block-level view of the device.

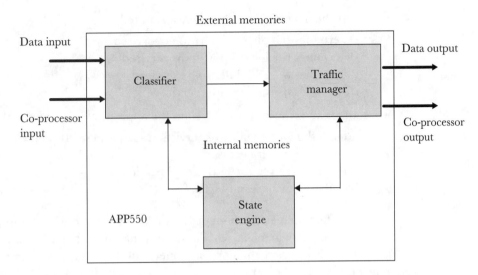

APP550 block-level view.

The APP550 classifies data as it comes in from the network or switch fabric using a two-pass process:

✦ The first pass processes the PDUs in 64-byte blocks. The first pass stores the data block offsets and links the blocks to reassemble the PDU.

✦ The replay pass processes the PDU as a whole. In the replay pass, the APP550 simultaneously performs pattern matching and passes the PDU to the internal traffic management logic.

The processing that occurs in both the first and replay passes is defined by programs written in a high-level classification language, Functional Programming Language (FPL). FPL is also used to program classification processing on Agere's other network processor offerings.

When replay processing is complete, a conclusion about the PDU along with the data is sent to the traffic management logic and processed in three major stages, where the APP550 performs the following.

✦ Prepares and queues the PDU for scheduling:
  • Assembles the blocks into a PDU in FCRAM.
  • Determines the destination queue for the PDU.
  • Determines if the PDU should be queued. If it should be queued, it is added to the appropriate queue for scheduling.

◆ Selects the next PDU block to be transmitted:

- Determines the physical port to be serviced
- Determines the logical port to be serviced
- Determines the scheduler to be serviced
- Determines the queue to be serviced

◆ Modifies and transmits the PDU on the appropriate output port:

- Adjusts the QoS (quality-of-service) transmit intervals and CoS (class-of-service) priority, if necessary
- Performs any necessary PDU modifications
- Calculates any necessary CRCs

The traffic manager component of the APP550 is responsible for implementing congestion management, scheduling and shaping, and packet modification. Figure 14.8 illustrates the major components of the traffic manager in relation to the other APP550 blocks.

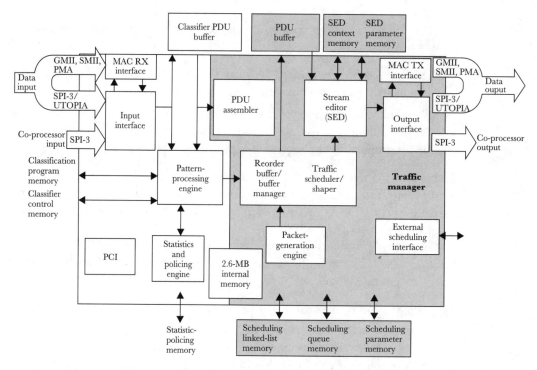

14.8   Traffic management components of APP550.

FIGURE

Traffic data from the classification block is assembled or reassembled into a complete packet in the PDU reassembly block. This procedure is necessary, given the fact that the classification block runs several threads in parallel and partial data from several packets are interleaved when sent to the traffic manager block.

14.3.1 Buffer Management

A buffer management mechanism is employed to manage and protect the system buffer resources in order to provide low delay and low loss to diverse types of traffic, from steady-stream fixed-rate to bursty, low long-term average-rate traffic. Buffer management functions are performed by programmable compute engines. C-NP is used to program the compute engines. Various buffer management schemes—such as RED, WRED, or any other type of congestion management scheme—can be implemented using the programmable compute engines.

The APP550 hardware maintains all the memory occupancies and handles all the queue management aspects of buffer management. Software running on the compute engines is invoked at every queue attempt. This program is provided with the memory occupancies at each level of the schedule hierarchy, as well as control plane setup parameters. The software implements the buffer management policy and returns a Boolean answer indicating whether the packet is accepted or discarded. In addition, the software can maintain statistics about packets accepted and discarded.

14.3.2 Scheduling and Shaping

Hardware mechanisms are built into the APP550 for common traffic shaping or rate strategies, including:

+ *Constant-bit-rate (CBR) traffic*. CBR scheduling allows the APP550 to support guaranteed rates only for cell-based traffic connections.

+ *Variable-bit-rate (VBR) traffic*. VBR scheduling supports dynamic adjustments to a traffic rate. The APP550 can be programmed to dynamically schedule VBR traffic based on a number of factors, such as rate changes and available traffic. The VBR scheduler can be used for packet or cell shaping. Software running in the APP550 computes the cell or packet interval at each scheduling event. This allows for flexible policies, such as GCRA, GFP, or single-rate shaping.

♦ *Programmable round–robin (PRR) scheduling*. Through the use of PRR scheduling using the Traffic Shaper compute engine, the APP550 supports SDWRR scheduling for packet-based traffic. For cell-based traffic, the PRR also supports SWRR (smoothed weighted round-robin) traffic. In addition, the PRR scheduler supports a maximum bandwidth per queue. Software running in the APP550 manages the weights and deficits per queue. In addition, this software can compute the minimum interval per queue to implement the maximum bandwidth function.

Traffic scheduling and shaping is defined by the APP550's scheduling logic and the programmable queue definitions. The high-level control of APP550 scheduling functions is provided by the internal logic; the traffic shaping is defined by the configuration of the APP550, the Traffic Shaper compute engine, and the programmable queue definitions.

14.3.3   Scheduling Hierarchy

To provide the control needed to schedule traffic for up to 256-K queues, the APP550 employs a set of configurable components. These components can be provisioned and programmed to service a wide range of applications. APP550 scheduling components include:

♦ *Queue*. Defines the destination and processing parameters for assigned protocol data units (PDUs). The APP550 supports two queue types: QoS and CoS. A set of CoS queues defines the priority levels for implementing CoS for a given QoS connection. Each set of CoS queues (up to 16 priorities) is assigned to a single QoS queue.

♦ *Scheduler*. Defines the type of scheduling for a queue and implements the rate for the queue, if applicable.

♦ *Logical port*. Defines a connection for a unique data flow.

♦ *Port manager*. Defines a rate for one or more logical ports, and monitors the available traffic on the logical port, the back-pressure signal, and a port manager group rate clock, if applicable.

♦ *Output ports*. The physical interface used to transmit traffic to the fabric or downstream logic.

The APP550 internal scheduler uses these components to determine the queue to service each time the APP550 is ready to send a block of data. Figure 14.9 shows the relationships between these PDU scheduling components.

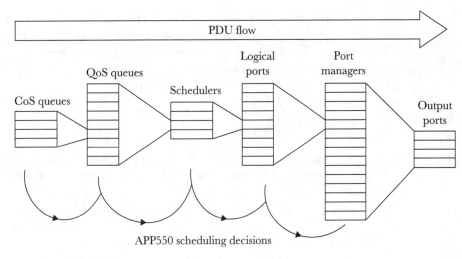

Scheduling hierarchy.

At every scheduling event, the Traffic Shaper compute engine executes a user-defined program. The actual queue-scheduling algorithm can be implemented in these scripts. Scheduling disciplines such as RR, WRR, SDWRR, and so on can be implemented in software that executes on these compute engines.

14.4 CONCLUSIONS

Traffic management is one of the most important functions performed by a network switching or routing system. It enables systems to adjust traffic flows, prioritize specific traffic, and react to a wide range of network traffic conditions. Sophisticated traffic management solutions are necessary for congestion management and differentiated services to maximize the value of traffic carried by the network during congestion.

While pure software implementations do not meet the required line-rate requirements, pure hardware implementations with no programmable parameters do not meet the scalability and flexibility needs of current and future networks. Finding the right balance is the key to building a system with the flexibility and performance to fulfill current and future network traffic management challenges.

A hybrid traffic management architecture is both flexible and scalable. A hybrid solution partitions traffic management functions into hardware-implemented mechanisms with software-programmable policies, yielding the right balance between performance and flexibility.

REFERENCES

[1] A. K. Choundhury and E. L. Hahne, "Dynamic Queue Length Thresholds for Shared-Memory Packet Switch," *IEEE/ACM Transactions in Networking*, vol. 6, Apr. 1998, pp. 130–140.

[2] Andrea Francini et al., "Enhanced Weighted Round Robin Schedulers for Bandwidth Guarantees in Packet Networks," *Quality of Service in Multiservice IP Networks, International Workshop*, QoS-IP 2001, Rome, Italy, Jan. 2001, pp. 205–222.

[3] J. C. R. Bennett and H. Zhang, "WF^{2}Q: Worst-Case Fair Weighted Fair Queueing," *Proceedings of IEEE INFOCOM '96*, Mar. 1996, pp. 120–128.

[4] D. Stiliadis and A. Varma, "Latency-Rate Servers: A General Model for Analysis of Traffic Scheduling Algorithms," *Proceedings of IEEE INFOCOM '96*, Mar. 1996, pp. 111–119.

[5] D. Stiliadis and A. Varma, "Design and Analysis of Frame-Based Fair Queueing: A New Traffic Scheduling Algorithm for Packet-Switched Networks," *Proceedings of ACM SIGMETRICS '96*, May 1996, pp. 104–115.

[6] D. Stiliadis and A. Varma, "Efficient Fair Queueing Algorithms for Packet Switched Networks," *IEEE/ACM Transactions on Networking*, vol. 6, no. 2, Apr. 1998, pp. 175–185.

[7] M. Katevenis, S. Sidiropoulos, and C. Courcoubetis, "Weighted Round Robin Cell Multiplexing in a General-Purpose ATM Switch," *IEEE Journal on Selected Areas in Communications*, vol. 9, Oct. 1991, pp. 1265–1279.

[8] M. Shreedhar and G. Varghese, "Efficient Fair Queueing Using Deficit Round Robin," *IEEE/ACM Transactions on Networking*, vol. 4, no. 3, June 1996, pp. 375–385.

[9] D. Stiliadis and A. Varma, "A General Methodology for Designing Efficient Traffic Scheduling and Shaping Algorithms," *Proceedings of IEEE INFOCOM '97*, Kobe, Japan, Apr. 1997.

15 AMCC nPcore NISC Architecture

CHAPTER

Robin Melnick, Keith Morris
AMCC Switching and Network Processing

The AMCC nPcore family, spanning four generations, consists of NPUs that differ mainly in the number of nPcores they contain, the line speeds they support, and the way traffic management is implemented. While some AMCC NPUs integrate a packet-oriented traffic manager for Ethernet-based applications, others combine with an AMCC traffic management co-processor for flexible, fine-grained admission control, bandwidth provisioning, queuing, and scheduling. The fifth generation of the nPcore architecture, dubbed nP^5, has a significant enhancement over the previous four generations [1] in that the chips in this generation integrate programmable nPcore-based packet and cell processing with the full capabilities of AMCC's traffic management co-processor family.

The nPcore is a RISC core supplemented with networking-specific instructions. While the company's first-generation NPUs had a single nPcore supporting four 10/100-Mb/s Fast Ethernet line interfaces, following generations increased the number of cores. The nP7510 10-Gb/s network processor, a fourth-generation nPcore-based device, utilizes six nPcores to support a half-duplex OC-192 or 10-Gigabit Ethernet connection [2]. The AMCC nP^5 family consists of fifth-generation nPcore-based devices, the first of which is the nP3700, having new performance capabilities and flexibility [3]. Table 15.1 describes AMCC's current NPU family for applications ranging from 100 Mb/s to 10 Gb/s.

The remainder of this chapter is structured as follows. In Section 15.1, the nPcore-based architecture is described. Section 15.2 introduces the software architecture and the nPsoft development environment. Section 15.3 concludes the chapter.

15.1 THE nPcore-BASED ARCHITECTURE

The centerpiece of the AMCC NPU is the nPcore cluster, where an nPcore is an application-specific RISC core. The cluster is surrounded by a variety of

NPU	Description
nP3450	24 x Fast Ethernet + 2 x Gigabit Ethernet stand-alone switch
	24 x Fast Ethernet line card
	Integrated MACs, packet classification, and traffic management
nP3454	4 x Gigabit Ethernet stand-alone switch
	2 x Gigabit Ethernet line card
	Integrated MACs, packet classification, and traffic management
nP3700	4 x GE, 2 x OC-48, 8 x OC-12, etc. line card
	Integrated MACs, programmable cell/packet traffic management
nP7510	OC-192 or 10 GE line card (two NPUs; one for ingress, one for egress)
	Combines with nPX5700 traffic manager co-processor

15.1 Overview of fourth- and fifth-generation AMCC NPUs.

TABLE

co-processing units, or "engines," that augment the cores, offloading certain specialized network data-flow-oriented processing tasks. Arrayed around these are a variety of memory and line I/O interfaces. In the remainder of this section, the nPcore-based architecture is described mainly in the context of nP3700 and nP7510 NPUs.

The nP3700 performs network processing and traffic management in a single package. Figure 15.1 illustrates the nP3700 NPU with integrated traffic management. It has 5-Gb/s full-duplex performance along with configuration flexibility for handling a wide range of multiclass, multichannel networking environments. Besides the integrated hardware-based traffic management, other new features include exception-channel processing, expanded memory options, an on-chip hardware algorithmic search co-processor, and new interface options. This gives both system and line card designers a greater degree of flexibility for implementing higher-speed network-processing functions within tighter space, cost, and power constraints while improving reliability through elimination of external interconnections between devices.

15.1.1   "NISC" = RISC + Network Co-processors

The AMCC NPU architecture integrates multiple nPcores with co-processor "engines" on the chip to accelerate network-processing functions, including traffic management with individual per-flow queuing and scheduling functions, packet transformations, classification, search, statistics gathering, metering, and

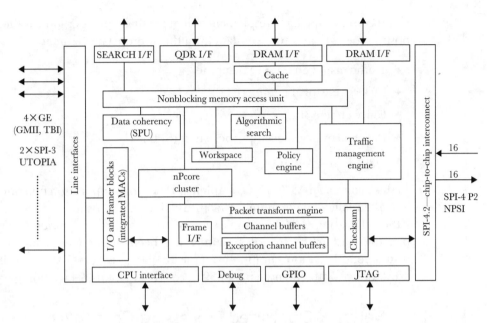

nPcore-based NPU architectural example: nP3700.

FIGURE

policing. The on-chip co-processor engines simplify the creation of software by providing single-instruction access to complex operations, creating a network-optimized instruction set computing (NISC) architecture. This approach significantly reduces the number of lines of code required to implement networking tasks.

To increase performance over time, the nPcore architecture relies both on splitting packet processing between nPcore tasks and special-function co-processors and on increasing the number of on-chip nPcores and faster clock rates. This approach contrasts both with architectures that achieve performance increases by hardwiring the flow order of certain functions, potentially limiting flexibility in the design of algorithms, and with those that may achieve flexibility by relying on off-the-shelf, general-purpose RISC cores, potentially limiting performance by implementing more functions in software or escalating complexity by increasing the amount of software that must be developed.

The nPcore-based approach offers the programmer the opportunity to offload common and complex tasks to specialized co-processors, yet it preserves software-programmable flexibility in terms of the structure and flow of packet processing. From the programmer's perspective, each of the following on-chip co-processors appears to implement a single-instruction operation as the nPcore posts requests to and receives data from the appropriate element:

+ Traffic management (TM) engine
+ Packet transform engine (PTE)
+ Policy engine (PE)
+ Data coherency/special-purpose unit (SPU)
+ Algorithmic search

In this manner, an AMCC NPU implements network application functions using a substantially smaller number of instructions than a more general-purpose RISC. Thus, simple MIPS comparisons of NPUs are not meaningful. For example, the "fast path" for IPv4 routing has been implemented in 43 nPcore instructions. In a more complex example, the fast path for ATM AAL5 CBR and UBR traffic is implemented in just 59 nPcore instructions, 94 including policing.

15.1.2   Network-Optimized Processing Core (nPcore)

The software-programmable nPcore is designed from scratch for high-speed packet and cell-based data plane operations. The nP3700 utilizes a cluster of three nPcores. The nP7510—one for each half (ingress and egress) of a full-duplex 10-Gb/s connection—employs six nPcores. The lower-bandwidth nP3450 and nP3454 devices use two nPcores each.

The nPcore has 64-bit registers that are byte addressable. Instructions use 8-, 16-, 32-, or 64-bit operands, which may lie entirely within a register, span registers, or reside in either internal or external memory without the need to preload data into registers. Also, the familiar 32-bit RISC instruction set is augmented with enhanced bit-manipulation and branch instructions—such as a single-instruction *CASE* statement—to optimize for network dataflow processing [4].

The NISC architecture yields a number of benefits that include simpler software implementations for the programmer (due to the need to create fewer lines of code) and smaller, lower-power NPUs. For example, AMCC's fourth-generation nP3454 NPU implements a four-port full-duplex Gigabit Ethernet stand-alone switch—or a two-port full-duplex GE line card (with a 2-gigabit full-duplex connection to a backplane) in a larger chassis-based switch—using two nPcores at 400 MHz or 800 MIPS. The nP3454 is implemented using the relatively conservative $0.18\,\mu$ fabrication process and a typical power dissipation of 6 watts.

The 800-MIPS rate may not be considered high. But if one takes a look at the 2 x GE line card example—where there are $2 \times 1.488M = 2.976M$ packets per second in the worst case of minimum-size (64-byte) frames at full line rate to maintain wire speed—the nP3454 must average 269 instructions per packet ($2 \times 400M/2.976M$). In the IPv4 routing scenario, this means the nP3454 implements this application at wire speed, and does so with 84% "headroom" (the additional cycles left for implementing further applications) over and above IPv4 routing. The nP3700 cores are at 700 MHz and can support twice the total line bandwidth while delivering one-third greater instructions per frame ($3 \times 700M/4 \times 1.488M = 359$ instructions per packet).

Single-stage, single-image programming

The fourth- and fifth-generation nPcores support 24 separate tasks/threads, yielding a total of 144 tasks available for packet/cell processing in the nP7510 NPU and 72 tasks in the nP3700. While earlier generations designated separate resources for ingress and egress channels, the nP^5 core used in the nP3700 makes all tasks available for either ingress or egress processing. This multitask, multicore architecture implements a simple, single-stage, single-image programming model. This is the logical inverse of multiple-processor-core models, where each core implements one stage of the processing algorithm. In a multistage model, any given cell or packet passes through multiple cores—whether software-programmed or hardwired—as it is processed (see Figure 15.2). It also contrasts with a single-stage, multi-image NPU model.

The packet transform engine co-processor of an nPcore-based NPU has an input controller block that assigns each incoming frame to an available (idle-state) task. From there, each individual frame is processed in its entirety, or "runs to completion," on this single task on a single core. While multiple cores and multiple tasks per core aggregate to increase total processing capacity, the

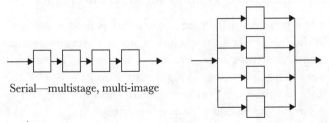

Serial—multistage, multi-image

Parallel—single-stage, single-image

15.2
FIGURE
NPU programming models: optimizing software flexibility versus hardware efficiency.

entire dataflow algorithm can be created as a single complete program, just as it would be on a uniprocessor system; the same program image is executed identically by each task on each core. This considerably simplifies programming, since regardless of the number of cores or tasks there is no code to be written or processor cycles spent on handoffs from task to task or core to core as a packet or cell is processed. More importantly, the programmer does not need to subdivide an algorithm into multiple serial stages, nor is any time spent load-balancing multiple stages or tuning the performance of multiple stages to avoid one stage overrunning another, potentially creating system bottlenecks.

This parallel processing structure also provides smoother performance scalability over the course of multiple generations. Because the same software runs on all tasks on all processor cores, there is no need to resubdivide or re-load-balance algorithms as more tasks and cores are added over time to increase line rates or application performance. An additional benefit of the nPcore single-stage parallel execution model is that performance is not sensitive to latency or bottlenecks in a multistage pipeline. Even in decision-rich network-processing environments, case statements and conditional jumps do not result in pipeline breakages. Regardless of the elapsed time needed to process a particular packet, cores are not left idle awaiting completion of a prior stage.

In earlier generations, separate program memories were maintained for each nPcore, even though in practice the same program image would be loaded into each memory. In the nP^5 generation, a single on-chip 64-KB program memory (16K x 32-bit instructions) is shared across all tasks across all cores, and an on-chip instruction cache improves memory performance. The nP^5 shared program memory is supplemented by the ability for host CPU applications to download less-frequently-used programs (applets) to be executed dynamically in runtime. For example, a program might be loaded periodically to flush aged-out entries from on-chip policy engine search databases.

Zero-cycle task switching and zero-cycle branching

A critical element of the nPcore architecture is its dynamic task control mechanism. In the nP^5 generation, each core simultaneously executes instructions for six different tasks using time-division multiplexing. The execution unit changes tasks every cycle, executing a single instruction for one of the six tasks in the active state before moving on to the next. This effectively implements an "overlapping virtual-processing pipeline," averting pipeline stalls by allowing each instruction six cycles to complete (see Figure 15.3). Even with *CASE* statements and conditional branches, no cycles are lost to fetching a new pipeline set of instructions. A different task executes in the next cycle, while the next instruction

T0	T1	T2	T3	T4	T5
				T0	T1
Task Sel	Task Sel	Task Sel	Task Sel	Task Sel	Task Sel
	Fetch	Fetch	Fetch	Fetch	Fetch
		Decode	Decode	Decode	Decode
			Read	Read	Read
				Execute	Execute
					Wr Back

15.3

FIGURE

Overlapping virtual processors: nPcore zero-cycle task-switching execution pipeline.

for the branched thread can be fetched before the next cycle opportunity for that task occurs.

When the current task suspends—for example, when accessing an off-chip resource such as a TCAM—the nPcore automatically switches to the next available ready-state task. No additional instruction is required to switch tasks. Each of the 24 tasks per core possesses its own non-shared state—a total of 8×8-byte-wide registers per task—resulting in zero-cycle task switching and branching. Thus, the nPcore utilization can approach 100%, supporting the goal of using fewer, lower-power cores in place of a greater number of less efficient, more general-purpose RISC engines.

15.1.3   Traffic Management

Demand for high-performance, flexible traffic management to support advanced services delivery in service-provider and enterprise networks has increased focus on dynamic per-subscriber provisioning, application quality of service (QoS), and other requirements for control of large numbers of traffic flows.

Current industry debate on traffic management centers on whether to implement admission-control, bandwidth provisioning, queuing, and scheduling in software within the NPU or in a separate, off-chip, configurable, hardware-based co-processor. The advantage of the former is flexibility in terms of software control over admission control and scheduling algorithms. The advantages of the latter are support for larger numbers of flows/queues and deeper buffers while maintaining higher performance. AMCC has traditionally utilized the hardware-based TM approach, offering solutions that included a software-programmable packet/cell-processing NPU and a separate, configurable traffic manager chip set. This approach generally better served AMCC's historical service-provider and access market focus, where fine-grained service provisioning is critical and performance cannot be sacrificed to provide it.

With the nP3700, AMCC has integrated on-chip the full capabilities of its hardware-based TM product line, offering the space, cost, power, and ease of system design advantages of greater integration. Software cycles are preserved for packet/cell processing, while hardware-based queuing and traffic shaping maintain wire-speed performance. Further, the on-chip integration allows greater software control over admission control and scheduling algorithms—enabling enhanced "programmable queuing," where the nPcore is able to take a flow of packets and perform functions such as reordering or assembling packets together and linking them back to the TM. The tighter interaction between the nPcores and TM can be particularly useful for efficiently implementing such advanced features as segmentation and reassembly (SAR), IP fragmentation, or TCP or even application-layer protocol (e.g., HTTP) termination functions.

The nP3700 traffic management engine co-processor handles both class-based and flow-based traffic management requirements. Its four-level control hierarchy has built-in support for a variety of scheduling and discard/admission-control mechanisms for packet and cell traffic—including strict priority, weighted round-robin (WRR), weighted fair queuing (WFQ), CBR and VBR rate shaping, minimum and maximum bandwidth limiting, XON/XOF flow control, weighted random early detection (WRED), early packet discard (EPD) and cell loss priority (CLP) marking—and additional mechanisms may be implemented in software by the developer.

The nP3700 TM supports per-flow queuing and scheduling in hardware for up to 128-K individual flows, 4-K pipes, and 512 subports, with payload memory that can store up to two million cells (see Figure 15.4). A flow is considered a unidirectional traffic stream from one port to another port using a virtual connection through the internal switching component of the NPU. Each flow can be a connection or a group of connections between two ports. All connections within a flow have the same traffic characteristics. The hardware provides the per-flow structure, but the developer determines how to identify each flow—typically using the policy engine co-processor to assist in classifying incoming traffic—and flags each frame to be queued in the TM block by appending a flow ID via the packet transform engine co-processor. Output scheduling and shaping are then supported on a per-flow basis or per-group-of-flows basis.

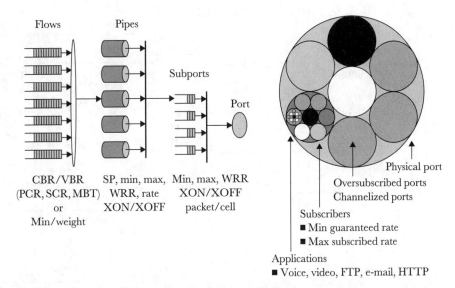

Flows   Pipes

Subports

Port

CBR/VBR   SP, min, max,   Min, max, WRR
(PCR, SCR, MBT)   WRR, rate   XON/XOFF
or   XON/XOFF   packet/cell
Min/weight

Physical port
Oversubscribed ports
Channelized ports

Subscribers
■ Min guaranteed rate
■ Max subscribed rate

Applications
■ Voice, video, FTP, e-mail, HTTP

15.4

FIGURE

Fine-grained, four-level admission control and scheduling for high-performance, hardware-based traffic management.

15.1.4   Flow-Through and Store-Forward Processing Within the nPcore Architecture

Earlier nPcore generations focused primarily on providing an optimized "flow-through" processing path, in which packets are received and buffered only briefly, with any required operations performed within time frames as small as 40 ns—the processing time allowed per frame in order to maintain wire speed with minimum-size 40-byte packet-over-SONET (POS) frames on a 10-Gb/s connection. The nP[5] NPUs additionally include an "exception process flow" for store-and-forward operations, enabling system designers to efficiently handle complex heterogeneous flows and deep channelization requirements without integrating a separate control plane CPU into the NPU, in addition to the primary nPcores.

As shown in Figure 15.5, the exception flow utilizes an on-chip exception buffer and associated channel service memory to temporarily store and/or accumulate packets or cells under specified conditions. By flagging frames that need special processing and moving them into the exception flow data path, the nP3700 can provide deterministic traffic flows through the primary path while simultaneously expanding the flexibility to handle special cases with the same set of nPcores. For example, in TCP termination functions the store-and-forward

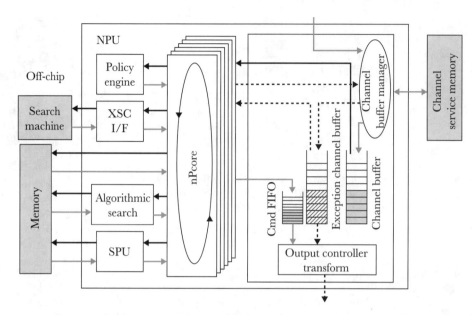

Exception path processing using same nPcores avoids cost and complexity of additional on-chip control CPU.

capabilities of the exception buffer are useful for accumulating all of the packets from a particular flow regardless of their arrival sequence, thus allowing the entire flow to be processed together. Similarly, preassembling the fragmented bits for a jumbo frame before subsequent operations can enhance overall processing efficiency. Another application of the exception buffer is streamlining communications with the system CPU by allowing fairly large packets, such as router table or software updates, to be transmitted and assembled in the background via the exception flow, without impacting the ongoing processes in the primary data path.

The impact of exception flow processing on overall system performance varies greatly with the complexity of the primary flow-through processing algorithms employed by an application, with the complexity of the exception processing algorithm(s), and significantly with the frequency of use of the exception path (i.e., with the percentage of traffic that is passed through such store-and-forward operations). Both types of processing ultimately use the same set of tasks and compete for the same set of processor core cycles. The advantage of this is that an additional control-type CPU core is not required for a number of applications, and handling these applications within an NPU does not require the size, power, and complexity burdens of an added core.

15.1.5   On-Chip Availability of Both Policy Engine and Lookup Table Capabilities

Each AMCC NPU includes a high-performance policy engine co-processor for handling sophisticated classification operations. The nP3700 adds an algorithmic search engine to accelerate low-cost alternatives for large-table search and lookup functions, such as routing tables implemented in external memory. This gives system designers options for tailoring implementations to meet specific cost and functionality requirements. The policy engine can then provide better responsiveness for deep or complex classification requirements, such as MPLS, *diffserv*, or content-specific traffic management.

The policy engine consists of an integrated ternary logic cell structure with network-optimized features. Specifically, it consists of a 512×68-bit ternary CAM (TCAM) and an associated best-match "weight array." The weight array logic block enables a pipelined weight comparison that prioritizes multiple policy-engine-based search matches, while maintaining one-clock-cycle searching throughput. There is also a secondary array, containing the local mask for each key entry, the local mask for each tag entry, and the control information associated with each entry. The advantage of the weight array concept is increased efficiency in implementing applications such as longest-prefix-match routing algorithms. With such algorithms, the search database may contain multiple entries that provide successful matches for a given key. A CAM-based search would ordinarily return the first record matching the key, so whenever new records are added the processor must spend cycles re-sorting the database to ensure the first match is the "best" match. With the weight array, new entries are simply added anywhere within the CAM—no sorting required—and are given an appropriate priority ("weight"). On a given search, all records matching the search key are compared, returning the matching record with the greatest weight; that is, the best match.

The policy engine can be used alone or in combination with a larger off-chip TCAM or search co-processor. However, when table sizes are large, the cost of CAM can be inappropriate for implementing relatively simple lookup requirements such as routing tables. In these situations, designers can achieve more cost-effective results by using the algorithmic search engine in conjunction with lower-cost off-chip SRAM memory structures. The co-processor provides a fast hardware-based mechanism to hash a key of arbitrary length, used to retrieve an external memory block associated with the hash result, and search that memory block for the key. For example, most L2 lookups typically require the rapid translation of a 48-bit MAC address to an input flow descriptor (IFD) or forwarding information.

15.1.6 Special-Purpose Unit for Managing Data Coherency

The nPcore architecture incorporates a special-purpose unit (SPU) that handles complex compound (multistep) functions within shared memory space as single-instruction atomic operations. It assures data coherency at high performance when shared state is accessed by multiple frames across multiple threads. This is key for high, sustained performance in the parallel multitask, multicore processing model. For example, as several packets from the same flow travel through an nP3700 via independent tasks, different tasks may frequently access the same locations in shared space simultaneously. These memory access operations must be handled and arbitrated efficiently. Also, accurate sequencing of access requests is critical for driving many sequence-dependent execution decisions in policing and packet discard algorithms.

The SPU automatically manages shared-space access requests and provides accurate sequencing information for execution decisions and statistics. It gives programmers the ability to manage complex compound functions—such as read-modify-write or provisioning algorithms such as dual leaky-bucket policing—as single atomic operations via simple co-processor commands. The SPU avoids creating complex memory-coherence or sequencing mechanisms in software, such as using semaphores to lock down memory during reads and writes in the shared space. This significantly reduces the programming complexity of implementing low-level shared-space management mechanisms and also reduces the potential performance degradation caused by individual processors locking down and holding memory locations. In effect, the SPU enables programmers to treat shared-space access as a relatively simple "post and forget" operation rather than low-level contention, coherence, and sequencing operations.

15.1.7 Packet Transform Engine—Receive, Modify, Transmit

The primary function of the packet transform engine co-processor is to offload frame content modifications from the nPcores. A single nPcore instruction is used to prepend, insert, or delete fields in a packet (or cell). The PTE also hosts built-in support for common functions, such as CRC calculation, and automatic generation of header elements, such as IP/UDP/TCP checksum.

The PTE is also responsible for the initial reception and final transmission of frames as they enter and leave the NPU. When a frame arrives at an input port, the PTE automatically reads the frame in and sets it up in buffer storage space. The programmer specifies a "high-water mark" for this data FIFO buffer. When this mark is hit (i.e., the specified amount of a frame's header has been received), an idle-state task is assigned to the frame and "kicked off" to begin processing.

There is no need to read the entire content of the frame into memory before beginning processing. The programmer does not need to create any code—nor are any software cycles spent—on these basics of packet reception and setup. Similarly, a single line of code instructs the PTE to transmit the modified frame content upon the completion of processing.

15.1.8   Standards-Based Interfaces

The nP3700 integrates on-chip support for both cell-based and packet-based protocols. It incorporates industry standard external interfaces to communications lines, switching fabric, system control processors, and a variety of memory products. The line interfaces are configurable at initialization as either four IEEE 802.3 Gigabit Ethernet ports, including integrated GE MACs, or a pair of Optical Interface Forum (OIF) standard SPI-3 or Utopia interfaces for connection to POS, ATM, or other appropriate framer products, totaling 5-Gb/s full-duplex line rate. For connectivity to switching fabric products supporting the Network Processing Forum's Streaming Interface (NPSI), the nP3700 supports the NPSI logical structure over industry-standard OIF SPI-4 Phase 2 physical connections.

The CPU interfaces include a memory-mapped PowerPC interface and a Gigabit Ethernet connection. A general-purpose I/O (GPIO) interface is available for other out-of-band signaling and control requirements. The nP3700 has an on-chip non-blocking memory access unit that manages both the internal cache and interfaces to external DRAM. External memory can be accessed via RLDRAM II controllers supporting RLDRAM II or DDR SDRAM operating at up to 250 MHz. The memory access unit also provides an interface to quad data rate (QDR) memory for high-speed data access. In addition, the on-chip traffic manager has direct access to external DRAM, with addressing capacity to handle as many as two million cells of storage.

15.2   SOFTWARE ARCHITECTURE

The AMCC nP^5 software architecture aims at rapid software development and multigeneration compatibility by making use of the same single-stage programming model and software architecture, dubbed nPsoft, used in previous versions of the nPcore-based family. nPsoft is designed to give software designers wide latitude in programming the nPcores while defining tightly linked relationships between the cores and on-chip co-processors. This relationship between the software and the underlying nPcore hardware is critical because of the need to

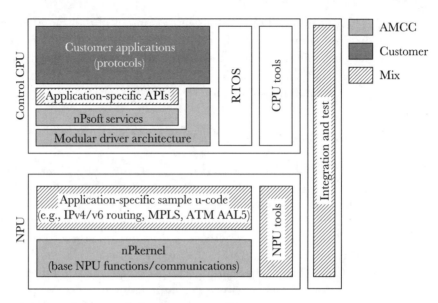

15.6   Elements of the nPsoft development environment.

FIGURE

provide deterministic processing results, even at very high speeds and regardless of peaks or spikes in traffic flow.

The nPsoft Workshop (nPWS) is a single integrated software bundle that includes all of the different components needed to develop, test, validate, and debug AMCC NPU software. The nPWS includes both runtime software that can be included in source code for customer products and development tools that are used to create or modify nPcore-based software (see Figure 15.6).

Development tools in the nPWS aid in code generation, debug, and test phases, including assemblers, compilers, simulators, debuggers, and performance analysis tools. The nPWS contains runtime components that include an "nPkernel," application libraries—which offer predeveloped code for many common NPU-based applications—and drivers and control CPU-resident APIs [5, 6]. To assist in integration of AMCC NPUs into overall system-level designs, nPWS incorporates a range of infrastructure software such as a modular driver for control of NPU, TM, fabric, and other non-NPU parts of the hardware platform, as well as bring-up and debug utilities.

The nPkernel provides API access to the nPcores' common services and co-processors. The nPkernel is a baseline framework of NPU-resident API code for nPcores and co-processors [7, 8, 9]. Through the nPkernel, the programmer can make use of most co-processor functions—such as classification, search, packet modification, flow synchronization, or statistics gathering—simply by using single-instruction atomic operations.

By providing API access to the most common functions and services, the kernel itself typically comprises more than 80% of the NPU-resident portion of most applications. Because the nPkernel contains the bulk of the runtime code and establishes a common framework for implementing application-specific requirements, it represents a major factor in the ability to shorten time-to-market cycles and optimize code migration from one generation to another.

Application libraries available for AMCC NPUs are designed to give system designers a foundation for implementing specific networking applications, including IPv4 and IPv6 routing, ATM processing, VLANs, and Layer 2 and MPLS switching. System designers can incorporate the code into their overall applications, typically adding their own customized features to these bases. Because the application libraries are pre-tuned to take advantage of the underlying hardware's specific capabilities and to make optimal use of available processing headroom, designers can rapidly develop additional high-speed functions.

The framework of the library code available to developers also provides a forward-migration path for reusability of code between different nPcore-based generations and offers a common foundation for implementing a variety of application-specific networking functions on the same basic hardware designs. This allows system and line card designers to leverage the same programming model across all ports within a system and also enables them to provide greater flexibility to service providers for supporting the convergence of multiple services across common hardware platforms.

15.3   CONCLUSIONS

The nP3700, the first member of AMCC's nP^5 generation, represents a significant step in the evolution of network processors by using a higher level of on-chip integration to improve performance and expand functionality. A key aspect of the nP3700 is the inclusion of high-performance traffic manager capabilities—based on AMCC's previous nPX5700 stand-alone TM co-processor—on the same device with multiple nPcores that use the effective single-stage, parallel-processing dataflow model. The nP3700 also incorporates a number of new features into the same chip-level design, such as exception path processing, more classification/lookup options, enhanced memory options, and an expanded range of standards-based interfaces.

An efficient nPcore instruction set that results in smaller application programs, coupled with fine-grained flow-based traffic management, small size, and low power consumption, make the nP3700 adaptable for a number of switching and routing applications at both the network edge and core. Specific examples include: high-speed multiservice switches, high-performance edge routers, DSL access multiplexers (DSLAMs), 2G or 3G wireless infrastructure systems, Layer 4 through 7 switches (such as content-based load balancers and firewalls), VoIP gateways, VPN gateways, multiservice access platforms, and remote access concentrators.

The nP^5 generation now makes it possible for designers to deliver virtually "any service, any port" within new multiservice system implementations. In addition, the ability to increase port densities while driving down power and cost means that these new systems can deliver universal port services at dedicated port economics. Furthermore, having brought these features together in a single chip with multiple nPcore processors, the nP3700 can establish a new architectural foundation for follow-on designs, which can leverage the same chip-level integration approach using additional nPcores to deliver even higher performance.

REFERENCES

[1]   "AMCC Unveils nP^5 Next-Generation Network Processing Technology Enabling Universal Port Services at Dedicated Port Economics," *www.amcc.com/Compinfo /PressReleases/nP5.htm.*

[2]   "nP7510 10 Gbps Network Processor," *www.amcc.com/networkprocessor.*

[3]   "nP3700 Network Processor Data Sheet," AMCC document # nP 2002–0058.

[4]   *nP3700 Programmer Reference Manual*, AMCC document # nP 2002–0071.

[5]   *nPsoft Application Services Libraries (nPASL) Programmer Manual*, AMCC document # nPS 2001–0004.

[6]   "nPsoft Services Overview", AMCC document # nPss 2000–0075.

[7]   *Network Processor Common Services Layer (nPCSL) v2.0 User Guide*, AMCC document # nPS 2002–0063.

[8]   *nPkernel Programmer Manual*, AMCC document # nPS 2002–0038.

[9]   *Common Coprocessor API (CoCoA) Reference Manual*, AMCC doc. # nP 2001–0070.

16 Adaptable Bandwidth Allocation for QoS Support in Network Processors

CHAPTER

Clark Jeffries, Mohammad Peyravian, Ravi Sabhikhi
IBM Corporation

In the past, Internet growth was enabled by using the transmission control protocol (TCP), in effect a "quality of connection" system that guarantees eventual delivery of information across a connectionless network. Future growth will be driven by ensuring QoS (quality of service) throughout the network by providing services that include automatic and uniform packet classification according to value and service expectations. A primary quality metric will be timely delivery, not just eventual delivery. At the network level, QoS will be much more difficult to achieve, but its rewards will be proportionally greater. In addition to network control tools and high-speed classification, a crucial part of network QoS is bandwidth allocation utilizing flow control techniques.

Flow control is the designed response of a network device to congestion. Although in Ethernet environments only highly overprovisioned systems will never be congested, in most networks occasional or even frequent congestion is inevitable. In response to congestion, flow control mechanisms must be activated. Often such mechanisms are based on intuitive or heuristic actions, such as thresholds that trigger discards of arriving packets. However, generally such methods, when not well tested, deal with stochastic queuing processes poorly and may lead to unpredictable network behavior and weak performance guarantees.

Consider, for example, a network provider selling two services: a Best Effort service that is at most 40-to-1 oversubscribed and a Premium service that is at most 20-to-1 oversubscribed. While this has some intuitive appeal, in practice such a service approach is often inefficient and unable to reliably deliver IP packets in a timely manner. The Internet is likely to remain underdeveloped until this situation is improved. RED (random early discard) [1] is an example of flow control based on using threshold methods and is discussed later.

In this chapter we address the problem of QoS support using network processors. We also present and discuss an adaptable bandwidth allocation and flow

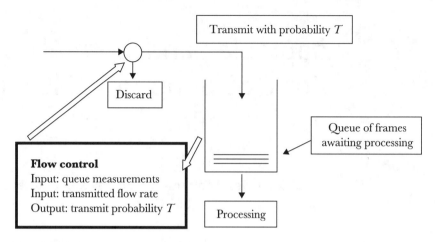

Transmit with probability T

Discard

Queue of frames
awaiting processing

Flow control
Input: queue measurements
Input: transmitted flow rate
Output: transmit probability T

Processing

16.1   Basic logic components of flow control.

FIGURE

control approach that was developed for the IBM PowerNP NP4GS3[1] [2, 3, 4, 7]
network processor. This approach, which is called bandwidth allocation technology (BAT) [4, 5], is compared with RED and WFQ (weighted fair queuing).
The chapter concludes with a discussion of BAT implementation on the IBM
PowerNP NP4GS3.

16.1   BACKGROUND

The overall logic of a generic flow control operation is shown in Figure 16.1. The
flow control logic monitors various dynamic properties of the system and produces a transmit probability T. T is the probability that a packet arriving within
a given time period is either queued (and thus proceeds eventually to be processed) or discarded. RED and other similar systems that use such probabilistic
decisions have the advantage of avoiding inadvertent synchronization of TCP
window adjustments among many sources that potentially result in TCP collapse.
However, the overall control paths for TCP congestion window adjustments may
take many tens or hundreds of milliseconds (ms) to reduce offered rates. Network
processors, however, having gigabit-per-second (Gb/s) arrival rates and ingress
data storage of a few megabits (Mb) must react in less than 1 ms to prevent

1. In this chapter we use the abbreviated term *PowerNP* for the IBM PowerNP NP4GS3, which is a
high-end member of the IBM network processor family.

RED algorithm:

$R1$:If $\quad Q(t) \leq 0.1$, then $T(t + \Delta t) = 1$;

$R2$:Else $\qquad\qquad\quad T(t + \Delta t) = 1 - [Q(t) - 0.1]/0.9$

SARED algorithm:

$S1$:If $\quad Q(t) \leq 1/4$, $\qquad$ then $T(t + \Delta t) = \min\{1, T(t) + (1/128)\}$;

$S2$:Elseif $Q(t) > 3/8$, $\qquad$ then $T(t + \Delta t) = (1/2) \times T(t)$;

$S3$:Elseif $Q(t + \Delta t) \geq Q(t)$, then $T(t + \Delta t) = (31/32) \times T(t)$;

$S4$:Else $\qquad\qquad\qquad\quad T(t + \Delta t) = \min\{1, T(t) + (1/128)\}$

16.2

The RED and SARED algorithms.

FIGURE

storage queues from becoming full. Thus, TCP-level adjustments are orders of magnitude too slow to prevent network processor buffers from overflowing. From a QoS perspective, such uncontrolled depletion of storage is unacceptable, since it forces arriving packets to be discarded under various circumstances when it is not necessary.

To understand this more fully we begin with a comparison of RED with a BAT component referred to as shock absorber RED (SARED). In this and all comparisons in this chapter (both simulations and reports of laboratory tests of NP hardware), the flows considered are constant and instantaneously go from no traffic to full offered rate. The observed reaction in terms of queue occupancy (for example) is presumably a worst case compared to system reaction to traffic with less extreme but more realistic bursts.

Figure 16.2 illustrates how each algorithm updates the value of the transmit probability T at time $t + \Delta t$, $T(t + \Delta t)$, as a function of its value at time t, $T(t)$, and the current and former values of the buffer (i.e., queue) occupancy fraction, $Q(t + \Delta t)$ and $Q(t)$ ($0 \leq Q \leq 1$). Note that the update time interval Δt is typically taken as:

$$\Delta t = (1/4) \times \frac{Maximum\ buffer\ capacity}{Maximum\ arrival\ rate}$$

This specification guarantees that the largest possible change of $Q(t)$ between updates is in the range of 1/4.

In the RED algorithm of Figure 16.2, all packets are transmitted (i.e., $T = 1.0$) until the value of Q reaches 0.1. If Q increases above 0.1, then T decreases linearly and reaches 0 as Q reaches 1. The threshold parameters 0.1 and 1 are typical but by no means universally selected.

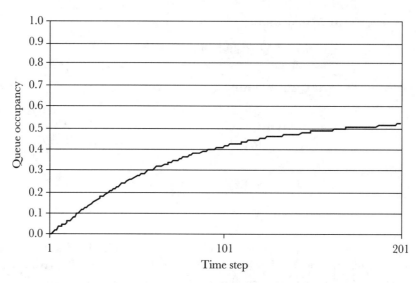

16.3

FIGURE

Response of queue occupancy to RED flow control for steady two-to-one congestion.

SARED improves on RED by making the transmit probability $T(t + \Delta t)$ a function not only of the current value of Q, $Q(t + \Delta t)$, but also on the prior values of both T and Q, $T(t)$ and $Q(t)$. In this way, SARED utilizes additional information contained in the rate of change of both T and Q.

Figures 16.3 and 16.4 illustrate the results from simple models of RED and SARED for a queue model with steady congestion at two-to-one (i.e., an offered load that is twice the available bandwidth/processing capability). As indicated in Figure 16.3, the RED queue occupancy is eventually 0.55. By contrast, as indicated in Figure 16.4, SARED queue occupancy reaches about 0.32 in 60 time steps; it eventually settles to 0.25.

In Figure 16.5, we see that the RED value for T starts to react when Q reaches 0.1 and then takes about 200 time steps to reach equilibrium. In Figure 16.6, SARED reacts after Q passes 0.25 at time step 40, and T then takes only about 35 time steps to reach an equilibrium that is near to the ideal long-term correct value of 0.5.

In summary, with two-to-one oversubscription and RED parameters (as defined above), SARED reaches an equilibrium transmit probability faster and has lower long-term queue occupancy. Different settings of RED parameters could result in lower long-term queue occupancy, but this would be at the expense of overreaction to low queue occupancy (burst shaving).

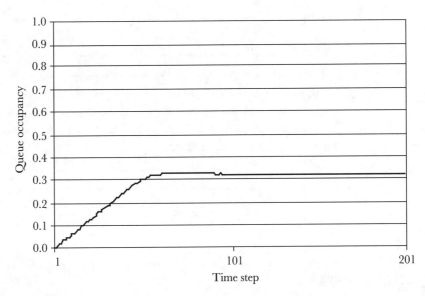

16.4
FIGURE

Response of queue occupancy to SARED flow control for steady two-to-one congestion.

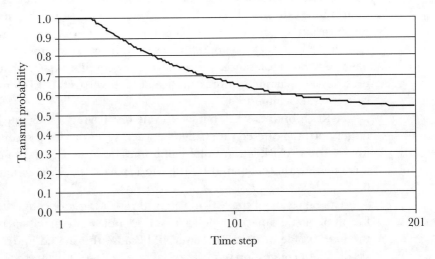

16.5
FIGURE

Response of transmit probability to RED flow control for steady two-to-one congestion.

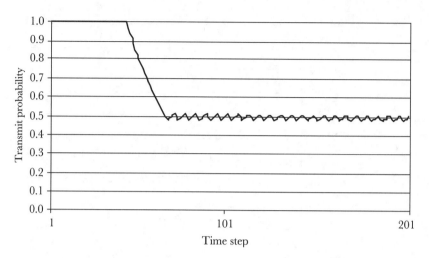

16.6

FIGURE

Response of transmit probability to SARED flow control for steady two-to-one congestion.

The results shown in Figures 16.3 through 16.6 are obtained from fairly straightforward queuing simulation models. The IBM PowerNP implementation, in the laboratory, has confirmed the model observations shown in the figures for both SARED and RED. Aside from adjusting thresholds, there are many variations on the RED theme, but we are not aware of any that robustly respond to high, steady congestion levels with fast convergence to the correct T, have good burst tolerance, and achieve a low equilibrium Q. That is, we feel the previous comparison is representative of RED versus SARED for the laboratory case of steady congestion.

SARED forgives small bursts. In one test having a flow into one 100-Mb/s target port, the offered rate cycled between 115 Mb/s for 2 seconds and 0 Mb/s for 1 second. SARED transmitted all frames because the peak queue occupancy was only 30 Mb, compared to 128-Mb capacity (i.e., a maximum Q value of $0.23 < 1/4$).

The behavior of the SARED algorithm is to ignore congestion below one-fourth of queue capacity, a policy that does not create much queuing latency in the ingress side of the IBM PowerNP because the shared ingress data store is small. Slight congestion (e.g., if arrival rate of Best Effort traffic is two times the processing capacity) results in Q settling to about 0.25. Heavy congestion results in Q stabilizing at about 0.38. If T is initially 1 and Q is 0.38, and if processing capacity suddenly becomes 0, then in subsequent time steps the queue builds in a serial manner. The transmit probability T remains 1 for one time step and then is divided by 2 on every subsequent time step. Under these extreme conditions Q finally reaches the value 7/8 (i.e., $3/8 + [1/4 * (1 + 1/2 + 1/4 + \ldots 0)] = 7/8$). Thus, with the SARED algorithm the various coefficients and the Δt value are chosen so that buffer overflow is mathematically impossible. Further problems with weighted RED (WRED) (i.e., two or more RED systems) appear in [5].

A common alternative to RED that also uses hand-tuned discard thresholds is called Taildrop. With Taildrop if Q exceeds a threshold, then $T = 0$, else $T = 1$. Taildrop is commonly used in conjunction with a scheduler that maintains calendars or other mechanisms to time service events for various types of traffic. A key scheduler's task is to determine the movement of packets from the receive (or transmit) queue. In doing this, it relies upon flow control to discard excess traffic when necessary, thus maintaining reasonable queue occupancy levels. When applied to only Best Effort traffic, a scheduler generally implements a first-in/first-out (FIFO) service mechanism.

The Taildrop and scheduler design can be applied to what is known as the 101% Problem. Suppose in the egress side of an NP, 101 Mb/s of Best Effort traffic is directed at a single 100-Mb/s target port and that, for the sake of illustration, there is no other traffic. In Taildrop flow control, all traffic arriving in egress is queued for processing until the data-store occupancy (buffer) reaches a certain threshold. What should the threshold be? If the buffer capacity is 128 Mb, then the threshold might be 50% of capacity, 64 Mb, making half the buffer unusable to Best Effort bursts. But this means in the 101% Problem that there are only two kinds of packets: a few are discarded and the rest suffer a queuing latency of 64 Mb/100 Mb/s = 640 ms. Such a high, steady queuing latency in a single NP egress is unacceptable and points to the desirability of using a lower threshold to initiate discards.

To solve the 101% Problem, the threshold may be set at a much lower level (e.g., 1% of capacity). This limits queuing latency in conditions of slight congestion to about 10 ms, solving the problem for steady congestion. However, this makes 99% of the buffer unusable for absorbing Best Effort bursts. Thus, a high Taildrop threshold implies high queuing latency during moderate, steady congestion, while a low Taildrop threshold excessively limits the ability of the system to absorb Best Effort bursts.

There are many QoS versions of the 101% Problem. For example, Premium traffic might offer 10 Mb/s and Best Effort might offer 91 Mb/s. The scheduler may correctly send all Premium traffic, but the problem of setting the Best Effort threshold high or low remains. In summary, continuous threshold tuning is an undesirable administrative burden, and it might actually be impossible to hand-tune RED or Taildrop thresholds to achieve optimal performance with changing traffic. We now show how the problem can be tackled with an adapt-able scheme (e.g., BAT) that attempts to use not only threshold information but other available information to reach decisions concerning packet discard.

16.2   QoS DESIGN FOR NETWORK PROCESSORS

Today, service-level specifications include limits on latency and loss across specified domains where differentiated services behavior can be consistently defined [6]. Such domains or network cores are usually not sources of high latency and loss because they are overprovisioned. Rather, the performance impact of congestion is typically felt at the network edge where high bandwidth domains connect to other domains or subnets. Some of the differentiated service performance goals that customers would like at such edges include:

+ Low loss of conformant Premium traffic, regardless of the demands of Best Effort traffic

+ Low port-to-port latency for all traffic during conditions of steady offered rates

+ Low latency for conformant real-time traffic

+ High utilization of network resources

These goals could be met by a system that organizes traffic at every point of potential congestion into groups of flows having common characteristics such as common loss and latency requirements. We refer to each class of equivalent pack-ets at each point of possible congestion as a *pipe*. Thus, *pipes* are local aggregates of packets having certain similar characteristics. This should be distinguished from *flows* (discussed later) that represent aggregates of packets associated with an end-to-end connection. A pipe may have a number of parameters (typically two to four) that characterize their operation. For example:

+ Each pipe has a minimum value such that if the transmitted rate is below this value, then the T associated with this pipe increases until it attains 100%.

+ Each pipe has a maximum value such that if the transmitted rate is above this maximum, the T associated with this pipe decreases until the maximum limit is eventually enforced.

+ Each pipe may have an absolute priority, so that bandwidth allocation for pipes between their respective minimum and maximum values respect this priority order and packets of higher priority get preference over packets with lower priority.

◆ Sets of pipes may also be organized administratively into aggregates, each with an aggregate maximum. Any pair of aggregates may have pipes in common.

There are only two constraints on the definitions of min (minimum) and max (maximum) rates for all pipes:

◆ If exactly one pipe is running and offers exactly and constantly its max rate, then the packets in the pipe should be processed without loss or undue latency.

◆ If all pipes offer exactly and constantly their min rates, then all the packets in the flows should be processed without loss or undue latency.

A network management tool must ensure that these two requirements are feasible before bandwidth contracts are sold. Of course, full understanding of system performance, including NP performance, is inherently part of this process.

Note that min and max parameters have no direct relationship with queue thresholds. In a well-designed infrastructure, the administrator should be called upon only to state the entrance and exit of each path of Premium traffic and the min and max, plus, if desired, priority or aggregate max values. A network control system that understands network assets and relies on bandwidth allocation would organize (and aggregate if needed) min and max values for all pipes at each point of congestion and then automatically communicate min, max, and other information to appropriate network processors. In fact, a multiprotocol label-switching (MPLS) prototype for this system has been developed for the IBM PowerNP [7]. Use of such a system over NPs could significantly improve the autonomic provisioning of network resources.

The general design of the PowerNP is described in [3] (see Figure 16.7). Within Figure 16.7, the specific instances of dataflow congestion in a network processor occur as shown in Figure 16.8. Metering, marking, logging, frame alteration, and other NP functions are not shown. Target blade refers to the particular network processor egress or other destination, such as an auxiliary cryptographic engine/chip to which traffic is routed. A router with N network processors would have N ingresses and N egresses.

Given a real-time queue and a non-real-time queue for each target blade, such a router would have $2 \times N$ target blade queues in each ingress. Also, other traffic could be sent to a control plane through additional other queues. Hence, the view of Figure 16.8 with only one target blade queue is highly simplified. Likewise, only one target port queue is shown in the egress path in Figure 16.8 while in the PowerNP there could be 40 physical ports (twice as many if there is both real-time and non-real-time traffic).

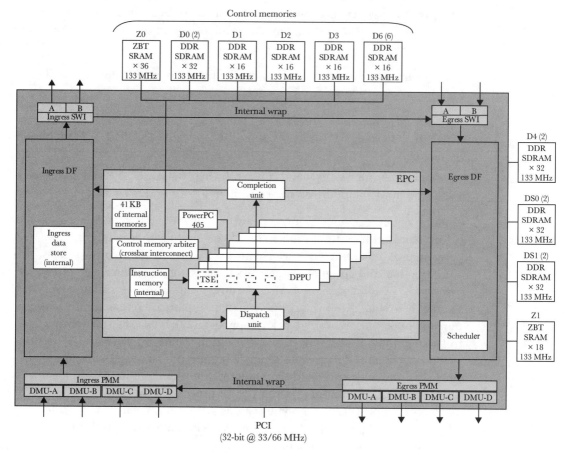

16.7   PowerNP hardware architecture.

FIGURE

In Figure 16.8, packets arrive and are identified by header values such as the differentiated services code point (DSCP) in the IP header using the packet classification function. The payloads of all arriving packets are stored and copies of fields in their headers, including DSCP, are used by the NP for classification, routing, and logging.

With each service event for the arrival queue, a packet is identified as Premium or Best Effort. Premium might include all real-time traffic and high-value non-real-time traffic, with this being designated by various DSCP bit combinations. The default designation is typically Best Effort. During network configuration, provisioning Premium traffic should take place so that ingress

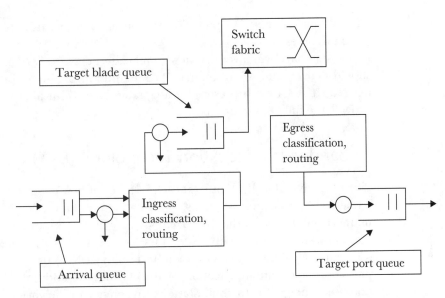

Location of flow control within simplified dataflow of network processor.

classification will never in itself cause overflow of the arrival queue by Premium traffic. At each service event for the arrival queue, a head-of-line Best Effort packet might be transmitted or dropped, depending on the state of the arrival queue. This seems backward, but if the entire discard mechanism is sufficiently fast, then discarding Best Effort packets is approximately as effective as not queuing them in the arrival queue in the first place.

Simple SARED acting only on Best Effort traffic is appropriate for the first instance of congestion in Figure 16.8, the arrival queue. In the IBM PowerNP, each arriving packet is either Premium (which may include all real-time traffic) or Best Effort. In our design, which must respond to the possibility of processing delay due to complex ingress classification, only Best Effort is subject to flow control. In a representative experiment with the IBM PowerNP, classification was artificially slowed to 1 Gb/s. The arrival rate of Premium traffic was set at 770 Mb/s, and the arrival rate of Best Effort was the same. The allocation was 770 Mb/s for Premium (very nearly all Premium packets were transmitted) and 220 Mb/s for Best Effort.

At the other two instances of congestion in Figure 16.8, the IBM PowerNP used the minimum of two transmit probabilities: a generic SARED T for all traffic and a per-pipe transmit probability Ti for pipe number i. Simple SARED is appropriate for Best Effort packets with min $= 0$ and max $=$ line rate (i.e., no effective min or max). Per-pipe Ti is appropriate for packets in pipes, especially Premium pipes.

In summary, we have seen how to manage Best Effort, what a QoS system should deliver, and where in an NP configuration planning for congestion is needed. It remains to present an adaptable bandwidth allocation scheme to provide the full QoS solution.

16.2.1   Bandwidth Allocation Technology (BAT)

Pipe i is defined locally; that is, at each instance of flow control. It consists of all packets with the same QoS status. Pipe i has a minimum called *mini* and a maximum called *maxi* such that [$0 \leq mini \leq maxi \leq$ link rate]. Conventional WRED sets the transmit probability Ti for pipe i using values associated with queue occupancy, Q. Bandwidth Allocation Technology (BAT) uses queue occupancy plus additional state information. With BAT and the additional state information used, the goal is to obtain faster convergence to the correct allocation for pipe i, higher utilization, and lower latency. BAT never attempts to calculate the algebraically correct Ti using only static threshold parameters. Instead, the BAT algorithm repeatedly determines if pipe i should get either more bandwidth (i.e., increase Ti if it is not already 1) or less bandwidth (i.e., decrease Ti toward 0) based on current values and rates of change of key parameters.

BAT uses a feedback mechanism to develop an *excess bandwidth signal Bi* that in turn is used to calculate Ti. Bi is 1 if there is excess bandwidth for pipe i, otherwise Bi is 0. If pipe i offers traffic at a rate between *mini* and *maxi*, then $Bi = 1$ implies that Ti should increase, while $Bi = 0$ implies Ti should decrease.

If different pipes represent different priorities, the definitions of Bi can be as follows. Thresholds *TH0, TH1, TH2,* and *TH3* are defined for priorities 0 (highest), 1, 2, 3 as 1/8, 1/16, 1/32, and 1/64 (respectively). Let Q denote the fraction of queue occupancy of the ingress or egress data store. Then:

IF $Q(t) \leq THi$, then $Bi(t + \Delta t) = 1$;

Elseif $\{Q(t) \leq 2 \times THi\}$ and $\{Q(t + \Delta t) < Q(t)\}$ then $Bi(t + \Delta t) = 1$;

Else $Bi(t + \Delta t) = 0$

The precise values of *THi* are not important, only their relative values per priority. For the given values, the effect of the low *TH3* value is that in steady congestion, queue occupancy for Best Effort traffic (with *mini* $= 0$) will keep decreasing until it is less than 1/64.

The concepts of *mini* and *maxi* are related to the excess bandwidth signal *Bi* as follows:

+ If *Bi* is constantly 1, then pipe *i* is allowed to increase its rate up to *maxi* (if its offered load is sufficiently high).

+ If *Bi* is constantly 0, then pipe *i* is compelled to decrease down to *mini* (if it has enough offered load).

More sophisticated versions of *Bi* feedback might be used. For example, in resilient packet ring [8] technology the previously cited *Bi* could be combined with a congestion signal from the ring.

Thus, for BAT QoS, each pipe *i* (including Best Effort as a default pipe) has a minimum bandwidth guarantee *mini* (possibly zero) and a maximum bandwidth limit *maxi*. Also, each potential bottleneck has a maximum possible send rate *S* and all flow rates (*mini*, *maxi*, and transmitted flow rate *Fi* for pipe *i*) are expressed as fractions of *S*.

An excess bandwidth signal $Bi = 0$ or 1 is calculated as previously at each time step Δt for pipe *i*. The full BAT algorithm [5] follows.

B1. If $Fi(t) < \min i$, then $Ti(t + \Delta t) = \min\{1, Ti(t + \Delta t) + (1/16)\}$;

B2. Elseif $Fi(t) > \max i$, then $Ti(t + \Delta t) = (31/32) \times Ti(t)$;

B3. Elseif {pipe $i \subset$ an Aggregate over Aggmax},

then $Ti(t + \Delta t) = (31/32) \times Ti(t)$;

B4. Elseif $Bi(t + \Delta t) = 1$,   then $Ti(t + \Delta t) = \min\{T(i), Ti(t + \Delta t) + Ci\}$;

B5. Else $Ti(t + \Delta t) = \min\{T(t), \max\{0, Ti(t + \Delta t) - (Di \times Fi(t))\}\}$

A pipe can be included in a grouping or Aggregate (step B3), with the Aggregate having a maximum permitted bandwidth (denoted by Aggmax). *Ci* (step B4) is a coefficient of linear increase of *Ti*, while *Di* (step B5) is a coefficient of exponential decrease. The control method thus implements a linear increase in *Ti* when excess bandwidth is available, and exponential decrease otherwise. This same method is used in TCP congestion window control, signal timing feedback in chips, and numerous other control applications where stability is important (i.e., regardless of initial state, the system will be eventually driven toward the same equilibrium conditions). The assembly language program for BAT takes about 50 lines of code on the IBM PowerNP. BAT calculation cost is discussed further in Section 16.3.

The values for *Ci* and *Di* are determined by the priority of pipe *i* with the IBM PowerNP using the following parameters (repeating the previous thresholds for *Q* to determine *Bi*, with 0 the highest priority):

Priority	C_i	D_i	TH_i
0	1/128	1/32	1/8
1	1/256	1/16	1/16
2	1/512	1/8	1/32
3	1/1024	1/4	1/64

The precise values are not critical. However, the relative values need to be maintained roughly as shown. This ensures that priority pipe i traffic (step B3) obtains excess bandwidth about twice as fast as priority pipe $(i + 1)$ traffic, and gives up (step B4) excess bandwidth about half as fast as priority pipe $(i + 1)$ traffic. Also, pipe i tolerates queue occupancy more than pipe $(i + 1)$ by virtue of the TH_i values. The effect of these differences is numerically close to that of a strict priority scheduler.

For example, if four pipes have priorities 0, 1, 2, and 3—and have offered loads of 40, 40, 40, and 40 Mb/s each into one egress 100-Mb/s target port—then BAT will allocate approximately 40, 39, 20, and 1 Mb/s of bandwidth to each of them, respectively. By comparison, the mathematically ideal allocation would be exactly 40, 40, 20, and 0 Mb/s. However, while BAT is not as precise as a priority scheduler, BAT will keep queuing latency low for all priority classes. The observed value of Q averages about 2% for such constant offered flows.

Regarding BAT when Aggregate max values (Aggmax in step B3) are used, the following experiment illustrates how we approximate ideal allocation. Figure 16.9 depicts a simulation of BAT in which four flows (F0, F1, F2, F3) are fed into a single 100-Mb/s target port. All flow mins are 0, except that the min for F0 is 5 Mb/s. All flow maxs are 100 Mb/s (in effect turning off max testing per flow in BAT steps B1 and B2). Let us assume there are three Aggregates:

Aggregate number	Member flows	Aggmax
0	F0, F1	20 Mb/s
1	F0, F2	30 Mb/s
2	F0, F3	75 Mb/s

Suppose initially offered flow rates instantaneously go from 0 to F0 = 17, F1 = 50, F2 = 30, and F3 = 50 Mb/s (i.e., total offered traffic=142 Mb/s). Also,

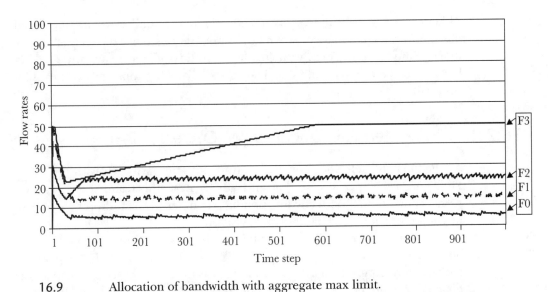

16.9   Allocation of bandwidth with aggregate max limit.

FIGURE

all flows are assumed to have priority 0 (highest), except flow F3 with priority 3 (lowest).

Consider next what the mathematically ideal allocation should be. Note first that flows F0, F1, and F2 have highest priority and offer a total load of 92 Mb/s. However, due to Aggmax, the total offered rate of F0 and F1 is limited to 20 Mb/s. Since F0 and F1 have equal priority, and F0 offers a third as much as F1, the correct allocation is 5 Mb/s to F0 and 15 Mb/s to F1. This also conforms to the min = 5 for F0. So a tentative allocation is 5, 15, and 30 to F0, F1, and F2. However, the Aggmax constraint F0 + F2 ≤ 30 must be satisfied, thus F2 is constrained to 25 Mb/s. Therefore, 45 Mb/s are allocated, leaving 55 Mb/s for F3. Since F3 has an offered load of 50 Mb/s, it is allocated 100% transmission even though it has lowest priority. Hence, the final correct allocation is F0 = 5, F1 = 15, F2 = 25, and F3 = 50 Mb/s.

Figure 16.9 shows how well BAT approximates this ideal over 1000 time steps. Note that F3 reaches equilibrium slowly because it has low priority. That is, its linear increase coefficient C_i is relatively small and so it obtains excess bandwidth slowly.

Since congestion in the aggregate experiment is moderate (1.42), the SARED transmit probability T remained 1. Only the per-pipe portion of flow control was actually exercised. The value of Q throughout the simulation remained low, peaking at 1/8 at time step 20 and remaining under 1/16 after step 40.

Although Figure 16.9 represents a simulation, very similar results have been observed in our laboratory over many configurations that test aggregate max functionality. In particular, with steady, laboratory-offered loads, the queuing latency observed is typically very low—under 1 ms for constant flows causing congestion.

16.2.2 Weighted Fair Queuing (WFQ) Versus BAT

A scheduler in itself does not discard traffic. As we have seen with the 101% Problem, in the special case that all traffic is Best Effort and there is slight, steady congestion, a perfectly functioning scheduler plus Taildrop flow control might not provide good bandwidth allocation.

For QoS support, WFQ scheduling is a popular QoS feature. WFQ goals, however, can be viewed as being very similar to the BAT min and max per pipe specification requirements. The reasoning is as follows. If processing capacity is denoted by Cap, the weight of pipe i denoted by Wi, and the sum of all weights is W, then WFQ establishes a $mini$ value such that $min\ i = (Wi/W) \times Cap$.

In the case that Cap is constant, then the $mini$ values are also easy to provide with BAT. However, usually the WFQ flows take the bandwidth remaining after allocation to higher-priority flows. In this case, Cap is variable. The PowerNP does provide a hardware scheduler with WFQ for such cases, and it can be integrated with BAT to control queuing latency. That is, the hardware scheduler will choose frames to serve in accordance with WFQ, and BAT applied per flow queue will provide flow control with low latency and high utilization. Allocation by BAT without WFQ is "fair" in an alternative sense; that is, Best Effort flows of common priority are allocated bandwidth in proportion to their offered rates.

16.2.3 BAT for Security Support

For many years QoS has been proposed as a powerful enabler for the Internet. However, part of the implementation problem difficulty has been in the administration of system parameters and tables (e.g., WRED tables). The BAT algorithm, described previously, in conjunction with the IBM PowerNP makes QoS simple to understand and administer. However, another motivation perhaps more compelling than *promoting* Premium traffic may be *protecting* Premium traffic in the presence of increasing security threats.

In particular, high-speed user datagram protocol (UDP) worms such as Slammer (also called Sapphire) threaten the collapse of critical services at any time, with no warning [9]. Slammer was released 24 January 2003, slightly before 2230 hours UTC. The number of infected servers doubled every 8.5 seconds for about five minutes, and after ten minutes at least 75,000 servers worldwide were spewing copies of the Slammer worm with random IP destination addresses into the Internet. The rate of worm production of each server was limited by the bandwidth of its link to the network. This flood caused drop rates of 90% at some network nodes, and many critical network services collapsed for about 10 hours.

The application of flow control with min and max per pipe could solve the problem of high-speed UDP worm attacks such as Slammer. Every router and server could have a flow control mechanism that provides a min and max for each pipe in a coarse partition of flows. For example, all UDP with destination port ≥ 1024 could be a pipe with min and max. The max could be a reasonable rate but far below link speed. Network services that were overwhelmed by the extreme reproduction rate of Slammer could be preserved by application of BAT or similar QoS technology that enforces min and max per pipe. The same bandwidth allocation schemes can be applied to TCP and Internet control message protocol (ICMP) flows to reduce the impacts of malicious activities. In fact, most denial-of-service attacks are TCP or ICMP [10].

16.3   IBM POWERNP QoS SUPPORT

Implementation of BAT is available on the IBM PowerNP in the form of APIs (application programming interfaces) and assembly code [4]. Representative Layer 3 configurations and code are available. Using the base code, developers can devise additional code that meets QoS requirements defined by a particular business. Up to 32 pipe transmit probabilities can be computed for ingress target blade queues, and up to 2 K for egress.

PowerNP enables WRED by means of 128 ingress and 128 egress tables that are established by a bandwidth administrator. Which table is selected at every refresh of flow control is determined by free queue occupancy Q rounded to the nearest 1/128. (An exponentially weighted moving average of Q can be used.) In ingress, after classification of a frame, the probability of its being enqueued into a target blade queue (see Figure 16.8) is read for its class from the table. Five bits, called QQQCC, can be queue number and color (from *diffserv*), but how the 32 pipes are defined is flexible. Classes (rows) in the 128 egress tables likewise can be defined very flexibly. The associated *User's Guide* shows examples of two ingress and two egress tables, but the examples are not related to or interpretable as performance criteria such as min or max values per pipe. IBM can offer neither a rationale for the four WRED tables nor guidance for filling in the other 252. We are not aware that any other NP vendors offer much WRED guidance, either.

BAT uses the same tables, but in an entirely different way. An assembly language implementation of the BAT algorithm refreshes the tables, but queue occupancy no longer points to 128 different values. Again, queue occupancy Q is only part of the state information used in the Bi values by BAT, so the effect of the current Q value is certainly present, but not in the WRED sense.

Both WRED and BAT implementations use 32-bit-wide entries organized as four 7-bit probabilities. A transmit probability of $0 \times 7F$ is equivalent to 1. In ingress, three free-queue thresholds may be set to cause "emergency" discard actions when occupancy is almost full. However, BAT is designed to discard low-value traffic aggressively during heavy congestion to avoid complete depletion and use of emergency thresholds.

In egress, each of the 2-K (i.e., 2,048) non-real-time flow queue can have its own transmit probability. The value can again be determined by WRED or BAT. A flow queue count can be compared to a threshold. Also, a flow queue plus target port queue count can be compared to a second threshold. The two comparisons result in a 2-bit value that can trigger emergency discard action. Egress stack management hardware also maintains a queue count that egress Q can be compared to, and utilizes three thresholds to recognize degrees of emergency depletion of free-queue resources. But again, BAT is designed to avoid use of emergency actions. In laboratory tests, BAT gracefully stabilized even 100-to-1 oversubscription (1 Gb/s of Best Effort into one 10-Mb/s target port).

Another test with four 100-Mb/s Best Effort flows directed into one 100-Mb/s target port (all frames 64 bytes) compared use of high emergency discard thresholds and BAT. Both systems allocated bandwidth correctly (25 Mb/s to each pipe). However, the latency using thresholds was over 1 second, while the latency for BAT was 670 µs. Such very low BAT latency is only possible with laboratory constant traffic, but it suggests that whenever congestion is steady BAT will strive to proactively discard frames and eventually reduce queuing latency to a low value.

In our laboratory, the processing cost of BAT per pipe is under 2 µs (i.e., < 267 cycles). Refreshing 32 ingress pipes every 80 µs therefore costs about 107 M cycles per second, and refreshing 2-K egress pipes every 8 ms costs about 68 M cycles per second. By comparison, 16 picoprocessors running at 133 MHz generate together over 2-G cycles per second. Thus, BAT running on the maximum number of pipes would consume slightly more computational power than one of 16 picoprocessors. BAT could be fully implemented in hardware, but an advantage of software is of course the flexibility to accommodate novel allocation requirements such as hierarchical allocation of VLANs into virtual ports or correct reaction to resilient packet ring congestion signals.

The PowerNP hardware scheduler can be used in conjunction with BAT to allocate bandwidth to multiple non-real-time flows with the same priority by WFQ. The maximum ratio of weights supported is 32. For constant flows with min = max > 100 Kb/s, the hardware scheduler can be used to reduce jitter to less than ±1µs.

There is also prototype network management software called Traffic Engineering Reference Platform (TERP), developed by IBM Zurich Research Laboratory [7, 11]. It can be used as a starting point for comprehensive, integrated network management tools that rely on network processors at nodes to enforce min, max, and other functions. The ideal would be a network that could be administered very easily, even automatically. A bandwidth customer merely specifies endpoints, duration of contract, and QoS (min, max, priority), and the network automatically decides if the request can physically be met. If so, then the network automatically lays pipe, communicates new min and max values to the three instances of potential congestion in affected NPs, and enables the service with all the complexity hidden from the human administrator.

The IBM PowerNP also supports policing for up to 1-K flow queues in ingress in accordance with standard token bucket algorithms [12, 13]. The minimum constant information rate supported is about 104 Kb/s. A Policer flow is anything that the classifier can define. For example, in one NP solution, the Policer flow includes all the packets flowing in both directions of a voice session. Policer flows have twin token buckets for monitoring sustained and peak rates. Voice streams might be assumed to be usually well behaved and low bandwidth. This efficient mechanism would almost always do nothing, only reacting by demoting the color of some packets in nonconformant flows. For example, ingress flow control for such real-time traffic could be set to always transmit Green packets, always discard Red packets, and transmit Yellow packets (using a BAT probability), all regardless of the specific policer flow membership. Thus, BAT flow control resources need not be spent on slow but valuable voice streams.

The IBM PowerNP in egress enforces BAT flow control only on non-real-time flows. However, if total service of an aggregation of real-time and non-real-time flows is to have an aggregate max (Aggmax), then the count for real time can be added to non-real time and the total compared by BAT to Aggmax to arrive at flow control for the non-real-time portion. For example, in one laboratory test, three flows were aggregated. Two offered 64 Kb/s and 6 Mb/s, respectively, values under their mins. A third in the aggregate offered 6 Mb/s with min = 0. The specified Aggmax was 10 Mb/s. BAT transmitted all of the first two flows plus 3.830 Mb/s of the third flow for a total utilization of 99%. The observed port-to-port latency of all transmitted frames was under 1 ms. Again, such low latency was a consequence of precisely determined offered rates and would not be the case for the third flow (data) if it were real traffic. But even with real data traffic, if the first two flows were real time and conformant, their latencies would remain very low.

16.4   CONCLUSIONS

Bandwidth allocation technology (BAT) is an important feature of the IBM PowerNP. It is valuable because it endows networks with predictable bandwidth allocation, thus increasing the value of other, much more complex services. It carries the potential of automation and simplification of QoS capabilities.

It is possible to provide network QoS without BAT or any other intelligent flow control; that is, merely by overbuilding all network components. However, some low-bandwidth flows are disproportionately valuable, and if any congestion can result in some loss or delay for any flows, then low-bandwidth Premium customers can be disappointed.

Of increasing importance are security issues. It is vital to protect essential network services in the face of fast-spreading worms. Today, security frequently involves information flowing from a sensor to a human, to another human, to a response mechanism. But UDP worms with very fast propagation rates make the human part of this exchange untenable. An adaptable bandwidth allocation scheme with min and max per class might save essential services in the presence of malicious attacks.

REFERENCES

[1]   S. Floyd and V. Jacobson, "Random Early Detection Gateways for Congestion Avoidance," *IEEE/ACM Transactions on Networking*, vol. 1, no. 4, Aug. 1993, pp. 397–413.

[2]   IBM Corporation, "NP4GS3 Datasheet," *www.chips.ibm.com*, Feb. 2002.

[3]   M. Peyravian, J. Calvignac, and R. Sabhikhi, "IBM PowerNP Network Processor," in *Network Processor Design: Issues and Practices*, ISBN#1-55860-875-3, Morgan Kaufmann, 2002, pp. 249–258.

[4]   IBM Corporation, "Advanced Software Offering 1.3.3," *www.chips.ibm.com*, Sept. 2002.

[5]   E. Bowen, C. Jeffries, L. Kencl, A. Kind, and R. Pletka, "Bandwidth Allocation for Non-Responsive Flows with Active Queue Management," *Proceedings of International Zurich Seminar on Broadband Communications Zurich*, Feb. 2002, pp. 13-1-13-6.

[6]   K. Nichols and B. Carpenter, "Definition of Differentiated Services per Domain Behaviors and Rules for Their Specification," *IETF Request for Comments (RFC) 3086*, Apr. 2001.

[7]   IBM Corporation, "NP4GS3 Network Processor Solutions," *www.chips.ibm.com*, June 2002.

[8]   IEEE Resilient Packet Ring 802.17 WG, *http://grouper.ieee.org/groups/802/17 /documents/presentations/sep2001/ka_ietfaug_01.pdf*.

[9]   D. Moore et al., "The Spread of the Sapphire/Slammer Worm," CAIDA (Cooperative Association for Internet Data Analysis), technical report, *www.caida.org/outreach /papers/*, Feb. 2003.

[10]   D. Moore, G. Voelker, and S. Savage, "Inferring Internet Denial of Service Activity," *www.caida.org/outreach/papers/2001/BackScatter/usenixsecurity01.pdf*.

[11]   R. Haas et al., "Creating Advanced Functions on Network Processors: Experience and Perspectives," *IEEE Network*, July 2003.

[12]   J. Heinanen and R. Guerin, "A Single Rate Three Color Marker," *IETF RFC 2697*, Sept. 1999.

[13]   J. Heinanen and R. Guerin, "A Two Rate Three Color Marker," *IETF RFC 2698*, Sept. 1999.

17

CHAPTER

IDT Network Search Engine with QDR LA-1 Interface

Michael J. Miller
Integrated Device Technology, Inc.

In an effort to support the continuing evolution of networks, network-processing units (NPUs) are being designed to simultaneously provide flexibility and performance. The key task of an NPU is to receive network packets, classify them using header fields, modify the headers as needed, queue, and retransmit the packets. The classification process involves extracting a key from the header fields of a packet and searching databases that contain network-specific information, such as forwarding address or access policy rules. One of the factors that constrain the performance of NPUs is the time required to search databases stored in off-chip SRAM or DRAM. These memories impose a fundamental limitation on performance due to the number of times they must be accessed in order to complete a single database search. Often up to four or five memory accesses are required to find a network address in a database. While NPU clock frequencies have increased following Moore's law, I/O technology and memory access latency have not kept pace. Furthermore, as network functionality and complexity has continued to grow, so has the size and complexity of database search keys, which further slows down database searches. Therefore, despite the design objectives of greater flexibility and performance, NPUs will remain limited by the performance of off-chip memory database searches.

To overcome these inherent design limitations, IDT has developed network search engines (NSEs) that utilize IDT's ternary content-addressable memory (TCAM) technology and high-performance logic technology. An NSE can dramatically reduce the time required to search complex databases by acting as a search co-processor. Content-addressable memories (CAMs) are specialized memories that provide the address (result index) of a memory location whose content matches a key value present on an external data bus. CAMs are typically designed to perform a search operation in a single clock cycle and often use a global mask that identifies search key bits that are to be ignored during a database lookup. Ternary CAMs are specialized CAMs that associate a mask value with each data word, allowing each data word in the CAM to identify search key bits that are to be ignored during a database lookup. Today's TCAM core technology can achieve up to 133 million searches per second (Msps), which for minimum-size packets allows four database searches at OC-192 line rates.

An NSE with a TCAM core and a quad data rate (QDR) interface may be connected directly to the QDR interface of an NPU. Within a single clock cycle, the NPU may initiate an NSE search via the QDR write data bus and obtain a search result via the QDR read data bus. To accommodate the complex multi-threaded execution environment of today's NPUs, NSEs incorporate schedulers and mailboxes so that requests, results, and exceptions associated with various NPU threads can be properly handled. Today's multithreaded NPUs can require up to 128 outstanding operations to be managed by an NSE. Beyond the basic search operation, additional NSE performance may be gained through architectural features such as reducing the number of NPU off-chip accesses by initiating multiple database searches using a single key as well as returning multiple match results from a single-database search. Further performance gains are possible through better implementation of address caches and flow tables by using intelligent learning operations, activity monitoring, and the notification of stale or aged database entries.

The remainder of this chapter focuses on IDT's NSEs for QDR: the IDT75K62134 (128-K × 72-bit) and IDT75K52134 (64-K × 72-bit) devices [1, 2]. The next section describes the architecture and operation of these devices. This is followed by an overview of IDT's NSE development and runtime system support tools. Finally, in the last section the benefits of NSEs are compared with alternative database search solutions that utilize SRAMs.

17.1   NSE DEVICE DESCRIPTION

The IDT75K62134 and the IDT75K52134 NSEs will be described on several levels: system, device interface, internal architecture, and TCAM organization. Starting from a top-level system perspective are NSEs designed to connect to NPUs with look-aside (LA-1)-compliant interfaces (QDR burst of 2) operating up to 250 MHz. Up to four NSE devices can be directly connected to one QDR interface, and up to eight devices can be cascaded from each of the four NSEs connected to the QDR bus using point-to-point cascading. Point-to-point cascading allows databases to contain up to two million 36-bit entries or one million 72-bit entries while maintaining only a single device load on the QDR bus. In this way, up to 32 devices can interface to one NPU, providing support for up to

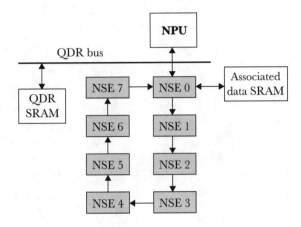

Bank of NSE devices.

eight million 36-bit entries. Figure 17.1 shows an NSE bank consisting of eight cascaded NSEs, connected to the QDR bus of an NPU.

Each NSE bank (one to eight devices) supports 16 databases, 128 contexts, and 64 72-bit global mask registers (GMRs) that are shared across all contexts. The width of each database can be selected to be 36, 72, or 144 bits wide or can be programmed to be from 32 to 576 bits wide in increments of 32 bits. Associated with each context is an instruction memory that holds operations to be initiated to the NSE and a results mailbox that holds operation results. Each results mailbox can store up to eight 32-bit results.

17.1.1   NSE Device Interfaces

The NSE has four major interfaces: the LA-1 bus, a cascade bus, a ZBT interface, and a JTAG interface. The LA-1 bus allows an NSE to be connected to an NPU and is composed of separate double-data-rate read and write data buses that share a common address bus. The set of NSEs that form a bank are chained in a ring with a point-to-point cascade bus. This bus is used to transmit operations and potential results to the next device in a bank, and send results to the last device in the cascade chain so that they may be returned to an NPU. The zero bus turnaround (ZBT) interface allows an external ZBT SRAM, which can be used to store associative data, to be connected to an NSE. Finally, an IEEE 1149.1-compliant JTAG interface is provided to facilitate board manufacturing tests.

The data array of the QDR NSE is divided into multiple segments, as shown in Figure 17.2. The IDT75K62134 has 32 memory segments, while the

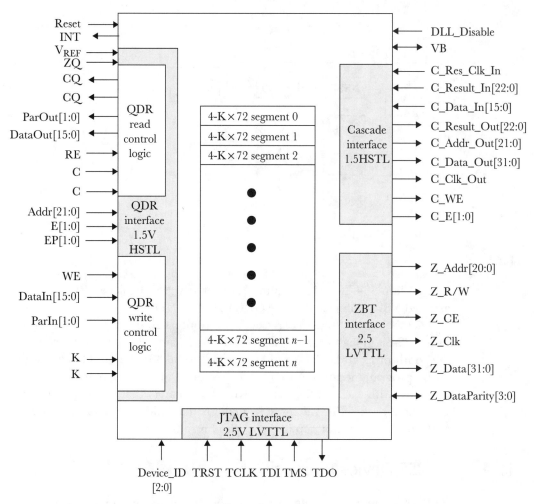

Simplified block diagram of IDT QDR NSE.

IDT75K52134 has 16 memory segments. Device power is minimized during operation by powering up only the segment(s) specified in the database to be searched.

17.1.2   NSE Internal Architecture

Figure 17.3 illustrates the internal architecture of the IDT NSE. The NSE can perform a number of operations to support database maintenance and searches,

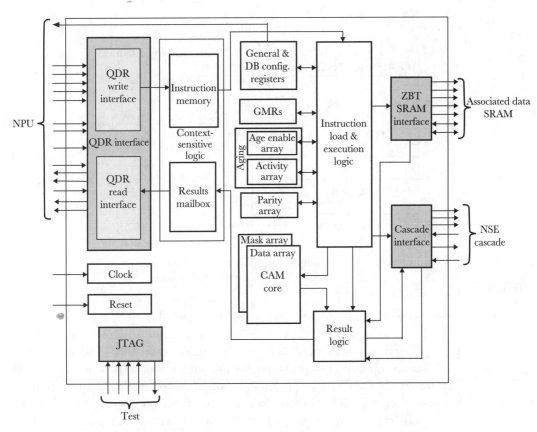

Architectural block diagram of the IDT NSE.

FIGURE

including a full-featured set of commands, such as *lookup*, *multi-hit lookup*, *multi-database lookup*, *re-issue multi-database lookup*, *learn*, and *multi-hit invalidate*. Each data entry in the NSE has a valid bit that can be set, cleared, or left unchanged by using the appropriate instruction. Additional database maintenance support includes aging with *age enable* and *activity* arrays that provide independent aging control per data entry. A separate aging count interval is supported per database.

NSE search and maintenance operations are initiated by writing to the NSE using the QDR LA-1 interface. The operation is nominally encoded on the address lines, and the search key is presented on the data bus. The operation is placed in the instruction memory, where it is associated with a specified context that is often connected to a specific thread of execution in the NPU. The association of an execution thread with a context is left up to the designer. Once a thread places a request in the instruction memory, the execution logic block

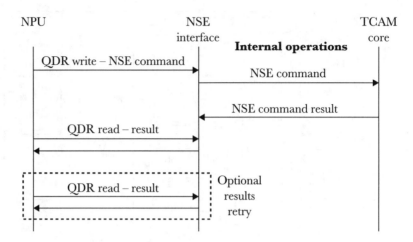

Transactional ladder diagram of basic search command.

presents the search operation, consisting of the global mask, the search key, and a CAM instruction to the TCAM core. The index results are stored in a mailbox for fetching by the associated thread of execution in the NPU (with *multi-hit* or *multi-database* operations, up to eight results can be returned). When a search is performed, the NSE can be optionally configured to fetch a 32-bit entry from the associated data SRAM. The execution block is also responsible for monitoring activity and indicating the lack of activity of entries being monitored. In addition, the execution unit maintains parity on the TCAM array, which can be interrogated through a background scrub operation using the *parity check* instruction. A transactional ladder diagram of basic search commands is depicted in Figure 17.4.

Results are read from the mailbox using the QDR LA-1 interface. When the execution thread receives the result word, a "done" bit indicates if the rest of the result is valid. If the result's read operation occurs before the NSE operation completed, the done bit is not set, and the application must reissue the *read* command. *Hit* and *multi-hit* bits further qualify the result. The NSE can operate in a deterministic fashion such that the *done* bit is a cross-check for correct operation and is normally set. Alternatively, the *done* bit can be used in an asynchronous polling fashion.

All maintenance is performed inline through the QDR LA-1 interface, reducing the pin count at the expense of requiring the operations to be funneled through the LA-1 interface. Since the same interface is used, coherency can be easily maintained between database search and maintenance operations.

17.1.3   TCAM Organization

The IDT75K62134 core has 128-K × 72 data cell entries, with 128-K × 72 associated mask cell entries; the IDT75K52134 core has 64-K × 72 data cell entries, with 64-K × 72 mask cell entries. This combination of data and mask cell entries, shown in Figure 17.5, enables the IDT75K62134 and IDT75K52134 devices to store 0, 1, or X ("don't care") in each bit of a data word. During a lookup operation, both arrays are used, along with a selected global mask register, to find the highest-priority match to a requested search key. The NSE core is a big-endian component, meaning the lower the value of the physical address the higher the priority of the entry. Thus, the address space is contiguous, with the physical address 0 having the highest priority.

The internal core of the NSE is divided into 4-K × 72-bit segments. There are 32 segments in the 75K62134 and 16 segments in the 75K52134. Databases are composed of a subset of these segments. As mentioned previously, to conserve power only the segments that belong to the database being searched are powered up. The NSE instruction specifies a unique database on each operation. Thus, the NSE devices consume minimal power per application, since only the segments being searched use power.

Each data cell in the NSE has a valid bit that is set when the data cell is written. Valid bits for individual data cells can be set, cleared, or left unchanged by using the appropriate instruction. In this way, entries that are unused do not participate in the search operation, thus eliminating unexpected results.

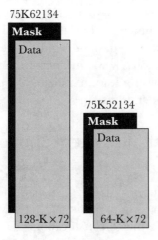

| 17.5 | IDT NSE mask and data cells. |

FIGURE

17.2   DEVELOPMENT AND SYSTEM SUPPORT TOOLS

The IDT NSE comes with a set of comprehensive software packages for development support that include system-level architectural models (SLAMs), data plane macros, complete product development diagnostics, and operational example applications, as well as a robust, production-quality control plane software library called the initialization, management, and search (IMS) library for runtime support.

17.2.1   NSE Development Support Tools

A detailed discussion of the SLAMs provided by IDT are NPU-specific and beyond the scope of this chapter. However, at a high level a SLAM provides both cycle- and data-accurate models of the NSE that dovetail with the workbench of the NPU. They not only provide a simulation of the operation of the NSE in the NPU environment but include tools for analyzing QDR bus (BusTracker) and power utilization (PowerTracker).

Data plane macros are provided for specific NPUs that are used to implement search engine operations. The IDT macros not only generate microinstructions that control the NSE but validate parameters. The current offering supports Intel's IXP NPUs. As more processors support the LA-1 interface, other packages will be provided. The product development diagnostics are a set of routines that allow the system designer to test the integrity of the device and the connections with the rest of the system at power-up. The operational application examples, such as the IPv4 POS, allow the system designer to get a quick start evaluating NSEs in an NPU environment. While the data plane macros and application code can provide a quick start, designers often achieve higher levels of performance for specific applications by writing new macros optimized for the unique requirements of each new application utilizing the pipelined nature and overlapped execution of NSE operations.

17.2.2   NSE Control Plane Runtime System Support

The remainder of this section describes the IMS library that is comprised of components that work together to support database management functions for three types of databases: exact match, longest prefix match (LPM)/classless inter-domain routing (CIDR), and range match/classification. The database management functions performed include device initialization, advanced database configuration, database entry addition and deletion, power minimization,

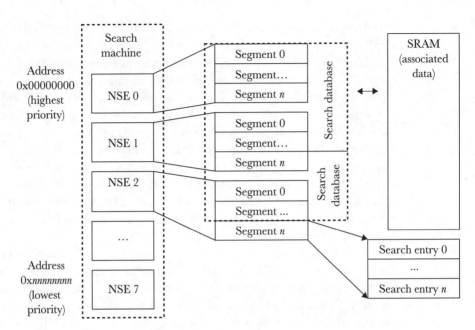

17.6

FIGURE

Search machine and logical database structure.

directly attached or NPU co-located associated data management, GMR provisioning, aging, and exception handling.

The IMS library also includes a well-defined application-programming interface (API) that is consistent across all IDT NSE product families, thus providing a common interface to the entire family of NSE devices. This common API enables single-source application development, cross-platform application reuse, and centralized OS-specific functionality while reducing the effort required to port to new OS environments. In addition, the IMS library also works seamlessly with the IDT SLAM: a cycle- and data-accurate model of the NSE with a QDR interface that enables developers to design and test solutions prior to hardware availability, accelerating both time-to-market and productivity.

The NSE software development environment support includes project-specific makefiles, cross-compilers, and UNIX environments, along with integrated development environments (IDEs) such as Microsoft Visual Studio and Wind River Tornado II for VxWorks.

The IMS software creates a logical architecture for a bank of NSE devices that consists of three elements: search machine, search database, and search entry. As shown in Figure 17.6, a search machine is a logical grouping of one or more NSEs cascaded together to form a single addressable lookup array. Each search machine is a contiguous address space, in which the address is a location in an NSE and device ID is the identification number assigned to the NSE. Each search machine is subdivided into one or more logical tables, called search databases. Typically, a search database is defined to contain one particular set of search data. For example, one search database might be a set of IPv4 addresses that comprises the currently active routing table, while a second search database may be a list of MAC addresses, and a third might be an access control list (ACL).

Search databases are comprised of search entries: individual logical records that are stored in the NSE core data array and the core mask array. Typically, a search entry may have associative data stored in an SRAM attached to the search machine, or in a separately accessible SRAM or DRAM. Search entries within a search database usually all have the same entry width, which is the number of bytes comprising the search entry.

Search databases can generally be classified into three different types: longest prefix match (LPM)/classless inter-domain routing (CIDR), exact match (binary/no ternary requirement), and range match (exact match with ternary characteristics, also known as classification). Each database type has different storage and organizational requirements, and the search database configuration characteristics are unique to each database type. In addition, each database type can be optimized to use a different maintenance algorithm where the add, delete, and modify operations are collectively referred to as TCAM maintenance.

The LPM database takes advantage of the ternary capability of the NSE TCAM core. Typically, the TCAM core mask array entry associated with an LPM entry is set to the bits corresponding to the IP address's network or subnetwork (subnet) mask. Thus, only the network portion of the IP address is matched by the search algorithm. The LPM database requires an ordering be maintained where the more specific route takes precedence over a general route. However, there are groups of routes that all have the same relative priority and within these priority classes only a single route should match. Together, the NSE and LPM characteristics require intelligence in the maintenance algorithm. Forwarding and routing of IPv4 and IPv6 are the most common examples of LPM databases.

For an exact match database, the maintenance algorithm requires significantly less intelligence, since all search entries can be treated as having equal priority and only one entry will match. Consequently, the solution is significantly simplified. Exact match databases essentially operate the NSE device as a binary CAM, and the TCAM core mask array bits are usually all enabled for this database type. Typical examples of exact match databases include layer 2 (L-2) media access control (MAC) address matching as part of an Ethernet bridge, and a 5-tuple specific match commonly referred to as a flow cache.

Range matches are typically referred to as classification databases. Range matching is accomplished by heavily relying on the TCAM ternary capability. One or more entries are added to the TCAM to create a representation of the range being searched and matched. Five or more tuple ACLs are good examples of wildcard and/or range matches.

17.3 DATABASE SEARCH SOLUTIONS, ANALYSIS AND COMPARISON

There are many ways to implement database searches with an NPU. While the NSE provides the highest performance, an alternative database search implementation is the use of an off-chip SRAM or DRAM together with sophisticated data structures and algorithms running on an NPU. For analysis and comparison purposes, this section will explore two approaches: algorithms using SRAM and NSEs using TCAM technology.

When considering algorithm approaches, the designer can consider: hashing algorithms for exact match applications, such as L-2 addresses or flow caches; multilevel trie searches for applications such as LPM of IPv4; and heuristic algorithms for complex field best-fit matching for ACLs. There are different trade-offs among these approaches. The performance of different kinds of search mechanisms can be measured in at least four dimensions: required bus bandwidth, number of devices, execution time, and number of NPU instructions. Maintenance must also be compared. The next few subsections describe algorithms utilizing SRAM to perform different types of network database searches.

17.3.1 Direct Index Mapping and Hashing/Exact Match Used in Flow Caching

At its simplest level, a "search key" can directly address an SRAM. The search key consists of the packet header fields used to locate each database entry. The memory location addressed by the search key contains an index (bit field) that can be used to locate the relevant database information. This approach is fast (an index is obtained in a single memory access), but limited by its inefficient use of memory. As a search key of W bits requires 2^W memory locations, keys much beyond 20 bits are impractical.

Hashing algorithms provide a fast method of indexing large tables with wider keys (even where W equates to several hundred bits). Hashing "randomizes" the search key and performs a search on just the first 16 to 20 bits (possibly using a direct index map). One method of hashing/randomizing the search key is to use an encryption algorithm (e.g., DES) with fixed keys.

It is possible that two search keys when randomized equate to the same bit sequence for the first ~20 bits. They would therefore clash (i.e., generate the same index). A hashing algorithm must therefore include further steps to resolve these cases. Typically this involves a direct comparison of the search key against the two (or more) clashing table entries. While resolving these cases slows down a hashing algorithm, the probability of a clash may be quite low. The performance hit may therefore not be significant.

Of greater significance is the fact that "hashing" is limited to "exact match" operations. This means that every bit in the search key must match the search criteria. This is suitable for some router operations (such as flow caching), but by no means all. Layer 3 route tables need to support LPM. In addition, classification, access control, and security policy databases invariably use wildcards. These introduce numerous "don't care" bits to the search key.

17.3.2   Trie-Based Tree Search—Longest Prefix Math

Multiple-level trie algorithms are a common means of implementing searches for LPM forwarding tables and narrow ACL. This approach breaks down a key into multiple bit groupings and sequentially examines each grouping on subsequent algorithm cycles. The bit grouping is used to walk down a tree of nodes. Each node stores pointers for all bit combinations examined; that is, if K bits are examined per cycle, 2^K pointers are required for each node (note that K is sometimes referred to as the "stride factor").

Increasing the stride (K) speeds up search performance, but involves a geometric increase in the amount of SRAM required to store node data. This can be an expensive way of improving search performance. A variable stride can be used to optimize between speed and memory utilized, as shown in Figure 17.7. In this figure, the variable stride factors K0, K1, and K2 describe the number of bits of the 32-bit search key examined at each level (or cycle) of the search.

The number of pointers needed per node = 2^{K0} for level 0, 2^{K1} for level 1, and 2^{K2} for level 2. At level 0 there is only a single (root) node, so it makes sense to make this as large as possible (e.g., 2^{16}). The number of nodes at each level is determined by the number of pointers in the previous level. This is shown as the number of "geometric nodes" in Table 17.1 due to its rapid expansion at each level.

In practice however, the number of nodes at each level will not exceed the number of table entries (N). With small tables, N determines the overall size of

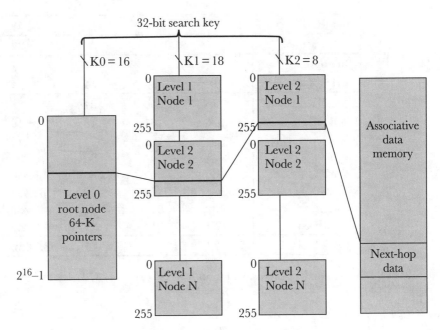

17.7

FIGURE

Variable-stride trie structure (16, 8, 8).

Detailed		N	Levels
calculation		**4,096**	**3**
Stride factors	**K0**	**K1**	**K2**
	16	**8**	**8**
Cumulative stride	16	24	32
Node size	65,536	256	256
Geometric nodes	1	65,536	16,777,216
Actual nodes	1	4,096	4,096
Words	65,536	1,048,576	1,048,576
Words used	65,536	1,048,576	1,048,576
Word size	32	32	32
Mbits used	2.1	33.6	33.6
Total Mbits	**3.1**	**35.7**	**69.2**

17.1

TABLE

Detailed storage calculation for best-case (16, 8, 8) trie structure.

Detailed		N		W	Levels
calculation		**4,096**		**32**	**5**
Strides	1	1	1	1	1
Stride factor	16	4	4	4	4
Cumulative stride	16	20	24	28	32
Node size	65,536	16	16	16	16
Geometric nodes	1	65,536	1,048,576	16,777,216	268,435,456
Actual nodes	1	4,096	4,096	4,096	4,096
Words	65,536	65,536	65,536	65,536	65,536
Words used	65,536	65,536	65,536	65,536	65,536
Word size	32	32	32	32	32
Mbits used	2.1	2.1	2.1	2.1	2.1
Total Mbits	**2.0972**	**4.1943**	**6.2915**	**8.3886**	**10.4858**

17.2

TABLE

Detailed storage calculation for best-case (16, 4, 4, 4, 4) trie structure.

the trie table. For comparison, a similar calculation is provided for a 16, 4, 4, 4, 4 structure in Table 17.2.

17.3.3   Trie Additions/Deletions (Maintenance)

If an IPv4 address is added with a /12 prefix, then all entries in the root node identified by the first 12 bits of the IP address need to be assigned pointers. This equates to $2^{(16-12)} = 16$ locations. On this basis, a /8 prefix requires 256 location updates, and a /16 prefix just one entry update (i.e., this occurs on the boundary of level 0). Data from the MAE-EAST routing table (*www.merit.edu*) shows that prefixes lower than /8 are not used, so the possibility of a /7 prefix requiring 512 location updates (or worse) never occurs.

For the 16, 8, 8 structure shown previously, prefixes between /16 and /24 will require a single update to the root node, and between 1 and 256 updates to the relevant level-1 node. Likewise, prefixes between /25 and /32 require single updates to the root and relevant level-1 node, and between 0 and 255 updates to the level-2 node.

Care should also be taken not to overwrite pointers relating to existing table entries (with different prefixes). A memory map for the level 0 (root) node for the 16, 8, 8 trie is shown in Figure 17.8. The location relating to 128.65.122.107/16 has to store two prefix pointers (for both /16 and /8 entries). Simply deleting

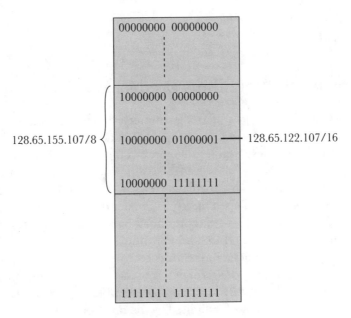

17.8

FIGURE

Memory map for root node (16-bit stride factor).

the /8 pointer might seem attractive, as this value will never be returned (assuming LPM). This cannot be done, however, as the /16 entry may be deleted at some time in the future. This would leave the /8 entry as the required search result. Each pointer must therefore store separate pointers for all /8 to /16 possibilities. A more detailed explanation of this problem is described in [2], which also presents a detailed algorithm for handling table maintenance in trie structures.

In relatively static networks, 256 memory updates per table addition/deletion may not be an issue. Border gate protocol (BGP) additions run as high as 3-K to 10-K entries per second during a route "flap." More typically, the update rate is hundreds of updates per second. This translates to just 6-M memory accesses per second (~2% of QDR bus running at 250 MHz). For more dynamic applications, table updates may be an issue. The flow table update or allocation of VLAN traffic to switched VCs may result in 100-K+ table updates per second. This translates to more than 25% of a QDR bus's capacity and may induce a significant bottleneck in the lookup algorithm.

In summary, the use of the large stride factors (e.g., 16, 8, 8) provides a three-stage lookup for an IPv4 address, compared to the five cycles required for a 16, 4, 4, 4, 4 structure. This speed improvement is, however, purchased at the expense of a 7-fold increase in SRAM storage requirements (70 Mbits instead of

10 Mbits) and a 16-fold increase in maintenance cycles (256 locations compared to just 16).

17.3.4 Heuristic Algorithms Used in ACL

Efficient multiple-field search algorithms are an area of active research. Typically, these algorithms reduce storage and/or access cycles by limiting search key configurations. These techniques require a thorough understanding of the classification and/or access rules used in an application, and often use precalculated tables. An example of one such algorithm is shown in Figure 17.9.

The IPv4 five-tuple search key is broken down into 16- (or 8-) bit chunks. Variations in each chunk are represented by a 2-, 3-, or 4-bit "equivalency ID." The functions f1, f2, and f3, and the indexing tables can therefore be configured to produce a unique index for each rule that needs to be encoded. These techniques are used in the recursive flow classification algorithm [3].

In certain conditions, this technique can offer fast classification for relatively small storage. It is, however, limited by the number of rules that can be encoded

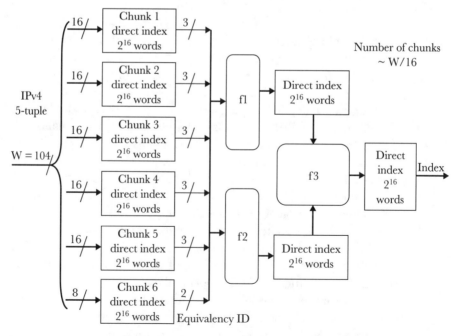

17.9   Heuristic classification algorithm.

FIGURE

Application database requirements	Configuration			Million access cycles for each		Min pkt. bytes	Line rate Gb/s				Memory usage	
	K entries N	Width W	Search method				0.6	2.5	5.0	10.0	M SRAM cells	Total device
				App. DB	Packet		Million memory accesses per second					
ACL 1	8.0	269	HEUR	17	49	64	60	239	479	957	49	3
L3 IPv6 forwarding	4.0	128	TRIE	32	32	64	39	156	313	625	40	3
L3 IPv4 forwarding	64.0	53	TRIE	13	19	64	23	94	188	376	38	3
Flow caching	8.0	104	HASH	6	6	64	7	29	59	117	2	1
	Max bus I/O MHz			250	333		M cells per device				18	
	Solution		**SRAM**	**K=4**			Bus width				36	

17.3

TABLE

Using 18-Mbit QDR SRAM.

(only a handful of variations in each 16-bit chunk). The number of rules and their format therefore have to be closely examined for each application. Further work is also required on how IPv6 5-tuples can be managed. A further limitation is the significant preprocessing of the tables and functions (potentially thousands of cycles per table addition). This limits the approach to static tables. Dynamic table management (typical for much next-generation equipment) requires fast table updates.

17.3.5   Comparing Search Methods: SRAM Versus NSE

Several algorithms conceived for the purposes of searching databases were described in the previous section. While there are many different scenarios for comparison [4], this section compares two different scenarios: the first uses algorithms with SRAM only, and the second uses an NSE. The SRAM-based algorithms utilized for comparison purposes are hashing (*HASH*) for an exact match key, such as a flow 5-tuple; a multilevel trie (*TRIE*) tree to implement an LPM search; and a heuristic (*HEUR*) algorithm constructed in a hierarchical search of a tree-like structure to perform ACL searches. The second example uses an NSE with a TCAM (*TCAM*) core for all searches. Tables 17.3 and 17.4 highlight the results of calculations that estimate the memory and bus cycle utilization of devices connected to an NPU with a QDR LA-1 bus.

Each database is specified by the number (N) of thousand entries, width (W bits), and a specific search method (*HEUR*, *TRIE*, *HASH*, or *TCAM*). For the

Application database requirements	Configuration			Million access cycles for each		Min pkt. bytes	Line rate Gb/s				Memory usage	
	K entries N	Width W	Search method				0.6	2.5	5.0	10.0		
				App. DB	Packet		Million memory accesses per second				M TCAM cells	Total device
ACL 1	8.0	**252**	TCAM	7	12	64	15	59	117	234	8.4	1
L3 IPv6 forwarding	4.0	128	TCAM	4	5	64	6	24	49	98	6.2	1
L3 IPv4 forwarding	64.0	53	TCAM	2	5	64	6	24	49	98	5.6	1
Flow caching	8.0	104	TCAM	3	3	64	4	15	29	59	1.1	1
	Max bus I/O MHz			250	333		M cells per device				9.0	
	Solution		**SRAM**	K=NA			Bus width				36	

17.4   Using 9-Mbit NSE.

TABLE

SRAM algorithms, a stride of K bits must be specified. From there, estimations can be made for the number of QDR bus cycles for each application database (*APP DB*) and a cumulative cycle count per packet specified in millions of cycles. Given the minimum packet size (*min pkt*) in bytes (64) and the line rate in Gb/s, the required cumulative QDR memory cycles per second can be calculated in millions of memory accesses per second.

To complete the analysis, the designer must assume types of tables and sizes. From there, the QDR memory bus accesses per database as well as the cumulative for each packet are calculated. Next, the cumulative memory accesses (starting with flow caching at the bottom of the table, working up the table to ACL for a single QDR bus) can be calculated for each possible line rate (see Table 17.3). When the cumulative number of cycles exceeds the max bus I/O MHz, the designer must consider an alternative (e.g., replicating the memory structure on another QDR bus), thus raising costs and board complexity. In each example, it is assumed that there are 8-K flows, 64-K IPv4 addresses, 4-K IPv6 addresses, and 8-K ACL rules. In the access cycles for each packet column, the larger number of accesses required for IPv4 and IPv6 is selected.

Whereas the 18-Mbit QDR SRAM solution uses three devices to achieve 2.5-Gb/s performance, the 9-Mbit NSE provides a single-chip solution at 10 Gb/s on a single QDR bus (see Table 17.4). The use of three QDR SRAM devices will furthermore be a challenge to operate at the 250 MHz necessary to meet the requirements.

As 36-Mbit QDR SRAMs become readily available, 18-Mbit NSE will be entering the market, keeping an advantage of nearly four to one.

17.4 CONCLUSION

The IDT NSE with an integrated QDR (LA-1) interface provides a comprehensive architectural solution that is supported with system-level support tools that enable the best time-to-market available. NSEs utilizing TCAM technology can provide enhanced NPU system performance that enables flow caching, IPv4 or IPv6 forwarding, and ACL at a 10-Gb/s line rate utilizing one QDR bus. As NPU designs strive to meet the ever-increasing demands of modern networks, NSEs will continue to be essential tools for offloading database table searches and allowing higher levels of functionality.

REFERENCES

[1] IDT, "4.5M and 9M Network Search Engine (NSE) with QDR Interface, Data Sheet," 2002.

[2] IDT, "Network Search Engine (NSE) TCAM with QDR Interface, User's Manual," 2002.

[3] P. Gupta, "Algorithms for Routing Lookups and Packet Classification," Ph.D. dissertation, Stanford University, Dec. 2000.

[4] M. Miller, S. Cochrane, and B. Tezcan, "Optimum Search Methods for Switch/Router Databases," IDT white paper, Mar. 2003.

18

Implementing Voice over AAL2 on a Network Processor

**Jaroslaw Sydir, Prashant Chandra, Alok Kumar,
Sridhar Lakshmanamurthy, Longsong Lin,
Muthaiah Venkatachalam**
Intel Communications Group, Intel Corporation

Programmable network processors (NPUs) offer telecommunications equipment manufacturers a flexible platform for building a variety of different equipment. The power of NPUs is that they can be programmed to perform many different packet-processing functions to support a variety of different protocols and standards. This flexibility allows equipment manufacturers to utilize the same NPU or family of NPUs across different product lines. It also allows them to easily evolve their products to support evolving standards and to provide unique value-added features within these products.

Until recently, most network processors have been designed mainly to perform basic IP packet processing, as described in RFC 1812 [5], at very high line rates. This basic IP packet processing is fairly simple and deterministic. All packets are subject to roughly the same processing. Quality-of-service (QoS) guarantees are either not provided at all or provided on a coarse, per-class granularity with no guarantees on packet delay or packet delay variation (jitter).

Unfortunately, real-world packet-processing applications are much more complex and diverse than this basic IP processing application. IP processing performed by today's routers includes many additional features (such as *diffserv* QoS, policy-based routing, and packet filtering) that make the packet-processing applications much more complex and less uniform. Other packet-processing applications deal with real-time traffic and therefore have stricter real-time processing requirements.

To provide the level of flexibility sought by equipment manufacturers, an NPU must be able to support diverse packet-processing applications dealing with connectionless and connection-oriented protocols with a variety of quality-of-service models and requirements. Different applications require different programming models, which must be supported by an NPU.

An example of an application that presents a different set of requirements than the basic IP forwarding application is the Voice over AAL2 (VoAAL2) application. In this chapter we discuss the special requirements and challenges presented by the VoAAL2 application. We describe the architecture and design of a VoAAL2 application that we have developed for the Intel IXP2400 processor and discuss the features of an NPU that are required to support this type of application.

18.1   IXP2400 NETWORK PROCESSOR

The IXP2400 is a next-generation network processor developed by Intel Corporation. It is fully programmable, offering a very flexible programming model and support for a broad range of diverse packet-processing applications. In this section we highlight some of the IXP2400 features that are utilized by the VoAAL2 application. *Network Processor Performance Analysis Methodology*, by Sridhar Lakshmanamurthy et al., provides a complete overview of the IXP2400 architecture [1].

The IXP2400 is a multithreaded multiprocessor system. Packets enter the IXP2400 through a configurable industry standard interface that supports packet-over-SONET and UTOPIA interfaces. Packet processing is performed by eight packet-processing engines, called microengines (MEs). Each ME has eight hardware execution contexts (also referred to as threads). Each context has its own register set, so that swapping between them is a very fast (one instruction cycle) operation. The MEs use a non-preemptive context-scheduling model, where the swapping out of contexts occurs under software control, and ready-to-run contexts are scheduled using a round-robin scheduling discipline.

Each ME contains an arithmetic logic unit (ALU) and a content-associated memory (CAM) unit, which allows the application to compare a key value to the keys of all CAM entries in one instruction cycle. The MEs also provide byte-alignment support to allow applications to manipulate packet headers and data that are not always aligned on 4-byte boundaries. Each ME contains 640 long-words of local memory, where packet headers can be stored temporarily while they are processed. Finally, the MEs provide real-time timers, which allow a thread to specify a time in the future when it should be awakened.

The IXP2400 contains interfaces to external SRAM and SDRAM memories.

18.2   VOICE SERVICE REQUIREMENTS

Transmitting voice signals over a network places some specific real-time requirements on the network. Voice (for example, a telephone call) is sampled at periodic intervals, and those samples are transmitted across the network and replayed at the other end at the same rate. Each voice sample is subject to a transmission and propagation delay as it traverses the network. This delay cannot be too large if the conversation is to flow at a normal pace. More importantly, variations in the delay experienced by different samples (referred to as jitter) cannot cause the replay of those samples to occur at a variable rate, or the quality of the voice experience by the listener will degrade.

Traditional voice networks, time-division multiplexing (TDM) networks, solve this problem by reserving the capacity for the voice samples of a call at the time the call is set up and synchronizing the transmission of voice samples throughout the network. This provides a very predictable environment for voice applications and guarantees that the jitter and delay experienced by voice samples is within specified limits and yields the voice quality that we are used to when using the telephone. The drawback of this approach is that a 64-Kb/s channel is reserved for the duration of the voice call and cannot be used to carry voice samples from other calls, even during periods of silence.

Transmitting voice over packet networks, such as ATM, can solve this resource usage efficiency problem because voice samples from different calls are allowed to use the bandwidth from a call during periods of silence. The challenge is to allow this type of bandwidth sharing while still providing the same delay and jitter guarantees in order to maintain the same level of voice quality as a traditional voice network.

18.3   VoAAL2 SERVICE

18.3.1   Typical VoAAL2 Deployment

Figure 18.1 illustrates the typical configuration of a VoAAL2 service in a network. Voice calls originate on the time-division multiplexing (TDM) network.

The analog voice signal is sampled and digitized in the VoATM gateway to produce a stream of voice packets. (Note: TDM networks also carry digitized voice and other traffic.) These voice packets are transported across the ATM network in AAL2 trunks. An AAL2 trunk is an ATM virtual circuit (VC) used to

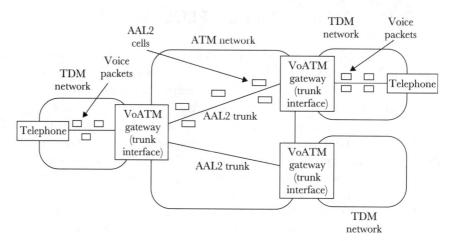

18.1

FIGURE

18.1   Configuration of a VoAAL2 service.

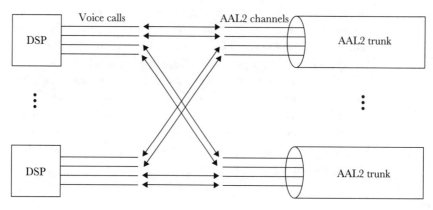

18.2

FIGURE

18.2   Relationship between voice calls and AAL2 channels.

transport AAL2 traffic. At the far end of the ATM network, the voice packets are converted back to an analog signal and transmitted over an analog voice network.

Figure 18.2 illustrates the relationship among voice calls, AAL2 channels, AAL2 trunks, and ATM VCs. There are many digital signal processors (DSPs) within a VoATM gateway. Each DSP processes a given number of voice calls. Each voice call is mapped to an AAL2 channel within an AAL2 trunk. There are 256 AAL2 channels within each AAL2 trunk. The AAL2 channel is identified by the channel identifier (CID). There are many AAL2 trunks in the system. Different voice calls from a given DSP can correspond to AAL2 channels within the same or different AAL2 trunks. The inverse relationship holds at the far end of the ATM network, where packets from each AAL2 channel are transformed into voice packets destined for a specific DSP. The VoAAL2 application transforms voice packets to AAL2 packets and transmits them on the correct AAL2 channel. At the other end of the ATM network, the VoAAL2 application performs the inverse operation.

18.3.2   AAL2 Standards

The VoAAL2 service is specified by the International Telecommunications Union (ITU). AAL type 2 is subdivided into the common part sublayer (CPS) and the service-specific convergence sublayer (SSCS). Recommendation I.363.2 specifies the CPS layer for all AAL type 2 applications [2]. This layer defines a packet format with a 3-byte packet header, which contains the length of the packet, a user-to-user indication (UUI) field, whose content is specified by the layer above, and a header error correction field. Recommendation I.366.2 specifies an SSCS layer for trunking of traffic from narrow-band networks (ISDN or analog networks) over AAL2 [3]. I.366.2 defines a number of services for transporting audio and data traffic, and signaling over an AAL2 network. For the audio service, the SSCS layer does not define its own header. It simply specifies the format and values that are passed to the CPS layer and transmitted in the UUI field of the CPS header.

18.4   PACKET PROCESSING IN THE VoAAL2 APPLICATION

Figure 18.3 illustrates the relationship among the different types of packets. In the digital signal processor (DSP) to asynchronous transfer mode (ATM) direction, digitized voice packets are received from the DSP chip. Each voice

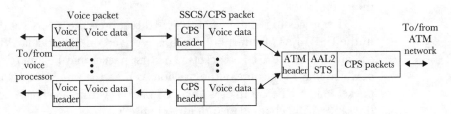

18.3   VoAAL2 packet transformations.

FIGURE

packet is mapped to one service-specific convergence sublayer (SSCS)/common part sublayer (CPS) packet. Multiple CPS packets are multiplexed within an AAL2 cell.

The voice packets contain a header that indicates the identity of the voice channel, the length of the packet, and the encoding algorithm that was used. The voice header is a software convention established between the VoAAL2 application and the DSP and is not part of the standards. The information contained in this header could also be communicated by some out-of-band communication mechanism.

The application looks up the AAL2 channel, within a specific ATM VC, which is used to transport this call. The DSP header is stripped from the voice packet and SSCS processing is performed. SSCS processing involves generating the proper sequence number that is carried in the user-to-user indication (UUI) field of the CPS header. This sequence number is maintained on a per-voice-call basis.

Next, CPS processing is performed. This entails the creation of the CPS header and the generation of a CRC-5-based header error correction field. Multiple CPS packets can be packed into the payload of an ATM cell, and the content of a given CPS packet can be split across successive ATM cells (within the same VC). The first byte of AAL2 ATM cells contains a field called the start field (STF), which indicates the length of the data and offset to the start of the first CPS packet within the cell.

CPS packets destined for the same VC are accumulated until either a cell is completely filled or the *timer_CU* has expired. Recommendation I.363.2 specifies the use of the *timer_CU* to force a cell to be sent after a certain amount of time, even if it is not full. The *timer_CU* is used to make certain that the processing delay incurred by a CPS packet (voice packet) is less than a specified number. A *timer_CU* is maintained for each VC. When the first CPS packet is received (for a cell on that VC), the *timer_CU* is started for that VC. When additional CPS packets are received and the cell is filled, the *timer_CU* is canceled (or restarted if there is enough data to start a new cell). If the timer expires before the cell is full, the empty part of the cell is padded with zeros and the cell is sent even though it is not full.

The processing in the ATM to DSP direction is the inverse of the processing in the DSP to ATM direction. A cell is received on a particular VC. Within the cell are one or more CPS packets. The first packet may be a partial packet, part of which may have come in the previous cell on the same VC. Also, the last CPS packet may not be complete. The CPS packets within a cell can be destined for the same AAL2 channel or different channels.

The CPS packets are extracted from the ATM cell and reconstructed, and the CPS headers are verified using the CRC-5 value in the header. For each packet the voice channel to which it belongs is determined as a function of the VC and AAL2 CID. The SSCS sequence number is also verified, and the packet is discarded if it is corrupted or misordered. The DSP header is prepended to the payload of the SSCS packet to create a DSP packet.

Each voice packet encodes a specified time interval of the voice signal. The timestamp for a packet represents the beginning of this interval. The SSCS sequence number captures the time of a packet relative to the time of the previous packet. The timestamp for packet $n(Tn)$ is given by the formula $Tn = Tn - 1 + ((Sn - Sn - 1) * I)$, where $Tn - 1$ is the timestamp of packet $n - 1$; Sn and $Sn - 1$ are the sequence numbers of packets n and $n - 1$, respectively; and I is the interval length for this call.

When a packet is received, its SSCS sequence number is used to generate a timestamp, which is used to perform jitter removal from the stream of voice packets that make up a call. Jitter is the variable inter-packet gap caused by network queuing and transmission delays experienced by successive packets or cells from one connection. Network jitter causes voice packets from a channel to be either bunched or spread out in time, thereby making the inter-packet gap smaller than or greater than the codec sampling interval. Before the voice packets can be played out to the listener or transmitted over a TDM link, this variability in the inter-packet gap must be removed. Removing jitter requires collecting enough voice packets from a channel in a buffer so that the voice packets can be played out with a constant inter-packet gap corresponding to the codec interval. This dejittering operation must be performed individually for each voice call.

18.5   QoS CONSIDERATIONS

Traffic management in asynchronous transfer mode (ATM) networks is specified by the ATM Forum in the traffic management specification [4]. The TM4.1 specification defines six service categories that are used to provide different levels of QoS guarantees to different types of traffic. Each service category is defined in terms of the characteristics of the traffic that can be afforded this service (called the traffic contract) and the types of QoS guarantees that traffic that conforms to the traffic contract will receive.

The constant bit rate (CBR) service category provides a service similar to that provided by a TDM network. CBR traffic is characterized by a peak cell rate.

A conformant CBR traffic stream cannot exceed its peak rate or a maximum cell delay variation. The traffic is guaranteed very low losses and a maximum cell transfer delay. Voice and circuit emulation services are potential users of this service.

The real-time variable bit rate (rtVBR) service category provides loss and delay guarantees to traffic whose bit rate is variable. The traffic is characterized by a peak rate, a sustainable rate, and a maximum burst size. A conformant traffic stream must not exceed its sustainable rate over long time scales; it can burst at rates up to its peak rate, up to its maximum burst size. The traffic is guaranteed very low losses and a maximum cell transfer delay. Real-time applications, such as voice and video, are potential users of this service.

The non-real-time variable bit rate (nrtVBR) service category is intended for non-real-time applications with a bursty traffic pattern. The traffic and conformance criteria for this service are characterized in the same way for the rtVBR service category. The network offers a loss guarantee, but no packet delay guarantees.

The unspecified bit rate (UBR), available bit rate (ABR), and guaranteed frame rate (GFR) service categories are intended for the transport of data traffic. UBR is a best-effort service, where no restrictions are placed on the traffic and no guarantees are provided by the network. ABR provides a loss guarantee and utilizes closed-loop feedback control to throttle the traffic sources in order to avoid losses in the network. Finally, GFR is intended to provide a service similar to that offered by frame relay for IP applications.

The TM4.1 specification describes a number of mechanisms for implementing traffic management within the network. Call admission control (CAC) is used to determine whether the network has the resources to support a connection and to reserve these resources for the connection. Policing is performed at the edges of the network to make certain that the traffic entering the network conforms to its traffic contract. Shaping is used to transform a traffic stream into one that meets a different traffic contract. Finally, scheduling is used to ensure that the resources reserved by a connection are made available to the cells traversing that connection.

From a traffic management perspective the VoAAL2 application is a user of the network. AAL2 trunks (VCs) are generally established as CBR or rtVBR connections, and the traffic stream produced by the VoAAL2 application for each VC must conform to the traffic contract for that VC. TM4.1 uses the generic cell rate algorithm (GCRA) for defining the conformance of a traffic stream to its traffic contract. GCRA has two parameters T, and τ. T is the inverse of the rate allocated to the flow by the network. The rate here could mean either peak rate or average rate, depending on the service class. The second parameter τ

represents the deviation from the theoretical arrival times of the cells in a flow that can be tolerated by the network. The algorithm maintains the theoretical earliest arrival time for the next cell. When a cell arrives, its actual arrival time is compared to the theoretical arrival time. If the cell has arrived later than the theoretical earliest arrival time or less than τ units of time earlier than this time, then the packet conforms. Otherwise, it does not. The theoretical arrival time is calculated as a function of the actual arrival time of the current cell and the parameter T.

18.6   VoAAL2 APPLICATION ON IXP2400

We have implemented the VoAAL2 application on the Intel IXP2400 processor. In this section we describe the design of this application and discuss some of the challenges involved.

18.6.1   DSP to ATM Processing Design

Figure 18.4 illustrates the major components, data structures, and control and dataflow for the DSP to ATM direction. Thin dotted lines within the figure represent a relationship between data items. Solid lines represent dataflow, and thick dashed lines represent control flow.

The *DSP Rx* component receives voice packets from the DSPs. It reads the header that is created by the DSP and extracts the relevant metadata that describes the voice packet. It then places this metadata into a message to the SSCS Tx component. It is important to separate the processing of voice packets from the voice processor because in other versions of this application the voice packets may come from a different source, such as another AAL2 connection (AAL2 switching), or from a voice-over-IP connection.

The *SSCS Tx* component receives messages from the DSP Rx component, indicating that a voice packet is ready to be processed, and performs SSCS processing to produce the value of the UUI and length fields that go into the common part sublayer (CPS) header. It accesses two main data structures in performing this processing. First, it looks up the entry in the *SSCS channel table* that corresponds to the AAL2 channel over which the voice packet is to be transported. The SSCS channel table contains an entry for each SSCS channel. Each entry contains the CID of this channel, the VC within which it exists, the profile for this call, and the SSCS sequence number. Next, the SSCS Tx component searches the profile table that describes the profile used for this channel for the

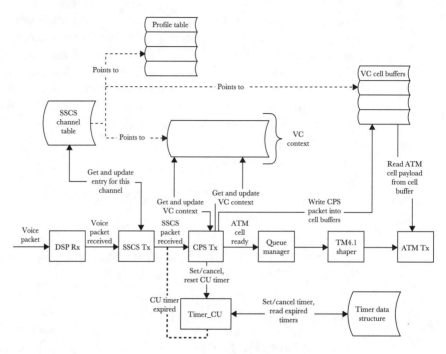

DSP to ATM processing.

entry that corresponds to this voice packet. The *profile tables* are read-only tables that describe the UUI field encoding, sequence number interval, and length for each audio-encoding algorithm that can be used within the profile. Within a profile table there is an entry for each encoding algorithm supported in the profile. Each voice packet must match one of the entries with the profile. A profile table exists for every profile supported by the application.

When it has completed the SSCS processing, the SSCS Tx component sends a message to the CPS Tx component indicating that an SSCS packet has been received.

The *CPS Tx* component encapsulates SSCS packets in CPS packets and packs CPS packets into AAL2 cells. It is driven by the arrival of two types of messages. Messages indicating that an SSCS packet has been received are sent by the SSCS Tx component. In response to these messages, this component gets the VC context that corresponds to the VC on which the packet has arrived. The *VC context* stores the state of an AAL2 VC. It contains information that is required to determine if the timer for a VC should be set, canceled, reset, or left alone, and information about the cell buffer in which the current cell is being assembled.

The CPS Tx component first performs the bookkeeping in order to determine what should be done with the *timer_CU* for this VC, and sends a message to the *timer_CU* component indicating the required action. The *timer_CU* can be set, canceled, reset, or left alone, depending on whether it was previously set and whether the data from the new packet have partially filled a new cell. The CPS Tx component then creates the CPS header to produce a CPS packet that contains an SSCS packet, which contains the voice packet. The CPS packet is written into the current cell buffer immediately following the previous CPS packet destined for this VC. The packet may not entirely fit into the current cell, in which case the part that fits into the current cell is written there and a message is sent to the queue manager component, indicating that the cell is ready to be sent. The remainder of the CPS packet is written to the next cell buffer. (A maximum-size CPS packet can fill up two ATM cells.) The VC context is updated and written back to memory.

Messages indicating that the *timer_CU* for a VC has expired are sent to the CPS Tx component by the *timer_CU* component. In response to these messages, the CPS Tx component gets the VC context that corresponds to the VC whose *timer_CU* has expired. It determines how many bytes of padding must be written to complete the cell, writes this padding to the cell buffer, and sends a message to the queue manager component indicating that the cell is ready to be sent. Finally, it updates the VC context to account for the actions that were taken.

The *timer_CU* component implements the *timer_CU* functionality. It accepts requests to set, cancel, and reset the timer for specific VCs. It is also responsible for firing the individual *timer_CUs* that are set (and canceled) for individual VCs. The *timer_CU structure* is a calendar queue data structure used to store the *timer_CU* entries for active VCs. The timers are stored in buckets, and each bucket is associated with a time interval. The *timer_CU* component wakes up at the end of each time interval and sends *timer_CU*-expired messages to the CPS Tx component for each VC that had a *timer_CU* set to go off during the previous time interval.

The *queue manager* component manages a set of queues in SRAM. There is a queue for each ATM VC. Cells are placed into the queue by the CPS Tx component and removed by the TM4.1 shaper component.

The *TM4.1 shaper/scheduler* component consists of three blocks. The TM4.1 shaper block receives input from the queue manager when a cell from a particular VC queue (VCQ) has been dequeued and there are cells remaining in that VCQ (this is called *cell dequeue without transition*) or when cells are queued into an empty VCQ (this is called *queue with transition*). The shaper computes the *earliest* departure time for the cell using the generic cell rate algorithm (GCRA) traffic

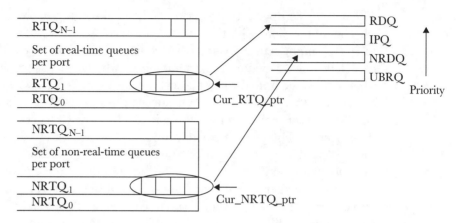

18.5   TM4.1 scheduler time queues.

FIGURE

descriptors. It passes on the *earliest* departure time, the VCQ number, and the
service category for the cell onto the TM4.1 write-out block.

The design uses time queues to achieve compliance and provide TM4.1
functionality. Time queues are depicted in Figure 18.5. The time axis can be
divided into small units of cell transmission slots. In each slot, one or no cells
depart.

A time queue is the aggregation of several cell transmission slots and hence
represents an interval of time. The time queue holds the cells that are meant
to be transmitted during this time interval. There are a fixed number of time
queues in the system (that can be derived based on the link rate), the slowest
VC bit rate, and the aggregation level of the time queue. The sum total of all
the time intervals represented by the all-time queues would constitute the time
horizon. The time horizon is nothing but the time after which the time queues
wrap around. There are two sets of time queues: one for real-time traffic (called
the *real-time time queue*), such as CBR and rtVBR, and the other for non-real-time
traffic (called the *non-real-time time queue*), such as nrtVBR and GFR.

The TM4.1 write-out block computes the time queue into which the cell
needs to be written based on the *earliest* departure time. Once the time queue
is computed for the cell, it writes out the cell into the real-time time queue if
the traffic is CBR or rtVBR, and the non-real-time time queue if the traffic is
nrtVBR. If no space is available in the time queues, the write-out block writes
into a different data structure called the intermediate-priority queue (IPQ).

The scheduler block schedules out cells from the time queues, IPQ, and the
UBR queues. It is essentially a priority scheduler with the highest priority for

the real-time time queue, the next priority for IPQ, next for non-real-time time queue, and the lowest priority for UBR. When scheduling from a time queue, the scheduler is always in sync with or behind the real time. The design ensures that cells are not scheduled ahead of real time, since this would violate the traffic contracts of the VC and create unfairness in the system.

Finally, the *ATM Tx* component performs the ATM header processing and transmits the cell.

18.6.2 ATM to DSP Design

Figure 18.6 illustrates the major components, data structures, and control and dataflow in the ATM to DSP direction. The *ATM and CPS Rx* component receives ATM cells. When a cell is received, the ATM and CPS Rx component determine the VC to which this cell belongs. The *VC context* for this VC is then read in from SRAM. Since it is possible that a CPS packet was split across cells, this context contains information about such a split CPS packet. The ATM and CPS Rx component reads the content of the ATM cell into the microengine and steps through the CPS packets contained within. It copies each CPS packet into a packet buffer, maps the virtual path indicator (VPI), virtual circuit indicator (VCI), and CID fields to the channel ID, and queues each packet buffer for the SSCS Rx component to process. If a CPS packet is split across ATM cells, the

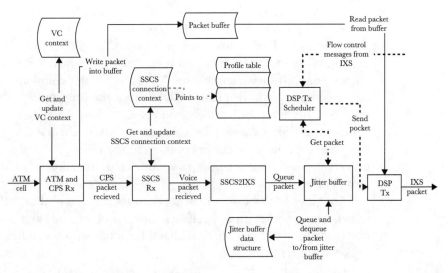

18.6   ATM to DSP processing.

FIGURE

ATM and CPS Rx component stores the reassembly context in the VC context, to allow the packet to be completed when the next cell for this VC arrives.

The *SSCS Rx* component performs the SSCS processing. It uses the channel ID to access the *SSCS connection context* for this channel. The context contains the sequence number of the previously received SSCS packet and a pointer to the table that describes the profile for this connection. The structure of the profile tables was described in the previous section. The SSCS Rx component accesses the entry in the profile table that corresponds to the UUI field and length of the SSCS packet (in the CPS header). This entry specifies the encoding algorithm that was used, along with information used to determine the expected sequence number and corresponding timestamp for this packet. SSCS Rx checks the sequence number against the one received in the packet and generates the timestamp. If there are no errors, the packet is passed to the SSCS2DSP component.

The *SSCS2DSP* component creates a DSP packet header from the information that the ATM and the CPS Rx and SSCS Rx components have extracted from the packet and profile table. It then passes the packet to the jitter buffer component.

The *jitter buffer* component enqueues the packet into a per-channel queue. The purpose of the jitter buffer component is to eliminate some of the jitter introduced into the voice packet stream in the ATM network. It does this by placing packets into proper time-sequential order, applying a specified jitter delay, and playing them back at the proper rate (with jitter removed).

The *DSP Tx scheduler* component is responsible for scheduling the transmission of DSP packets to the DSP. This component registers itself with the MSF in order to receive flow control messages from the DSP. In each flow control message, the DSP indicates one or more channels, on which it is ready to receive a packet. For each such channel, the DSP Tx scheduler component asks the jitter buffer component to dequeue a packet from the jitter buffer. The jitter buffer returns either a buffer handle or an error. If the jitter buffer returns a buffer handle, the DSP Tx scheduler component passes this handle to the DSP Tx component. If the jitter buffer component returns an error, the DSP Tx scheduler component creates a DSP packet that indicates silence (an SID) and passes it to the DSP Tx.

The jitter buffer component receives requests from the DSP Tx scheduler to dequeue a packet on a specific channel. It determines if a packet is queued and ready to send for that channel and responds with the buffer handle of that packet or an error.

Finally, the *DSP Tx* component transmits voice packets to the voice processors.

18.7   CHALLENGES AND LESSONS LEARNED

In this section we discuss some of the challenges that must be surmounted in developing a VoAAL2 application on an NPU.

18.7.1   Processing Asynchronous Inputs Within Many Contexts

The VoAAL2 application must support a large number of AAL2 VCs. There is a requirement that within each VC cells/packets be processed in the order in which they were received. (In the DSP to ATM direction voice packets destined for a VC should be processed in order, while in the ATM to DSP direction ATM cells received on a VC must be processed in order.) The data rates within VCs can be fairly small, so at any given moment the application is holding/processing cells/packets from a small subset of this total number of VCs. Because there are many VCs, the packets that the application is processing/holding at a given time are most likely all from different VCs, although this is not guaranteed and cannot be assumed by the application. The challenge is how to serialize the processing of cells/packets within each VC, while allowing cells/packets from different VCs to be processed in parallel.

Another problem is that the CPS Tx component must process voice packets received by the system as well as react to the expiration of the *timer_CU*. *Timer_CU* expiration events are not regular or predictable, since they are a function of the traffic patterns on individual VCs. The amount of processing required to process a packet that has arrived is much larger than that required to react to the expiration of the *timer_CU*.

We solve the problem of having to serialize the processing of packets/cells within each VC by dynamically binding VCs to threads. A thread receives a packet or message, determines which VC it belongs to, checks to see if any other thread is already processing packets/messages for that VC, and locks the VC if it is not already locked by another thread. The thread then processes the packet or message. When it has completed processing the packet or message, it checks to see if any other packets or messages have been queued for it to process (associated with this same VC). The thread processes any packets or messages that have been queued, and when there are none left it unlocks the VC. On the other hand, if another thread has already locked the VC, the packet or message is queued for this other thread to process.

The process of locking a VC, unlocking a VC, and checking to determine if a VC is locked must be performed in an atomic fashion in order to ensure that two threads do not lock the same VC. In our design the entire component is implemented within a single ME, so we use a built-in CAM for storing the identity of the VC that is locked by each thread, allowing the operations of locking, unlocking, and checking to see if a VC is locked to be performed in one operation.

We found that the IXP2400 provides good support for the asynchronous programming model used in the VoAAL2 application. Central to this support are the CAM and local memory that are included in each ME. The IXP2400 also provides the basic support required to distribute this type of processing across multiple MEs. It provides atomic test and set operations in the shared SRAM, which can be used to implement locks. However, SRAM operations have a fairly large latency, making it difficult to use this mechanism for locking in high-performance applications. Additional hardware support for performing distributed locking from threads on multiple MEs would make it easier to implement such multi-ME asynchronous applications. On the other hand, it is generally possible to partition an application into components in such a way as to avoid asynchronous components that run on more than one ME.

18.7.2   Bit- and Byte-Level Memory Access

The CPS header and AAL2 cell are tightly packed structures, where fields are not aligned on 4-, 8-, or even 1-byte boundaries. This means that the VoAAL2 application must read and write from/to arbitrary bit and byte addresses as it creates/parses CPS packet headers and packs/unpacks CPS packets from AAL2 cells. This presents a challenge for any processor because memory systems generally support reads/writes of 4- or 8-byte chunks of data, addressed on 4- or 8-byte boundaries.

Our implementation utilizes specialized byte alignment hardware of the IXP2400 processor to merge and align the CPS packets as we pack/unpack them into/from AAL2 cells. Bit fields are accessed utilizing mask and shift operations provided by the ALU. Efficient support for such data access is critical to support applications such as VoAAL2, where packets are small and protocol overhead must be minimized.

The problem of having to access unaligned data is solved by some combination of providing specialized hardware instructions and simply providing sufficient processor speed to allow the applications to perform the required data manipulations within the required time budget. We found that the IXP2400 provides a reasonable combination of processing speed and specialized instructions to support this application.

18.7.3   Jitter Buffer

The purpose of the jitter buffer is to receive voice packets, place them in proper time-sequential order, provide a specified jitter delay, and then present them for transmission. The jitter buffer must be large enough so that the slowest packets can arrive in time to be played out in the correct sequence. On the other hand, the jitter buffer must be small enough such that the delay introduced is minimized. To address these conflicting requirements, the jitter buffer can be dynamically resized based on measurements of actual network jitter. On lightly loaded paths, this allows for a minimum jitter delay and a higher quality of speech with less noticeable turnaround delay. On congested paths, the jitter delay can be increased so that fewer packets are missed or dropped due to the irregularity of their timing but with a more noticeable turnaround delay.

Implementing a jitter buffer offers some new challenges when compared to traditional first-in/first-out (FIFO) queues. The jitter buffer is a sorted queue based on the timestamps of arriving voice packets. Therefore, packets can be inserted in the middle of the jitter buffer. Packets can be dropped from a jitter buffer for two reasons: (1) the buffer is full, or (2) the packet is received too late. When packets are dropped because the queue is full, they are dropped from the front of the queue (packets with the oldest timestamp are dropped). Because the queue is allowed to contain packets representing a fixed time interval (the jitter delay value), the arrival of one voice packet may cause multiple older voice packets to be dropped if the time difference between the newest packet's timestamp and the oldest packet's timestamp is greater than the jitter delay value. Packets with duplicate timestamps are dropped. A further challenge is that a separate queue must be maintained for each of the many thousands of voice channels that are handled by the application.

Our implementation uses circular queues to implement the jitter buffer. Each circular queue has pointers to the packets with the oldest and newest timestamps. The position into which a new packet is inserted is a function of the difference between the packet's timestamp and the oldest packet's timestamp, along with the codec interval. To calculate this position we need to divide the timestamp difference by the coded interval. We implement this using fast reciprocal multiplication utilizing the multiplier of the IXP2400 MEs. Once the position is calculated, the insertion of the packet into the jitter buffer is the same as an insert into an array of the order O(1).

The circular queues may have "holes" (positions with no packets). When a packet must be removed from the jitter buffer, it is necessary to quickly skip over the holes to get to the position with a valid packet. We implement this search for a valid packet in O(1) time by making use of the *find first bit set* (FFS) instruction provided by the IXP2400 MEs. By maintaining a bit mask of positions in the circular queue with valid packets, and using the FFS instruction, we can remove the next valid packet from the jitter buffer in constant time.

In summary, the jitter buffer implementation takes advantage of the hardware features provided by the IXP2400 network processor to implement, insert, and remove operations in O(1) time. This allows for an efficient jitter buffer implementation that scales to a large number of voice channels.

18.7.4 TM4.1 Real-Time Scheduler

There are many challenges that must be overcome in developing a TM4.1-compliant scheduler. TM4.1 requires per-VC shaping and scheduling, and the number of VCs can be very large. Also, the implementation must scale with increases in line rate, as well as numbers of VCs.

The most interesting challenge is in providing the real-time scheduling required to support the CBR and rtVBR service classes. When servicing CBR and rtVBR traffic, the packet scheduler must transmit each cell within a certain time window in order for it to conform to the traffic contract.

Because the IXP2400 performs non-preemptive round-robin scheduling, it is difficult for the software to perform such real-time scheduling. When a thread sets a timer and goes to sleep, expecting to be awakened when the timer has expired, it cannot be guaranteed that it will get awakened the instant that the timer expires, because another thread might be executing at the time that the timer expires, and other threads might be ahead of this thread in the round-robin schedule. We found that TM4.1 scheduling is still possible, although the software must be carefully tuned to place an upper bound on the time between the expiration of a timer and the time that the thread is awakened, and the schedule must take this bound into account when setting its timers.

18.8 CONCLUSIONS

The flexibility and programmability of next-generation NPUs will make them a key component of next-generation telecommunications equipment. NPUs can support a variety of packet-processing applications, with a variety of different requirements. The VoAAL2 application discussed in this chapter presents a number of challenges. We have demonstrated that these challenges can be overcome and that applications such as VoAAL2, with strict QoS requirements and asynchronous inputs, can be performed on an NPU.

The VoAAL2 application is most naturally implemented using an asynchronous programming model. We found that the IXP2400 naturally supports such a programming model. Support for asynchronous components that span MEs could be improved by adding support for a distributed lock manager.

The AAL2 application requires a lot of bit- and byte-level data access. The IXP2400 provides all of the necessary facilities to perform these operations while meeting the performance requirements of the application. Finally, the VoAAL2 application requires real-time scheduling to conform to the TM4.1 traffic contract. Although the IXP2400 does not support preemptive scheduling, the software can be tuned to perform the required scheduling in conformance with TM4.1.

REFERENCES

[1]   S. Lakshmanamurthy et al., "Network Processor Performance Analysis Methodology," *Intel Technology Journal*, vol. 6, issue 3, Aug. 2002.

[2]   ITU-T Recommendation I.363.2, Series I: B-ISDN ATM Adaptation Layer Specification: Type 2 AAL, ITU, Geneva, Switzerland, 1997.

[3]   ITU-T Recommendation I.366.2, AAL Type 2 Service Specific Convergence Sublayer for Trunking ITU, Geneva, Switzerland, 1999.

[4]   The ATM Forum, "Traffic Management Specification Version 4.1," af-tm-0121.000, Apr. 1999.

[5]   F. Baker, "RFC 1812 Requirements for IP Version 4 Routers," *IETF*, June 1995.

19 Implementing QoS Mechanisms on the Motorola C-Port C-5e Network Processor

Pranav Gambhire
Motorola, Inc.

Quality-of-service (QoS) mechanisms are used in packet networks to ensure that some packet flows get preferential treatment over other flows. The demand for QoS mechanisms is being driven by the increasing multimedia packet traffic and by the business proposition of an Internet service provider (ISP) being able to deliver differentiated service guarantees. QoS mechanisms can be applied end-to-end on a packet flow or on a per-hop basis. The end-to-end QoS mechanisms, such as Reservation Protocol (RSVP) [1] and the integrated services framework (*Intserv*) [2], require every network element on a flow's route to fix QoS guarantees for the flow before the flow starts. This requires every network element to maintain extensive state information per flow. In contrast, per-hop QoS mechanisms apply QoS locally without the need for maintaining the same extent of flow-state information. They are more popular because they are simple and because they naturally complement the per-hop routing mechanism in packet networks. Most of the popular QoS mechanisms, such as the differentiated services framework (*diffserv*) [3], ATM traffic management (TM) [4], and multiprotocol label-switching (MPLS) traffic engineering (TE) [5] fall into the per-hop category.

By their definition, per-hop QoS mechanisms need to be implemented on the data path in switches/routers. As a commonly used data path technology, network processors must be programmed to support per-hop QoS mechanisms. This chapter analyzes the design criteria for popular QoS mechanisms in software on a network processor, including the ability to provide resilient service guarantees in the event of severe congestion and even in the event of oversubscription. The design and implementation of a QoS mechanism involves several trade-offs in the amount of available buffer space, number and depth of available queues, processor speed, and egress interface line rate. All of these trade-offs are explained and analyzed. Programming the Motorola C-5e network processor for ATM TM and *diffserv* is used as a practical example of the concepts involved in implementing per-hop QoS mechanisms.

19.1 THE MOTOROLA C-5e NETWORK PROCESSOR

The data path resources of the Motorola C-5e network processor include 16 channel processors (see Figure 19.1). Each channel processor has a RISC core (CPRC) based on the MIPS architecture and two serial data processors (SDPs). The RISC core provides the ability to run four concurrent threads and provides hardware support for zero-overhead context switches. In the absence

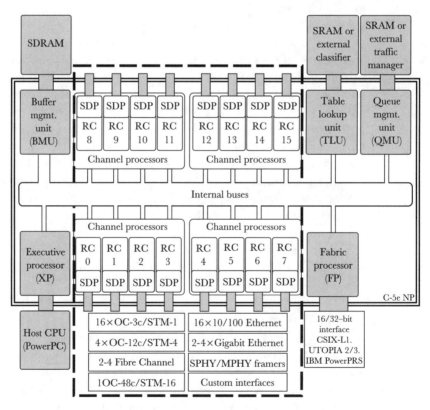

19.1

FIGURE

C-5e network processor block diagram.

of hardware-assisted thread facilities, each of these modules would need its own CPRCs. However, with the C-5e network processor, a single CPRC can deliver the necessary throughput.

Each channel processor is full-duplex, where one of the two SDPs is used for transmit and the other for receive. Channel processors can be configured for a number of different interfaces at different speeds. For example, each channel processor is capable of supporting 16 TDM ports (i.e., E1/T1 ports) with external multiplexing or one OC-3c/STM-1 port where an E1 link has a raw bandwidth of 2.048 Mb/s, a T1 link has a raw bandwidth of 1.544 Mb/s, and the OC-3c or STM-1 link has a raw bandwidth of 155 Mb/s.

19.2   IMPLEMENTING ATM QoS

The ATM approach to QoS leans toward preventing congestion using bandwidth provisioning. Bandwidth is provisioned using service-level agreements (SLAs) at the virtual circuit (VC) level.[1] The SLA consists of the following elements:

+ Peak cell rate (PCR)

+ Sustained cell rate (SCR)

+ Maximum burst size (MBS)

+ Maximum permissible cell delay variation tolerance (CDVT)

The PCR specifies the absolute maximum bandwidth to be apportioned to a VC. The sum of PCR of all VCs on a link could potentially exceed the link bandwidth. The common understanding is that the traffic rate averaged over a long period of time is limited to the SCR, though it may spike over short time intervals. The traffic rate spike is limited to the PCR, and its time duration is limited by the MBS. MBS is specified in number of bytes or number of cells. Determining the PCR, SCR, and MBS enables a fine level of control over bandwidth apportioning with ATM. Restricting link transmission rate to the SCR is called traffic scheduling. Hence, the SLA includes a parameter called CDVT, which specifies the maximum tolerated jitter on a VC. ATM switches typically drop cells that cannot be delivered within these latency requirements.[2] Otherwise, they can either drop traffic that violates the SLA or buffer it up for scheduling, provided sufficient buffer space is available.

1. Bandwidth could be provisioned at both VC and virtual path (VP) levels, though the former is more popular.
2. ATM switches are designed such that this tends to be a very rare event.

ATM TM 4.1 [4] defines the following classes of ATM traffic:

+ Constant bit rate (CBR) characterized by a PCR, very low burst requirements, and low CDVT.

+ Real-time variable bit rate (rtVBR) characterized by PCR, SCR, and low CDVT.

+ Non-real-time variable bit rate (nrtVBR) characterized by PCR, SCR, and moderate to high CDVT.

+ Unspecified bit rate (UBR) characterized by an absence of the SLA.

+ UBR+ specified by a PCR, a minimum cell rate (MCR), and an arbitrary CDVT. Traffic exceeding the PCR is dropped immediately. Traffic exceeding MCR should be shaped to a rate no lower than MCR.

+ Guaranteed frame rate (GFR) for AAL5 traffic. Like UBR+, a PCR, MCR, and CDVT specify a GFR stream. In addition, it requires the traffic manager to recognize AAL5 service data unit (SDU) boundaries. If a cell belonging to an AAL5 SDU on a GFR VC is dropped, the traffic manager is required to drop all subsequent cells to the end of the current SDU. This saves bandwidth and resources, as the entire packet SDU will most likely be retransmitted anyway.

An ATM QoS implementation consists of the following canonical modules:

+ *Input rate policer*. For every cell that arrives at the input of the QoS component, based on the time of its input, this module decides whether it is conformant with the SLA. This conformance can be tested using the generic cell rate algorithm (GCRA), as detailed in ATM TM 4.1. This module gives a three-point conformant/shape/drop decision on every cell.

+ *Traffic shaper/dropper*. This module uses the decision from the policer to transmit the packet immediately, schedule it for later transmission, or drop it. A cell may be dropped because it severely violates the SLA or because its transfer delay requirements can no longer be satisfied.

+ *Traffic scheduler*. The module buffers up traffic spikes and restricts the VC transmission rate to the SCR.

19.2.1   ATM QoS on the Motorola C-5e Network Processor

The QoS component for the C-5e network processor has been designed to meet the requirements of cellular telecom equipment, typically 2.5G and 3G base transceiver stations and base station controllers. The ATM TM design supports the six traffic categories as specified by ATM Forum TM 4.1 (described previously). It implements integrated shaping and scheduling based on the generic cell rate algorithm (GCRA) mechanism. It needs to support multiple ATM ports with different port speeds.

The C-5e network processor shown in Figure 19.1 provides adequate resources to handle ATM QoS at low line rates (like E1 and T1) for which a dedicated traffic management co-processor engine would be excess. Four concurrent threads supported by a channel processor simplify the division of QoS functionality. One thread handles ingress for all the ports, one thread performs policing and shaping, and a third thread handles egress traffic scheduling for all ports, as shown in Figure 19.2. Since an E1 link has a raw bandwidth of 2.048 Mb/s and 16 of these can be supported by a channel processor, the QoS egress should be able to handle cells coming in at an effective port rate of 16×2.048 Mb/s and should never generate traffic at a rate consistently higher than the port's line rate.

The C-5e network processor manages external SDRAM as a collection of buffer pools, using a hardware buffer management unit (BMU). The software, therefore, does not have to do any buffer maintenance. ATM QoS requires, per VC SLA conformance, that data be accessed on the application data path. To take care of table management, the C-5e network processor organizes fast-access SRAM into tables with the table lookup unit (TLU), which provides hardware acceleration of this task. The block diagram of Figure 19.2 illustrates the canonical architecture of ATM TM mapped to three threads on a single CPRC on the C-5e network processor.

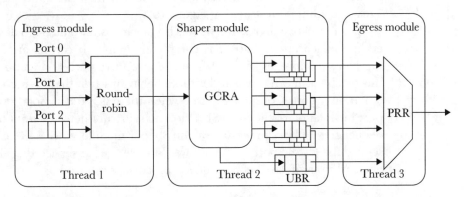

19.2   ATM QoS high-level design.

FIGURE

The following sections discuss the design and implementation of the ATM QoS system on a single CPRC using the modules Ingress, Shaper, and Egress. Each of these modules runs in an independent CPRC context.

19.2.2   ATM QoS Ingress Module

The C-5e network processor has a hardware queue management unit (QMU) that provides message-passing services between the CPRCs. Each CPRC is allocated a certain number of queues at system start-up.[3] To send a message to a CPRC, the source CPRC sends it to the QMU, which in turn signals the message availability to the destination CPRC. The QMU maintains bitmaps to track message availability on the queues dedicated to CPRCs. The CPRC periodically examines this bitmap and removes the messages from those queues whose bit is set. This bit is automatically reset when the message is removed from the QMU.

Messages are formatted as cell descriptor structures. A cell descriptor contains the BMU buffer number of the buffer holding the cell payload, the cell's VPI, VCI, and egress port number. The QoS CPRC is allocated 18 queues—one for each serviced ATM port. The first 16 queues are for the TDM ports, while the last two are for the OC-3c ports. A cell destined for TDM port p will be sent to the pth queue on the QoS CPRC.

All input queues should be served in a strictly fair manner. The input queue service algorithm runs an infinite service loop. Each iteration of the service loop logically examines each input queue. When it finds a nonempty input queue, it dequeues exactly one message descriptor from it and passes it on to the Shaper module, and then proceeds to the next queue. At the beginning of the iteration, the bitmap is read into a local copy maintained on the CPRC. For every set bit in the local bitmap, the corresponding queue is dequeued and the bit is reset. This algorithm is illustrated in Figure 19.3.

An alternative ingress queue service mechanism would be to dequeue packets from each queue until it is completely empty. It can be argued that this mechanism improves latency between consecutive packets on a port. However, this mechanism can cause undesirable behavior when there is a gross SLA violation on a port. Consider the case when there is a traffic flood on the OC-3c port in violation of the SLA. SLA violations are not detected until the packet is dequeued and later processed by the Shaper module. If we were to continually service the OC-3c port queue, we would never get to service the TDM queues. Such arbitrary delays between queue processing can lead to *maxCTD* violations

---

3. The number of queues is decided by configuration code running on the C-5e network processor's XP (executive processor).

```
While (true)
{
    mask = 1;
    qsBitMap = QMU queue bitmap;
    for (queueNum = 0; queueNum < 33; queueNum++)
    {
        if (qsBitMap & mask)
        {
            msg = dequeue(queueNum);
            giveToShaper(msg);
            mask <<= 1;
        }
    }
}
```

19.3   ATM Ingress software module.

FIGURE

on the underserviced queues, if not outright queue overflow. SLA violations on offending ports cannot be allowed to affect service on well-behaved ports.

As most of the ports are slow TDM ports, the queues are empty for most of the iterations. The actual implementation of the Ingress module takes advantage of this by starting the *for* loop in Figure 19.3 from the first nonempty queue number. The "count leading zeroes" (*clz*) hardware instruction is used to count the first non-zero bit in the *qsBitMap*, and the starting *queueNum* and *mask* are set accordingly.

19.2.3   ATM QoS Shaper Module

The Shaper module is responsible for determining the SLA conformance of a cell based on its time of input. The CPRC does not have support for floating-point arithmetic or for any form of multiply or divide instructions. The Shaper module has to live with these restrictions when representing time and determining conformance. Time is always represented in number of clock cycles, to avoid floating-point numbers. It implements GCRA as explained in ATM TM 4.1. The GCRA state is maintained for each VC in the external SRAM, under the control of the hardware TLU.

GCRA works with four parameters: theoretical cell arrival time (TAT), ideal intercell arrival time (called the *increment*), the *limit* (which characterizes the tolerated violations of intercell arrival times), and the maximum tolerated cell transmission delay (*maxCTD*). These parameters are derived from SLA parameters using the equations outlined in Table 19.1.

	CBR	rtVBR and nrtVBR	UBR+ and GFR
Increment	1/PCR	1/SCR	1/MCR
Limit	CDVT	$CDVT + (MBS - 1)$ $\times (1/SCR - 1/PCR)$	$CDVT + (MBS - 1)$ $\times (1/SCR - 1/PCR)$
MaxCTD	0	CDVT	CDVT
TAT	0	0	0

19.1

Deriving GCRA parameters from the SLA.

TABLE

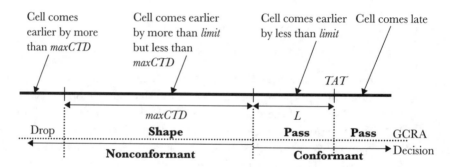

19.4

Using GCRA for SLA conformance checking.

FIGURE

The first cell coming on a VC is always declared as conformant. On every conformant cell, the *TAT* for the VC is increased by the *increment* parameter. If a cell arrives at a point of time earlier than *TAT*, it is a part of a burst. If it arrives before *TAT* but after ($TAT - limit$), it is a part of a legitimate burst that does not need to be shaped. If it arrives earlier than ($TAT - limit$) but later than ($limit - TAT + maxCTD$), then it is part of a burst that needs to be shaped. A cell arriving before ($limit - TAT + maxCTD$) is construed to be too far ahead of its time, and a decision is made to drop it. A cell arriving after *TAT* is conformant. Figure 19.4 shows various zones, on a time axis, where a cell can arrive with respect to its theoretical arrival time.

Note that the *maxCTD* is used to differentiate between excess traffic that can be buffered and that to be dropped. This heuristic limits the buffer requirements and simplifies the buffer maintenance logic, as discussed in following sections. This heuristic could be improved or changed in the future if better buffer management algorithms are found to be applicable to this scenario. Also, the cell loss priority (CLP) bit from the ATM header could be made a part of the heuristic.

For GFR traffic, the frame-level GCRA (F-GCRA) is used. F-GCRA differs from regular GCRA in that it recognizes frame boundaries and bases its drop decision at AAL5 SDU level rather than at ATM cell level. If the first cell of the SDU passes the regular GCRA, F-GCRA declares all the remaining cells in the SDU as conformant. However, it updates the *TAT* and *increment* with each cell, as with regular GCRA. If there was a GCRA SLA violation in the middle of an AAL5 SDU, it is propagated to the beginning of the next SDU, and all the cells of the next SDU are dropped. This complete SDU discard saves bandwidth as compared to partial SDU discard because the entire SDU will typically need to be retransmitted even if a single cell is dropped from it.

The GCRA decision is used by the next part of the shaper. A cell that has passed GCRA is immediately queued to the CPRC that handles its egress port. The shaper discards a cell that has been classified for drop. All other cells are buffered using per-port ring buffers called soft queues. A soft queue is an SDRAM buffer that can hold a fixed number of message descriptors. It is accessed as a circular FIFO queue. The "front" and "rear" pointers, along with the pointer to the SDRAM buffer, constitute a soft queue descriptor. Each soft queue descriptor occupies 4 bytes of space in the on-chip data memory (DMEM). To restrict the descriptor to 4 bytes, 8-bit array indices are used for the front and rear pointers. Only the 2-byte buffer number is stored rather than the complete 4-byte buffer handle, which includes both the buffer pool number and the buffer number.

A CPRC timer is set up to generate a timer interrupt every cell period for the fastest egress port. It maintains a time counter that is incremented on the cell period timer expiry. This counter is used as a "wall clock" to determine the current time. Every port is associated with a *time_to_service* variable. This variable is initialized as *(cell rate of this port/cell rate of fastest port)*. On every wall clock tick, this variable is decremented. When it hits zero, it means that a new cell period has begun on this port and hence it should be provided with a cell for transmit.

The shaper maintains 30 soft queues per traffic category for the purpose of storing cells away for future transmission. A different set of per-traffic category soft queues is used per egress port. Among the 30 soft queues, one queue in each category is marked as the current queue. When the *time_to_service* variable for the port is zero, a cell is dequeued from one of the set of current soft queues, as explained in the section on the Egress module. The current queue pointer in every category is updated to point to the next soft queue after every *max_queue_depth* tick of the wall clock (i.e., after a potentially full soft queue has been completely drained).

By design, the current queue contains all those cells that need to go out during the current cell period. However, only one cell can be transmitted during the current cell period. The transfer delay (or latency) experienced by a cell is equal to the number of cells ahead of it in the current queue. To track this number of cells, a depth counter is maintained for every soft queue. It is incremented for every cell queued and decremented for every cell dequeued.

For a cell determined to be "shaped" by GCRA, a destination queue is chosen using the following equation:

$$dest\_queue = (TAT - wall\_clock)/max\_queue\_depth$$

Let $Q_{i,j}$ denote soft queue i in pool j. A priority round-robin algorithm is used to dequeue cells from the soft queues. Hence, the time spent by a cell in the soft queue (i.e., its transfer delay) is determined as:

$$transfer\_delay = Depth(Q_{j,j}) + Depth(Q_{j,j-1}) + Depth(Q_{j,j-2})$$
$$+ \cdots + Depth(Q_{j,1})$$

Pool 0 is the CBR soft queue pool, pool 1 is the rtVBR soft queue pool, and pool 2 is the nrtVBR soft queue pool.

The transfer delay is determined this way before a cell is queued. If it exceeds the *maxCTD* for the cell, it means that the *maxCTD* cannot be satisfied and the cell is hence dropped. If the dropped cell belongs to a GFR VC, all subsequent cells up to but not including the last cell in the current AAL5 SDU are dropped. The PTI field in the cell header identifies the last cell in the current SDU.

The shaper module design involves a number of trade-offs, including the following:

✦ The number of soft queues allocated per traffic category per port defines the amount of available buffering capacity. It could be increased arbitrarily (at the cost of greater SDRAM requirements) if greater burst (traffic spike) tolerance is desired. Note, however, that the availability of external SDRAM is not the only capacity-limiting issue. Each soft queue descriptor needs 4 bytes in DMEM. There are only 12 KB of DMEM for each CPRC. Given these restrictions, it was determined that 30 soft queues per traffic category happens to be a good trade-off.

✦ A soft queue can hold a maximum of 256 cell descriptors. This implies that no more than 256 cells can contend for the same cell period. Typical *maxCTD* values are less than 256 for ATM traffic, and hence this is often not a limitation. Should it be necessary to allow more than 256 cells to contend for the same cell period, the soft queue descriptor range can be increased by increasing the size of the front and rear pointers. This will lead to increased DMEM requirements.

✦ The GCRA and Shaper modules do not look at the CLP bit in the ATM header with this design. The GCRA heuristic could be enhanced to include the CLP bit value. For example, a cell that arrives before ($limit - TAT$) and after ($limit - TAT + maxCTD$) but has the CLP bit set in the header could be marked for drop rather than for shape. The use of the CLP bit in traffic shaping and policing is optional according to ATM TM 4.1, and hence this design does not tie it into the GCRA heuristic.

✦ The BMU logically arranges SDRAM into buffers and buffer pools. The program cannot access any arbitrary location in SDRAM. It accesses SDRAM by requesting a DMA read/write of a buffer's content. Such DMA reads/writes need to be aligned to 16-byte boundaries within the buffer. Because of this restriction the size of message descriptors in soft queues needs to be a multiple of 16. The FIFO soft queue discipline is an ideal abstraction given these restrictions.

19.2.4 ATM QoS Egress Module

The Egress module runs in a separate thread. It is responsible for dequeuing cells from the shaper soft queues and transmitting them at the port's line rate. For each port and each traffic category within the port there is one soft queue marked '*current*'. The Egress module does a priority round-robin dequeue from the four current queues. The CBR queue has the highest priority, followed by rtVBR, which has a priority higher than nrtVBR, which in turn has a higher priority than the UBR+ and GFR queues. The CBR queue is completely drained before visiting any lower-priority queues. This behavior ensures that CBR and rtVBR cells are processed with the least possible latency.

The Egress module algorithm consists of an infinite loop of port visitations. A port is visited only when its *time_to_service* variable hits zero. On visiting a port, exactly one cell is dequeued from its '*current*' set of soft queues using the priority round-robin dequeue mechanism. The current queue pointer in every category is updated to point to the next soft queue after every *max_queue_depth* ticks of the wall clock (i.e., after a potentially full soft queue has been completely drained).

The egress algorithm has the hard real-time requirement that the fastest port needs to be serviced at its full line rate. Visitations on a port necessarily need to examine the set of its current queues in decreasing order of priority. If all current queues are empty, no cell will be transmitted. As ports are visited in a fixed order, the last serviced TDM port would always end up taking a higher latency hit than all the other ports. To minimize this dynamic latency, a list of all those ports that have at least one nonempty current queue is maintained. The egress algorithm visits only the ports tracked in this list. A port is removed from this list when all of its shaper queues are empty. The shaper context adds a port to this list when it queues a descriptor to one of its shaper queues. Besides reducing the latency, this also prevents wasteful soft queue examination when there is no traffic.

19.3   IMPLEMENTING *diffserv*

The *diffserv* approach to IP QoS focuses on making minimum service-level guarantees to IP traffic streams. When spare link capacity exists, it is shared across all traffic streams. *diffserv* categorizes traffic into six forwarding classes:

+ *Expedited forwarding (EF)*. This class of traffic needs to be forwarded with the least possible queuing delay.

+ *Four assured forwarding classes (AF1, AF2, AF3, and AF4)*. These classes of traffic are associated with a minimum bandwidth guarantee and can tolerate longer latencies.

+ *Best effort (BE)*. This class is characterized by the absence of an SLA.

The *diffserv* design on the C-5e network processor provides six classes of service, as specified by RFC 2475 [3], with intelligent scheduling and discard policies. It can enforce QoS guarantees over 16 E1/T1 ports and two 10/100 Ethernet ports or two OC-3c/STM-1 ports.

RFC 2697 [6] describes the parameters for specifying the *diffserv* SLA. The *single-rate three-color marker* specification is being used in this design. It consists of the following elements:

+ *Committed information rate (CIR)*. This is the minimum long-term average bandwidth guaranteed to a traffic flow.

+ *Committed burst excess (CBS)*. This parameter specifies the permitted short-term burst over the CIR.

+ *Peak information rate (PIR)*. The minimum long-term peak bandwidth guarantee.

✦ *Peak burst excess (PBS)*. This parameter specifies the permitted short-term burst over the PIR.

A *diffserv* implementation first needs to partition the incoming traffic into streams that get differential treatment according to their SLAs. It then checks each stream for SLA conformance. Based on the stream's current conformance state, it then marks packets. Nonconformant packets are buffered subject to buffer space availability, and dropped otherwise. Usually an intelligent drop algorithm like RED [7] is used to minimize the impact of dropped packets at the TCP layer. Finally, the buffers need to be drained at the line rate in a fair manner. A *diffserv* implementation, therefore, consists of the following canonical modules:

✦ *Classifier*. Using custom rules on the IP header fields, the classifier assigns the IP packet to a forwarding class. The forwarding class is encoded into the TOS field of the IP header, as specified by RFC 2474 [8].

✦ *Meter*. The meter is responsible for determining SLA conformance using token buckets. It gives a three-point decision for each packet. The decision points are low drop precedence (meaning that the packet is within the SLA), medium drop precedence (meaning that it is within burst characteristics), and high drop precedence (meaning that this packet transmission would require bandwidth in excess of the minimum specified by the SLA). The drop precedence is also encoded as a part of the TOS field in the header.

✦ *Shaper/dropper*. The shaper/dropper maintains buffer space to absorb bursts. It is also responsible for implementing an intelligent drop policy based on buffer occupancy levels and the drop precedence value from the meter.

✦ *Egress*. The Egress module drains the buffers at the output port's line rate.

The *diffserv* design presented here maps the previously cited canonical modules to the following thread-level modules:

✦ *Ingress module*. The *diffserv* component is responsible for providing service to the 16 TDM ports and the two Fast Ethernet ports. The Ingress module imposes a fair round-robin discipline to service each of these ports and then runs the classifier function to determine the traffic category.

✦ *Meter and Shaper module*. This module gets the classifier function results and implements a single-rate three-color marker token bucket (SRTCM) (RFC 2697 [6]) to determine SLA compliance. Based on the SRTCM results, it writes a new label in the TOS field of the packet's IP header. Based on the

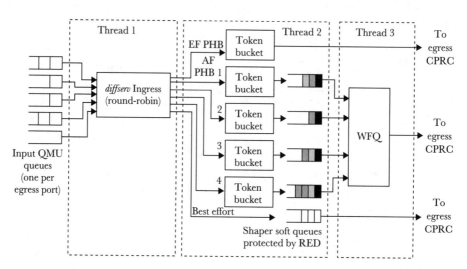

19.5 *diffserv* high-level design.

FIGURE

label, it queues the packet to a soft queue that is protected from overflow by the RED algorithm.

+ *Egress module.* This module dequeues the shaper soft queues for each port at the port's configured line rate and forwards the IP packet descriptor to the appropriate CPRC for link transmission.

The block diagram in Figure 19.5 illustrates the functional components of the *diffserv* engine.

19.3.1   *diffserv* Ingress Module

The *diffserv* CPRC has one input QMU queue for each egress IP port. IP packet descriptors are dequeued from these queues in a strict round-robin fashion using the algorithm of Figure 19.3. Packets coming to the *diffserv* CPRC already have the complete IP header. The first 64 bytes of the packet contain all the protocol headers. They are DMA transferred into a DMEM buffer. As with ATM, the strict round-robin discipline ensures that a misbehaving port does not cause a denial of service on any other port.

The Ingress module maintains a global multifield (MF) mask. This mask specifies the specific fields from the IP header that are used in determining the packet's traffic category. The structure of this mask is shown in Figure 19.6.

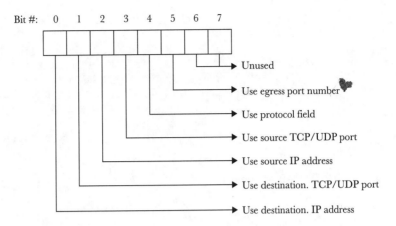

Multifield mask format.

The header fields specified by the MF mask are concatenated to form up to a 14-byte TLU lookup key. A longest-prefix-match table (IP flow table) is maintained at the TLU to match these keys to a flow ID and a *diffserv* forwarding class. The longest-prefix-match table enables a wildcard prefix pattern matching on the MF mask.

Nonprefix pattern matching is not supported in this design. The TLU does not provide wildcard matching and the CPRC cannot do pattern matches on an arbitrarily large set of rules because of processing power and SRAM bandwidth limitations. Wildcard pattern matching can, however, be delegated to a general-purpose host processor that maintains the SRAM IP flow table. This is, however, beyond the scope of the current design that focuses purely on the network processor aspects of implementing *diffserv*.

19.3.2 *diffserv* Meter and Marker Module

After launching a flow table lookup, the Ingress module switches context to the Meter module, which waits for the results of the flow table lookup. The meter context implements the single-rate three-color marker scheme specified by RFC 2697. It maintains a TLU data table containing the RFC 2697 parameters per flow. This meter table is indexed by the flow ID. The entry structure for the meter table is shown in Figure 19.7.

Time is measured in ticks of 2.84 microseconds, which translates to 512 cycles at 180 MHz on the C-5e network processor. The *increment* entry in Figure 19.7

```
/* The single rate three color marker RFC 2697 */
struct Srtcm
{
    int16u  cbs;          /* The committed burst size */
    int16u  ebs;          /* The excess burst size */
    int16u  increment;    /* The number of tokens added to
                             token buckets at every tick */
    int16u  tc;           /* The green token bucket */
    int16u  te;           /* The yellow token bucket */
};

struct TokenBucket
{
    int32u  cir;          /* The committed information rate */
    Srtcm   srtcm;
    int16u  lastUpdateTime;
};
```

19.7

FIGURE

RFC 2697 token bucket structure.

is the number of tokens that need to be added to each of the buckets at the end of 512 cycles.

The table entries are initialized in the following manner:

✦ Increment is calculated as CIR/(time equivalent of 512 cycles). CBS and EBS are obtained as the maximum burst sizes over the time period of one increment.

✦ TC is initialized to CBS, and TE to EBS.

✦ The *lastUpdateTime* member is set to 0.

When an IP packet arrives for this TLU entry, the current cycle count is divided by the number of cycles per tick to get the number of ticks elapsed since system start time. The *lastUpdateTime* from the table lookup is compared to this tick count. If they are not equal, the tokens need to be added to TC and TE or TP. TC is incremented by the number *Increment* $\times$ *(curr_tick_count−lastUpdateTime)*. If TC exceeds CBS, it is reduced to CBS. Similarly, TE is incremented by *Increment* $\times$ *(curr_tick_count − lastUpdateTime)* and capped at EBS.

If $(TC - packet\_size >= 0)$, then the packet is within the committed information rate and is colored green. If $(TE - packet\_size > = 0)$, the packet is within the permitted burst excess and is colored yellow. Otherwise, the packet is nonconformant and colored red. If the packet is colored green, TC is decremented by packet size. Similarly, if it is colored yellow, TE is decremented by packet size.

If the traffic category is an AF category, then green packets are marked using the low drop precedence label, yellow are marked using the medium drop precedence label, and red are marked with high drop precedence label within the traffic category. The appropriate DS code point (RFC 2474 [8]) for the traffic category and drop precedence is determined and updated in the TOS field of the IP header (stored in SDRAM).

If the traffic category is EF, any packet not marked green is dropped. Green packets are marked with the EF label [9] and immediately queued to the QMU queue for their destination egress CPRC.

If the category is the best-effort category, none of the previous actions are taken. Instead, the packet is queued directly into the best-effort shaper queue.

19.3.3 *diffserv* Shaper Module

Packets mapped to the AF classes are processed through the shaper function. There is one soft queue per AF class per egress IP port. This single soft queue simulates the three queues required by RFC 2697. The token bucket scheme ensures that all yellow packets follow the green packets and all red packets follow the yellow packets. This means that green packets are serviced before the yellows, and yellows are serviced before the reds. This behavior is equivalent to having three soft queues—one for each color, and priority servicing the green queue over the yellow and yellow over the red. Packets are not dropped on the basis of their color or the token bucket's state. Instead, the RED algorithm is used to decide drop behavior on every soft queue.

Random early detection (RED) algorithm

After marking a packet, it is run through the RED algorithm [7] before queuing it to the soft queue. RED works by tracking the average depth of a queue and dropping packets so that this average never exceeds a threshold. This average is maintained as an exponential weighted moving average—typically measured using the characteristic equation of a low-pass filter. If adding a packet causes this queue depth to exceed the minimum threshold queue depth, the packet is dropped with a certain probability. As the average queue depth keeps building beyond the minimum threshold, packets are dropped with increasing probability. If the average queue depth hits the maximum threshold, all subsequent packets are dropped until the average queue depth goes below the maximum threshold.

There is one instance of RED for each AF traffic category and one for the best-effort category. The RED parameters are set as follows.

+ Minimum queue depth threshold *(MinTh)*: 128 packets
+ Maximum queue depth threshold *(MaxTh)*: 256 packets
+ Queue weight (Wq): 2^{-9}
+ Maximum drop probability: 2^{-7}

These parameters are chosen to be optimal for the maximum soft queue depth of 256 packets. If the soft queue depth is changed, these parameters have to be recomputed. RED ensures that the drop behavior is sufficiently randomized to avoid all TCP connections to increase and decrease their window sizes at the same time. It also makes sure that no connection is given unfair drop preference in the event of congestion.

An ideal RED implementation would use floating-point numbers to store the parameters and to calculate the exponential weighted moving average. However, the CPRC does not provide floating-point number support, so a 32-bit representation is used to store numbers at a higher resolution. The 8 most significant bits of the word represent the integer part of the number, and the remaining 24 bits are the fractional part. As the soft queue max threshold is fixed at 256, the average can never exceed 256 and hence 8 bits are sufficient to represent the integer part of the average. The following examples illustrate this number format:

+ The number 1 is represented as 0x01000000, and the number 255 as 0xff000000.
+ The number 7.5 is represented as 0x07800000. Note that 0x0F000000 is 15; 7.5 is $15 \gg 1$ (i.e., $0x0F000000 \gg 1$).
+ The number 127 is represented as 0x7F000000, and 63.5 as 0x3F800000. Note that 127 is $63.5 \ll 1$ (i.e., $0x3F800000 \ll 1$).

This representation gives enough bits to represent the fractional parts of a number while retaining the equivalence of left and right shift operations to multiply and divide, respectively.

The RED algorithm is implemented as follows:

1. Initialize *count* to 0xff (i.e., -1) and *average* to 0. Build a 256-entry table of random numbers between 0 and 1 (in the special RED number format) offline and load it into DMEM. Repeat through step 7 for every packet arrival event.

2. If the soft queue for the traffic category is not empty, calculate the new average as $average\mathrel{+}= (curr.\ Queuedepth - average) \gg (-1 \times \log(Wq))$. Note that Wq is a negative power of 2 and hence $\log(Wq)$ is an integer.

3. If the soft queue is empty, according to the RED specification, the average needs to be updated using the equation

$$average = (1 - Wq)^{(\text{time\_now} - \text{last dequeue time})/s} \times average,$$

where s is the number of packets dequeued from the soft queue in a unit time at the line rate. This equation causes the average to decay over periods of queue inactivity. It can be approximated by the following behavior: If no packet was seen for duration $t1$ or less, then the average remains unchanged. If no packet was seen for duration greater than $t1$ but less than $t2$, the average is reduced to half. If no packet was seen for duration greater than $t2$ but less than $t3$, the average is reduced by one-fourth. If no packet was seen for duration greater than $t3$ but less than $t4$, the average is reduced by one-eighth. The points $t1$, $t2$, $t3$, and $t4$ are calculated by solving the equation for the average decaying to half, one-fourth, and one-eighth, respectively. The Egress module writes the *last_dequeue_time* for a traffic category. If the average exceeds maximum threshold, drop the packet and set *count* back to -1, and if the average is less than minimum threshold, queue the packet and set *count* back to -1.

4. Calculate the drop probability Pb as $Pb = (average \ll \log(C1)) + C2$, where $C1$ is *(maximum drop probability/(maximum threshold − minimum threshold))* and $C2$ is given by *(maximum drop probability × minimum threshold)/(maximum threshold − minimum threshold)*. $C1, C2$, and $\log(C1)$ are calculated at compile time. Note that they are powers of 2, as all the numbers involved in their calculation are powers of 2.

5. If *count* equals 0, fetch the next random number R from the table.

6. Approximate the factor *(R/Pb)* as $R \ll$ *(# of leading zeroes in the fractional part of Pb)*. Coarsely, the number of leading zeroes in the fractional part of *Pb* approximates to $-\log(Pb)$. If the *count* exceeds this approximation, drop the packet and set *count* to 0. Otherwise, queue the packet and increment *count*.

7. If the soft queue was empty before the packet queue, its descriptor is added to an active list. The WFQ Egress module picks queues for dequeue processing from this active list in FIFO order.

19.3.4   *diffserv* Egress Module

The egress function runs in a separate context and performs deficit round-robin dequeue [10] from the AF soft queues. In accordance with the AF specification (RFC 2474), each traffic category is associated with a minimum guaranteed bandwidth. Based on this bandwidth, a quantum is associated with each soft queue. The quantum is the maximum number of bytes that may be transmitted out from the soft queue for every round of the round-robin visitation. It is initialized to the average packet size times the ratio of the bandwidth apportioned to the traffic category.

A *next_service_time* variable is associated with every port. After transmitting a packet on the port, this variable is updated by adding the transmission time for the packet size at the port's line rate. This port will be serviced the next time the current time equals or exceeds this variable. This ensures that the *diffserv* engine does not overwhelm the QMU queues to the egress port and uses the soft queue to buffer up traffic spikes.

A deficit counter is associated with each PHB soft queue. It is initialized to 0. At the beginning of the round-robin visitation, this counter is incremented by the quantum. If the packet at the head of the soft queue is smaller in size than the deficit counter, then the packet is dequeued from the soft queue and shipped to its destination CPRC. The deficit counter is decremented by packet size. If the packet is larger in size than the accumulated deficit count, the round-robin procedure visits the next soft queue. A queue is serviced only after it has accumulated a sufficient number of deficits.

When the egress function finds that a soft queue has gone empty, it removes the soft queue from the active list and resets the deficit counter for this soft queue to 0. It also sets the last queue time variable in the RED state entry to the current time. If the soft queue is not empty, its descriptor is added back to the active list at the tail. When the active list is empty, the egress function services the best-effort soft queue.

19.4   DESIGN ALTERNATIVES

Line rate processing is achieved for ATM QoS and *diffserv* in the C-5e network processor implementations described in this chapter. However, the C-5e network processor architecture has a great deal of flexibility that enables other design approaches.

The designs in this chapter provide QoS for low-speed TDM links. The ATM QoS design supports 16 TDM links and one OC-3c link. The *diffserv* design supports 16 TDM and one 10/100 Ethernet link. One CPRC is sufficient to implement these QoS mechanisms in both ATM QoS and *diffserv* designs. The designs can be scaled to support higher-speed links, such as OC-3c and OC-12, by pipelining multiple CPRCs. For example, one CPRC could be used for Ingress and Shaper modules, and another CPRC for the Egress module.

The number of soft queues that can be held in the local on-chip memory limits the amount of burst or SLA violation tolerance. One way to overcome these limitations is to move the soft queue descriptors to the TLU-controlled SRAM. This will enable support for an extremely large number of shaper queues per flow, which will provide an even finer granularity of QoS.

To support more extensive QoS requirements than can be handled through soft queuing and to support higher bandwidths, Motorola provides alternate implementations, such as use of an external traffic management co-processor that can be connected to the QMU memory interface. This external traffic manager provides hardware acceleration for QoS mechanisms and operates in the same programming environment as the C-5e network processor.

19.5   CONCLUSIONS

The primary objectives of any QoS system in a packet network are to curb congestion arising out of short-term packet bursts, to minimize the latency through the network, and to improve network utilization by minimizing packet loss. ATM approaches QoS from the perspective of strict bandwidth apportioning to avoid congestion build-up, even at the cost of some loss in utilization. Strict cell shaping and cell scheduling is needed, and the design presented in this chapter illustrated the mechanism used to achieve it. The *diffserv* approach to QoS in IP networks emphasizes a minimum service guarantee. It does not discard packets until a point is reached when there are not enough resources left to hold them. Upon reaching this congestion point, packets are intelligently dropped on the basis of their drop precedence. The *diffserv* design illustrated this non-compromising position of maximum network utilization. The architecturally unique features of the Motorola C-5e network processor enable wire-speed implementation for ATM TM and *diffserv* as described in this chapter, with capabilities to modify and scale the design to address other design criteria, such as finer granularity of QoS or higher bandwidths.

REFERENCES

[1]   R. Braden, L. Zhang, S. Berson, S. Herzog, and S. Jamin, "Reservation Protocol (RSVP)—A Functional Specification," RFC 2205, Sept. 1997.

[2]   R. Braden, D. Clark, and S. Shenker, "Integrated Services in the Internet Architecture: An Overview," RFC 1633, June 1994.

[3]   S. Blake et al., "An Architecture for Differentiated Services," RFC 2475, Dec. 1998.

[4]   ATM Traffic Management Specification Version 4.1, ATM Forum, Apr. 1996.

[5]   J. Boyle et al., "Traffic Engineering with MPLS," RFC 3346, Aug. 2002.

[6]   J. Heinanen and R. Guerin, "A Single Rate Three Color Marker," RFC 2697, Sept. 1999.

[7]   S. Floyd and V. Jacobson, "Random Early Detection Gateways for Congestion Avoidance," *IEEE/ACM Transactions on Networking*, Aug. 1993.

[8]   K. Nichols, S. Blake, F. Baker, and D. Black, "Definition of the Differentiated Services Field in the IPv4 and IPv6 Headers," RFC 2474, Dec. 1998.

[9]   V. Jacobson, K. Nichols, and K. Poduri, "An Expedited Forwarding PHB," RFC 2598, June 1999.

[10]   M. Shreedhar and G. Varghese, "Efficient Fair Queueing Using Deficit Round Robin," *Proceedings of ACM SIGCOMM '95*, Aug. 1995.

20

CHAPTER

A C-Based Programming Language for Multiprocessor Network SoC Architectures

Kevin Crozier
Teja Technologies, Inc.

Multiprocessor system-on-a-chip (SoC) silicon devices are being adopted for their programming flexibility and high performance. For example, the Intel IXP2400 and IXP2800 network-processing units (NPUs) support full software programmability of up to eight independent threads on each of up to 16 RISC microengines [1,2]. Developers benefit from the expanded programming options but face the challenge of extracting maximum performance from such multiprocessor architectures. The challenge is heightened when one also considers the overall distributed system in which the SoC resides.

Conventional "sequential" programming languages are inadequate for extracting high performance from the parallel, distributed architectures of multiprocessor SoCs. The Teja NP Software Platform from Teja Technologies, Inc., solves these issues with a programming model based on ANSI C, with a set of minimal but necessary extensions to handle the multiprocessor SoC architecture [3].

20.1 SOFTWARE DESIGN CONSIDERATIONS

An important challenge faced by the developer in NPU-based system design is architecting the functionality to use the various processing elements (PEs) in the complete system in an optimum manner. In some applications, such as a single-board network appliance, a network processor may be used stand-alone. In this simplest of cases, the decision of partitioning the application logic is between the different on-chip PEs. More typically, an NPU is used in conjunction with an external host CPU for control and management, multiple NPUs are used together through a switch fabric (separate ingress/egress NPUs, for example), or co-processors such as classifiers and content-addressable memories (CAMs) may be added to boost performance. Furthermore, OEMs designing a scalable product family, rather than a single point product, will want to use these hardware building blocks configured in various combinations to meet a range of price/performance targets.

In the absence of a systems-level development environment, OEMs would have to program each of these various PEs in its own separate target language in isolation. This approach requires an a priori assignment of logic to PE, locking the developer into a particular system configuration. For example, a software implementation of a classifier is considerably different from the code required to configure a classifier co-processor. Thus, moving functionality from one PE to another would require manual recoding—leading to multiple software code bases and increasing the probability of errors, and hence loss of investment leverage in developing a product family that targets different price/performance points.

20.2   THE TEJA NP SOFTWARE PLATFORM

How then to provide an approach that does not require a priori partitioning and coding each PE separately? Teja provides one solution to this problem by providing a platform in which the application logic is developed at the system level in a manner that is independent of any specific targeted hardware. Multiple realizations are achieved from a common code base by mapping the application logic to the target hardware architecture corresponding to each price/performance point.

The Teja NP software platform introduces an architecture framework for parallel and distributed applications and a programming methodology that abstracts the application logic over specific hardware features. The architecture framework is capable of expressing the architecture of a distributed multiprocessor application, and the programming methodology is capable of expressing the application logic.

The application is mapped to the processing and storage elements of the targeted hardware. This mapping is not unique. Different mappings for the same target hardware produce different performance results, from which the best must be chosen. This mapping step takes on all the more significance when one considers the changing relationship between memory bandwidth, processor speed, and network media interfaces. With the mapping completed, code generators (a unique one for each unique type of PE) are employed to convert the application logic into high-performance production code.

20.3 THE TEJA C PROGRAMMING LANGUAGE

Rather than introducing a completely proprietary programming language, Teja's guiding principle in the development of its approach has always been to introduce the minimum set of new concepts, necessitated by the silicon and application needs, and reuse existing software methods everywhere else. Basing Teja NP's programming model on the C language was a natural choice. C is universal, low level, and widely understood by nearly all programmers. Thus, the incremental learning curve for a C programmer on Teja NP is limited to the minimal set of Teja C extensions.

Teja C allows the use of the usual C programming constructs. C programs have structs, global functions, and a "sequential" programming model. Teja C supports full arithmetic and logical C expressions, including the . (dot) and → (arrow) operators, and supports C statements such as assignment, conditionals, and loops. Standard C and C++ commenting styles are supported. Target-specific assembly code can be handled with the Teja C *native* code block, which facilitates inline source code inclusion.

Teja C extensions to ANSI C can be described in three feature set groups:

✦ System view

✦ Flexible mapping

✦ Scheduling and communication

20.3.1 Teja C System View Extensions

To enable the flexible partitioning and assignment of the application logic to the target hardware, a system-level view is needed. This is broken down into software architecture, hardware architecture, and application mapping.

Teja C provides software architecture constructs for thread and memory space, and API primitives for signaling. Threads allow the user to map their algorithms (functions) to threads of execution. Memory spaces allow the user to map their data structures to shared or private memory areas. Signaling provides a mechanism for inter-thread synchronization.

Teja C provides hardware architecture constructs for processor, memory bank, and bus, along with a means of specifying their associated properties. A processor can have specific properties, such as processor speed. Memory banks can have properties, including size and starting addresses. Buses connect memory banks to processors and have speed and data width properties. A collection of processors, memory banks, and buses forms a hardware architecture. Hardware architectures may be nested to form more complex systems. For example, at the lowest level an architecture could describe the processors, on-chip memory, and buses within an NPU, while a higher-level architecture describes multiple NPUs and other elements comprising a blade. In addition to providing a means of describing common hardware elements, Teja NP also provides a chip support package for the architectures supported by the Teja platform. These chip support packages include a prebuilt hardware architecture and valid properties for the selected target.

In application mapping, the software architecture threads and memory spaces are mapped to hardware processors and memory banks, respectively. This separate mapping phase allows the same software architecture to be mapped to a variety of hardware architectures, providing a high degree of software reuse across multiple projects and NPU generations without altering the logic section of the program. An additional benefit of this approach is that by mapping the entire software architecture to an Intel Pentium target configuration the application can be functionally simulated and debugged on a desktop PC before moving to the actual hardware.

We illustrate the Teja C extensions in Figure 20.1 using a simple producer-consumer example. The application consists of a producer that creates a data item and passes that data item to the consumer.

In this example, we see that functions and data structures are declared using standard C syntax. Then we see the addition of the software architecture. Note that static instances are declared and later mapped to memory spaces. Memory spaces and threads are declared as well. Then we see the declaration of the Intel IXP2400 hardware architecture. This example shows the declaration of one microengine, the embedded XScale, and the SRAM memory bank. Finally, the application mapping provides the connection between the software architecture and the hardware architecture.

The user creates a queue data structure, global functions for queuing and dequeuing, along with the producer and consumer functions. The producer and consumer functions are mapped to software threads.

20.3.2   Teja C Flexible Mapping Extensions

One key feature of Teja NP is the ability to write an algorithm once in a single, target-independent language regardless of its final destination. To obtain high performance despite this hardware abstraction, the Teja NP code generators are required to avoid runtime branches and emit appropriate production code based on the application's architecture configuration and hardware mapping.

```
typedef struct queue_t {
  data *first; /* pointer to the first data element */
  data *last;  /* pointer to the last data element */
  int mutex;   /* mutex for maintaining synchronization */
} queue;

typedef struct data_s {
  int data_item; /* the data item */
  data *next      /* pointer to the next data element */
}data;

/* function for placing data d into queue q */
void enqueue(queue *q, data *d) {
   ...
}

/* function for removing data from queue q and return it */
data * dequeue(queue *q) {
   ...
}

/* "main" function for the producer :
 *  Allocate a data item and set the data value
 *  Enqueue the item.
 */
void producer (queue *q) {
   ...
   data *d;
   d = malloc(sizeof(data));
   d->data_item = 7;
   enqueue(q, d);
   ...
}

/* "main" function for the consumer :
 *  Dequeue the data item
 *  Process the data item as needed
 *  Deallocate the data item
 */
void consumer (queue *q) {
  data * d = null;
   ...
```

20.1   Teja C code with language extensions for system view.

FIGURE

```
      /* Wait for something to appear in the queue. */
      while (d == null) {
          d = dequeue(q);
      }
      free d;
      ...
  }

  swarch sa {
      /* initialize the static instance of the queue */
      queue data_queue = {0, 0, 0 };
      /* declare a memspace for the queue to reside in */
      memspace ms;
      /* declare threads for the producer and consumer */
      thread t1, t2;

      swmap {
        /* map the producer function to a thread 1 */
        producer(&data_queue) => t1;
        /* map the consumer function to a thread 2 */
        consumer(&data_queue) => t2;
        /* place the static instance of the queue in ms */
        data_queue => ms;
      }
  }

  hwarch ha {
      chip IXP2400_I ixp2400.IXP2400Chip;
      // Properties for the IXP2400 chip
      IXP2400_I.chip_rev = "A1";
      IXP2400_I.clock_frequency = "600.0";

      // Specify the processing elements inside the chip
      processor p1 IXP2400_I.ue0;
      processor p2 IXP2400_I.XScale;

      membank mb ixp2xx.QDRSRAM;
      // Specify the properties for this memory bank
      mb.size = "0x400000";
      mb.bit_alignment = "32";
      mb.reserve_word_0 = "true";
      mb.physical_address = "0x90000000";
```

20.1   Teja C code with language extensions for system view (*continued*).

FIGURE

```
            bus b ixp2xxx.QDRSRAMBus;
            // properties for the sram bus
            b.width = "32";
            b.frequency = "100";

            connection p1 sram_bus b;
            connection p2 sram_bus b;
            connection mb sram_bus b;
            ...

        }

        application app sa ha {
            /* map swarch t1 to processor 1 (microengine 0) */
            t1 => p1;
            /* map swarch t2 to processor 2 (XScale) */
            t2 => p2;
            /* map swarch ms to the SRAM memory bank */
            ms => mb;
        }
```

20.1

FIGURE

Teja C code with language extensions for system view (*continued*).

In ANSI C, such an effect is typically obtained by using preprocessor directives for conditionally including the required code. However, in a production application with numerous mapping choices, such a technique does not scale well. In C++, such an effect is achieved using templates, which provide type genericity (i.e., generated code depends on the type of the variable used in the class template).

In Teja NP applications, selection of the generated code depends not only on the type of data variables but on the value of constants assigned during the application's hardware mapping. Such constants are known in Teja C as late-binding constants.

Teja C implements late-binding constants in the manner of C++ class templates. With this extension to classes and templates, Teja C supports the typical features found in object-oriented languages, including classes with member variables, member functions, constructors and destructors, inheritance, and late-binding constants in the form of templates.

The concept of a memory pool is added to the software architecture for dynamic memory management. Also added are the following base framework classes, which provide initial implementations of elements needed in a multiprocessor application:

✦ *TejaClass*. Base class from which all Teja NP applications are derived, used to describe any data structure

✦ *TejaAux*. TejaAux provides reflection, typically used for dynamic function dispatching and higher-level memory management

✦ *TejaQueue*. Queue implementation for producer-consumer synchronization

✦ *TejaMutex*. Mutex implementation for mutual exclusion synchronization

We illustrate these features in Figure 20.2 by reworking the previous producer-consumer example.

Note that the queue data structure is no longer in the user's code; the *TejaQueue* system class is used instead. Member functions *enqueue* and *dequeue* are used instead of global functions. Note the use of constructors in the case of the *Data* class. Constructors allow the initial value of the data to be set in a simple manner. Both the producer and the consumer have *q* as a late-binding constant. The producer also has a late-binding constant for the memory space in which the memory pool for the data object resides.

The declaration of a memory pool for the data items is shown in the code example of Figure 20.2. The *mempool dataPool* will hold 10 nodes that are the size of class *Data*. This allows 10 data items to be allocated in the system at once. If the producer attempts to allocate more than this, *new* will return null. When this condition occurs, the user can either wait until a data item is freed up or do some type of error processing.

Now instead of global functions being mapped to threads, member functions from the *Producer* and *Consumer* classes are mapped instead.

The application mapping shows an additional section that specifies the implementation of the queue. In this case, the queue will be implemented as a software linked list. The mutex implementation guarding the queue is also specified.

This added flexibility allows quick and easy remapping of data structures and algorithms. These language features also lead to a more structured software design, making the software easier to maintain and easier to debug.

20.3.3   Teja C Scheduling and Communication Extensions

In many high-performance applications, the multiple processing elements are used in a pipeline. For example, a router has an algorithm for receiving packets, another for processing those packets, performing an IP address lookup for forwarding, and the final pipeline stage transmitting those packets.

```
class Data : TejaAux {
  int data;  // The data item

  // Constructor for Data - sets data to d
  Data(int d) {
    data = d;
  }
}

// Producer class with 2 late binding constants
//   TejaQueue q - the queue to place the data in
//   memspace ms - the memory space to allocate the data
class Producer<TejaQueue q, memspace ms> : TejaAux {
  produce() {
    Data d = null;
    while (d == null) {
      // attempt to allocate data from a mempool in ms
d = new Data(10) in ms;
    }
    q->enqueue(d);

    ...
  }
}

// Consumer class with 1 late binding constant
//   TejaQueue q - the queue to receive the data from
class Consumer<TejaQueue q> : TejaAux {
  consume() {
    Data d = null;

    ...
    while (d == null) {
      d = q->dequeue();
    }
    // Process the data as necessary
    ... = d->data;
    // Return the data node to the mempool
    Data::delete d;
  }
}

swarch sa {
  // Create an instance of TejaQueue
  TejaQueue dataQueue();
```

20.2

FIGURE

Teja C code with language extensions for flexible mapping.

```
          // Create an instance of the Producer specifying the late
          // binding constants
          Producer<dataQueue, ms> P();
          // Creat an instance of the Consumer
          Consumer<dataQueue> C();

          // Declare the memspace for the mempool and the dataQueue
          memspace ms;

          // Declare the threads for the producer and the consumer
          thread t1, t2;

          // Create a memory pool that will hold 10 Data
          // sized elements.
          mempool dataPool(10, Data);

          swmap {
            // Map Producer P to thread 1
            P->produce() => t1;
            // Map Consumer C to thread 2
            C->consume() => t2;
            // Place dataQueue in ms
            dataQueue => ms;
            // Place the memory pool in ms
            dataPool => ms
          }
      }

      hwarch… { … }

      application app sa ha {
          // Map the software arch elements to the hardware
          t1 => p1;
          t2 => p2;
          ms => mb;

          // Specify the implementation for the queue
          // using a linked list and fair
          // as opposed to a priority mutex.
          implementation instantiation dataQueue
            TejaQueueCodeGenSwLinkedList {
                mutex_algorithm = "fair";
            }

      }
```

20.2   Teja C code with language extensions for flexible mapping (*continued*).

FIGURE

To facilitate pipelining, quick asynchronous communication is needed. Teja C implements the software architecture concept of channels that are an asynchronous communication mechanism for structured messages. The medium over which a channel communicates is set by its hardware mapping. However, the interface to the channel remains the same independent of the actual communication medium. These media can include registers, memory, hardware rings, PCI bus, or even TCP/IP.

The logic for receiving and processing messages typically operates in phases. For example, the algorithm waits for one or more messages or events to be triggered. These messages may arrive on channels or a mask of signals. Once triggered, the logic for receiving and processing messages performs computations, issues I/O commands, and signals other threads. Then it waits for the next condition, and so on.

Such behavior is best depicted using state machines. State machines are similar to classes in that they have member variables, functions, and constructors. They also contain states and transitions. States can either be transient or nontransient. Transient states create control flow without waiting within the state machine. Nontransient states wait for events to trigger a transition. Transitions connect states together and provide their scheduling conditions and the body of actions to be executed when taken.

State machines also provide another important performance benefit. Consider the following logic flow written in pseudo-C.

```
while (1) {
  if (cond)
    f1 ();
  else
    f2 ();
}
```

Typical code generators for this program snippet will insert a branch in every execution path of this logic. In Teja NP, using a state machine description of this logic, a priority can be given to each transition. For example, the call to *f1* can be prioritized higher than the call to *f2*. The Teja NP code generator will then generate the high-priority transition loop with no branches. When the loop contains multiple *if-then-else* decision points, the state machine-based code generator performs significantly better. The trade-off made is that the lower-priority paths are generated with two branches. However, in most situations, this is an acceptable, even desirable, trade-off.

Scheduling of the state machine logic is handled by the Teja NPOS runtime system. NPOS also enables time-driven scheduling of state machine logic in addition to the event-driven execution.

Framework classes supporting scheduling and communication are *TejaEvent*, *TejaAlert*, and *TejaComponent*. *TejaEvent* and *TejaAlert* are the base classes for structured messages. *TejaComponent* is the base class for state machines.

The example in Figure 20.3 contains two state machines that communicate over a channel. The state machines are event driven. Thus, explicit polling of a queue is not necessary. In the consumer, the NPOS runtime system will execute the transition upon reception of *myevent*. When the event is received it is placed in an implied structure called *event*. The user can then cast it to the expected class and act on it as necessary.

The *Data* class is now a subclass of *TejaAlert*. This allows *Data* to be sent over a channel, since the *TejaAlert* class has the necessary bookkeeping information, including the *eventid*.

An instance of each component is created in the software architecture. A channel is created with the consumer specified as component c. The channel producers are inferred from the components that specify them as late-binding constants or constructor parameters. Two threads are declared, and in the software map each component is mapped to a thread.

Note that the implementation of the channel is not set until the application mapping. This particular channel communicates using the next neighbor registers (a specific high-performance feature of the Intel IXP2400 and IXP2800 NPUs). Specifying the implementation in this phase allows users to easily tune their application for highest performance.

Notice that these extensions, summarized in Table 20.1, further simplify the design by reducing the logic (no polling of queues) and actually increase flexibility (multiple implementations of channels) while maintaining high performance.

20.3.4   Limitations

Certain limitations of the target SoC devices are reflected in Teja C. For example, the '&' operator typically cannot be applied to data structures in general-purpose registers (GPRs). Some other limitations that may be relaxed on a case-by-case basis include structures within structures, unions, arrays of structures, and static structures within functions.

20.4   PLATFORM SUPPORT

The Teja NP software platform consists of an application development environment (ADE), network-processing operating system (NPOS), and a library of foundation applications, including TCP termination, IPv4 forwarding, and ATM.

```
        // Data will be a subclass of Teja Alert so it
        // can be passed through a channel.
        class Data : TejaAlert {
          int data;  // the data item

          Data(int d, int event) {
            super(event); // Call the superclass constructor
            data = d;
          }
        }

        class Producer<channel ch, memspace ms> : TejaComponent {

          start state s;  // declare the discrete state s

          // Create a transition that loops around state s
          transition produce_data from s to s {
              // allocate the data element
              Data *a = new Data(10, myevent) in ms;
              // send the data element to the consumer
              teja_send_alert(ch, a);
          }

        }

        class Consumer : TejaComponent {

          yield start state s;  // declare discrete state s

          // Create a transition that loops around state s.
          // The transition will be executed when ever the
          // the event "myevent" is received.
          transition consume_data from s to s on myevent {
              // Cast the event data to the Data Class
              Data d = (Data *) event;
              // Process the data as necessary
              ... = d->data;
              // The runtime system handles free'ing the Data
          ...
          }
        }
```

20.3

FIGURE

Teja C code with language extensions for scheduling and communications.

```
swarch sa {
    // Declare the producer and the consumer
    Producer<ch, ms> p();
    Consumer c();

    // Thread to run the components in.
    thread t1, t2;

    mempool alert_pool(10, Data);

    // A memory space for the alert_pool to reside in
    memspace ms;

    // A communication channel with c specified as a consumer
    channel ch(c);

    swmap {
        p => t1;
        c => t2;
        alert_pool => ms;
    }
}

hwarch   .. { .. }

hwmap app {
    t1 => p1;
    t2 => p2;
    ms => mb;

    // Specify the implementation of the channel using
    // the next neighbor registers of the IXP2400
    implementation channel ch {
        channel_code_generator {
            medium = 'NEXT_NEIGHBOR';
        }
    }
}
```

20.3

FIGURE

Teja C code with language extensions for scheduling and communications (*continued*).

The ADE provides front-end tools for parsing Teja C text programs, and GUI tools for developing applications graphically. It also provides back-end tools for application validation, optimization, code generation, and tool chain integration. Finally, it provides multiprocessor debugging tools for graphical, Teja C source-level debugging with event-driven breakpointing. The debug tools are

	Feature set 1: system	**Feature set 2: flexible mapping**	**Feature set 3: scheduling and communication**
Programming style	Procedural C	Object-oriented C++	Model-based
Programming constructs	Struct Global function	Class Member variables Member functions Late-binding constants	State machine
Software architecture constructs	Thread Memory space Send/wait signal	Memory pool Get/put node	Channel Send/receive alert
Hardware architecture constructs	Processor Memory bank Bus		
Framework constructs		TejaClass TejaAux TejaQueue TejaMutex	TejaEvent TejaAlert TejaComponent

20.1   Summary of Teja C extensions to ANSI C.

TABLE

integrated with and extract performance data from the cycle-accurate simulators supported by the target hardware. NPOS provides the runtime environment and APIs used by the application and the generated code. NPOS is deployed on all processing elements. Whether on processors where an operating system (such as Linux or VxWorks) is present, or on bare silicon in the absence of such an OS, NPOS is used as a library that is linked into the application code. The foundation applications provide production examples of high-performance applications developed in Teja C. Initially supported SoC devices are the Intel IXP2400 and IXP2800 network processors.

Figure 20.4 shows the design flow using Teja NP. While for purposes of illustration the design sequence is shown using screens from the ADE, all of these user steps can be accomplished within the Teja C language syntax in textual format, with the exception of the interactive debug step.

20.5   CONCLUSIONS

Conventional "sequential" programming languages are inadequate for extracting high performance from the parallel, distributed architectures of multiprocessor SoCs. The Teja NP software platform introduces a programming

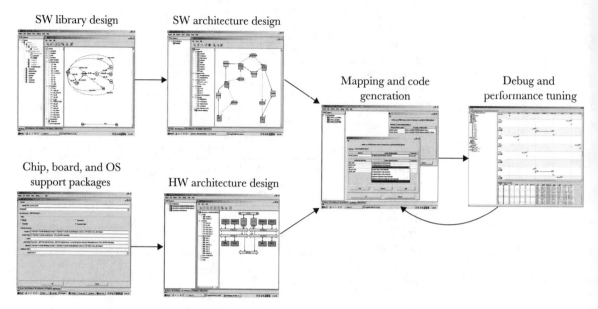

SW library design   SW architecture design

Mapping and code generation

Debug and performance tuning

Chip, board, and OS support packages

HW architecture design

20.4   User design flow illustrated using Teja NP ADE tool suite.

FIGURE

model that is based on ANSI C, with a set of minimal but necessary extensions to handle the multiprocessor SoC architecture. Teja NP has been successfully used by network equipment manufacturers to create software for a variety of networking devices, including high-performance switches/routers, wireless gateways, distributed denial-of-service security appliances, network monitoring and billing systems, and others. Many of these products are already in production and are operational in enterprise and service provider networks.

REFERENCES

[1]   "Intel IXP2400 Network Processor," *www.intel.com/design/network/products/npfamily/ixp2400.htm*.

[2]   "Intel IXP2800 Network Processor," *www.intel.com/design/network/products/npfamily/ixp2800.htm*.

[3]   Teja product descriptions and technical white papers, *www.teja.com*.

Index